Window on
GOA
A History and Guide

Window on
GOA

A History and Guide

MAURICE HALL

Quiller Press
London

NOTE ON SPELLINGS USED FOR PLACE NAMES

The local language Konkani was only given the status of an officially recognised Indian language in 1976. Marathi, the language of a large neighbouring state (Maharashtra) is also widely used. Portuguese is still spoken and understood by a large part of the population and now Hindí and English are also official languages, as in the rest of India.

The previous paragraph makes apparent the complexities of choosing which spelling or version of place names to use. It has been decided to use none of them exclusively, but to use the version that seems to be most appropriate or in common use. Accents on Portuguese words have been omitted.

First published 1992
by Quiller Press Limited
46 Lillie Road
London SW6 1TN

Text, photographs and drawings
© 1992 Enid Hall

ISBN 1 870948 71 8

Produced by Hugh Tempest-Radford *Book Producers*
Printed in Great Britain by Jolly & Barber Limited, Rugby

CONTENTS

Shipwreck memorial, Caranzalim

PREFACE

Maurice Hall described the genesis of *Window on Goa* in these terms:

> From my first visit to Goa eleven years ago, frustration grew at not being able to find any sort of travel book that even began to provide sufficient information to enable any appreciation of the many delights that Goa obviously had to offer. There are several large 'coffee-table' books, concentrating more on photography than text, with a big gap between them and pamphlet-type guides that concern themselves mainly with lists, things to see, accommodation, transport facilities, postal rates etc.

> As a result, being an enthusiastic tourist, I began to search and accumulate information to satisfy my own needs. I reached a point where I seemed to have more than sufficient for the sort of book I myself was looking for. . . .

After Maurice's death it was decided to proceed with the publication of *Window on Goa* and it has been with the support of British Steel that we were able to produce it with so much colour, which anyone who knows India will appreciate to be of the utmost importance.

Enid Hall
March 1992

PRACTICAL INFORMATION FOR A VISIT TO GOA

CLIMATE

The best months to visit Goa are from early November to the end of March – with October and April also possible. May is extremely hot; June to September is the monsoon which, nevertheless, will hold its own charm for some.

The winter temperatures are between 32°C and 21°C; in the summer between 32°C and 24°C.

CLOTHING

Light cotton clothing is the order of the day, with the possibility of needing a shawl or light cardigan during December and January. It is easy to buy relatively cheap cotton garments, T-shirts, dresses, shorts, skirts and trousers. There are wonderful straw hats, from the ubiquitous fisherman's hat to some more exotic varieties. It is possible to have dressmaking and tailoring done, but this is not for the faint-hearted and one must be armed with very definite ideas and firm instructions.

HEALTH

Medical facilities are quite good. Pharmacies abound and the local pharmacists are most helpful. Most hotels have a local doctor available or can arrange for you to see one. For the best advice, before setting out, any airline regularly travelling to India will have details of injections and other medication currently advised.

CURRENCY

Currency in use is the Indian rupee. The rupee is divided into 100 paise. There are coins of 1, 2, 5, 10, 20, 25 and 50p and also 1 and 2 rupee coins. Notes are of 1, 2, 5, 10, 20, 50, 100 and 500 denomination.

During the recent past the exchange rate has been exposed to startling variations and as the rupee is not quoted on the foreign exchange markets possibly the best place for up-to-date information is the travel agencies. It is not legal to take rupees into India nor yet to take them out. Foreign exchange, both currency and traveller's cheques, may be taken into the country but the amount is to be declared on entry.

On changing money at banks or hotels (where the exchange might not be as favourable) a currency exchange form is issued. One of these at least will be necessary in order to exchange money on departure.

As the physical act of changing travellers cheques can be quite time-consuming it is helpful to exchange as infrequently as possible.

Credit cards are accepted in hotels and in some shops.

FOOTNOTE: Torn or damaged notes are likely to be refused so take care when accepting change.

TELEPHONES

Goa has recently gone onto the STD service which has enormously improved the situation. Within Goa itself there are still problems but one gets by. Calls can usually be made from hotels and cafés as well as from the post office.

POSTAL SERVICES

Internal mail is very cheap to send and the service is very quick and reliable.

Mail to and from overseas is also pretty good.

Stamps can also usually be purchased from hotels.

PUBLIC HOLIDAYS

India has possibly more public holidays than anywhere else in the world – if not, it must come close. Christian, Hindu, Muslim and Sikh must all be accommodated and there are approximately 20 holidays each year. In Goa not all of these are observed, but details need to be established locally.

CALENDAR OF SOME OF THE FESTIVALS IN GOA

January – *The Feast of the Three Kings* held only at Chandor, Reis Magos and Guirdolim.

February/March – On the few days preceding Lent, *Carnaval* is celebrated. Also 2 February the *Feast of our Lady of Candelaria* – Pomburpa. *Shigmo*, the Goan version of Holi, happens over five days, culminating in Rang Panchani, where coloured water is thrown and folk theatre is enacted in towns and villages throughout the territory.

Sixteen days after Good Friday a mass is held at Mapusa followed by a fair, this is the *Feast of Our Lady of Miracles*.

June – There are two festivals associated with the monsoon at the *Feast of Saint Anthony*, when St Anthony is entreated to bring rain. Followed by the *Feast of St John*, a boisterous affair with young men jumping into village wells after having begged drinks of feni (the national drink) from their neighbours.

August – In August the *Feast of St Lawrence* celebrates the coming end to the monsoon and the re-opening of the sand bar that annually silts up the Mandovi, which means that ships can once more ply their trade up-river. Also in August, Krishna's birthday is celebrated at the festival of *Gokul Ashtami* and *Novidade*, a harvest festival, is held in the churches.

On the third Sunday in October, the *Fama of the Menino Jesus* is held at Colva. *Divali* is also in this month. Divali is the Hindu Festival of Light, and the triumph of Good over Evil.

December brings *Christmas*, which is traditionally celebrated everywhere with families coming together; the midnight masses make an impressive spectacle.

The only Muslim festival of note is held in Ponda during the month of February.

There are many more festivals going on throughout the year.

EATING OUT IN GOA

Goan food is excellent and there are innumerable restaurants where food is quite safe. As for water, ask for boiled, filtered water, although mineral water is now widely available. The quality of restaurants obviously varies from season to season. There are also North Indian and Chinese restaurants.

One or two of those tried and tested are:
The Mandovi, Panjim
O'Coqueiro, Porvorim
Longhuinos, Margao and also at Colva
Hotel President, Ponda

TRANSPORT

Travel to Goa – The airport in Goa is Dabolim, 5 km from Vasco da Gama and 29 km from Panjim.

The Indian Airline's office is at Dempo Building, D. Bandodkar Marg, Panjim.

The Air India office is at the Hotel Fidalgo, Panjim.

V.S. Dempo and Co. Ltd. at Campal, Panjim are shipping agents – hopefully the service from Goa to Bombay will soon be reinstated.

Buses are cheap, mostly overcrowded, but great fun and for shortish journeys to be well recommended. There is an amazing bus network and even the remoter parts are almost always accessible.

Tourist Taxis can be hired from ranks in the town and there is a standard rate per kilometre. These can also be hired on a daily or half daily basis at reasonable rates.

Three-wheeled auto-rickshaws and *black and yellow taxis* can also be hired. They both have meters but it is prudent to establish the fare structure before beginning the journey.

There is another quite common form of transport and that is travelling as a passenger on a fully fledged *motor bike taxi*; this is apparently speedy and cheap.

In spite of the numerous bridges that already exist, and are being added to, Goa is still, to a large extent, reliant on its ferries. These vary in size but most seem to encapsulate the feeling of travelling at the pace most suited to this land.

CHURCH, TEMPLE AND MOSQUE ETIQUETTE

In churches, expectations are similar to those in Europe; it is not necessary for women to cover their heads. In temples and mosques, it is necessary to shed one's shoes.

HOTELS

There are a few well-established hotels and new ones are springing up all the time.

The Taj group have three complexes, all at the Aguada Headland. The original hotel *Fort Aguada* has air-conditioning, a swimming pool, shops, hairdressing, tennis courts, etc. *The Hermitage* consists of up-market bungalows which were built at the time of the Commonwealth Heads of Government Meeting in 1983. These two are five-star deluxe. Then there is the *Taj Holiday Village* which consists of Goan-style cottages set in a coconut grove; this has a good swimming pool and is right on the beach. The Taj operates a private bus service which is available for trips into Panjim, as well as a service to Dabolim Airport.

Cidade de Goa at Dona Paula. Facing south-west onto the mouth of the Zuari River, this five-star hotel has a swimming pool, a sandy secluded beach and good mooring.

The Fidalgo, Panjim. This modern hotel situated in the town with good bars and restaurants is three-star, as is *The Mandovi*. This is the oldest of the hotels. Centrally situated, this colonial-style hotel has a large first-floor balcony – an ideal meeting place – overlooking the Mandovi River and has an excellent bar, restaurants and bookshop.

The Majorda Beach Resort – Another five-star deluxe hotel, this one is situated on the northern-most beach of the Salcete coastline.

The Oberoi Hotel, Bogmalo Beach – This five-star hotel is part of the Oberoi Group, has a swimming pool and good restaurants, a safe sandy beach and is within three km of the airport.

From north to south there are many more places to stay: *The Tourist Resort*, Terekhol. *Vagator Beach Resort*, Chapora. Several hotels on Baga and Calangute Beaches. At Dona Paula there is *Prainha cottages by the sea*, a family-run hotel, newly renovated, which is well established over many years, has good food and service and helpful owners. There is a secluded beach in a quiet cove. Colva has the *Hotel Silver Sands* and *Longuinhos Beach Resort*.

Beyond Cavelossim the narrowing peninsula formed by the approach to the sea of the Sal River is the site of extensive hotel development, which will provide a wide range of first-class hotel facilities to this southern stretch of Salcete's coastline.

The Directorate of Tourism, Government of Goa, produces a leaflet *Accommodation in Goa* which covers all kinds of hotels, guest houses, tourist hotels and even paying-guest accommodation.

Post Offices and Banks operate in the main towns, with branches in some of the other towns and villages. Note that these close from 12 noon until 3 p.m.

PRIVATE HOUSES IN GOA

There are several important houses in Goa. These are not usually open to the public, but in some cases this can be arranged.

Margao The Da Silva House – Borda – 1785; The Miranda House – Rua Abade Faria; The Lorenzo House – Rua Abade Faria.

Loutolim The Salvador Costa House – has an elaborate altar and is outside the village; The Miranda House – outside the village; The Vicente Joao De Figuerdo House – a 300 year-old house, with a 150 year-old façade and a fine furniture collection; The Saluzin Monteiro House; The Roque Caetan Miranda House.

Chandor The Menezes Braganza House – 1730.

Panjim The Ferreira Martin's House; The Visconde De Pernem's House; The Alfredo Gamma's House; The Mhamai Kamat House.

Calangute The Afonso House – with stained glass in an enclosed balcao.

Candolim The Abbé Faria House – now destroyed.

Aldona The Elsa Rocha's House; The Diva Alvares.

Guirim The Sousa Gonsalves House; The Braganza Cunha House.

Chinchinim The Furtado House.

Pernem The Deshprabhu House.

Anjuna The Albuquerque House – built in the 1920s by a doctor returned from Zanzibar.

Saligao The 'Madame Rosa' Vaz House – built 1933.

USEFUL ADDRESSES

GOVERNMENT OF INDIA TOURIST OFFICE, Church Square, Panjim.
DEPARTMENT OF TOURISM, GOVERNMENT OF GOA, Tourist Home, Pato, Panjim.
TOURIST INFORMATION BUREAU, Government of Maharashtra, Tourist Hotel, Panjim.

INTRODUCTION

In terms of size, in the context of the immensity of the Indian sub-continent, it has to be allowed that Goa is insignificant. It is only 100 km from its northern to its southern border and, at its widest, only 50 km from the coast on the west to the mountain peaks that form its border on the east.

But here is where any thoughts of insignificance must end.

Washed by the Indian Ocean, 400 km south of Bombay, it lies well within the Tropic of Cancer. At 15° north of the equator, it is at roughly the same latitude as Hawaii, Acapulco and Barbados together with the other islands of the southern Caribbean. In the southern hemisphere it has the island of Mauritius in the Indian Ocean and Tahiti in the Pacific as its counterparts in this respect.

One of earth's tropical paradises, it is also unique in India in terms of atmosphere and the character of its people. Arriving in Goa, one has the feeling of having been transported on to an island and, in a sense, this is true, for Goa, certainly the western coastal area, is a distinctive cultural island, largely the result of the impact of four-and-a-half centuries of Portuguese rule. The intensity of this impact derives from the interaction of several factors: the great length of time the Portuguese occupied Goa, the nature of their colonial approach and the geography of the territory, which meant that these forces were directed at a small area physically isolated from other outside influences.

The Portuguese ruled Goa for 450 years. They had been there for more than a century before the British even obtained their first trading concession from the Moghul Emperor and many more years would pass before the British could build their first fort – this in Madras where they established their first territorial foothold. They were still there when the British left more than 300 years later, and Danes, Dutch and French had come and gone before, eventually, in 1961, the Indian army moved in. It was definitely a case of first in but last out.

Perhaps of even greater significance than the length of their involvement was the nature of their approach to their colonies. More than any other European invader they stamped their character on their Indian possessions. They arrived fanatically determined to convert the entire population to Christianity and went a long way towards succeeding, at least outwardly, in the areas they first conquered. In contrast to British India, Portuguese influence was concentrated on a minute area over which they exerted total control and where, though small in number, they constituted a much higher proportion of the population, certainly in the early centuries.

Compounding all this was the geographical isolation of the territory, resulting from the physical barriers of mountains and wide rivers that separate Goa from the interior, making it difficult of access and insulating this little coastal enclave from the vastness of India stretching beyond the ghats to the east.

So the Portuguese imprint was powerful and deep-rooted – and even determined Goa's name. Before their arrival, the name Gowapuri, or Gove, was only applied to the port on the River Mandovi. This was abbreviated by them to Goa and, as they expanded their territory, the use of the name was extended to cover all the area under Portuguese control. However, even within the confines of Goa itself there are two distinctive areas reflecting different degrees of Portuguese impact.

The Velhas Conquistas, the Old Conquests, comprise the territory brought under Portuguese control soon after the taking of the port of Goa itself in 1510 and consist of only four of the present talukas, or administrative districts. Tiswadi, Bardez, Salcete and Mormugao taluka[1] cover an area of less than 700 square km (270 square miles), only a fifth of the total area of modern Goa (Map B). It is these Velhas Conquistas that form the especially distinctive Goan Goa, and it is truly Goan not Portuguese for, although the Portuguese factor is an essential ingredient, it is also important to remember that, at that time of distant conquest nearly 500 years ago, the conquered themselves already had a long history and a well-founded culture of their own. Subsequently, they subtly adapted all that was thrust upon them so that it has been merged with, rather than been allowed to usurp, their past.

Here is an area of impressive but gentle natural beauty. Behind a coastline of glorious palm-fringed beaches, interrupted now and then by thrusting rocky headlands, low rolling hills encircle basins of rich green paddy-fields laced by wide slow-flowing waterways. Superimposed on nature's benevolence are gleaming white churches, colourful and distinctive houses set amidst tropical shrubs and flowers and, occasionally, the striking remains of long-abandoned fortresses. Apart from its visible charms, there is something less easily definable but powerfully evident: the Goan 'air' that stems fundamentally from the nature of the people, lively but easy-going and welcoming, with an inimitable cultural heritage of which they are proudly aware and which extends beyond mere history into customs, language, music, food and even drink – all of which they are anxious to share. Here the essence of Goa is distilled into something tangible. Here a lush and languid environment has combined with the quirks of history to produce a small world apart, quite distinctive and until now unspoiled.

The other part of Goa, the Novas Conquistas, the New Conquests, has something quite different to offer. These areas were not added to Portuguese territory until the end of the 18th century, more than 250 years after the first invasion. Not only therefore were they subjected to Portuguese influence for a much shorter time compared with the four-and-a-half centuries of the Old Conquests, but, in addition, were acquired almost unintentionally and at a time when Portuguese administrative vigour and religious fanaticism, were considerably diminished. As a result, these outlying areas were left relatively little affected by their new masters. Most of the people were Hindus and, together with a small number of Muslims, were put under little pressure to change their religion – a far cry from the early years of conquest. All of this, together with geographical differences, results in two areas contrasting in atmosphere to the extent that one can sense, quite distinctly, the crossing from one to the other.

This part of Goa is a land of deep valleys with fast-flowing rivers cutting through wooded hillsides. Bare rocky uplands open up wider horizons and the peaks of the Sahyadri range that form Goa's eastern border are never very far away. It is in this area that the opencast ore-mining operations make their presence felt as a feature of the landscape. This too is a land where temples rather than churches are in the ascendancy and the villages also assume a different aspect.

All these contrasts, and the way in which many different influences have interacted to produce them, are part of Goa's fascination and, running true to form in terms of Goa's ability to provide intriguing paradoxes, so too is the fact that overriding all these differences there is a fundamental unity – all are Goans first and foremost. When the very elements that distinguish the Old from the New Conquests are examined more closely, it becomes evident that this underlying unity stems from the pre-Portuguese past which, together with Goan ability to adapt things seemingly forced on them from outside, has produced this end result. It is this unity that, against heavy odds, has brought ultimate success in the long political battle to prevent Goa's absorption into its giant neighbouring states of Maharashtra and Karnatika, at last giving it recognition as a separate state in its own right. It will be this unity that must surely enable this small corner of a vast country to continue to preserve its own special identity.

Throughout history, Goa always seems to have inspired magical-sounding names from those appreciating its unique qualities. Perhaps the prize should go to the Buddhists who, over 2000 years ago, demonstrated considerable perception in foreseeing Goa's continuing individuality when they referred to it as Aparanta, 'Beyond the End'.

MAPS

INDIA

A

PAKISTAN

•Srinagar

NEPAL

●DELHI

•Agra

I N D I A

CALCUTTA

Diu

Damen

Bassein

BOMBAY

ARABIAN
SEA

Bijapur

+

•Hyderabad

BAY OF
BENGAL

GOA

Vijayangar

+

Bangalore

Mangalore

•

MADRAS

Calicut

Cochin

Trivandrum

SRI
LANKA

B   GOA: THE OLD AND NEW CONQUESTS

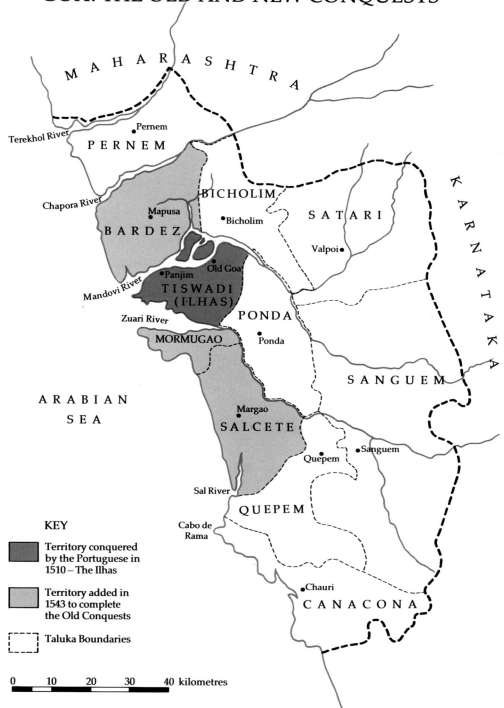

MAHARASHTRA

Terekhol River

•Pernem

PERNEM

Chapora River

BICHOLIM

SATARI

BARDEZ

Mapusa

•Bicholim

Valpoi•

Mandovi River

•Panjim   Old Goa•

TISWADI
(ILHAS)

Zuari River

PONDA

MORMUGAO

•Ponda

ARABIAN
SEA

KARNATAKA

SANGUEM

Margao•

SALCETE

Quepem•   •Sanguem

Sal River

QUEPEM

Cabo de
Rama

•Chauri

CANACONA

KEY

Territory conquered
by the Portuguese in
1510 – The Ilhas

Territory added in
1543 to complete
the Old Conquests

Taluka Boundaries

0   10   20   30   40 kilometres

C THE FORTRESSES OF GOA

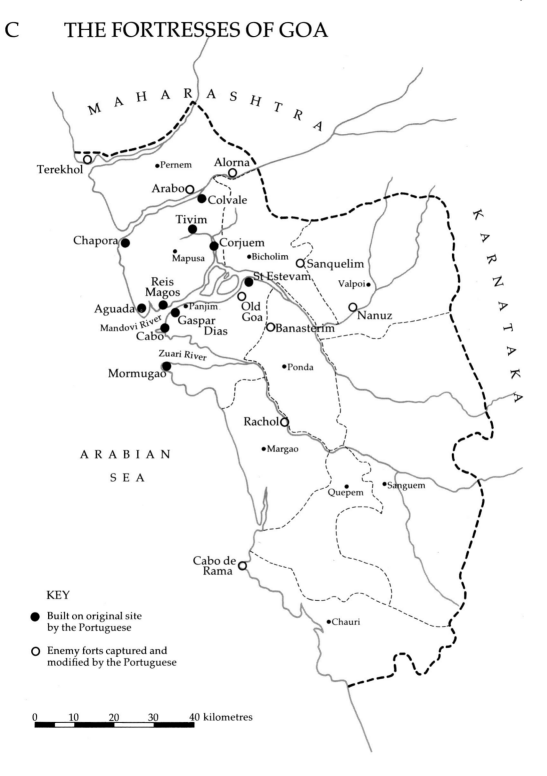

MAHARASHTRA

KARNATAKA

Terekhol

•Pernem

Alorna

Arabo○

●Colvale

Tivim

Chapora●

•Mapusa

Corjuem

•Bicholim

Sanquelim○

Reis Magos

St Estevam

Valpoi•

Aguada●

•Panjim

Old Goa○

Gaspar Dias

Mandovi River

Nanuz○

Cabo●

Banasterim○

Zuari River

Mormugao●

•Ponda

ARABIAN SEA

Rachol○

•Margao

•Sanguem

Quepem•

Cabo de Rama○

•Chauri

KEY

● Built on original site by the Portuguese

○ Enemy forts captured and modified by the Portuguese

0   10   20   30   40 kilometres

1 PANJIM

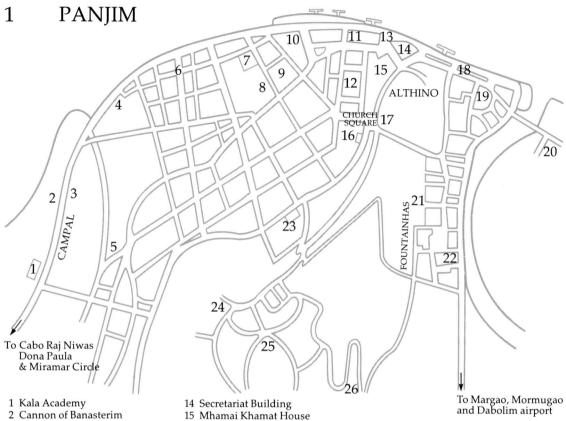

ALTHINO

CHURCH SQUARE

CAMPAL

FOUNTAINHAS

To Cabo Raj Niwas
   Dona Paula
   & Miramar Circle

To Margao, Mormugao
and Dabolim airport

1 Kala Academy	14 Secretariat Building
2 Cannon of Banasterim	15 Mhamai Khamat House
3 Statue of Louis Gomes	16 Jama Masjid
4 Medical College	17 Church of the Immaculate Conception
5 Museum	18 Church of San Thome
6 Municipal Market	19 Post and Telegraph Office
7 Menezes Braganza Institute	20 Department of Tourism
8 Police Headquarters	21 Church of San Sebastian
9 Azad Maidan	22 Historical Archives
10 Mandovi Hotel	23 Mahalaxmi Temple
11 High Courts	24 All India Radio
12 Municipal Gardens	25 Patriarchal Palace
13 Statue of Abbé Faria	26 Maruti Temple

2   OLD GOA

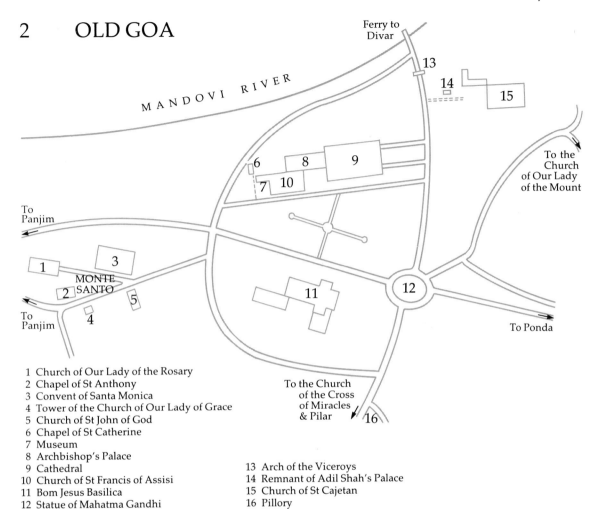

1 Church of Our Lady of the Rosary
2 Chapel of St Anthony
3 Convent of Santa Monica
4 Tower of the Church of Our Lady of Grace
5 Church of St John of God
6 Chapel of St Catherine
7 Museum
8 Archbishop's Palace
9 Cathedral
10 Church of St Francis of Assisi
11 Bom Jesus Basilica
12 Statue of Mahatma Gandhi

13 Arch of the Viceroys
14 Remnant of Adil Shah's Palace
15 Church of St Cajetan
16 Pillory

3 TISWADI – THE ILHAS
SKETCH MAP OF THE OLDEST CONQUEST

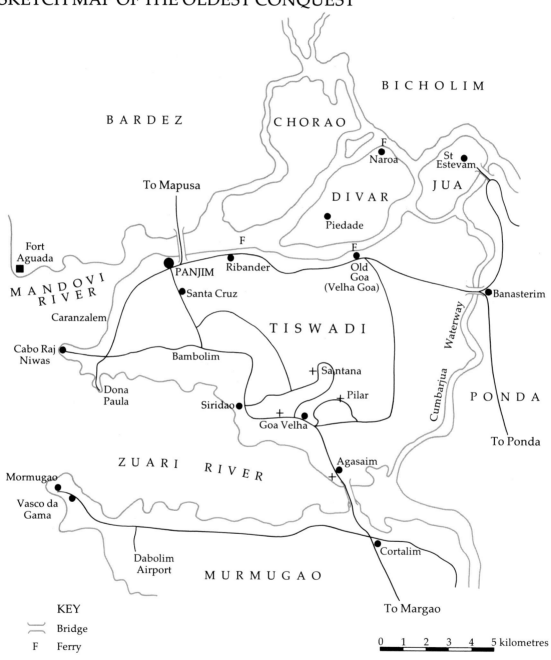

B I C H O L I M

B A R D E Z

CHORAO

Naroa

St
Estevam

J U A

To Mapusa

D I V A R

Piedade

Fort
Aguada

F

F

M A N D O V I
R I V E R

PANJIM

Ribander

Old
Goa
(Velha Goa)

Banasterim

Santa Cruz

Caranzalem

T I S W A D I

Cabo Raj
Niwas

Bambolim

Santana

P O N D A

Dona
Paula

Pilar

Siridao

Goa Velha

To Ponda

Z U A R I   R I V E R

Agasaim

Mormugao

Vasco da
Gama

Dabolim
Airport

M U R M U G A O

Cortalim

To Margao

Cumbarjua Waterway

KEY

Bridge

F   Ferry

0   1   2   3   4   5 kilometres

4 PONDA – THE OTHER SIDE OF THE RIVER
HINDU PONDA

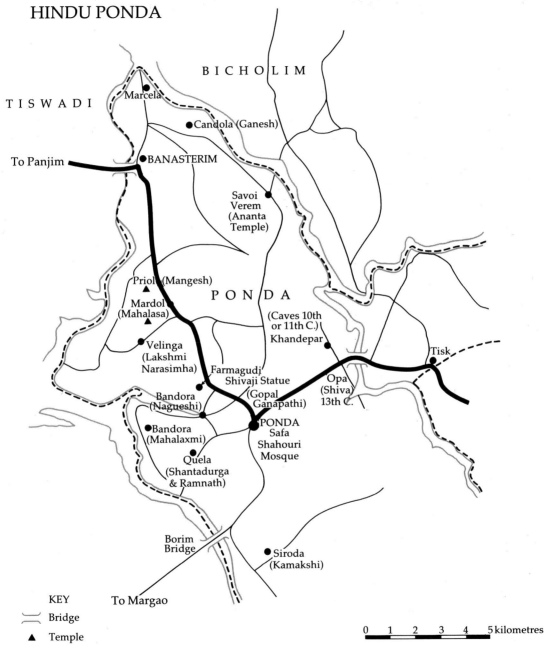

B I C H O L I M

T I S W A D I

Marcela

Candola (Ganesh)

To Panjim

●BANASTERIM

Savoi
Verem
(Ananta
Temple)

Priol (Mangesh)
▲

P O N D A

Mardol
(Mahalasa)
▲

(Caves 10th
or 11th C.)
Khandepar

Tisk

Velinga
(Lakshmi
Narasimha)

Farmagudi
Shivaji Statue
(Gopal
Ganapathi)

Opa
(Shiva)
13th C.

Bandora
(Nagueshi)

●Bandora
(Mahalaxmi)

●PONDA
Safa
Shahouri
Mosque

Quela
(Shantadurga
& Ramnath)

Borim
Bridge

●Siroda
(Kamakshi)

KEY

To Margao

Bridge

▲ Temple

0   1   2   3   4   5 kilometres

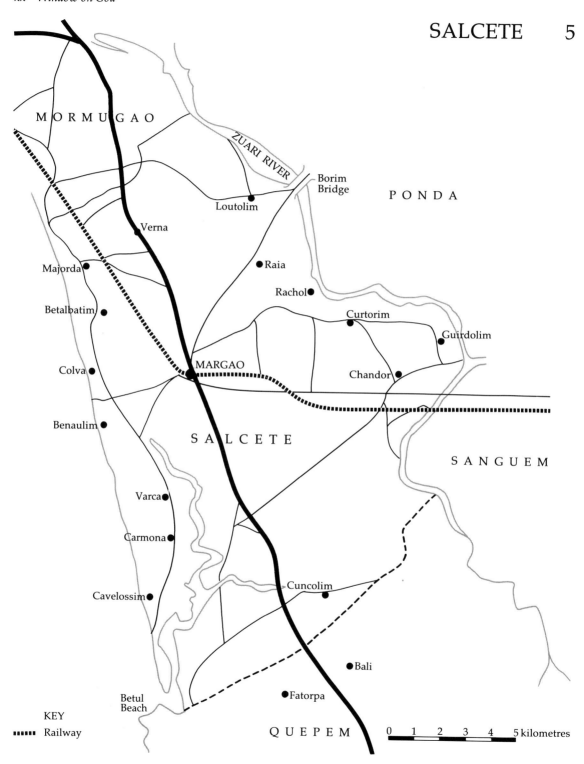

SALCETE 5

MORMUGAO

ZUARI RIVER

Borim
Bridge

PONDA

Loutolim

Verna

Raia

Majorda

Rachol

Curtorim

Betalbatim

Guirdolim

Colva

MARGAO

Chandor

Benaulim

SALCETE

SANGUEM

Varca

Carmona

Cavelossim

Cuncolim

Bali

Betul
Beach

Fatorpa

KEY

QUEPEM

0 1 2 3 4 5 kilometres

▪▪▪▪▪ Railway

6 MARGAO

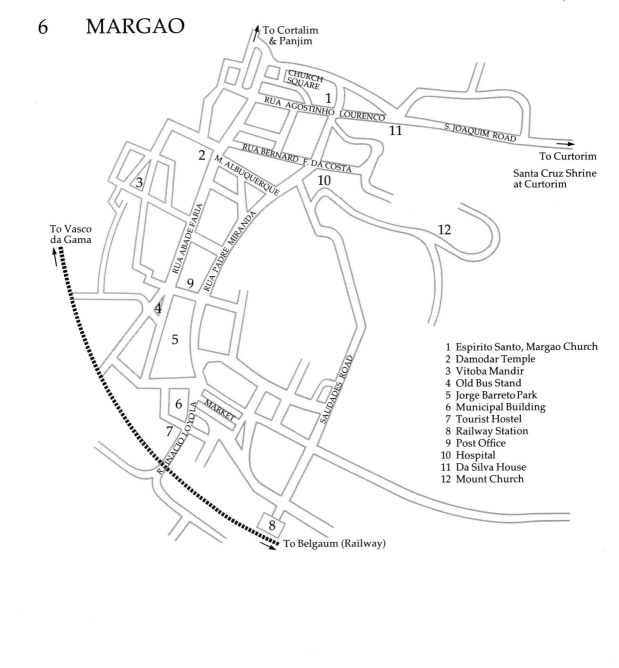

To Cortalim
& Panjim

CHURCH
SQUARE

RUA AGOSTINHO LOURENCO

1

11

S. JOAQUIM ROAD

To Curtorim

Santa Cruz Shrine
at Curtorim

RUA BERNARD F. DA COSTA

2

M. ALBUQUERQUE

10

3

12

To Vasco
da Gama

RUA ABADE FARIA

RUA PADRE MIRANDA

9

4

5

MARKET

6

R. INACIO LOYOLA

7

SAUDADES ROAD

8

To Belgaum (Railway)

1 Espirito Santo, Margao Church
2 Damodar Temple
3 Vitoba Mandir
4 Old Bus Stand
5 Jorge Barreto Park
6 Municipal Building
7 Tourist Hostel
8 Railway Station
9 Post Office
10 Hospital
11 Da Silva House
12 Mount Church

7   BARDEZ

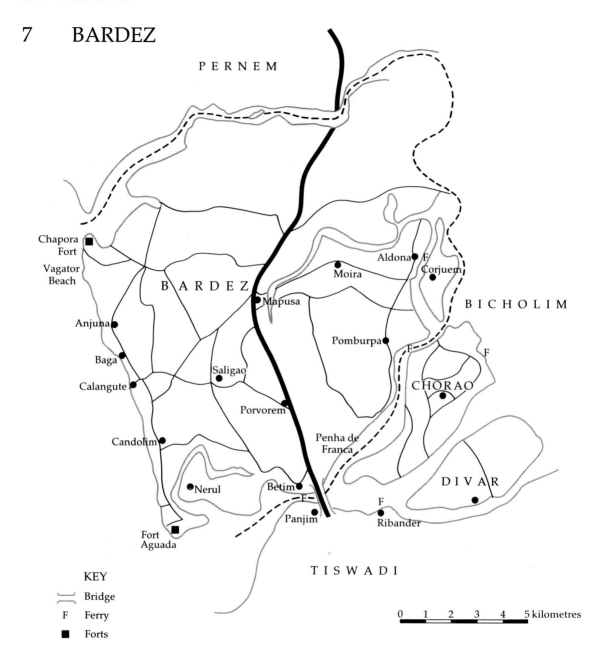

PERNEM

Chapora
Fort

Vagator
Beach

BARDEZ

Aldona ● F
Moira ●

Corjuem ●

Mapusa

BICHOLIM

Anjuna ●

Baga ●

Pomburpa ●

Calangute ●

Saligao ●

CHORAO

Candolim ●

Porvorem

Penha de
Franca

DIVAR

Nerul ●

Betim ●
F

Panjim ●

F
Ribander ●

Fort
Aguada

TISWADI

KEY

〜   Bridge

F   Ferry

■   Forts

0   1   2   3   4   5 kilometres

8 BICHOLIM

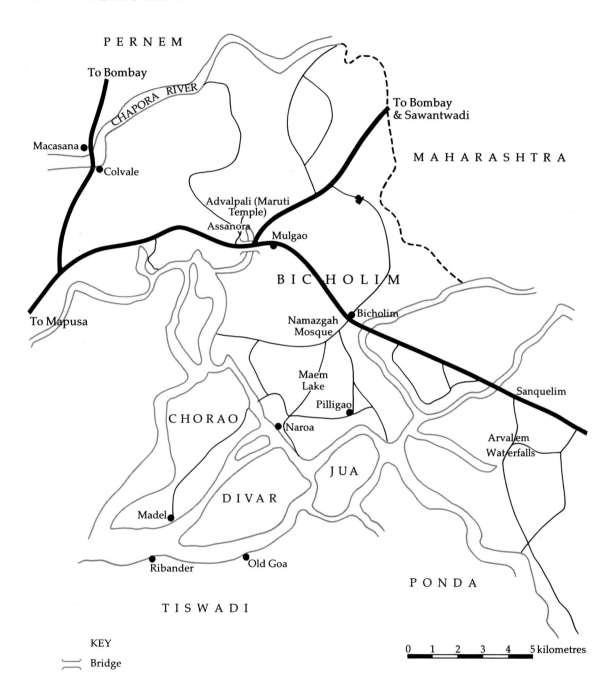

PERNEM

To Bombay

CHAPORA RIVER

Macasana

Colvale

To Bombay
& Sawantwadi

MAHARASHTRA

Advalpali (Maruti
Temple)

Assanora

Mulgao

BICHOLIM

To Mapusa

Namazgah
Mosque

Bicholim

Maem
Lake

Sanquelim

CHORAO

Pilligao

Naroa

Arvalem
Waterfalls

JUA

DIVAR

Madel

Ribander

Old Goa

PONDA

TISWADI

KEY

Bridge

0   1   2   3   4   5 kilometres

9   GOA – FRINGE BENEFITS

MAHARASHTRA

Terekhol fort ▲

▲Keri ▲Pernem

P E R N E M

Arambol Beach

Agarvarda• •Colvale

•Siolim

BICHOLIM SATARI

Mapusa•

B A R D E Z •Bicholim ▲Brahma Temple
Carmoli

Valpoi•

•Panjim

T I S W A D I

Bondla Tambdi
Sanctuary Surla

P O N D A

Mormugao• Bhagwan Bondia
Vasco de Gama• MORMUGAO •Ponda Mahaveer
Sanctuary
Molem•

Colem• ▲Dudhsagar
Falls

A R A B I A N

S E A Margao• •Chandor S A N G U E M

SALCETE

Chandranath ▲

•Quepem •Sanguem

Cuncolim ▲ ▲Zambaulim

Rivona ▲Curdi

QUEPEM

Cabo de Rama ▲
Fort

KEY

▲ General location of places
of interest mentioned
in this section

—————— Railway Line

•Chauri

C A N A C O N A

Cotigao
Sanctuary

0   10   20   30   40 kilometres

K A R N A T A K A

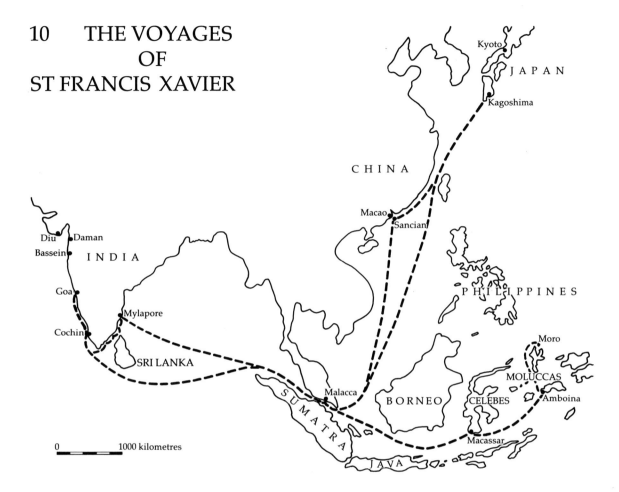

10 THE VOYAGES
OF
ST FRANCIS XAVIER

PART ONE

SETTING THE STAGE

Look-out post, Chapora Fort

1 THE HISTORY

BEFORE THE PORTUGUESE

Goa's history stretches back into the centuries before Christ when it formed part of the domains of the Buddhist Emperor Asoka Maurya. Subsequently, it was ruled by a series of Hindu dynasties, although for much of the time these were vassal states of one of the more powerful rulers beyond the mountains to the east, only its geographical isolation giving some degree of independence.

Towards the end of the 6th century the great Badami Chalukyan king, Pulekesin II, took Goa into his territories and put his son, Chandraditya, at its head with his capital – coincidentally, at the already ancient site of Chandrapur, present-day Chandor. This was heavily fortified and grew into a fine city. It was to be the capital for the next four centuries, but even in these early days, sea-bound trade was developing rapidly and a port grew up on the north bank of the Zuari River at a place called Gopakapat-tana or Gowapuri.

In the later part of the 10th century a new dynasty was established as overlords of the area, still feuda-tories of more powerful rulers beyond the ghats, but a line of kings that would consolidate the foundations of Goa's future development. The Kadamba dynasty would rule for nearly 400 years and leave their firm imprint on Goa. Soon sea trade was booming and a huge volume of international traffic was going through the port of Gowapuri. Just as important, Kadamba power had as its basis a strong naval fleet and so in 1052 they transferred their capital to Gowapuri, the port in the Zuari, known to visiting seamen simply as Gove. Trade continued to flourish, with Arab Muslim traders, who had played such an important role in its growth, settling there and becoming an integral part of the community.

Goa's Arab traders were very different from their fellow Muslims that fought their way into India from beyond the mountains of the north-west in about AD 1200. These northern invaders were the overspill from power struggles that had been going on in Afghanistan and the lands beyond the North West Frontier, and their objective was not only loot but new territory over which to rule. They routed the combined armies of the Hindu Rajas of the north and established their capital at Delhi. From there, the treasure-seeking expeditions of the Sultans of Delhi took them further and further afield, leaving a trail of devastation in their wake. These warriors of the Prophet were as fanatically committed to the destruction of heathen temples as any Portuguese conquistador would later prove to be.

The palaces and temples of the deep south offered rich pickings and it was on one of these looting expeditions that Goa experienced its first unhappy encounter with the warlike side of Islam. In 1312 the troops of Ala'ud-din-Khilji under Malik Kafur virtually razed Gowapuri to the ground. The Kadambas retreated to Chandrapur, but, in 1327, Muhammed Tughluq's army attacked and this time it was Chandrapur's turn to be ravaged and its population slaughtered.

In 1347 a new Muslim power was established in the northern Deccan, the Bahmani Sultanate being a breakaway group from their now enfeebled Delhi overlords. It was under the Bahamanis that Goa 'enjoyed' direct Muslim rule for the first time, being taken over by them in 1352. Further Bahmani expansion southwards was blocked by another newly formed kingdom, the great Hindu Vijayana-gar Empire, and a state of constant war existed between these two. Meanwhile Goa had to suffer the further destruction of its temples by dedicated Muslims and the extraction of heavy tribute, with many Hindus fleeing the areas under control of the invaders – a foretaste of things to come.

The relief can be imagined when in 1378 the

Vijayanagar general, Madhav Mantri, took Goa from the Bahmanis and there followed nearly a century of peaceful Hindu rule. Trade thrived, particularly the import of Arab horses. Southern India bred no horses of quality of its own and they were a vital factor in maintaining military supremacy. This also encouraged the reverse trade of local goods across the Arabian Sea, pepper, betel nut and calico being in great demand. However, Gowapuri never recovered its former absolute dominance as the supreme west coast port and was already experiencing the problem that would ensure its demise. The mouth of the Zuari River was beginning to silt up.

It was not until 1470 that Mahmud Gawan, the Bahmani Chief Minister and General, took Goa back into the Muslim fold. There was a repeat of Hindu temple destruction, the secreting away of their deities and the flight of refugees. In addition, the Muslim forces obliterated what was left of poor Gowapuri. The site of this first Gowapuri is at the northern end of the new road bridge over the Zuari River, now as a result of continued silting of the river a little way inland and known as Goa Velha to distinguish it from Velha Goa that was about to be born.

Even before the Zuari port's decline, a new port had begun to emerge on the clear, deep waters of the Mandovi at the village of Ela on the northern side of the island and shortly after the Muslim takeover, the functions of capital, along with its name, were transplanted to the site of what was to become 'Golden Goa'.

The Bahmani Kingdom itself soon broke up, its western territories being formed into another Muslim Sultanate, powerful Bijapur under its Sultan Yusuf Adil Shah or Khan. As a port, the new Gowapuri or Gove continued to prosper under the new and much more liberal regime, with added importance as a departure point for pilgrims to Mecca. It was a favourite resort of the Sultan who built a great palace overlooking the river and, at one time, even considered making it his capital. Gove was already a beautiful and thriving city. Contemporary visitors praised its impressive buildings, wide streets and gardens with an abundance of that feature of all Persian town-planners – flowing water. Apart from its function as an international trading centre, again with Arab assistance, it added ship-building to its talents.

1510–1600 THE CONQUEST AND THE GOLDEN YEARS

In 1498 Vasco da Gama landed at Calicut on the Malabar Coast, the first to negotiate the sea route from Europe to India round the Cape of Good Hope. He came, as he himself said, 'seeking Christians and spices'. The Christians he hoped to find, the subjects of the legendary Prester John who were believed to be under Muslim threat and whose alliance against the common enemy was one of the objectives of the mission, were not there. The Syrian Christians who were, and who claimed their origin in the mission to India of Thomas the Apostle in the 1st century, constituted a poor substitute from the Portuguese Roman Catholic point of view, being highly unorthodox in their practices.

The spice trade, however, was very real and the Portuguese were determined to break the monopoly of the Arab Muslims who had a stranglehold on supplies to Europe from the East Indies and from India itself, shipping the spices across to the Red Sea and the Persian Gulf for sale to Egyptian and Venetian merchants.

Spices were not a luxury in the Europe of the 16th century. With the lack of winter fodder necessitating the slaughter of all cattle each autumn, spices were essential for the preservation of meat through the winter and to counter the increasingly overpowering smell and taste of decay, while wine, in the absence of effective maturation techniques, was only made palatable by mulling with spices. To the Portuguese it was a highly valuable business, made all the more attractive by the fact that it was currently in the hands of heathen unbelievers.

Thus the Portuguese were inspired by a high degree of religious and commercial zeal, crusading romantics with an overpowering sense of mission and destiny that would characterise all their colonial enterprises.

Following Vasco da Gama's epic voyage, they built a fort on Anjediva Island, just south of Goa, and established another base to the north of Calicut at Cannanore. Neither fully met their needs and, after an initial visit to reconnoitre the situation, the inimitable Afonso Albuquerque was sent back in 1508 to take over as Governor with orders to establish a Portuguese trading empire in the East.

Strong vantage-points from which to control Arabian sea-traffic and close down the Red Sea spice route were the first requirement and Albuquerque set out to capture Ormuz, the key to the Persian Gulf and the Red Sea itself. He was diverted by information laid by Timoja, a Hindu sea captain pirating the Muslim horse trade and pilgrim traffic on behalf of Vijayanagar. Timoja not only gave a graphic picture of the excellence of Gove's port facilities but also of the substantial shipyard where the Sultan, with Arab assistance, was building large, high-quality ships with which to oppose the Portuguese. He clinched matters with the news that the powerful Yusuf Adil Shah was in his capital across the ghats and on his death-bed, the last an inaccurate piece of information, as Albuquerque would soon discover to his cost.

In March 1510 Afonso Albuquerque, with 20 ships and 1200 men, occupied Adil Shah's fortress-palace at the mouth of the Mandovi River and the rest of the island fell with little opposition. However, it did not take long for Sultan Yusuf Adil Shah to recover from this surprise and, barely two months after their arrival, the approach of a powerful army 60,000 strong caused Albuquerque and his men to retreat onto their ships to spend an uncomfortable monsoon anchored just out of range of the Sultan's guns. This sad situation was tempered only by the fact that they had taken with them local provisions and as many beautiful ladies as could be accommodated on board as hostages. The provisions did not last long, and the crews were in dire straits by the time, as soon as the weather permitted, Albuquerque could retreat south to re-fit. This was in August.

Three months later, reinforced by more ships and men, Albuquerque attacked again and, on 25 November, St Catherine's Day, re-took Gove after a brisk and bloody battle. He sacked the city and ordered the wholesale massacre of the Muslim inhabitants, the one blot on his otherwise liberal record. Yusuf Adil Shah himself died ten days after the fall of the city. Albuquerque then set about building his base, the first Indian territory to be brought under European control since Alexander the Great left in 326 BC. Gove was further abbreviated by the Portuguese to Goa.

The next step was to extend the Portuguese trading empire eastwards. Initiated by the vigour and enterprise of Albuquerque, this was accomplished in a remarkably short space of time. He at once sailed for the East Indies, the source of the spice trade, conquered Malacca and built a fort there, returning to Goa in time to direct resistance against attempts by the youthful Ismail Adil Khan, who had succeeded his father, to regain his territory. He then went west across the Arabian Sea, conquering Aden in 1513 and Ormuz, the key to the Persian Gulf, in 1515. It was while in Ormuz that he fell seriously ill and at once sailed for Goa. Legend has it that as his brigantine sailed up the Mandovi, he struggled from his cabin clad in his imposing uniform to an armchair on the deck, so that he might see Goa for the last time. Here he died on 15 December 1515.

While expanding their commercial empire, it was also essential that the Portuguese consolidated and strengthened their position in their base in Goa. Initially, their territory was confined to the Ilhas which constituted the main 'Island of Goa', Tiswadi, together with the small islands in the Mandovi River. Both the north bank of the Mandovi and that of the Zuari were in hostile hands and not only threatened the entrance to the two great rivers but put Ismail Adil Khan's armies at uncomfortably close quarters across the narrow stretches of water.

The long-running conflict between Vijayanagar and Bijapur had been going on for nearly 200 years, and it so happened that in 1520 a surge of Hindu successes led to the capture of the fort of Rachol and Muslim control over the areas surrounding the Ilhas being considerably weakened. Handing over Rachol Fort to the Portuguese, Vijayanagar encouraged them to occupy Bardez, Ponda and Salcete, an opportunity they seized with alacrity. Adil Shah soon re-took Ponda and Bardez and most of Salcete, but Rachol provided a core of resistance in the south and a lengthy period of fierce fighting ensued.

Soon another opportunity presented itself for the Portuguese to expand beyond the Ilhas. A dispute between Adil Shah and his Governor of Belgaum, who included Bardez and Salcete in the territories under his control, led to the errant governor offering these areas in exchange for Portuguese support. The offer was accepted and the Portuguese again moved in. Two years later, on the death of Ismail Adil Shah in 1534, one of the contestants for the title, Ibrahim, put himself on the throne and demanded the return of Bardez and Salcete. The Portuguese refused, but soon Ibrahim's superior armies forced them to negotiate yet another withdrawal, the Viceroy destroying the Fort of Rachol before retreating. However, diplomatic manoeuvring succeeded where force of arms had failed. Ibrahim was still struggling to establish himself as Adil Shah and the Portuguese applied pressure by bringing to Goa his strongest rival claimant, threatening to give him their support. Ibrahim gave in and handed back Bardez and Salcete in return for the Viceroy agreeing to send Mir Ali, the pawn in this political game, to Malacca. Although this part of the bargain was never kept, Bardez and Salcete were formally ceded by treaty in 1543, establishing the boundaries that would define Portuguese Goa for almost two-and-a-half centuries (map 2).

Meanwhile Macao, the link port with China, was established, while the addition of the fortress ports on the west coast of India at Bassein, Daman and Diu not only confirmed control of the spice trade to the Red Sea and the Persian Gulf, but also enabled the Portuguese to control all other maritime operations in the Arabian Sea. Heavy tolls were levied on all cargoes carried, in return for guaranteeing protection against Portuguese attack. This included the lucrative extortion of protection money on all pilgrim traffic to Mecca.

The Portuguese were on top of the trading world and Goa, the hub of this eastern empire, was the recipient of incredible riches from this wildly flourishing commercial enterprise. A profitable trade in gold, silver, pearls and silks, together with the Vijayanagar horse trade, was added to the wealth derived from acting as middle-men and shippers in the East Indies spice trade. They also controlled the trade in the limited spices available from the Malabar Coast itself, cardamom and pepper. A bonus was the enormous profit to be made from acting as bullion brokers, taking advantage of the variations in exchange values of gold and silver between China, Japan and India. 'Golden Goa' was truly a name to be conjured with throughout the civilised world in the second half of the 16th century.

This meteoric rise was, in fact, almost brought to an abrupt end. Vijayanagar, long-standing ally of the Portuguese, had at last been crushed by Muslim forces whose attention turned once again to Goa. Bijapur, Ahmednagar and Calicut planned a combined assault and in 1570, for ten long months, the tiny garrison withstood a siege against overwhelming odds. Inspired by the leadership and courage of Viceroy Lous de Ataide, Goa survived to continue its headlong progress to its zenith.

However, there was another aspect to the Portuguese occupation apart from the heady commercial success, one that was to have a longer-term impact on its people. This was the total commitment of the colonists to convert all their subject peoples to Christianity and to a pure form of Roman Catholicism in particular. They were absolutely and utterly convinced that this was their rightful mission in life and many of their excesses in this regard can perhaps be excused to some extent by the sincerity of this belief. The process started at a gentle pace, Albuquerque himself being particularly liberal for his time and, in any case, more concerned with commercial rather than religious objectives. However, the subsequent approach to the conversion of the local people was anything but liberal.

The Franciscans were early arrivals, but it was not until after 1540, when representatives of other religious orders arrived on the scene in considerable numbers that missionary activity began in earnest. With the Dominicans and Augustinians in particular thirsting for converts, the vigour and

competitive element of the missionary process rapidly gained in tempo. A notable arrival in 1542 was the Spanish priest Francis Xavier, disciple of the founder of the Jesuit Order, Ignatius Loyola. Francis, although he himself was to live in Goa for only a few months in all, was to become one of the most famous names in Goan history and the Jesuits were to play a leading role. It was at the instigation of the Jesuits that the Viceroy was given sanction by the King of Portugal, to destroy all Hindu temples within the boundaries of Goa and build churches in their place. The area of the Old Conquests was cleared from end to end of all outward manifestations of Jewish, Muslim and more particularly, in view of their numerical superiority, Hindu practices. Several hundred Hindu temples or shrines are believed to have been destroyed. Images were, in some cases, rescued, taken across the border and re-established in areas at that time outside Portuguese control.

In 1560, 'celebrating' fifty years of Portuguese occupation, the horrors of the Inquisition were inflicted on Goa. Any outward expression of other faiths was made illegal. Most Muslims had been dispersed or disposed of, and some Hindus had fled the territory, though many remained to practice their forbidden rites in secret, it being now a crime even to worship their gods within their own homes. The most punitive measure, in economic terms, was that land tenure by succession, a system well established in Goa, was only allowed if descendants could prove their rights to inheritance by Christian church marriage records. Thus, for this reason alone, at least some representatives of each family remained and 'converted'. In practical terms, cremation, so fundamental to Hindu philosophy, was, as can be imagined, the most difficult to perpetuate without discovery – yet even this continued.

Balancing the religious oppression and fanaticism, which was undoubtedly there in abundance, was another aspect to the approach to conversion, no less sure in its dedication. Religious concepts imposed by fear and threats alone, could not possibly have survived the centuries to produce the deep-rooted Christian ethic that is so evident in Goa today, just as the destruction of temples, and administrative edicts imposed by force, failed to suppress Hindu beliefs and practices.

Goa was fortunate in its share of missionaries who devoted their lives to establishing means of communication that would lead to understanding. That this was a means to an end cannot detract from the ensuing benefits that would have lasting effects on Goan life. The first printing press in India was at

St Paul's College, introduced as early as 1556, soon to be followed by two more, one of these at Rachol. From this press came a Konkani Grammar, the first to be produced in any of the modern Indian languages, together with many more linguistic studies as well as philosophical and medical works. Just as the religious orders competed in terms of church building as part of the conversion process, so did they compete in education and learning, with almost each one establishing a seminary or college. The first hospital in Asia is another item on the credit side, and, on a different plane, but still important, Indian life without the chilli would hardly be the same and the Portuguese can take the credit for introducing that, along with the cashew, papaya and pineapple, not to mention the establishment of techniques for cross-breeding mango varieties that produced the Alfonso as its first achievement.

1600–1660 THE DREAM OF EMPIRE FADES

In no way connected with the Christianisation process, which in any case was to continue in a varying degree for another 200 years or more, the end of the century saw the first signs of decay that presaged the rapid collapse of Portugal's eastern commercial empire with its inevitable effect on Goa.

In political terms, the annexing of Portugal by Spain in 1580 following the death of the youthful and impetuous King Sebastiao in his foolhardy attack against the Moors in North Africa, had deprived Goa of the European government's direction and support that its importance to Portugal had warranted. Spain demonstrated little interest in the eastern colonies and this would continue even after Portugal regained her independence sixty years later in 1640.

In commercial terms, the reversal began in 1600 when the English and Dutch began to take an interest in eastern trade. On the last day of 1600, Queen Elizabeth granted a trading charter to 'the Governor and Company of Merchants of London trading into East Indies', and in 1602 the United East India Company of the Netherlands was founded.

Dominance at sea was all-important and lack of competition during the 16th century had led to a stagnation in Portuguese seamanship in all its aspects, navigation, quality of crews and naval warfare techniques, all compounded by poorly designed and unwieldy vessels.

The first major disaster for the Portuguese came in 1612 when, off the coast of Surat, they suffered a heavy defeat at the hands of the fleet of the East India Company of the Merchants of London. Six years later the Company obtained a firman from the Moghul emperor Jehangir granting them trading rights in the Port of Surat in return for English defence of Muslim sea traffic in the Arabian Sea. This struck at an important source of Portuguese income as well as influence and put the first of many nails into the coffin of Goa's prosperity. But it was the Dutch who were really responsible for the downfall of the Portuguese commercial empire in the East. The heaviest blow was the loss of the East Indies spice trade to the Dutch, initially operating from Batavia but in 1641 taking the Portuguese base of Malacca itself. To the south, the Malabar Coast was no longer a factor in the East–West spice trade. In 1657 the Dutch took Cochin and other Malabar ports but in any case their ships were already by-passing India on their way to Europe round the Cape of Good Hope. Portuguese fate was sealed once the English, themselves having failed to usurp the Dutch in the East Indies, turned their full attention towards India as their next best commercial option.

At this period of Goa's history, religious fervour was at its peak, showing no signs of flagging in the face of degeneration in other aspects of Goan life. It was a 'museum of 16th-century imperialism, more plentifully supplied with churches than trade and with monks than soldiers'. With the progressive deterioration in civil administration, the 'monks' assumed considerable importance and influence, and the conversion process continued with frenetic vigour. Of Hindus, Muslims, Syrian Christians and Jews there was hardly a remaining outward relic.

A great surge of ecclesiastical building had followed the arrival of the religious orders after 1540 and religious fervour, backed by the accumulated wealth of Goa's commercial heyday, now carried this architectural exuberance throughout this period of economic and political disarray, on an even grander scale than before. This was the time when the great churches of Old Goa were completed, in particular, the Cathedral and the Bom Jesus Basilica, and the city itself continued to present a brave social front, flaunting ostentation and luxury in defiance of economic circumstance. Be that as it may, by the middle of the 17th century Goa's importance as an international trading centre had vanished and, in addition, their landward connections had deteriorated to the point where it was by now commercially irrelevant to the Portuguese which power held the hinterland, their main concern being the threat of aggression and their survival.

1660–1813 THE YEARS OF SURVIVAL

Soon after the first conquest, the Portuguese had held on to their territory in the face of determined counter-attacks by the new Sultan of Bijapur, Ismail Adil Khan, and subsequently in 1570, as already mentioned, the tiny garrison had survived a lengthy siege by the army of one of his successors. Early in the 17th century, two Dutch attacks on Goa from the sea had been beaten off, but soon after the second of these, which took place in 1640, a new power emerged beyond the ghats to threaten their territory. Shivaji was bringing the Marathas out of obscurity to terrorise much of western India.

In 1664, adopting the guerrilla tactics that became his hallmark, and the means of his success in the face of much stronger, more formally organised forces, Shivaji took possession of many of the outlying Bijapur territories including Bicholim and Pernem. This brought him to the very borders of Goa and it was with relief that the Portuguese saw him withdraw, in some haste, to meet a threat to his own territory from the army of the Great Moghul, Aurangzeb, who was beginning to realise the growing significance of this outstanding leader, originally no more than a brigand chieftain.

The Portuguese found themselves walking a diplomatic tightrope. Their Indian possessions were small and scattered and it was vital that they maintained good relations with the great Moghul Emperor. However, Shivaji had demonstrated that the Marathas were also a force to be feared and could not be ignored. So, they signed a treaty of friendship with the Marathas as well! Being allies of two deadly enemies was no simple matter, but the Portuguese managed this until soon after Shivaji's death in 1680, when his son and successor, the headstrong Sambhaji, decided to remove what he regarded as the Portuguese irritant factor. Before long, he and his troops had penetrated so deeply into Goa that in 1683 his forces were at the limits of the island of Tiswadi itself, even the Fort of St Estevam having fallen, bringing them virtually to the gates of the city. It seemed that nothing now could save Goa, but it is recorded that at this moment of ultimate peril, the coffin of St Francis Xavier was opened, the Viceroy, Count D'Alvor placed his baton of office and his Royal Warrant of Appointment at St Francis's side, and committed the city to his protection. Almost immediately afterwards, news came that Sambhaji had withdrawn his troops, threatened by powerful Moghul forces in his rear. The miracle had happened. It

would not be for another fifty years that Goa would again be subjected to Maratha attacks.

Following Aurangzeb's death at the beginning of the 18th century, the rapidly diminishing power of the Moghul Empire, coinciding with a revival of Maratha strength, enabled the Marathas once again to cast covetous eyes on the wealth of Portugal's Province of the North centred on Bassein, and, in 1737, they began what was to become a protracted attempt to take the great fortress there. In 1739, having failed to overcome the strong defences, they sent a large force to Goa to cut off support being sent from there into Bassein by sea. Here success was rapid and they were soon in control of most of the territory. In Bardez, only the forts of Aguada and Reis Magos held firm and in Salcete only Mormugao and Rachol. This time, however, a vigorous new Viceroy, the Marquis of Lourical, together with substantial reinforcements, arrived just in time to prevent the fall of the territory, but the terms of the negotiated peace that followed were devastating. Except for Daman, all the Province of the North was handed over to the Marathas and crippling financial compensation was agreed to persuade them to withdraw from Goa.

So, looking back to 1660, this had been a disastrous time from the point of view of loss of Portuguese dominions in India. The Dutch had taken Ceylon and all the Malabar ports including Cochin, Bombay had been handed over to the British in 1665 as part of the dowry of the sister of the King of Portugal, Catherine of Braganza, on her marriage to Charles II, and now Bassein was irrevocably lost to the Marathas. This left only Goa and the tiny bases of Daman and Diu in Portuguese hands.

During this period the crusading religious spirit at last showed some signs of abating, and although, in general, proceedings in Goa were followed with scant attention by the parent government, even after Portugal regained its independence from Spain, there was the occasional flutter of interest that resulted in legislation being initiated in Europe. Two edicts in particular had important effects on the life of the colony. The first resulted from the fact that, although the Portuguese government were not prepared to involve themselves too whole-heartedly in the affairs of what many now regarded as a parasite territory, they were equally determined that others should not usurp their authority, an attitude that would typify their later dealings with their Indian colonies. They were particularly concerned at the growing influence of the religious orders, especially the powerful Jesuits whose direction came from Rome rather than Lisbon and whose large-scale acquisition of land ran contrary to Portuguese colonial practice. Accusing the Jesuits in Portugal of involvement in an assassination plot against the King, the authorities decreed the suppression of the Society of Jesus throughout their overseas territories and in Goa in 1759 many were arrested and deported and their properties confiscated. However, it was difficult effectively to enforce such edicts at a time of general maladministration and it was not until 1773 that they were finally suppressed. Other religious orders continued in existence for another sixty years until 1835 when they too were banned.

Yet another edict, this issued in 1774, abolished the Inquisition and yet again its implementation took over-long, the dreaded institution only being finally vanquished once and for all time in 1812.

The end of the century witnessed an important incident, the first real revolt against Portuguese rule. In 1787, perhaps encouraged by the mood in Lisbon, and dissatisfied with the severe discrimination against Goans on the question of promotion in the clerical hierarchy, it was a group of priests who hatched a plot to overthrow the government, even sending representatives to Lisbon to try to enlist support. Known as the Pinto Revolt, as the conspirators met in the Pinto family house in Candolim village near Fort Aguada, the priests were joined by army officers and others. The plot was discovered and forty-seven of the conspirators were arrested and tortured. Fifteen of them were executed in Panjim.

Two other significant events marked this period of Goan history, one the final abandonment of the once great city of Old Goa, the second, astonishingly, the expansion of the territory under Portuguese control.

Ill-drained and pestilential, the site of the city of Goa was not a healthy one and, as numbers grew, the situation deteriorated rapidly in the tropical climate. The first cholera epidemic had struck as early as 1543, and these scourges became so frequent that, by the end of the 17th century, official proposals were being made that the site of the capital should be moved. By this time the population had, in any case, dwindled rapidly to less than 20,000 – only a tenth of what it had been at its peak earlier in the century. Mormugao was the first site selected as an alternative, but, in 1759, it was to Panjim that the Viceroy finally moved, taking up residence in the building that had been Adil Khan's palace.

After this there was a progressive drift of population out of the city and, although the Senate continued to meet there until 1835 and the Royal Decree declaring Panjim the capital was not issued until 1843, the city had long since died.

The second event, the expansion of territory which took place in the second half of the 18th century, was admittedly achieved fortuitously rather than by design and took place in two stages.

In 1764 the Raja of Sonda, Goa's neighbour to the east, under threat from Haider Ali of Mysore, fled to Goa, asked for asylum and requested the Portuguese to occupy his territories until the threat had passed. The Portuguese obliged, moving into what are now the districts of Ponda, Sanguem, Quepem and Canacona. The wrath of Haider Ali was diverted only by the news that a joint force of Marathas and British were moving against him. Once again Goa had been saved by the unexpected but timely intervention of outside forces. Inevitably the occupation of the Raja's territories became permanent and his descendants still live in Bandora, in Ponda, in the house the Raja had the Portuguese build for him.

The three northern districts that completed the Novas Conquistas and established the present territorial boundaries of Goa, were added between 1781 and 1788. Pernem, Bicholim and Satari formed part of the territory of the Bhonsles, the Rajas of Sawantwadi Goa's northern neighbour. To put it mildly, Portuguese relations with successive Bhonsle rulers had been strained since the beginning of the century, at times breaking into open conflict with brisk military action when the Bhonsles attempted to take territorial liberties, notwithstanding the existence of a treaty of mutual assistance in the event of attack. In 1781, in spite of his own previous total disregard for their alliance, the Raja called for such assistance against his traditional enemy, the Raja of Kolhapur. The Portuguese agreed with alacrity and moved north to occupy Bicholim and what is now Satari. Instead of an ally the Raja found another enemy at his back. Efforts to regain his territory proved unsuccessful and when, in 1788, he came under attack once again from the north he resignedly ceded Pernem to the Portuguese in exchange for their support. The New Conquests were complete.

By this time, as has been seen, religious fervour had subsided and the newly added territories were not subjected to the Christianisation process that had been the lot of the Old Conquests. They remained mainly Hindu and also retained much of their original character.

Following a long period of isolation from the troubles of the world beyond the ghats, yet another incursion incurred. Paralleling the conflict in Europe the French and British were battling for supremacy in India and, in the south, allied with the French, Tippu Sultan of Mysore, one of the most successful and charismatic leaders the British had yet faced, was emerging as a major obstacle to British success. In order to deny the French, and Tippu Sultan, a port on the west coast, a British force occupied Goa in 1798. After the defeat of Tippu a year later the troops withdrew, only to return in 1802 on rumours of an impending invasion of India planned by Napoleon. The threatened invasion never materialised, but the British remained based in Goa until 1813 when any French sea threat that may have existed had been removed. After this, there were no further threats by the British to interfere in the affairs of this territory of a long-standing traditional ally, apart from an offer made in 1839, to purchase it for half a million pounds, an offer that was contemptuously refused.

All in all, this period of 150 years from the middle of the 17th century had been a testing time for Portuguese India, certainly not without incident, and though considerably diminished in size and influence, it had at least survived the many threats to its very existence.

1813–1961 HANGING ON

From this point on, there was little external threat and Portugal clung on to its Indian colonies, administering them in desultory fashion. It was the threat from within that gradually took centre stage, as the combination of a lack of commitment, coupled with a tendency towards a liberal approach on the part of Lisbon, fired Goan thoughts of freedom.

Portugal had shaken off the supremacy of monarchy in 1820 and had elected a parliament for the first time. Associated with this first flush of enthusiasm for democracy, Goa was given a Constitutional Charter and three seats for their representatives in the Lisbon parliament. No legislation affecting Goa could be introduced without the consent of these deputies and this, together with such measures as the freedom of worship being restored to Hindus in 1833, was welcomed by many as the dawn of a new age.

Not so by some. Satari, a province that had always gone very much its own way, its affairs pushed onto the sidelines by events of greater moment taking place elsewhere, began to make more than just a nuisance of itself. Something of a backwater far away in the north-east, an area mainly of forested foothills and mountain slopes with a scattered and scanty population, it had been the feudal territory of several powerful groups, by

far the most prominent of these being the Sardessais of Rane, a family of Rajput descent and nominal feudatories of the Bhonsles of Sawantwadi. An almost unwanted area of responsibility, Satari had been ceded to Portugal by the Bhonsles with something approaching eagerness, and the Ranes had sworn allegiance to Portuguese Goa as early as 1746. But treaties and sworn allegiances, as with the Bhonsles themselves, were flexible arrangements as far as the Ranes were concerned. They were accustomed to managing their own affairs without too many constraints or too much outside interference. Adept at guerrilla tactics and with the jungles and mountains as their operating base, the Portuguese found them more than a little difficult to manage and from the time Satari was acquired, all the way through the 19th century, they appear to have been in an almost perpetual state of revolt. It seems that to the Ranes, anything was a good enough excuse for an uprising, whether it was an attempt to make them pay more taxes, or at times any taxes at all, or to prevent them from exercising their right to levy heavy taxes on others, or even to raid and loot surrounding areas. Whatever the reason they were a constant thorn in the viceregal flesh.

There were one or two occasions when their uprisings posed a serious threat, such as in 1852 when they took the fort at Nanuz and engaged Portuguese troops for three years before a negotiated settlement restored all Rane privileges and their leader Dipu Rane was awarded the title of 'Captain of Sepoys'! But of much greater significance was the fact that in the second half of the 19th century, with thoughts of increasing Goan say in their own affairs emerging as a major issue, the revolts of the Ranes, whatever their original motives, assumed symbolic importance to Goans beginning their freedom struggle. The importance of this aspect of the conflict with the Ranes increased so that, in 1912, when yet another rebellion broke out in Satari, this time against increased land taxes, a major military operation was mounted, the Ranes suppressed and the leaders deported to Portuguese colonies in Africa.

In 1910, Portugal had dispensed with its monarchy altogether, declaring itself a republic, and, in tune with the times and with all these factors contributing, a new deal for Goa was worked out giving some degree of autonomy and a real chance at last to manage its own affairs. In 1918, on the very day of Goa's rejoicing, doubts and second thoughts caused the suspension of the decree putting these new proposals into effect. This was all that was needed to re-kindle the flame that this time threatened to sweep throughout the land, and men like Luis de Menezes Braganza moved into the spotlight, crusading for Goa's rights to self determination. Hurriedly, it was agreed to establish a legislative council and developments could still have moved forward steadily had not Salazar with his dictatorial approach taken power, first as Finance Minister in 1926, then as Prime Minister from 1932. From the moment he took office conflict was inevitable. In 1928 Tristao de Braganza Cunha founded the Goa National Congress Committee, which he affiliated to the Indian National Congress, and the struggle was launched in earnest.

Between 1939 and 1945 Portugal's neutrality ensured Goa's non-participation in hostilities but hardly left it untouched by the war. In many ways, Goa matched the role of Lisbon in Europe as an intelligence centre and was the scene of an astonishing incident, the story of which has subsequently been made into an exciting film, *The Sea Wolves*, based on James Leasor's novel *The Boarding Party*. German ships, having taken refuge in a neutral port but engaging in espionage activities, were scuttled by their crews during an attack mounted by part-time soldiers of the Calcutta Light Horse, a British territorial regiment.

At the end of the war Goa was economically resurrected, operating as an independent port and restoring a certain glamour to its existence, but it was already being subjected to a different set of political pressures. The Indian freedom movement was nearing victory and looking to bring Goa into the fold. In Goa in 1946, the activities of the Jai Hind movement, a non-violent movement along Gandhian lines, led to the arrest and imprisonment of many of its leaders, some being deported to Lisbon or Angola.

After the British left India in 1947 Goa and the other tiny Portuguese area, Daman and Diu, along with French Pondicherry, remained as isolated enclaves, anomalies from an independent India's point of view. Still the Portuguese refused to accept the situation, the Salazar regime maintaining its historical right to the territories. India began to take practical steps to resolve the situation and in 1951 the landward frontier was blockaded and diplomatic relations with Portugal severed.

Meanwhile the French handed over Pondicherry in 1954.

In Goa, batches of satyagrahis, unarmed Indian demonstrators, demanding the withdrawal of the Portuguese and Goa's incorporation into India, crossed the border and several ugly incidents resulted from clashes between demonstrators and the Portuguese military. A section of Goa's National Congress decided more militant action was needed, the Azad Gomantak Dal was formed to initiate armed struggle and a long series of violent incidents followed over the next few years.

Eventually India's patience was exhausted and, in December 1961, 'Operation Vijaya' saw Indian tanks move in and the Portuguese move out. Panjim with its pleasant, country town atmosphere, became the capital of the Union Territory of Goa, Daman and Diu and the centre of an area determined to preserve its individuality, a concept soundly based on its historical background and furthered when, in 1987, the struggle for full statehood was at last won, removing fears of absorption into one of the vast states that constitute its neighbours.

2 THE CHURCHES

Churches are a dominant element in the landscape, particularly in the area of the Old Conquests, with white domes, towers and crosses rising from the green sea of waving palms and paddy-fields wherever one looks.

Those Portuguese arriving on the Malabar coast at the beginning of the 16th century were certainly not venturing into an architectural wilderness. They even found Christian churches already in existence, those of the Syrian Christians who had been established in small communities there for several centuries, possibly from the 1st century after the arrival of Thomas the Apostle in AD 52, but more certainly from a century or so later when Syrian missionaries visited the coastal area. Their oldest surviving church, that at Crangonur, to the north of Cochin, is believed to date from the 4th century.

Of much greater importance than the already established Christian presence was that there existed a fund of well developed constructional and decorative skills, even though the Malabar coast could not be compared with the Tamil culture of the eastern seaboard in this respect. The invaders utilised these skills to reproduce European styles, which in turn were themselves modified by strong local influences.

On the east coast, Christianity was never imposed with the fanatical fervour of the Portuguese in western India, and Tamil Christian church building was always overshadowed by the magnificent achievements of Hindu temple construction, both in architectural and sculptural terms.

On the west coast, especially in Goa, we have a totally different picture with a great flowering of Indian versions of European architectural forms. In the course of 300 years, this progressed through local variants of several styles and in the Indian Baroque produced something that was no mere imitation, but something powerful and unique, the result of the original being moulded by local factors to create a distinguishable school of its own.

There are **four main stages** of church architectural development in Goa, followed by a period of modern church building to the present day:

1 The Early Churches, built soon after the arrival of the Portuguese in 1510.
2 The Developmental Stage, from 1550 to 1660, during which a great surge of building activity launched on a tide of missionary zeal, produced the great churches of the city of Old Goa. During this stage, ideas were imported from Europe, providing the framework within which Indian builders began to develop their own form and style. It was at this time that Goa truly earned its acclamation as 'Rome of the East'.
3 The flourishing of the Indian Baroque from 1660 to 1760.
4 The splendiferous, though appropriately degenerate, ornateness of the Rococo in the second half of the 18th century.

THE EARLY CHURCHES 1510–1550

On their arrival, the Portuguese had more to occupy them than building churches. The occupation and establishment of the Goa station was but the first stage in Albuquerque's plans for trading links throughout the east and, in addition, it was to be some time before priests and missionaries descended on Goa in any numbers. Even so, one of Albuquerque's first acts was to order the building of several small votive churches in thanks for his initial success. The first was a mud and palm thatch church on the site of his breakthrough into the city itself, a church dedicated to St Catherine on whose feast-day victory had been won. This was soon rebuilt of stone and was accompanied by other churches on important battle sites; Our Lady of the Rosary on the hill from which he had directed the battle; Our Lady of the Mount on the hilltop on which enemy artillery had been concentrated and St Anthony's, where a particularly heroic action had taken place. Another notable church built at that time was that attached to the Jesuit College of St Paul. Francis Xavier used this church as his base and it was here that his body lay at rest when first returned to Goa. With one exception, all have been rebuilt, some several times over, although their historical associations remain strong.

The exception, and as a result the oldest surviving church in Goa, is Our Lady of the Rosary on Old Goa's Monte Santo, the Holy Hill. It was built in Manueline style, a style peculiarly Portuguese, an amalgam of Gothic and Renaissance developed in the reign of Dom Manuel right at the end of the 15th century as the great voyages, initiated half a century before by Prince Henry the Navigator, were being brought to a successful conclusion by the skill and courage of such men as Columbus, Bartholomew Dias and Vasco da Gama. Celebrating Portuguese eminence at sea, the decorative motifs of this style centred on ships and sailing, using cables and anchors together with sea shells and waves. This church was built by, or under the direction of, Portuguese masons and is a replica of its many counterparts being built at the same time in southern Portugal.

This same style survives in a fragment from another of the early churches in the Church of St Francis of Assisi, also in Old Goa, the Manueline central doorway standing out in contrast with the rest of the façade. The Franciscans were the first of the religious orders to arrive, building their first church on this site in 1521. It was from this church that the doorway was retained during rebuilding of the larger church in 1661.

From these, some hint can be obtained of what must have been the dominant style among the early churches, but it was a style that did not last, not being well suited to the west coast of India and in any case to be superseded by influences from other parts of Europe, notably Italy, that were already making their impact on Portugal itself.

There were other small churches built, especially towards the end of this forty years of Portuguese rule, accelerated by the arrival of more and more missionaries. The destruction of all Hindu temples in the occupied territories was authorised and in 1541 it was agreed that income from lands belonging to destroyed temples should go towards the construction and upkeep of Christian churches on these sites. Churches already built at this time included the first church at Panjim, that on the Cabo and the church on the hilltop on the island of Divar. With the addition of Salcete and Bardez to Portuguese territory in 1543, the destruction of temples and their replacement by churches would later spread, but by this time, because of two important factors, church building was beginning to take on a new flavour. The two factors were the rapid development of Goa's commercial success, providing unthought-of riches, and the flood of missionaries anxious to utilise them as a weapon in their battle for converts.

THE ROME OF THE ORIENT – IMPORTED GLORY

Missonary activities were by this time in full swing and the various orders, Dominicans, Augustinians, Franciscans, Theatines and Carmelites were demanding churches of sufficient size and impressiveness to support their efforts. The Jesuits in particular were soon planning grander edifices as settings for the pageantry of their ceremonies. Backed by the now considerable wealth available, church building went ahead with enormous vigour and resulted in Goa's largest churches.

In Europe at the end of the 16th century, the Renaissance, with its revival of the classical orders, Tuscan, Doric, Ionic and Corinthian, having been subjected to a degree of formalisation by the severe Mannerist style, was moving towards the flamboyance of the Baroque as a direct reaction to these constraints. So this important period, when European architecture on the grand scale was being introduced into Goa, coincided with a declining Renaissance, perpetuated mainly in exterior design, together with the introduction of rampant Baroque into interiors. This was particularly evident in the retables or reredos, the backdrops to the altars, which assumed vast and elaborate proportions.

Although in these first substantial buildings, the fundamental designs were provided more or less wholesale from Europe, these rules could never be imposed unaltered and, from the outset, local craftsmen, and later architects, developed their own interpretation of these basic concepts. In the early stages this was mainly evident in fashions and techniques of decoration, but this was truly the developmental period when Indian builders were imbibing the spirit of the new forms and refashioning its expression. The groundwork was being laid from which would emerge a genuine Indian version of Christian church architecture.

As in the case of the early churches, many of this epoch have disappeared, but there are three outstanding examples in Old Goa, all demonstrating the dramatic change in scale as well as design that took place. All three are in excellent condition, offering a wide range of contrasting architectural styles, their construction being spread across the whole of this period of over a hundred years. These are:

The Se Cathedral	built 1562–1619
The Basilica of Bom Jesus	built 1584–1605
The Church of St Cajetan	built 1656–1661

There were several other massive churches built at this time, the first being the Church of the Dominicans, begun in 1550, now heaps of rubble, its only memorial being some of its columns used to construct what was originally Albuquerque's monument in Panjim. St Paul of the Arches was the first great Jesuit church in the east. Built in 1560 it was once the heart of the great seminary and college, but now only the central doorway of the façade survives, standing amidst swaying palms in serene isolation, similar in design but larger than that of Bom Jesus. What was the biggest of Goa's churches, Our Lady of Grace, the Augustinian monastery church, 1597–1602, stood high on the Monte Santo, all that remains being a solitary tower, or rather half of one, soaring over forty metres above the overgrown wreckage of its church.

Outside Old Goa, other only slightly less imposing churches were also built at this time, each making its own contribution to the awareness of this new architectural spirit. The outpost church of Rachol Seminary was rebuilt in 1596 followed shortly by the rebuilding of Panjim Church itself, Our Lady of the Immaculate Conception, in 1619.

Architectural considerations apart, the greatest visual impact came from the reredos, the backdrops to the altars already mentioned. Though introduced early to Goa, one of the first examples being that in Our Lady of the Rosary, it is in these grander churches that the full potential is revealed. It is at this time that Goan reredos attained their extravagantly monumental excellence. This was a vehicle that immediately appealed to the Indian craftsman, giving him full scope to demonstrate his skills. The dazzling effect of intricately carved wood, heavily gilded and of vast proportions, awed Goan congregations, devout or otherwise, and still has that effect on visitors today.

The European development of reredos through Gothic, Renaissance and Mannerist to the Baroque can be broadly traced through changes in styles and by characteristics specific to each phase. In terms of composition, many-storeyed compartments are characteristic of both Renaissance and Mannerist styles, contrasting with the large central space of the Baroque, both the compartments of the earlier styles and the central space of the Baroque being defined by columns and entablatures. The columns or shafts are themselves insignificant. Earlier columns tend to be less ornate, divided into two by a ring, the bottom half being relatively plain, at most decorated with rosettes or light floral designs, while the upper half is simply fluted. Later examples have the bottom half heavily decorated with cherubs while by the time we reach the Baroque period, the swirling salomonic column is the essence, an exotic spiral covered with vines laden with grapes and even on occasion clustered with birds.

However, in India, the introduction of the reredos came mid-way through the European sequence. Inevitably 'the rules' were broken and a great mixing of forms took place. So, we can find in the reredos of Goan churches every conceivable blend and permutation of the various style elements. Basic classifications can be made but it is better to take each masterpiece as it comes. From the traveller's point of view, little is to be gained from too analytical an approach.

It was from the great churches of this golden era that the lessons were learned that enabled the subsequent emergence in full flower of what is known as the Indian Baroque.

THE INDIAN BAROQUE 1660–1760

The next hundred years saw the culmination of the art of church building in Goa and the climax of Indian Christian tradition in terms of architectural development.

This is particularly well represented in four churches, two easily accessible, two well worth any trouble to see:

The St Francis of Assisi Church in Old Goa –
  built 1660–1668.
The Church of the Holy Spirit in Margao –
  built 1675–1684.
The Church of St Anne (Santana) in Talaulim –
  built 1681–1689.
The Church of Our Lady of Compassion on
  Divar Island – built 1700–1724.

The churches of the period all introduced elements that fathered the Indian Baroque and in these four churches it can be seen fused and refined into a distinctive style with a character of its own.

There are several distinguishing architectural features but two, the façade and the ceiling design, are of particular interest.

By this time Goan architects, masons and sculptors had assumed full command of this new field for their crafts and were pursuing their own inspiration. Western classical orders were still fundamental but, as is obvious in these churches, were freely adapted, deviating widely from traditional forms and proportions in order more nearly to meet Indian ideas.

Decorative motifs, which at first had shown only faint signs of local influence subtly introduced by craftsmen working under the direction of the conquerors, were by this time more positively Indian with palm, lotus, shell and tropical fruit themes proliferating. The resemblance of angels to the apsaras and gandharas of Hindu mythology was now even more marked!

The interiors of these Indian Baroque churches live up to expectations, that in the St Francis of Assisi church in Old Goa being particularly impressive, while that of the other church of the Holy Spirit, in Margao, is notable because of its unusual composition, making use of paintings to present its theme.

These churches, an important part of Goa's heritage, have received very different treatment in recent years. The church in Margao is superbly maintained and in constant use. The St. Francis of Assisi church in Old Goa has benefited from sympathetic restoration and remains one of the most, or perhaps the most, beautiful of churches in Goa. The Piedade on Divar Island is in full-time use as a parish church and is currently undergoing a full-scale restoration programme that will take some time to complete while enabling the church to maintain its active role in the community. Sadly, what is perhaps the finest of them all, the Santana, having lost its congregation, was falling into decay due to neglect but recently efforts have been made to remedy this.

THE ROCOCO PERIOD
1760–1800

The second half of the 18th century was one of disruption and complexity with political and religious upheavals. The stuttering anti-climax of the end to Maratha threats saw Portugal safely in control again, but lack of interest in the welfare of her colony continued, punctuated only by bouts of interference such as the suppression of the Jesuits.

It saw the first significant attempt at internal revolt, instigated by Goan priests beset by frustration at racial discrimination, and there was continuous bickering conflict with the rajas on their borders, which eventually led to an almost unwanted expansion of the territory under Portuguese control. It also saw the abandonment of Old Goa.

Amidst all this, there was the contradiction of yet another surge in church building, characterised by an even greater degree of ornateness and splendour, though on a smaller scale. The time had passed when crusading religious orders were competing to impress potential converts with their grandiose edifices. Perhaps of greater significance, funds were drying up at last. The luxury of the Rococo suited the mood of the time. It reflected the relaxation of religious intensity, with the removal of constraints that allowed Indian craftsmen to give full vent to their natural inclination towards exotic adornment and freeing them still further from western traditional constraints although, even in the Indian Baroque, local architects had already declared their independence.

They were not entirely free from constraints, however, practical considerations imposing limits on the expression of Rococo exoticism in exterior design. The local red laterite does not lend itself to detailed sculpting and wood, while excellent for carving, does not survive outside for long in this tropical climate. Stucco, although an important feature of Rococo art, was hardly practical for the adornment of exterior surfaces on a large scale, although it was used to a limited extent on facades and, more particularly, on roadside shrines, chapels and the crosses to be found in village squares.

There was one large church yet to be built, St Stephen's, Santo Estevam, on the island of Jua, 1759, acting as a bridge between the great Baroque churches and those that would follow. In fact, some of the late-18th-century churches adopted the Santo Estevam façade design, with its false domed central tower topped by a substantial lantern, between twin towers themselves having domes and lanterns. The Church of Our Lady of the Immaculate Conception at Moira is a typical example, though there are many others. In the façades of still smaller churches the towers were omitted to maintain balance and proportion achieving a slenderness that makes some of these amongst the most attractive small churches in Goa. Rococo represented elegance as well as ornateness. In others of this period the architects almost seem to have shrugged their shoulders in resignation, adopting plain, almost severe exteriors and transferring their attentions indoors.

So Rococo luxuriance flourished mainly within, and flourish it did. The reredos of these churches were obvious subjects for the new freedom with a mass of dazzling and elaborate decoration at times almost submerging the essential components, which inevitably led to a loss of solidity and the controlled design evident in earlier styles. Pulpits also offered great potential and there are some exquisite examples to be found from this period. The decoration of the vaulting in the chancel also received attention in some cases.

As already mentioned, this was not a time of church building on a grand scale and the Rococo is represented in a large number of churches and chapels spread all over the Old Conquests. Not all Rococo features appear in every church, but there are an interesting array of examples from which to choose. Some of the more accessible, depending on where you happen to be, are, from north to south:

Assagao – St Cajetan
Calangute – St Alex
Moira – Our Lady of the Immaculate Conception
Pomburpa – Our Lady Mother of God
Agasaim – St Lawrence
Curtorim – St Alex
Margao – Our Lady of the Rosary
Colva – Our Lady of Mercy
Benaulim – St John the Baptist
Carmona – Our Lady of Help
Cavelossim – The Holy Spirit.

Apart from the churches themselves, an important feature of Goa's ecclesiastical landscape are the crosses, so typical of every village square, and the roadside shrines that seem to appear around every corner. Both can be seen throughout the Old Conquests, both vary from the utmost simplicity to the highly ornate.

Roadside shrines can be a simple roof sheltering a crucifix, or impressive 18th century structures with domes and lantern towers surmounted by crosses, with columns, arched entrances and altars inside.

In much the same way, crosses too appear in various forms and sizes, hidden in hedgerows or dominating a large square. As in the case of shrines, the larger and more ornate crosses are also mainly the product of the 18th century. The cross in the square in front of the Church of the Holy Spirit in Margao is a classic example; that in front of St

Alex in Curtorim equally fine. Most village crosses are more recent and the work of local people in design and construction.

THE CHURCHES OF THE 19TH AND 20TH CENTURIES

Along with the shrines and crosses, Goa abounds with small churches dating from the 19th century to the present day for which architects, perhaps not of the conventionally qualified variety in terms of classical church design, drew on any and every example that appealed to them, giving a whole host of combinations from Saligao's spiky 'gothic' to Siridao's concrete modernity.

So we have a white painted church, shrine or cross in view at almost every turn, abruptly confronting us as the centre-piece of a village, appearing intriguingly on a far river bank, or standing proud among the greenery of a distant hillside. These delightful contributions to the Goan scene all have their roots in the great classical architectural tradition that was Goa's enforced but privileged inheritance that it took to its heart and expressed in its own image.

Church of Nossa Senhora Madre de Deus, Saligao.

3 THE TEMPLES AND MOSQUES

Far back in the mists of time, the land that is now Goa earned fame among Hindus as an especially holy place. Long before the Muslims or the Portuguese sought to change things, this crescent on the shores of the Indian Ocean had its Hindu traditions so well rooted that their survival through all subsequent trials and tribulations was assured.

More than a thousand years before the Portuguese even arrived, Buddhism had fluttered into near oblivion after six centuries of tentative survival in this shielded corner of the sub-continent. The lingas of Shiva were planted in the Buddhist rock-cut caves. In true Goan fashion, however, some Buddhist statues appeared in Hindu temples, adopted and given a new name. There are examples to show that the Tirthankaras, the images of Jainism, suffered a similar fate. Assimilation is a fine art, developed early here.

Hindu mythology and legend surrounding this place stresses its ancient significance, all three members of the Hindu Trinity having associations. Its very origin is attributed to Vishnu who, as Parashurama, his sixth incarnation, came to free the worlds from Kshatriyas under their thousand-armed king. After twenty-one campaigns in which he 'thrice seven times' slew every Kshatriya on earth, Parashurama, wanting virgin soil on which to perform yajna, the fire sacrifice and the greatest of all purification ceremonies, shot an arrow, or some say cast his axe, his trademark and the terrible weapon with which he slew his enemies, into the sea from the peaks of the Sahyadri Mountains that now form Goa's eastern boundary. He then commanded the sea to withdraw beyond where it fell, thus creating this sliver of new land. There is still a 'Mountain of Ash' in Pernem marking the

exact site of the fire sacrifice! Having created the land, it is not surprising that Vishnu could not resist a return visit, and Cabo de Rama commemorates time spent here during his exile with Sita.

In happier circumstances, he came yet again, this time as a youthful Krishna and, after watching the beautiful *gopis*, the girls who herd the cows, bathing in the sea, he beguiled them with music from his flute. They in turn further entranced him with their dancing and so he gave this land of milk and honey its name, Gowapuri, the place so richly endowed with cows, and of course those who tended them.

Shiva too chose Goa as his place of exile when, in a game of dice with his wife Parvati, he staked everything he had, including his home on Mount Kailasa, on one throw. He lost and had to leave. Parvati eventually went to look for him and they were reunited in Goa. They both stayed on the banks of the Zuari River for a few million years before returning to Mount Kailasa. Goa had, as usual, cast its spell. Not only mere mortals are susceptible to its attractions.

Brahma, the third member of the Hindu Trinity, Creator of the World and of mankind, also has associations with Goa. His temple here[1] is one of only very few in the whole of India dedicated solely to him, and where they do exist it is in only the most holy of holy places. Brahma in his role of the Creator is regarded as having completed his task in this existence, while Shiva, the Destroyer, and Vishnu, the Preserver, are both still very much in action.

There is also one temple in Goa dedicated to the Trinity itself, the Trimurthi of Brahma, Vishnu and Shiva.[2] However, it is Shiva who is in the ascendancy here, even Vaishnavite temples and deities

FIG A. SYMBOLS OF SHIVA IN GOA:

Dharalinga, faceted linga. Lamgao, Bicholim.

Mukhalinga, linga with face. Parshem, Pernem.

Kalbhairava (with Brahma's fifth head) Manguesh Temple, Ponda.

Betal – with necklace of human heads and scorpion on his belly, the most horrific form of Shiva.

being drawn into the Shiva fold in some way. In a way, this is poetic justice, in that it was Shiva who originally gave Parashurama the axe with which he performed his task of slaying the Kshatriyas, after which the need to purify himself led to his creation of the virgin land of Goa!

The image of Shiva that is worshipped in the temple can be either in the form of the linga, the phallic symbol, or of Shiva in one of his human forms. In both cases the images are given a wide variety of names, some of them unique to Goa (Fig. A).

The linga, by which Shiva is mainly symbolised, can be seen in Goa in all shapes and sizes, either carefully fashioned and smoothed or roughly formed. The most common form is cylindrical or it can be flat sided, when it is called a *dharalinga*, or with a human face carved on it, when it is a *mukhalinga*, regarded as a rarity. Within the sanctuary, the linga itself is often hidden by a human mask and garlands of flowers. Mangesh, Chandernath, Saptakoteshwar and Ramnath are some of the names used for Shiva in Goa.

Although mainly represented by the linga, Shiva is also worshipped in some of the human forms he adopts. In Goa the three most important are:

Ravalnath – who has his origins as a folk deity of ancient lineage.
Bhairava or Kalbhairava – a form so fierce that even Kala the Lord Death cringes before him.
Vetal or Betal – even fiercer than Bhairava, Vetal's horrific image is the only nude god in Goa.

Temples to Shiva in these three forms can be found all over the area of the New Conquests and his eminence is underlined by the fact that these three are all members of Goa's 'Village Five', the Grampanchatayana, the five deities at the core of village worship. Even in temples to other gods, one or more of these three, especially Kalbhairava, are often present as an affiliate deity. Affiliate deities or parivar devatas are an important feature of Goan temple life. They are the supporting cast, the 'family' of the principal god or goddess to whom the temple is dedicated. They can be numerous, six or seven is not unusual, and any of the gods perform this role depending on their local popularity. For example, Ganesh, the elephant-headed God of Prosperity, is worshipped widely as an affiliate deity though he only has two temples of his own. Affiliate deities can occupy shrines within the main temple building or have separate small shrines within its precincts.

Shiva's consort is as widely worshipped in Goa as he himself, also in many forms and under different names. These range from the Goddess of Peace, Shantadurga, through several of the many other aspects of Durga to Bhagavati and finally the yet more formidable Chamunda, the skeleton-like tusked consort of Kalbhairava. They are well matched. Shantadurga is the most popular of all, especially as Goans relate her with Shanteri the local folk goddess who is another member of the 'Village Five'. The prominence in the Goan Hindu scene of these two goddesses, both representing peace and security, in itself says much about Goa. Significantly, Chamunda, though patronised by the royal Kadambas from the 10th to the 14th centuries, has only two temples dedicated to her here. As well as her role in the countryside, where she is often represented by an ant-hill, Shanteri is present almost everywhere as an affiliate deity.

There are few temples in which Vishnu himself is the principal deity, being more popular as Lakshminarayana when he is in partnership with his consort Lakshmi. This is in fact the fifth member of the 'Village Five'.[3] Some of the most important temples are dedicated to Lakshmi in one of her forms such as Mahalasa and Mahalaxmi.

Brahma, as already mentioned, has only one temple in his name in Goa and so has his consort Saraswati.

But all these members of the Hindu Pantheon, even Shiva, have to contend with more primitive forms of worship, for country folk everywhere tend to look to their local spirits as the main arbiters of everyday matters. These spirits, residing mainly in special trees or natural objects if anywhere in particular, are respected and receive their due regard.

For obvious reasons few ancient Hindu temples have survived in Goa and these are confined to the more remote areas of the New Conquests. The edict of 1540 gave the Viceroy the authority to destroy all Hindu temples and shrines within the area of Portuguese control, 'not leaving a single one on any of the islands'. He was also ordered to confiscate temple estates for the maintenance of the churches that were ordered to be built on the temple sites. With the acquisition of Bardez and Salcete in 1543, these areas were also subjected to an orgy of temple destruction. The orders were carried out assiduously, and in the old Conquests virtually all traces were swept away, never to be replaced. Pressing home their point, the fervent Portuguese forbade Hindus to cross the border to worship at shrines and temples outside the area of their control and were not averse themselves to organising regular forays to continue the destruction beyond their own conquests.

FIG C. DEEPASTAMBHAS: THE LAMP TOWERS OF GOA:

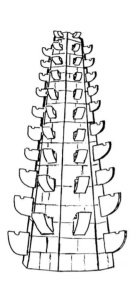

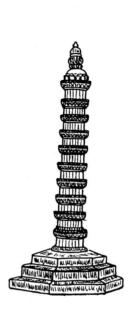

Maratha Lamp Tower: mid - 17th century - from which basic concept the Goan temple architects developed their ideas.

Lamp Tower of the Saptakoteshwar Temple, 1668. Typical of Goa's elegant first step away from the crude Maratha form.

Shantadurga Temple, Quela, 1743. Typical of the Ponda-style lamp tower, with its strong Christian Baroque influence, developed in the 18th century.

The oldest temples still intact to be found in Goa, are the rock-cut caves at Arvalem in Bicholim, with lingas installed in what might have been a Buddhist sanctuary, but which some believe were purpose-built as temples to Shiva, having been variously dated between the 1st and the 5th centuries AD. There are also rock-cut caves of Buddhist origin at Rivona in Sanguem Taluka, although this seems to have been more a religious retreat than a temple. Also in the rock-cut category are some simple shrines at Khandepar in Ponda. These are much later, and contemporary with the first stone-built temples that would come to characterise the Kadamba period.

Of these Kadamba temples there is now little to be seen, but, happily, there is one fine example

from this period. This is the 13th-century Shiva temple at Tambdi Surla, right on Goa's eastern border beyond Sancordem in Sanguem taluka. Built from black basalt amidst the red laterite of the district that must have given Tambdi (Red) Surla its name, this hard stone which enables delicate carving must have been brought from some distance away. It is a traditional Hindu temple in concept, having much in common with the temples beyond the Western Ghats, although there are refinements that mark its own distinctive character. Though small by comparison with some of the temples that once existed in the Old Conquests, now known only through shattered remnants and the descriptions of travellers, it is beautifully constructed and decorated, a reminder of what must have been widespread architectural splendour under the Kadamba kings.

There are other sites with historic temples long established there, but where the buildings themselves have been replaced at some stage. Such a temple is that at Chandranath on the border between Salcete and Quepem in the south. Standing conspicuously high on its hill, the temple is one of the oldest on record, being referred to in 5th century inscriptions. Its original garbhagriha, the sanctuary, and even the linga itself, is carved out of the living rock of the hill and the temple built round it. The famous Nagueshi Temple of Bandora in Ponda is another of ancient lineage, there being an inscription in the courtyard there dated 1413, recording a grant of land to local families for the worship of Naganatha. Again, however, the temple has been rebuilt in relatively recent times.

Another group of temples, a large and important group, are those that result from their deities having been smuggled to safety out of the Old Conquests in the second half of the 16th century because of the destruction of their temples by the Portuguese. Altogether, there are almost fifty temples in the New Conquests in which the principal deity is a refugee from the Ilhas, Bardez or Salcete, this apart from many affiliate or subsidiary deities as, almost without exception, every temple has its supporting cast of several such parivar devatas. Within the insecurity resulting from the danger of continuing raids across the border by the Portuguese, these 'migrant' deities were originally either kept hidden or set up in modest buildings of wood and thatch, discreetly concealed in nooks and crannies in wooded valleys. However, the fact that their devotees still wished to worship them and were prepared to risk the border crossing in order to do so, meant that they had to be accessible, resulting in a concentration on the very doorstep of Portuguese territory. The main group was in Ponda Taluka, beyond the Cumbarjua waterway and the Zuari River, which in the 16th century together formed the eastern border, and in Bicholim north of the Mandovi River.

In these precarious locations it was not for some time, until people felt more secure, that these deities were properly housed. There was some difference between the two areas in that in the second half of the 17th century the northern shore of the Mandovi, Bicholim, was firmly under Maratha control in the person of Shivaji, who himself made expeditions when his authority, and especially his tributary dues, were challenged. In Ponda, it was very nearly three quarters of a century later before Maratha influence was positive enough to provide sufficient security, not to mention funds, to encourage the building of substantial temples. Late in the 18th century both of these areas would come under Portuguese control as part of the New Conquests, but by that time there were the beginnings of change in terms of relaxation of attitudes towards the Hindu religion.

So this meant that in Bicholim temples were being re-built somewhat earlier than in Ponda, illustrated by Shivaji being responsible for the Saptakoteshwar Temple in Naroa in 1668, while his grandson sponsored the Shantadurga Temple at Quela in 1738, seventy years later.

In both areas, most of the temples conformed in plan to the conventional temple in that their layout consisted of an entrance hall or porchway leading to a pillared hall, the mandapa, and a small inner sanctum, the garbhagriha. Above the inner sanctum was a tower, the shikara proclaiming the presence of the deity. But from here on there was a dramatic break with tradition and, in architectural terms, these temples of Goa are unique in India. This uniqueness derives from the way in which Hindu architects and craftsmen utilised distinctive Muslim features, together with the astonishing degree to which they were influenced by the Christian church architecture of Portuguese Goa.

There were several fundamental variations from conventional temple design, but two were of particular significance:

1 The replacement of the traditional pyramid form of the shikara, the tower over the sanctuary, by a dome resting on an octagonal base or drum.

2 The introduction of a deepastambha or dipmal, a lamp tower which could be transformed into a pillar of light on festive occasions. This exists hardly at all in any other part of India.

TEMPLE DOMES

The dome is totally foreign to Hindu temple architecture and rarely occurs outside Goa in this context. First introduced into India by the Muslims arriving from beyond the mountains of the northwest at the end of the 12th century, it was soon a familiar feature in the architecture of the successive cities of the Sultans of Delhi. Muslim power and influence soon expanded southwards into the Deccan, and the Konkan came under their rule with the establishment of Bahmani control here in 1352. After Vijayanagar's rule ended here in 1489, the Bijapur Sultanate of Yusuf Adil Shah ruled until the arrival of the Portuguese, taking particular interest in the city that was to become Old Goa. So, there would be direct Muslim influence over a considerable period and, even after the Portuguese took the Ilhas, the Adil Shahs continued to dominate the surrounding areas, at least until the arrival on the scene of Shivaji with his Marathas one hundred and fifty years later. The dome rising from an octagonal base was a well established and prominent feature of Muslim architecture and had even been used by the Hindu Raja of Gwalior, Man Singh, in his famous fortress-palace built just as the Portuguese were in the process of conquering Goa. Some domes rested on a shallow plain base while in others, where height was required, an elongated drum was decorated with blind niches.

These basic designs were taken up early by Goan temple architects. Good authority has it that the dome became a feature on Goan temples as early as the Vijayanagar occupation of the 14th century but it is more certain that it was in evidence by the 17th century, when the rebuilding of temples in the area that was to become the New Conquests began in earnest. Saptakoteshwar at Naroa, Chamundi at Piligao and Chandreshwar-Bhutnath at Paroda were perhaps some of the earlier examples, although as a feature, the dome had soon penetrated the far corners of what would become Goa. The boom and ultimate development came in the 18th century with the Ponda temples such as Manguesh and Mahalaxmi. Dome profiles vary widely, some of the earlier ones having especially obvious Muslim feeling but from then on subject to the whim of Goan architects (Fig. B).

This period was also marked by the development of the design of the towers on which the domes rested. In the 17th century, temple builders had quickly superimposed on their towers modified Christian Baroque decorative forms of pilasters, round arched niches and balustrades. By 1665, the first substantial domed Christian church, St Cajetan, was under construction to make its contribution in terms of influencing design. This type of temple tower would develop through to the impressive double-storeyed tower of the Shantadurga Temple at Quela, built in 1738, that is its finest example.

The domes themselves were in turn crowned by a variety of finials, sometimes based on the European lantern, sometimes on Indian symbols. These were either the amalaka, a flattened globe vertically grooved all round to represent a fruit, or a pinnacle built up of spheres to represent water pots, sometimes a combination of both. Here again there is enormous variety which provides an entertaining study. The lotus motif is frequently introduced

round the base of the finial or around the base of the dome itself (Fig. D collage).

Another distinctive feature of this period of Goan temple construction was the introduction of the lamp tower. The Marathas had introduced the concept of a separate tower of light, but it was hardly a thing of beauty, a sturdy pillar on which oil lamps could be placed. The Hindus of Goa found the idea of a lamp tower an attractive one, and indeed it was surprising that it was not adopted more widely in other parts of India, but they could not accept unaltered the crude Maratha product. Their first efforts produced the version typified by the Saptakoteshwar and Chandranath Temples and perpetuated to this day over much of Goa. However, in 18th century Ponda the architects, looking for something more impressive, once more turned to the octagonal form that so obviously appealed to them, influenced by earlier temple towers as well as, by this time, having octagonal piazza crosses to draw on for inspiration. Also by this time, designs based on Christian Baroque elements were well developed in terms of the use of a wide variety of columns and pilasters with complex capitals together with entablatures and round-arched niches and windows and these were used to the fullest extent. In order to provide an adequate number of niches for the lamps, the whole tower was composed into many layers, a reversion to the age-old Hindu architectural principal as expressed in the south Indian gopuram. The combination produced a striking result (Fig. C).

Steeply sloping roofs of red tiles are another characteristic, with tiled pyramids often taking the place of domes.

In front of the porch, some temples have been extended in more recent times to provide another larger hall, mainly for music, dancing and dramas that are performed at festival times. These often destroy the harmony of the original proportions although no doubt they are necessary in functional terms.

FIG B. THE TEMPLE DOMES OF GOA:
Every type of dome is to be seen, straight-sided and smoothly rounded, high-standing and flattened, grooved and segmented and some, as seen over the porches of Mahalaxmi, two-tiered. Sources of inspiration are many and diverse and the Goan architect has contributed his own flair and imagination.
Above, adorning the domes, rise an equal variety, in several combinations, of European lantern towers and Indian finials. The Indian symbols used in these are either the amalaka, a flattened globe vertically grooved all round to represent a fruit, or a pinnacle built up of spheres representing water pots.

Fig B. THE TEMPLE DOMES OF GOA.

1. *Chandranath Temple, Paroda.*

3. *Naguesh Temple, Bandora.*

2. *Mahalaxmi Temple, Bandora.*

4. *Mangesh Temple, Priol.*

5. *Mahalasa Temple, Mardol.*

Fig B. THE TEMPLE DOMES OF GOA. (continued)
6. Vithal Temple, Sanquelim, Bicholim.

One feature common to almost all temples in Goa, regardless of their deity, is a tulasi or tulsi plant, named after one of Vishnu's lovers who Lakshmi out of jealousy turned into a flowering bush. The plant, a type of basil, is kept at temples or outside any Brahmin home, in a vrindavan. They can be seen all over Goa, and daily circumambulation, a lovely word, much better than 'walking around', is a meritorious act. It is included in many Hindu ceremonies such as the Thread Ceremony when a young Brahmin makes his obligations and is forever accepted into his community. Tulsi vrindavans are usually set to one side of the front entrance to the mandapa. In the case of those temples with a modern extension, it will be found somewhere near where the old and new buildings are joined. The vrindavans themselves vary from the majestic example, its ultimate architectural form, at the Mahalasa Temple at Mardol, may it be preserved during the new building taking place there, to the elaborately tile-decorated pedestal at the Manguesh Temple and from there to the multitude of every-day often brightly painted versions to be seen wherever you go, especially in the area of the New Conquests. Some of these domestic examples are of considerable size with carved figures in niches in between columns, the whole pillar rising from a lotus petal pedestal. Others are quite small and plain, decorated only with a painted 'OM' symbol or a swastika. There is every graduation in between and, in less prosperous circumstances, a rough, baked clay version serves the purpose honourably (see Fig. D).

Both inside and out of these temples, colour is of the essence. The Portuguese may have painted their churches all white, and in fact ruled that all other buildings had to be of some other colour, apart from door and window surrounds, but the Hindus wanted colour in their temples. Although domes and lamp towers may be white, the rest is usually enlivened by strong colours.

An interesting decorative method, examples of which can still be seen in Bicholim and more especially in Pernem, is 'graffito'. This is not the scratching of names and verses, but an art form in which a layer of coloured plaster, usually red, is

FIG D. TULSI VRINDAVANS OF GOA:

Tile-decorated vrindavan. Mangesh Temple, Priol, Ponda.
Also showing dharmasalas, living quarters for pilgrims.

Simple clay tulsi vrindavan. Lamgao village, Bicholim.

Village extravagance. Candola village, Ponda.

The ultimate example, Baroque-inspired and seven metres
high. Mahalasa Temple, Mardol, Ponda.

Ravalnath Temple, Mulgao.

applied before the final white layer and, before this top white layer hardens, patterns are created by scratching this away to expose the red underneath. The 'scratching', the literal meaning of 'graffito' in Italian, is delicately carried out and as well as solid, basic patterns some intricate work can be seen. The German archaeologist, Gritli V. Mitterwallner considers these graffito-decorated Hindu temples as representing 'the most important contribution Goa has made to the folk art of India'.[4]

Water plays an important part in Hindu ceremony and water tanks for ritual ablution are an essential part of large temples. Some of them are particularly attractive in their setting just outside the main courtyard, and if seeking a moment's peace away from the crowds, these offer the ideal solution, except of course on festival days.

The interiors also display distinguishing aspects. The pillared hall was an essential feature of traditional temples and there are many 'Thousand Pillared' halls in south India, few actually living up to their ambitious description. However, the arrangement adopted here of providing a central space

with aisles either side relates to the Christian church plan and the round arches that link the columns are certainly inspired by the buildings of Portuguese Goa, always preferred, it would seem, to the pointed Muslim arch. The mandapa of these Goan temples usually has twin rows of six to eight columns, these being either round or square and, especially in the case of wooden columns, decorated with intricate carving. In later temples, at the end of each aisle flanking the entrance to the inner sanctum there is often a shrine to one of the supporting cast of deities and, with an entrance hall and porchway on either side in front of the sanctuary, the ground plan becomes cruciform. The whole interior design has links with both Christianity and Islam.

This continues in the decoration of one of the most striking details of these temples, the screen between the mandapa and the main shrine. This is often completely clad in silver fashioned into complex patterns, the inspiration for the motifs being drawn from many sources. Niches on either side of the central doorway hold statues or paintings of *dvarapalas*, the door-keepers or guardians of the sanctuary.

The ceilings are worthy of study, some of beautifully carved wood, some heavily stuccoed and all painted, with a dominant central panel that received special treatment from the artists responsible, sometimes with a raised central section decorated with carved and painted panels of gods and goddesses or illustrating events from Hindu mythology. Like some of the friezes of carved panelling that in some cases run along the side of the mandapa above the arches, the panels are often framed with Muslim cinque-foil arches. Clusters of chandeliers and lamps hang from the ceilings, Muslim influence this time, many quite unusual and ornate in concept, perhaps originating in Hyderabad away to the east, where such items were certainly produced for the Nawabs. Amidst the chandeliers hang the temple bells.

The *palki*, palanquin, in which the deity is carried out in procession on certain occasions is usually kept in one of the aisles. The other transport of the gods is the rath, the huge wooden chariot in which the image is hauled by human energy on only very

special occasions. This is kept outside in the courtyard and will be worth seeking out.

The huge courtyards in which these temples are enclosed, derive from their peculiar refugee status which required the extension of the usual functions of a Hindu temple. For example, the temples became centres where the marriage ceremony itself could take place, not at all usual in Hindu practice, but adopted because of the problems of organising marriages in the traditional way where Portuguese rule was paramount. A corollary of this was the need to provide places where the accompanying essential festivities could be held. Further still, because those involved had to travel some distance from beyond the border to reach the temple, accommodation had to be provided. This applied not only to wedding parties but for those attending festivals throughout the year as well as visits by individuals or groups of devotees on occasions special to themselves. Today, in a different context, this continues to be an important requirement.

As a result, ranged around the courtyard are the *dharmasalas*, or living quarters, available for pilgrims together with the offices of the administra-

Silver-clad screen in Mahalasa Temple, Mardol.

Naguesh Temple, showing carved and painted panels from Hindu mythology.

tors of the temple and its estates. Also in the courtyard is often a well, signifying the basic blessing of water within the compound. Talking of self-contained units and self-sufficiency, there is even the branch of a local bank inside the Shantadurga Temple, one of the largest and most frequented by visitors of all the temples in Goa.

Above and as part of the main gate into the courtyard is a *naubat khana*, more usually associated with Muslim rather than Hindu architecture, describing precisely its purpose, its literal meaning being 'a place for beating drums'. If you happen to arrive at the temple at an appropriate moment, the effect of the sounds on the atmosphere have an impact as significant as being in the temple when worshippers announce their fervent entrance with the ringing of temple bells, or of being alone with the soft silence of chanting priests.

But in spite of all these unique forms and the outward evidence of strong influences foreign to the Hindu tradition, nothing detracts from or diminishes the true Hindu spirituality and atmosphere of these places. On entering, one could be nowhere

other than a Hindu temple. Nor are they monuments to the past, but very much of today. The nature of their very beginnings meant that they were not established to meet the needs of a small local community and, from the first, devotees travelled some distance to worship their particular deity. This continues today and is now even more true with the dispersal of Goans all over India and even further afield, not this time driven from their homeland by repression but in search of fame and fortune. These migrant Goans still return to pay homage to their god, and there seems to be a never-ending stream of devotees in every temple.

Donations for the upkeep of particular temples flow in from all over India, indeed from across the world, and this brings us to another point – most of the temples are extremely well maintained. There is no question of them falling into decay, even in their often isolated sites.

Apart from the outside support they receive, this is largely due to a system first established as long ago as the 14th century. In 1378, Madhav Mantri at the head of the Vijayanagar army took from the Muslims the territory that would become Goa and, among the many reforms initiated during his twelve years as Governor, was the setting up of

Wooden chariot at the Shantadurga Temple, Ponda.

Temple at Naroa and the Chamundi Temple nearby at Piligao, both built in the 17th rather than the 18th century like the others, demonstrate interesting variations on the theme. Here, there are no large courtyards with the extensive accommodation found in the Ponda temples and, as already mentioned, the lamp towers are of a much simpler type. The domed tower over the sanctuary was however already a feature.

An exception to all this, is the Brahma temple at Carambolim (or Carmoli) in Satari Taluka. In this case, the deity was taken from Carambolim village in the Ilhas into the forests of the foothills of the ghats far to the east, well out of reach of any possible detection. Nor was a great temple to Brahma built here, even when less harrowing times would have allowed it. He is still housed in a small and modest temple in quiet countryside, the magnificent ancient image being served by a single priest to perform his rites.

With the growing atmosphere of tolerance, or rather indifference, many more Hindu shrines and temples subsequently appeared over the length and breadth of the New Conquests, often adopting the Goan 'Baroque' formula but also sometimes assuming a more conventional mantel as in the Dattaraya Temple at Sanquelim built in 1882.

By comparison with the New Conquests, there are still relatively few large Hindu temples in the area of the Old Conquests which, in spite of the initially harsh and forceful nature of its conversion, remained until recent times predominantly and devoutly Christian. However, once the Portuguese relaxed their religious attitudes in the 19th century, temples and shrines did make their appearance in the Old Conquests, mainly small and, interestingly,

estates for the temples to provide for their upkeep.

In the lands that were to become the New Conquests, this method of providing funds for temples was perpetuated even after these areas fell under Portuguese control. It is interesting that when, in 1764, the Raja of Sonda handed over the territory of Ponda, Sanguem, Quepem and Canacona to the Portuguese for 'safe-keeping', one of his conditions, accepted and honoured by the Viceroy, was that the Portuguese should continue the endowments and preserve the estates that supported the Hindu temples in his territory.

Important examples of temples of this type built for 'migrant' deities in Ponda are:

The Mangesh Temple at Priol
The Mahalasa Temple at Mardol
The Shantadurga Temple at Quela

Of the Bicholim temples, the Saptakoteshwar

Mahalaxmi Temple, Panjim

constructed on traditional lines. Modern Hindu temples are being built on a larger scale, a notable example being the Mahalaxmi Temple in Panjim. This was the first Hindu temple to be re-establish-red in Panjim, official Portuguese approval being given in 1818. It is only recently, however, that it was decided to rebuild and considerably expand the temple which was re-opened in 1983.

MUSLIMS IN GOA

Nor is there so much evidence of the Muslim faith, and today only four percent of Goa's population are followers of the Prophet. Even though the whole territory fell under Muslim domination for lengthy periods, the proportion of Muslims was never large and, on the arrival of the Portuguese, they were immediate targets for elimination. This objective was not confined to the Portuguese priesthood, but was the devout aim of every man among the conquistadors. Portugal itself had not long been freed from the yoke of Islam, it being only eighteen years earlier in 1492 that the Moors had been driven from neighbouring Spain; they were still threatening from the northern coast of Africa, so they were still the immediate foe. Thus it was that initially it was against the Muslims that their crusading spirit was mainly directed. On the fall of

Yusuf Adil Shah's city in 1510, Afonso Albuquerque, usually the most liberal of men for his time, ordered the wholesale massacre of the Muslim inhabitants and all the mosques were systematically destroyed. As in the case of Hindu temples, few ancient mosques have survived, but the Muslim contribution had already been made in the 15th century and their influence is still there for all to see in Goa's temples.

The most famous and accessible mosque is the half-ruined Safa Shahouri Masjid built in 1560 by Ali Adil Shah on the outskirts of the town of Ponda. Another of some antiquity is the Namazgah Mosque, built high above Bicholim by Prince Akbar, rebel son of the Moghul Emperor Aurangzeb, to commemorate a battle which he and the Marathas led by Sambhaji, a treasonable combination, fought against the Portuguese here in 1683. The mosque design is as intriguing as the alliance, and the siting is dramatic.

There are also two Dargahs, shrines of Muslim holy men, with their attendant mosques, one that of Hazrat Abdullah Khan in Ponda and the other the Dargah of Madal Shah in Cuncolim, far to the south of Salcete Taluka.

The old mosque in Sanguem has recently been completely rebuilt and there are newly erected mosques in most of the main centres.

4 THE HOUSES, VILLAGES AND TOWNS

Although this may seem a mundane topic, it is in fact fundamental to the atmosphere that is the irresistible attraction of Goa, one of the strands that distinguish it from the surrounding environment, at least as far as the Old Conquests are concerned. It has to be acknowledged that, in this particular respect, the rest of Goa is more akin to its neighbouring states. The palm heart of Goa is something quite different.

Apart from Old Goa, an unnatural phenomenon, which rapidly rose to become a great city of over 200,000 inhabitants only to shrink just as suddenly to practically nothing, Goa has never been characterised by urban development on any scale. Cities and large towns usually originate from commercial wealth, as did Old Goa, and the riches of Old Goa were created and managed by foreigners between and for themselves with the city acting purely as an *entrepôt*, its wealth deriving almost entirely from the trading of goods coming from outside the territory. When this trade dwindled, the city dwindled with it. During this period, any activity within the colony was so heavily concentrated on Old Goa that, in relative terms, all else was played in a minor key. The point is often made that during Goa's hey-day, Goans themselves escaped relatively unscathed by the whirlwind. By the time the centre of power had shifted to Panjim, taking this from the vice-regal transfer in 1759, the level of both commercial and administrative activity associated with the capital was considerably diminished and with it the potential for growth and its attraction to the local people.

Even now, Goa does not suffer from the problems associated with migration from rural areas to the towns that beset so many societies. Goans go further afield to seek a solution to their frustrated ambitions. It is true of the whole of Goa that the population has remained widely spread in the villages rather than concentrating on towns. In all, only about 20 percent of the population are genuine

city, or rather town, dwellers, even with the recent industrial and mining developments that have attracted immigrants from outside Goa and materially boosted the total population and, in particular, the urban figures.

The basis for the genuine domestic wealth of Goa was its natural resources and in particular, in the past, the fertility of its soil. It remained so throughout the period of Portuguese rule. The Portuguese did not come to acquire land; this was not part of their colonial strategy. The exception came when the Jesuit order began to take over more and more estates to provide themselves with financial support in a declining commercial environment. This was soon stamped upon by the government in Lisbon and was one of the factors leading to the Jesuits' suppression and expulsion in the 18th century. It will be remembered that, even when Hindu families were fleeing the territory under the fierce religious persecution of the 17th century, it was usual for at least some members to remain behind and convert to Christianity in order to meet the new inheritance laws, thus enabling them to retain their land rights.

So the land remained with the Goans and, importantly, the Goans remained with their land. They would continue to do so.

At the time of the arrival of the Portuguese, much of the land was held in joint ownership by members of village communities and administered by the Gaunkaris, the co-operatives or Comunidades, as the Portuguese called them. Over the years, the undermining by the Portuguese of this long-established community system led to the movement into private hands of more and more land and in many places changed the structure of village society. By the end of the 18th century, the presence of a middle or upper-middle class element would impart a unique social role and a distinctive character to the villages of the Old Conquests. Portuguese influence would also play a part in changing other aspects of village life. It was the adoption by upper-class Goans of a western-style social life that had its effect on the homes in which they lived, which in turn had consequential effects on domestic architecture generally.

This was not a 'from the beginning' development, in fact it took two-and-a-half centuries for it really to begin. There were good reasons why it was not until the mid-18th century that social and economic factors combined to take Goa along the path that would lead to its present highly distinctive style. By this time, there was a general easing of conflicts that had developed initially following the arrival of the Portuguese and, as the determination of the conquerors to initiate change diminished, so did the inclination of Goans to resist western influence. Another factor was that Christian Goans were more settled in their religion now after many generations, and were more united as a social group. Although the artificial wealth of Golden Goa was no more, the real wealth, based on the richness of the land as well as locally based trade, was developing rapidly. The great family estates of Goa began to crystallise. The famines and plagues of the first half of the century were forgotten and also there was a greater feeling of security. The threat of Maratha pillage and destruction was ended. In Portugal the celebration of a new prosperity was in full swing, with Brazilian gold funding Rococo elegance. Through vice-regal channels, this spirit overflowed into Goa and it so happened that Goans were in a receptive frame of mind and had the material wealth to indulge the new fashion to the full. There is also the fact that this new spirit had much to commend it to the Goan psyche. It struck a chord with their appreciation of life and its appeal is shown in the way that they took this opportunity not only to establish a clearly defined Goan style of domestic architecture, but, while they were at it, took the opportunity to develop new art forms in furniture, music and the culinary field.

THE HOUSES

It was this that led to the great houses of Goa as we see them today and because, as we have seen, the upper classes were village-based, village houses took their inspirational cue from the great mansion.

Grand and beautifully built houses were nothing new to Goa and, indeed, the basic materials used continued to be the traditional ones typical of the whole of this part of the west coastline of India, the Konkan and south into Kerala. Laterite blocks continued to be the essential component, with wooden beams and posts topped by roofs of steeply sloping

and overhanging red Mangalore tiles. However, the adoption of a life-style of grace and elegance with entertaining on a grand scale meant a change in emphasis in house design and decoration. The concept of rooms designated for a much wider range of specific functions was developed to a high degree and with a spaciousness not normally associated with Indian houses. Libraries, studies, music rooms, card rooms and with-drawing rooms were introduced, though not all in every house one hastens to add. More important, however, was the emphasis on the main reception rooms, splendid salons and grand dining rooms in order to cope with the formal entertaining, the balls and banquets, that became a feature of life in the late 18th and particularly in the 19th century.

To accommodate all these functions there was a major revision in the layout of the large house. The traditional Hindu house here had been planned round an inner courtyard, the larger ones with the undivided family in mind, and with very much an inward-looking philosophy for protection and privacy. Now, although the courtyard principle was retained, its exterior opened windows and doors on to the outside world with guests in mind.

The Miranda House, Loutolim.

The bigger houses were two-storeyed with the reception rooms usually on the first floor along the front of the house. The width of the frontage was simply decided by the size and number of reception rooms. Inner pillared verandahs round a courtyard provided outdoor living areas and the bedrooms opened off these. Below and behind were the kitchens, utility rooms and servants' rooms.

Façade design is distinguished by several features that derive from Portuguese, or rather Mediterranean, domestic architecture as many of the ideas current in Portugal at that time were Italian or French in origin. As in the case of Rococo church exteriors of the same period, there were constraints on what could be achieved in terms of exterior decoration, as, whether large or small, all are built from the local stone, the ubiquitous red laterite. Rich red in its natural state, heavily pitted and soft, it is used for this reason in blocks much larger than normal building bricks. It weathers on exposure to the tropical atmosphere to a darker colour and becomes much more durable. However it is not suitable for elaborate carving. Most buildings are plastered to protect the laterite further and smooth the rough surface, and decorative detail is limited to stuccoed pilasters and cornices with mouldings round the carved window frames and doors.

Tall handsome windows often occupy almost the full height of the rooms along the front of the house, Baroque in style with many variations on the form of the upper part, mostly round-arched but some pointed or trefoil, many with delicately carved tracery decoration, often with stained glass to add distinction. These are further decorated with plaster moulding where Rococo curves can be brought into play. The windows are enhanced with small balustraded balconies, a very Mediterranean feature not seen other than in this part of India. The balustrades in plaster, carved wood or wrought iron give further scope for the craftsman's skill and invention.

The windows themselves were paned in old traditional fashion with nacre, the indigenous substitute for glass, which was not available locally and was difficult to import. Tiny pieces of the translucent inner layer of oystershells are trimmed into squares and polished and are then fitted overlapping between vertical wooden slats providing a soft filtered light. After many centuries, glass has now taken over but there are still many examples to be seen in Goan homes.

Sadly, many of these windows have been fitted with a protective awning of incongruous corrugated iron sheeting such as are also fitted on some churches, a rusting and unsightly concession to the monsoon.

The steeply sloping and overhanging roofs of Mangalore tiles are also designed to cope with monsoon rains and there is particular interest in the way in which the overhang is achieved. A wide cornice is built up of layers of the curved tiles, which in itself provides an attractive decorative feature, an old traditional device seen also in temples. Also decorating the rooftops, on the ridge of the roof itself or on the tiled pyramid of the

Nacre window. Fontainhas, Panjim.

balcao, are terracotta figures, the most popular being smartly saluting Portuguese soldiers or proud, almost strutting cockerels. There are several others, even a Chinese dragon on a house in Margao. As decoration for gate posts, lions are the thing, perhaps harking back to when it was the royal emblem of the Kadambas, although Goan lack of first-hand acquaintance with the royal beast results in them tending to resemble plump friendly cats with somewhat vacuous expressions.

The greatest care and attention was given to the interior decoration of these elegant houses. Floors were of intricate patterns of tiles or gleaming polished wood, while the ceilings could be stuccoed and painted in the more elaborate rooms or of polished woods, sometimes with different types of wood inlaid to form delicate patterns. Gilded mirrors and chandeliers were imported from Europe and Chinese porcelain ordered in special patterns and designs. The famous Goan 'blackwood' furniture appeared at this time. At first furniture was also imported, but the skill of local woodcarvers soon rendered this unnecessary. Based on designs from Europe and Macao, Goan craftsmen soon established their own interpretations and a new local art form emerged. Genuine old pieces, deeply and elaborately decorated, mostly in Indian rosewood, though some in exotic woods brought in especially for the purpose, are

Smartly saluting Portuguese soldiers.

now much sought after. There are still fine examples to be seen, however.

Always included in the larger houses was a family chapel, in some cases gems of ecclesiastical architecture adopting the gilded splendour of their public counterparts, whose builders were rejoicing in the flamboyance of the Rococo. Not all family chapels were ornate, many being relatively modest, nor was it a feature confined to the houses of the wealthy, every Christian home having its shrine, however simple. This is obviously an inheritance from the Hindu practice of always having a shrine to the favoured deity in every house.

Unhappily, many of these larger mansions are now falling into decay, the cost of upkeep being too great for their sometimes absent 20th-century inheritors. However, the fading elegance is still there to be seen and the long-stilled strains of string instruments and harmonic voices providing the background to the graceful dance movements of the peculiarly Goan *mando* can still be summoned in the imagination.

Social demands often cause people to put up with incongruities in the name of style and fashion so it was fortunate that aspects of the domestic architecture of the sunny Mediterranean were so well

suited to the climate and social atmosphere of this dot on the shores of the Arabian Sea. Allied with Goan innate ability to adapt any imported influences to their own needs, this meant that features of the great houses would impact on the style of the whole range of the less imposing homes in the villages and towns, unifying them with their surroundings and creating a soothing harmony. Elements of window design were adopted and even smaller houses had their balconies, but it was the deep balustraded verandah that came to form an essential part of an outdoor living area usually extending along the full length of the front of the house. Even where there is no verandah there is certain to be one of the most distinctive features of the village house, the *balcao*, the dominant porchway.

The design of the balcao varies, but retains a fundamental similarity, with steps leading up to a pillared structure usually with bench seats along each side and covered with a pyramid-shaped tiled roof. This provides an outdoor but sheltered seating area and is a social focal point. This is no mere practicality as the term 'porch' would imply, a fleeting shelter until the house itself can be entered, but a Goan's window on the world, the stage upon which welcomes can be extended, partings prolonged and family or village dramas enacted and endlessly debated. Decorated with a family crest or even stained glass in some of the grandest, in others a simple cross or flowering plants.

In addition to all these architectural components there is one outstanding ingredient in the Goan recipe, the use of colour wash on all houses. This is where the householder can demonstrate his individuality and the colour combinations can be striking and certainly add to their charm, seeming entirely appropriate in their lush tropical settings. Everywhere, there are banana, papaya, bread fruit and mango trees together with many types of palms all interspersed with shrubs of endless variety. Bougainvillaea, frangipani and hibiscus are only a beginning. These villages can be a colourful experience.

Moving eastwards the atmosphere changes rapidly where, as has been said before, Portuguese Christian influence was not as strongly inflicted and for the most part people remained Hindu. Unlike in the western areas, the occasional church stands out on a hill-top as an unusual feature and is no longer the hub of the villages. This is a land of temples rather than churches and, too, a land of dusty hills and deep valleys, of forest and rushing rivers. The villages reflect these different environments and influences.

Typical balcao. Loutolim, Salcete.

Yet another different type of community has developed with the mining activities on the uplands to the north-east where huge open-cast iron and manganese ore mines superimposed on the landscape have brought with them their own unmistakeable form of settlement patterns.

In the far north, the taluka of Pernem, a land of bare rocky hills with areca palms filling the valleys, merges imperceptibly into its northern neighbour Maharashtra, and its villages are indistinguishable from those beyond the border.

THE TOWNS

For census purposes, technical definitions control when a village becomes a town, thus making its population urban instead of rural. Under such a classification, Chauri in Canacona in the far south, with its population of 1629, becomes a town and its population 'urban'. Leaving aside such anomalies, only about 20 per cent of Goa's population live in towns and nearly three-quarters of these are concentrated in the three main centres, Panjim, Margao and Vasco da Gama including Mormugao.

With the abandonment of Old Goa in the 18th century, the role as the seat of government was thrust upon Panjim only because it was the site of the small riverside palace of Yusuf Adil Shah, which provided a ready-made vice-regal residence, and, importantly, was nearer the open sea and therefore regarded as healthier.

There was little else other than the church, already rebuilt, the tiny fort of Gaspar Dias nearby and the country villas of some noblemen. It is now a pleasant thriving town and the seat of government for the State of Goa, Daman and Diu but, with its population of about 45,000, still hardly a great metropolis. This is eminently proper and entirely in keeping with the character and needs of the State. There is a distinct Mediterranean flavour to the atmosphere, some fine public buildings and fascinating sections of old residential areas remain together with other interesting features. Inevitably, modern buildings are encroaching at a rapid rate, but it retains its charm and is well worth exploring.

Margao, in contrast, has a history that goes back before the Portuguese and is the main commercial centre. Situated on Goa's only railway line that starts at Vasco da Gama and, crossing the Western ghats, links up with the Indian Railway's system, it is a bustling little town. The increased economic activity since 1961 is reflected in the fact that its population has more than tripled in this period and is now at about 55,000, perhaps more if this rate of growth has continued since the last census.

It is a town of some character. There are some particularly fine examples of Goan domestic and ecclesiastical architecture which are worthy of attention. Like Panjim it will be described in more detail later.

If the recent growth of Margao is impressive, that of Vasco-Mormugao is astounding. When the Portuguese left, it was a town of only just over 6000 people. Twenty years later it had exploded by more than ten times to over 70,000. Once considered as an alternative to Panjim as the capital, now the terminus of the railway and the site of Goa's airport, it has gained in importance with the dramatic growth of the mining industry and the rise of Mormugao as one of India's major ports in terms of volume of traffic. Its highly mechanised ore-handling terminal dominates the waterfront. In addition, much of the new industrial development has taken place in this area. Immigrant labour has played an important part in its rapid growth.

The rest of the towns of note grew up as market centres for their own area, and subsequently developed as administrative centres for their respective talukas. Of these, Ponda has had particularly rapid growth in the last twenty years because of an hotel and tourist infrastructure to cope with the greatly increased pilgrim traffic to the cluster of important Hindu temples nearby once the area became more readily accessible after Independence. In addition, three new major industrial units have opened there in the seventies. All this gives it an air of urgent activity.

Mapusa is the supreme example of a market town and Bicholim has grown as a centre for mining activity. Otherwise, the rest have changed little over a long period of time and perform their traditional functions. None of these have more than 10,000 inhabitants.

So, in spite of all the political and economic changes, the villages continue as the essence of Goan life and it is there that the true Goa can be experienced.

5 THE FORTRESSES

The forts are part of Goa's dead past, unlike the churches and temples which, while having a long historical past, are yet of the present, with an important role for the future. However, the forts are an essential ingredient of the Goan ambience, part of the backdrop and, where they survive, one of the stongest and most evocative symbols of Portuguese presence. They act as a reminder that although once a golden city founded on commercial wealth, it was fundamentally a far-eastern outpost in a hostile land, dependent on military strength for survival.

Survive it did, thanks to its forts and armies, even after its commercial demise. But most of these forts that enabled its survival are no more, now walls and rubble and in many cases not even that, only a mark on a historical map or a note in a treatise on successful conquests or repelled aggressions.

The Portuguese were great fort builders and, in terms of sites, Goa's rocky headlands provided dramatic scenic as well as strategic possibilities of which full advantage was taken. Added to this, Goa's local stone, the blood-red heavily pitted laterite, was fitting material for fortress building, lending itself to being quarried in massive blocks, and visually eminently appropriate, weathering almost to black. Of Goa's forts the Portuguese built only those in the Old Conquests, those in the New being either captured in battle or acquired from their neighbours in territorial transactions, although they were then modified and strengthened by them, sometimes almost rebuilt, turning their faces to confront their former occupants (map C).

It was not only church and domestic architecture that was imported through the Portuguese connection; defence architecture and techniques were, in fact, the most completely adopted, with little concession being made to local circumstances. The timing of Portuguese arrival in India dictated precisely the fort architecture that would become standard in Goa, and in its northern possessions, during the 17th century when most of the major forts were being built. In Europe, defensive architecture had had to undergo a revolution to deal with the arrival on the scene of more powerful weapons. This was the result of more efficient gun-powder together with improved cannon manufacture and, after 1480, the production of the tougher cast-iron cannonballs capable of wreaking much greater damage. Of necessity, medieval castles went out of fashion, giving way to new defensive systems that could cope with the new awesome cannonades. The answer was provided in Europe by Italian engineers, their solutions being rapidly adopted by the other European powers. Portugal was no exception and in 1580 employed an Italian, Filippo Terzi, to design new royal forts and modernise existing ones in their colonies. Another Italian adviser is mentioned in the inscription above the main gate at Fort Jesus in Mombasa on the East African coast, where the engineer responsible for its construction, Joao Batista Caireto, is described as 'Chief Architect of India'. The fort was completed in 1593. Caireto died in Goa in 1596, but principles of design had been established that would characterise all Portuguese-built forts in India from the great forts of the 17th century through to modifications to captured forts at the end of the 18th century.

High walls and impressive towers, difficult to scale but, with the new weapons, now easy to knock down, were replaced by lower and much thicker walls, thus offering attacking artillery a smaller target above ground level. The loss of height was compensated for by deeper and wider ditches in front. In some cases, the effectiveness of the walls was increased by using earth infill between two thick outer layers of stonework which helped absorb the impact of a shot. Walls were made sloping instead of vertical, to deflect round shot. Modifications were also required to allow

FORT AGUADA

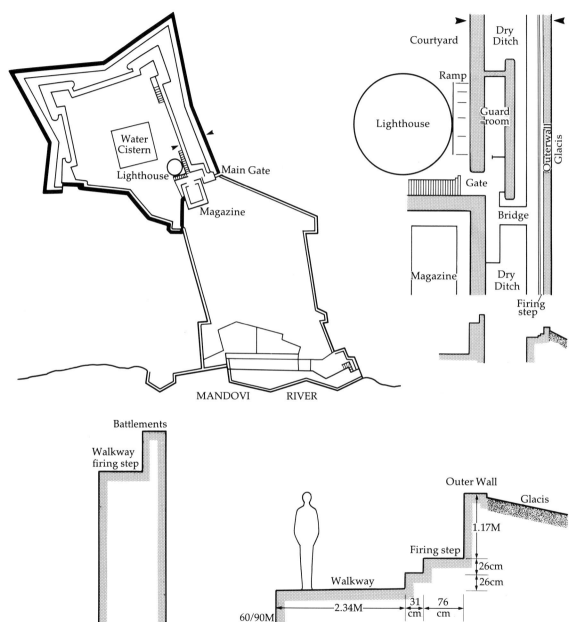

MANDOVI   RIVER

Cross Section of Defences of Fort Aguada

The Queen of Beaches. Calangute (Bardez) with one of the bastions of Fort Aguada in the foreground.

forts to use these new weapons themselves. Bastions, the projections from the lines of curtain walling, replaced high towers. They were enlarged to accommodate the bigger cannon on their wheeled carriages and their design became more sophisticated, round bastions giving way to arrowhead or vee-shaped design, which achieved maximum deflection of shot and also improved the field of fire, especially at close quarters. The exception was at sea level where round bastions were retained, being more effective in deflecting pounding waves. Fort building was becoming a mathematical science (see figure opposite).

Now, the only towers were low ones over the entrance to give sufficient height for defence of the gateways, which were arched for strength and with heavy iron-spiked doors. There are, of course, the distinctive cylindrical turrets that are such a typical feature of these Portuguese forts and add a pleasing decorative effect but they are small and their main purpose would have been to provide a sheltered lookout post from which sentries could obtain a good view of the surrounding countryside. There is little enough room for the handling of weapons to assist in defence.

Just as the reduction in the height of the walls above ground required deeper dry 'moats' on the outside, to restore the height obstacle for defence against hordes of foot soldiers or horsemen with hand arms, so it became necessary to have more depth inside to give protection to interior structures. There was some excavation to provide lower levels on which to build, but the main solution was to excavate the facilities themselves out of the solid rock. Underground stores, guard-rooms, shot and powder magazines and water storage cisterns were all linked by complex passages and staircases. This also provided a source of vast quantities of building materials. In Goa, *Fort Aguada* is a particularly good example of this as it was the source of water for visiting ships, apart from the usual need for self-sufficiency in case of siege, and the storage requirements were considerable.

At *Terekhol*, the most northerly of Goa's forts, a captured outpost on a tiny headland, converted by the Portuguese not originally built by them, another principle of Portuguese fort building is well illustrated. A church was considered desirable for a fort's garrison and for those who had to flee within its walls seeking protection. However, anything built just outside the walls would interfere with the field of fire and could, if captured, provide the enemy with a threatening stronghold at close quarters. Churches were, therefore, built inside the walls and at Terekhol the re-builders were prepared to discount the considerable disadvantages of having it occupy so much valuable space in order to achieve this. There was no room to expand, nor was there any possibility of further excavation, so the church not only takes up much of the courtyard, it also overtops the walls! At Aguada when another church was required on the headland, in addition to the small Chapel of Our Lady of Good Voyage within the walls of the fort, the new church, St Lawrence's, which Count Linhares the Viceroy founded in 1630, eighteen years after the completion of the fort, was sited at some considerable distance from the walls of the citadel though still within the outer defences.

In coastal forts, which constituted the majority of those built by the Portuguese, a safe mooring for loading and unloading men and supplies, or for use as an escape route by sea, was linked to the main part of the fort by a protected corridor, usually created by defensible walls or in some cases by cutting underground tunnels. Even at Rachol, far inland, there is a mysterious tunnel of which only the end at the seminary still exists and which was probably an escape route linked with some part of the fort.

Where built on a promontory it would always be regarded as ideal if the peninsula could be virtually turned into an island by linking the sea on either side, thus greatly strengthening the defensive position against landward attack. But, if this proved impractical the Portuguese fort-builders were willing to sacrifice better landward defences in order to create a sufficiently large defensible area into which the local population could flee for protection, another major consideration. This accounts for the large area covered by many of the forts. There was also their conviction that, in any case, the greatest danger came from the sea rather than the land, looking to their European trading rivals, especially the Dutch, as their greatest threat.

There was no standardised ground plan for Goa's forts, all these basic principles being applied as they fitted best to a particular site, with the outline of the fort following the contours of the ground and its size related to the nature of the area to be defended. This resulted in some strange and complex geometric patterns.

The first forts were on the cluster of islands, the Ilhas, that were their first foothold to protect their newly captured city from attacks along the rivers or from the east where Muslim armies still lurked. In the city itself the existing fort built by Yusuf Adil Shah was demolished and a European-style structure built on the same site overlooking the Mandovi River. Forts were also re-built on other islands in the river, *St Bartholomew's* on Chorao, at *Naroa* on Divar and at *St Estevam* on Jua. The bastion at *Banasterim*, captured from Ismail Adil Khan in 1512, was converted into an important Portuguese defence post against further Bijapur attacks and, like the other forts, was armed with cannon beginning to be turned out from the great Arsenal that was soon established in the heart of the city, local craftsmen quickly adapting skills to produce weapons equal in quality to the foundries of Europe. The Idalcao's Palace at Panjim near the mouth of the river was greatly reinforced with more artillery pieces. This still left the southern approaches up the Zuari River unprotected and, to remedy this, a gun emplacement was planned for the Cabo promontory. This would also give additional fire-cover to the Mandovi estuary.

Once the territory of the Old Conquests had been established, with the addition of Bardez and Salcete in 1543, the Mandovi River defences were further strengthened by the building of the *Reis Magos* Fort in 1551 on the newly acquired north bank. Later, in 1598, the somewhat inadequate fortress-palace of the Adil Shahs was supplemented by the small fort of *Gaspar Dias* carrying twelve guns.

The inland fortress of *Rachol*, captured from Muslim Bijapur by Hindu Vijayanagar in 1520, was relinquished by them to the Portuguese soon afterwards as encouragement against the common foe, but destroyed on orders of the Viceroy on their enforced withdrawal in 1536. Rebuilt after the territory was formally acquired by treaty in 1543, it was to prove a great stronghold in Portuguese resistance against the further attempts of the Adil Shahs to regain this territory and also, after modifications carried out in 1604, against subsequent Maratha attacks of the 17th and 18th centuries. One of Goa's key positions, it was often to be isolated but never taken.

Of these early forts, little is known of their architecture. An archway and a ramp surrounded by remnants of wall at *St Estevam*, and sections of wall at *Banasterim*, are all that survive. The fortress-palace of the Idalcao has been subsequently modified out of all recognition and the fort at *Reis Magos* was rebuilt at the beginning of the 18th century. The others have all disappeared.

It had always been from the sea that the Portuguese most feared attack, with the ever-growing threat from other European sea-faring nations. The Dutch did attack in 1604 and, though eventually repulsed, managed to penetrate the river mouth and set fire to Portuguese ships at anchor. So, in 1612 the huge *Fort Aguada* was built with another in 1624 on the headland of Mormugao that formed the dual estuary of the Mandovi and Zuari Rivers. River access to the heart of Portuguese territory now had formidable protection and it was to the sea that the Portuguese kept anxious and diligent watch against possible aggression.

This obsession was confounded in 1664 when the next assault on their territory came from landward with the Maratha Chief Shivaji, sweeping down into the Konkan virtually unopposed. He took Pernem and Bicholim, at that time areas under the rule of vassal chieftains subservient to the Sultan of Bijapur, but stopped short of entering Goa, distracted by the Mughul threat to his own homeland to the north. As soon as he had left, the two chieftains of Pernem and Bicholim, who had taken refuge in Portuguese Bardez, started raiding into their old territories. Infuriated, Shivaji mounted a punitive expedition into Bardez in 1667, wreaking considerable havoc before the Portuguese hastily negotiated for peace. Shivaji himself was on Goa's borders again a year later but contented himself with rebuilding the Saptakoteshwar Temple at Naroa.

All these alarms and excursions demonstrated the seriousness of the Maratha menace, but Goa was in decline and lacking real direction. The strengthening of the northern defences with the small forts of Tivim and Colvale was half-hearted and, in 1683, Shivaji's son Sambhaji proved their inadequacy, this time the Marathas reaching the gates of Old Goa before it was again saved by outside intervention and the assistance of St Francis Xavier (see p. 8). After this, a real effort was made to improve their defences. *Reis Magos* on its fine defensive site was completely rebuilt in 1707 and in 1717 the gesture of *Chapora Fort* was made, though it had no ditch in front of its walls and its strength was again to seaward.

Twenty years later, the Marathas subjected Portuguese possessions to the north of Bombay to a series of devastating attacks, all being overrun with the exception of Bassein which just managed to hold out with the aid of supplies coming in by sea

from Goa. To weaken Bassein's resistance and with the prize of Goa itself beckoning, the Maratha machine rolled south with the Bhonsles of Sawantwadi not slow to attach themselves to the victorious Maratha coat-tails, occupying Bardez once the Marathas had reached the Mandovi River. All the new fortifications of Bardez had proved ineffective and by 1739 only Fort Aguada and Reis Magos in the north were holding out, supported by Mormugao and Rachol in the south. The towns and villages of Bardez and Salcete had been plundered and for the second time Maratha troops were sitting at the gates of Old Goa.

At this moment of high drama, with the downfall of Goa's capital imminent, the term of office of the Viceroy expired and his successor arrived bringing 12,000 troops and sixty pieces of artillery. This was mid-May and with the monsoon approaching there was little time for action once celebrations of the new Viceroy's formal succession had been completed. But as soon as the first flooding downpours were over, the spirited counter-attacks of 1741 began in earnest. The new Viceroy, the Marquis of Lourical, was an energetic and determined leader but all he could do was to relieve the immediate threat and demonstrate sufficient strength to cause the Marathas to agree to peace negotiations. However, the terms were harsh. All Portuguese possessions constituting the Province of the North, with the exception of Daman and Diu, were relinquished to the Marathas and heavy financial compensation paid for their total withdrawal from Goa. There was some consolation in the restrictions imposed on the Bhonsles.

Viceroy Lourical died soon after this, after only a year in office, and during the next two years, with Goa ruled by an interim council, the Bhonsles, becoming restless, began probing sorties to test Portuguese determination. On his arrival, the new Viceroy, Dom Pedro Miguel D'Almeida e Portugal, Marquis of Castelo Novo, decided drastic action was required and struck at the heart of Sawantwadi, taking their strongest fort at Alorna in Pernem. This fell in 1746 and was followed by other Bhonsle forts including Terekhol, Arabo, Bicholim, Sanquelim and Nanuz. The Marquis of Castelo Novo added Marquis of Alorno to his other titles to celebrate the victorious campaign.

There were no further Maratha attacks – they were busy elsewhere – but there must have been a great sigh of relief throughout Goa when, in 1761, Maratha strength was shattered in a crushing defeat by the Afghan, Ahmed Shah Durrani, at the Battle of Panipat far to the north.

The ceding by the Raja of Sonda of Sanguem,

Ponda, Quepem and Canacona in 1764 gave the Portuguese the southern coastal fortress of Cabo de Rama. The less peaceful extraction of Bicholim, Satari and finally Pernem from Sawantwadi between 1781 and 1788 confirmed the Portuguese in possession of the northern forts, many of which had been strengthened or even rebuilt. Not that this had much significance by this time, as by the end of the 18th century there was little danger to Goa from outside.

The only ripple of excitement was the temporary occupation of Goa by British troops when the Anglo-French conflict of the Napoleonic Wars in Europe spilled over into India. In 1798, Napoleon himself sailed for Egypt with a powerful army, the preliminary move in a strategy for Oriental supremacy, with India a prime target. A thousand British troops were sent from Bombay to defend this vital port on the west coast and moved into Goa opposed only by diplomatic protest, occupying the forts of Cabo and Gaspar Dias. They did not interfere with the Portuguese civil administration but were obviously most unwelcome visitors. The troops were withdrawn in 1802 with the defeat of the French in Egypt and the Peace of Amiens in Europe, but were hastily returned with the resumption of hostilities in 1803, establishing themselves again in *Cabo Fort* and this time also in the forts of *Aguada* and *Mormugao* where they built barracks and a hospital and began to look like a permanent fixture. However, continued diplomatic protest from Portugal, long-standing and friendly ally of Britain, led to a British withdrawal of troops from Goa in 1813.

With this final flurry of activity the fortresses of Goa fell into disuse and decay. There were no further enemies to oppose. In any case, few of the inland forts were now on Goa's frontiers established as a result of the New Conquests. By the middle of the 19th century all these inland forts had been abandoned and either been allowed to fall into disrepair or their stone used for other buildings. Apart from *Alorna*, remote in the north-east, and *Corjuem*, secluded on its island in the Mapusa

River, both of whose gateways and walls still stand, all have virtually disappeared, only solitary stone remnants marking their previous existence.

The coastal forts fared better. *Terekhol* in the far north has been converted into a tourist hostel, maintained in excellent condition, and the battlements and bastions of *Chapora* loom over the northern end of Vagator Beach. The neighbouring forts of *Aguada* and *Reis Magos* are two of the best preserved, but the interior of both *Reis Magos* and parts of *Aguada* will hopefully be unseen by visitors as they now perform duty as prisons. However, the most interesting part of Aguada, its citadel on the headland, together with its lighthouses, is outside the confines of the jail and gives the best impression of this aspect of Portuguese presence, sited at Goa's hub and readily accessible. It also provides, as do all the coastal forts, a series of magnificent views in all directions. On the Calangute side of the fort, a five star hotel has edged inside what were the northern outer defences.

Of the other coastal forts, Gaspar Dias was completely dismantled and overbuilt by Panjim's expansion, the remnants of Cabo survive, also out of bounds within the grounds of the Governor's official residence, and the battlements of *Mormugao* still glower from its promontory in spite of being virtually swamped by the industrial development around Vasco. The collapsed gate-house and outer walls, together with a small chapel, are almost all that is left to be seen of the most southerly of the forts, that of *Cabo de Rama*, sprawling across its vast, open peninsula on a superb site, though recently a new road has at least made it more accessible.

Where appropriate the remains of all these forts are described later in more detail as part of the local scene, and what does remain makes a forceful impact on the senses. Their presence looms large, the occasional bastion, archway, tower or crenellated wall, vivid reminders of men-of-war and cannon smoke, pikes and muskets and of the fact that Goa's existence once depended upon the armoured guardians of this outpost of empire.

6 THE SCENERY AND THE NATURAL WEALTH

The Beaches – Sea and Sand, Fish and Tourists;
The Coconut and The Cashew – Nuts and Feni;
Areca Nuts and Betel Leaves – The Pleasures of

Paan; Mines and Forest – The Wealth of the Hills;
Fruits and Spices from Around the World;
The Rice Bowl.

For many, one of Goa's greatest attractions is the scenery. It is a beautiful land, restful on the eye and spirit, yet also full of colour and contrast.

The sharp ridge of the Western Ghats, so called because they run just inland along much of India's west coast, provides Goa with a well defined eastern border, never more than 55 km from the sea. An effective barrier with the Deccan beyond, crossed by only one road and the railway line in the eastern sector, they are wild and trackless in many places, less dramatic and tree-covered in others; again the emphasis is on variety. Here the ghats are known as the Sahyadri Mountains, with the peak of Sonsagad at 1666 metres – the highest point in Goa. Several supporting peaks only a little lower maintain its level for much of its curving length.

All of Goa's rivers rise in this higher ground and make their way by winding routes to the Arabian Sea in the west. There are many of them, from the Terekhol, forming the border in the north, to the Galgibaga, in the far south, a series of east-west links, though at the same time creating barriers to north-south movement. Within this small area, rivers have first cleft deep valleys through the mountains and forests and have then, on their wanderings to the sea, created wide, fertile flatlands, the higher areas of rock left between reaching out into the sea to break up the palm-fringed sands that run the full length of Goa's coastline.

Much of life in Goa has unusually strong links with water. Visually it is everywhere, an important part of the scenery, from sea and river to temple tanks and irrigation channels. Apart from dictating what will grow for nature and for man, and inci-

dentally being the source of Goa's soul-food, fish, it also controls movement. Changes in the waterscape mean changes in Goan life.

The very shape of Goa has changed over the geologically brief period of a few hundred years and continues to change, mainly because of the silting up of its waterways. In accord with the legend of its creation, Goa is still rising from the sea. Islands in rivers that were once distinctive features are growing and merging with the 'mainland' and villages that were once riverside settlements, once even ports of some consequence, are now distant from any water, Goa Velha being a prime example. The Mandovi River is closed to all but the shallowest draught of vessel between June and September, when the south-west monsoon drags up sand bars at its mouth – the stormy weather of these months completing its maritime isolation. In fact, both of Goa's main arteries, the great rivers of the Mandovi and the Zuari, will be kept in use only by a programme of dredging, and even the fortunes of Mormugao as a great port depend on keeping these main channels clear to ensure that it does not suffer the fate of the original Zuari port of Gopakapattana, Goa Velha. River transport in the form of ferries, launches, canoes, fishing boats and ore barges, amongst a host of water-craft, are part of life almost wherever you are in Goa and any changes in the water pattern can directly affect the lives of the people, just as can the building of bridges, as has been demonstrated by the crossing of several water barriers in recent years.

Man has made his impact on this landscape of infinite variety, so far mostly a sympathetic and kindly one, though with some notable exceptions that give some concern for the future. There are few large towns to intrude and the villages make a positive contribution, in many cases being an attraction in themselves. The landscape is essentially rural, dominated by wide stretches of paddy fields together with the varied outlines of commercial crops such as coconut palms, areca palms and cashew, with forest taking over on the hills of the fringes in the east and south. Industrial development is only just beginning to thrust itself on the Goan scene and, so far, has made little impact. The nature and extent of the further expansion will depend on how effectively the economy can be developed in other directions.

Since the commercial decline of 'Golden Goa' in the 17th Century, the territory has been given little chance of even approaching economic viability until relatively recently. Fundamentally agricultural, its food and commercial crops could hardly achieve a prosperous economy unaided, however well developed, because of the relatively small areas available to them. Little had been ventured by the Portuguese in other directions, hardly touching the mineral resources known to exist. In spite of this, a high standard of living was enjoyed then, only made possible by the much lower levels of population before 1961, the remittances from immigrants working mainly in British India and in Africa, the efficient utilisation of rural resources by the Gaunkari system and the high level of imports acceptable to the Portuguese.

In the last quarter of a century, things have changed, and Goa's economic achievements have been considerable. Great steps have been taken in terms of agricultural produce, although these have been frustrated by the constant upward revision of targets to meet even domestic demand, necessitated by the substantial increases in population resulting from immigrant labour and the explosion in the volume of tourist traffic. The number of tourists each year now equals the resident population.

It was natural that, after Independence, heavy manufacturing industry should be regarded as essential to Goa's economic growth, but fortunately not much had been ventured before it became apparent that the massive infrastructure required for large-scale industrial development was not available. As a result, not too many blots have yet appeared on Goa's fair scene from this source, the major exception being the monstrous chemical fertiliser plant established in 1967 on the headland near the airport. The heavy tyre plant and the iron ore pelletisation units are other examples, but they are few and scattered.

The most successful industrial progress has been made in smaller-scale secondary industries based on Goa's natural raw materials. Outstanding are the processing of cashew nuts, fish canning and the freezing of shellfish for export. There is some processing of coconut palm products, but with scope for much more if nuts in particular were available. The traditional commercial crops have been recently supplemented by rubber and sugar cane, and a sugar processing plant has been established to utilise the cane. In terms of associated industries, increased fish requirements have boosted boat building and the mining industry has spawned barge building and repair establishments, signs of which can be seen along the banks of both major rivers. Efforts are being made to establish light industry on industrial estates, attracting small-scale, high-tech products with the availability of educated, readily trainable labour. The production of Goa's own spirit, feni, from cashew and coconut palm, is a supreme example of a successful cottage industry related to local circumstances.

It has, however, been the mining and the tourist industries that have emerged as the main strands of the economy and which will, properly managed, together with expanded secondary industries based on local resources, enable Goa to look forward with optimism to its economic future.

THE BEACHES – SEA AND SAND, FISH AND TOURISTS

The beaches are the best known of Goa's attractions and they offer everything from a veritable hive of activity to solitude as deep as could be imagined. Nowhere do they begin to approach the congestion of beaches with much less to commend them in other parts of the world, even the busiest being quiet by modern standards.

Especially on the stretches of sand in the vicinity of the larger hotels, entertainment is provided by a cast of colourful characters who either set up a display at their favourite point or wander the beach offering a strange medley of services or items for sale. Ear pickers carry a leather satchel full of weird and wicked-looking implements of their trade and it would seem from the demeanour of its practitioners that, on the whole, this is a gloomy profession. In contrast, barbers and oily masseurs, usually a combined occupation, are of cheerful, open disposition, relievers of others' stresses and strains. Fortune tellers of necessity have a mysterious air. Smartly dressed jewellery salesmen with their suitcases, out of place amongst the sun-worshippers, operate in teams, no doubt for protection, while the brightly dressed ladies with their mirrorwork or colourful clothes for sale are the most silently persistent, unmovable for long periods once they have settled themselves with their bundles on the sand beside a group of potential customers.

In many places, tavernas and cafés, simple structures of poles and woven coconut palm fronds, have spread onto the sands, though they are still mainly to be found in the shade of the palm groves. In any case, this does not deter the original inhabitants, the fishermen who still operate from traditional stretches and whose comings and goings attract observers here as they do anywhere else in the world. Others to watch at work are the boatbuilders, still producing, as they have for centuries, small craft in their 'yards' just behind the beaches. Elsewhere, the fishermen and their entourage have little competition for the open shore, and there are yet still other places where the only distractions are the toddy tappers or coconut pickers, leaving the sands to scuttling crabs, seagulls and the hopping crows of India that are everywhere.

Apart from the sliver of gold at Keri, opposite Terekhol Fort, the most northerly of Goa's beaches is **Arambol**, succumbing slowly to the attentions of visitors determined to push further northwards away from the main beaches. Slumbering quiet and empty in front of their villages, the beaches at **Mandrem**, protecting the lagoons at its river's mouth, and **Morgim**, just beyond, offer little except to those assisting the fishermen to launch and later off-load their catch. They are the scene of the sorting and slow despatch of a great variety of fish, either balanced in baskets or in bullock-carts heavy in the sand, leaving the fishermen to dry and roll their nets ready for the next expedition.

To the south, across the Chopdem-Siolim ferry, is the headland of Chapora with its fort, above steep slopes looking down on **Vagator Beach** in its small, self-contained bay, with rocky fingers at each end creating small enclosures of sand. Here there has been a steady growth of hotels and accommodation under pressure from the south, which has by-passed **Anjuna Beach**, one of Goa's most attractive, long taken over by the hippy population as they evacuated northwards. Anjuna was once the home of the weekly 'flea market' closed down as part of anti-drugs measures.

Yet another headland separates this from **Baga Beach**, in reality the northern extension of **Calangute**, the queen of Goa's beaches, though Baga inclines towards a superior attitude towards its southern neighbour. Calangute, the beach for

which Goa is perhaps most famous, and which stretches in splendour for seven km southwards to the rocky promontory of Fort Aguada and the wide estuary at the mouth of the Mandovi River, despite being the scene of considerable building activity behind the sands and the fact that Calangute is now the most densely populated area of Goa, it is still a magnet that, understandably, draws more and more visitors.

Beyond the Mandovi, Tiswadi, the 'Island of Goa', is not without its own sands. Now more popularly known as **Miramar Beach** after an old hotel that once was here, rather than by its old name of Gaspar Dias, a Portuguese landowner, this is Panjim's own beach. The outskirts of the town now spread behind it and, along with shaded gardens, the shore is lined with Panjim's extensive sporting facilities. However, the mouth of the river is treacherous with currents. Round the corner to the south, **Caranzalem Beach** stretches to the rocks of Cabo Raj Niwas with the Governor's house on its headland and, further on is **Dona Paula**. This little peninsula with its delightful bays and sands ends in a rocky islet, its viewpoint looking down on the ferry across to Mormugao. Round the corner nestles the sheltered fishing village, beyond which the sands resume their golden sweep on into the Zuari River estuary in front of **Bambolim**. The next beach at **Siridao** is far enough inland to enjoy the fresh water of the river itself, a peaceful stretch with fine views across to Mormugao harbour and upstream to the wide spread of the road bridge that now links north and south.

The story is taken up again beyond the combined towns of Mormugao and Vasco da Gama, where at **Bogmalo Beach**, no great distance from the airport, swimming is good and, as is the case on beaches near all the major hotels, there are plenty of boating facilities. Beyond is **Colva Beach**, the collective name for more than 20 km of sand that extends to the Sal River in the south. To identify different sections of this long stretch, the villages behind the beaches have given their names to the part onto which they face: Majorda, Colva, Benaulim, Varca, Cavelossim and Mabor. The road from Margao, lying only five km inland from the shore, joins the beach at Colva and is the most often used point of access. Here is a hive of activity with hotels and cafés, stalls and gypsy markets, spreading even onto the sands. The large fishing fleet which operates from here adds to the hustle and excitement. But only a short distance either side the crowds disperse and there are many fine stretches of quiet beach in front of shielding groves of coconut palms, all accessible from the coast road

Caranzalem Beach, Tiswadi: On the headland is the Cabot, residence of the governor of Goa.

that winds just behind. Even the fertiliser plant is hazy against the northern headland. Fewer facilities for greater solitude is an exchange many would make; others would not hesitate to opt for comfort. All are catered for here.

Beyond Cavelossim to the Sal River and Betul Island, was once heavily biased in favour of solitude. Now, the balance has swung almost on the instant, with several luxury hotels marching shoulder to shoulder down to the sea and sealing off the whole of the peninsula, offering the ultimate in comfort.

On the other side of the estuary to the south, access once more restricts the number of visitors. Beyond the quaint village port of Betul, the headland of Cabo de Rama, with its sprawling fort, marks the beginning of the beaches of Canacona taluka. Here, the Western Ghats crowd near the coast forming a backdrop to the fringing palms, while on the beaches the sand is broken by upsurges of boulders and rocky outcrops. Here, **Palolem** is Goa's most idyllic beach, and between

here and the southern border with Karnataka are yet more, even smaller and quieter, but even more difficult of access. These are for the truly adventurous seekers of seclusion.

Tourists, together with the infrastructure that goes with the tourist industry, are obviously having a dramatic influence on Goa's coastline. Since Independence, the Indian government has singled out Goa as the area most worthy of attention in terms of tourist development. This reflects itself in more crowded beaches in certain sections though, until now, at their busiest they would still be classified as almost deserted by Mediterranean standards! Booming hotel and associated development has not yet reached the point where strict government management, and adherence to planning rules and environmental guidelines already in place, could not prevent the destruction and irrevocable loss of this most important of Goa's assets. At the same time it will be essential to ensure that the needs of the coastal villagers are met, to preserve their traditional livelihoods and guarantee their very necessary co-operation.

Long before they became magnets for visitors,

Colva Beach, Salcete.

the beaches and palm groves were the home of one of Goa's major primary industries – fishing. Substantial numbers of people are directly or indirectly engaged in supplying the vast quantities of fish so vital to the Goan diet and it has become an important export commodity. In Goa everyone eats fish, whether Christian or Hindu. It is the 'Fruit of the Seas' and few beaches are without their picturesque fishing boats in varying shapes and sizes, from small, crudely fashioned 'catamarans', consisting of two pieces of timber fastened together and the forerunners of modern twin-hulled boats, to more sophisticated sailing boats. Most of these boats have out-riggers to keep them stable in rough waters. All are built to traditional designs in tiny 'yards' the length of the coast, often ending up decorated with painted saints or gods, as the spirit moves their owners. They fish the waters relatively close in to the shore, sailing on the tides and still making a material contribution to Goa's rich sea harvest. Occasionally lone fishermen can be seen casting from the rocks or wading into the surf with

their nets, while in the rivers, fishing from canoes or a system of fixed nets along lines of poles are the favoured methods. These small-scale fishing operations mainly serve local demand, the women waiting for the catch to be sorted to take it fresh to local market places.

About 180 different varieties are said to be available, including the many fresh-water fish taken from rivers and lakes, but mackerel, the beloved bangda, and sardines dominate with pomfret, kingfish, baby shark, seer and catfish making up much of the rest of the catch. Shellfish are of course the prize, especially prawns. The women join in the hunt along the shore and amongst the rocks at low tide for clams, crabs and oysters.

Responsible for the considerable growth of the industry in recent years have been the mechanised trawlers, operating mainly from Mormugao and Panjim. These have grown substantially in number, fishing the deep waters off-shore and increasing the volume of catch far beyond local needs. The result has been the birth of a fish-canning industry that is growing rapidly and promises much. Sardines are most important from a canning point of

Fishermen preparing their nets on Caranzalem Beach, with the Aguada Fort in the background.

view, but the most profitable fish-processing enterprise is the freezing and packaging of prawns for export. This has led to rising prices and diminishing availability for the larger varieties in local markets, although up-market restaurants can still afford their share, along with the splendid lobsters that thrive in Goan waters. Happily, there are still ample supplies of the deliciously tender and flavoursome medium-sized prawns to go round. The relative contributions are interesting. Sardines and mackerel make up about half the total catch by weight and contribute a quarter of the total market value, while prawns constitute one eighth of the catch but half of the value. Japan is the main destination for frozen prawns.

THE COCONUT AND THE CASHEW – NUTS AND FENI

The importance of these two to the Goan scene can hardly be overstated. Between them they occupy almost half of the area under crops and wherever you are you are likely to have one of them within view – both in many places. Both are grown for their nuts, but both are also the source of the sap or juice from which Goa's 'national' drink is produced. They therefore assume added significance.

Strung out behind the beaches are the groves of coconut palms in which the fishing villages nestle. The palms thrive on sandy soil and further inland the groves diminish in size and density although they remain part of the scenery. The palm tree itself is a marvel in terms of its value to man, everything being used. Plaited fronds provide material for screens, thatching for roofs, fish traps and the multitude of baskets of all shapes and sizes that one sees everywhere, on heads, between knees at markets and piled on top of or thrust into the depths of buses. The thicker stems are used for fuel, as are those parts of the trunk not used for building, or even some furniture making. Tender young shoots from the tops are even sometimes used for exotic salads. However, it is the nut that is the most versatile product. The husks provide coir for the manufacture of mats, ropes and string – the separation of their fibres and their spinning into a tough yarn for rope manufacture being an ancient skill. It has long been important for fishing-boat rigging, nets and lines and in the past contributed much to Goa's reputation for building big sailing ships. The brown shells inside the husk contain the real treasure, copra, the white kernel, valued for its oil which is used as the base for edible oils and a wide range of cosmetic and industrial products.

Normally, this would provide the major reason for taking all the trouble involved in growing coconut palms – they do have to be given a lot of attention and fertiliser to produce healthy nuts. However, in Goa, only a relatively small proportion of the nuts are processed for their oil, there being two other motives for growing the palms. The first is that the coconut is vital to Goan cooking, the essential ingredient being the milk extracted from the grated white kernel by immersing it in boiling water, crushing and straining. This gives a distinctive flavour to many Goan dishes, in particular 'seet corry', the fish curry rice that is the 'national' dish, and the basic diet of many people. This milk is not

Coconuts being harvested.

to be confused with the coconut water which is not itself used much, except as a healthy refreshing drink straight from the nut. The domestic consumption of coconuts each year for cooking is considerable, most of the total production of more than 100 million nuts being sold in the local market!

The level of actual nut production is affected by another important factor and the second reason for growing coconut palms other than for the copra. This is the demand for palm feni. Unfortunately a choice has to be made. A coconut palm can produce nuts or it can be tapped for the sap from the base of young shoots that would otherwise have produced nuts. It cannot provide both at the same time. Toddy is the sap in its natural state. Unfermented it is a sweet and nourishing drink and also, when strained and boiled down to crystallising point, produces palm *jaggery*, the coarse brown slabs of sugar used in Goan sweet dishes – yet another demonstration of the palm's versatility. However, toddy ferments naturally within hours of tapping to about four percent alcohol and is often drunk soon afterwards. This is only the beginning of its alcoholic potential. If distilled, the first runs gives *urrack*, a popular drink sold in the bars of Goa. A second distillation results in the famous palm *feni*, a pure but powerful drink ranking with the strongest spirits. Feni in Konkani means 'froth', from its reaction during processing.

The whole process is carried out in literally thousands of small units scattered all over the state[1], using picturesque ancient copper stills. It is a perfect example of a successful cottage industry and their product is similarly distributed through the tiny tavernas, again numbered in their thousands, that are themselves a feature of the landscape.

So, a choice has to be made between nuts and feni, but it is one that can be reversed with each growth of the shoots, so growers can change from one to another, depending on demand. In fact, some tapping is held to be good for the tree, a sort of refining process. There is continuous growth throughout the year with the best results during winter months. Nuts can be cut every few weeks and it is a spectacular sight, the teams of cutters shinning agilely up the palms, razor-sharp knives sheathed on their backs and a rope harness around their ankles to improve their grip on the trunk, clearing out dead fronds and hacking out ripe nuts, sometimes in clusters, to come crashing down to the ground. Cutting comes to a standstill during the monsoon when wind, rain and slippery moss on the bark make it impossible to climb any but the shorter straight-growing trees. The availability of cutters is becoming a problem, as education and alternative employment opportunities reduce young men's inclination to take up this work.

The cashew, the other favoured commercial crop and another Portuguese introduction, this from Brazil, can be seen in all shapes and sizes, from low bushes to rather untidy trees up to ten metres high. Although described as a 'plantation' crop, there is no question of the cashew being grown in orderly rows, carefully maintained. They are scattered everywhere, sometimes in continuous dense masses, sometimes in small clumps, its dark, glossy, evergreen leaves making it easy to identify. The only attention it receives is the clearing of the undergrowth from around the bushes and trees to enable the annual picking of the fruit and nuts.

The first small, pink-and-white flowers appear in December and after a few weeks the fragrant scent of cashew blossom fills the air. In March the first fruit appears and they are picked as they ripen; the last in early June just before the onset of the monsoon. The cashew apple itself is highly distinctive, up to six or seven centimetres long with the nut growing out of its base, bright red or yellow and extremely soft and juicy, though not edible, except by pigs who, it seems, find them delicious. Anywhere other than Goa, pig food is the apple's fate, but here the juice provides the raw material for that other, even more sought-after feni, *caju feni*. But, more of that in a moment, it is the nut that is supposed to be the main object of the exercise.

This has become one of Goa's main foreign exchange earners, though with the prices obtainable in India itself, there is domestic competition for supplies. Nuts are even imported from Africa into India for processing. The nuts are first roasted, then shelled and sorted into size grades, a job still done by hand with great skill and dexterity bewildering to the eye.

A by-product is cashew nut oil which is extracted from the shells. It has water-proofing qualities with several industrial applications.

To return to caju feni, there is no need, as in the case of the coconut, to choose between nuts and feni, as it is the juice of the apple in which the nut grows, elsewhere discarded once the nut has been extracted, that provides the liquid from which the feni is made. Cashew growers and their customers can have the best of both worlds and, as there is one apple to every nut, these are available in abundance. The juice is extracted by crushing, often by treading, as in the traditional foot pounding of grapes in European wine making. It is then distilled twice, as in the case of palm sap, the first run producing urrack and the second the more potent feni. Goans acknowledge a debt to the Portuguese,

The cashew apple (with nut) from which feni is made.

not only for the introduction of cashew but also to the brothers of the religious orders who brought with them, and passed on, the secrets and the art of distilling.

ARECA NUTS AND BETEL LEAVES – THE PLEASURES OF PAAN

Something that never fails to strike a visitor, soon after arriving in India, is the habit of chewing paan. The impact of reddened mouths and red marks in and around spittoons in public buildings can be startling. Yet this is not a habit confined to India, one estimate being that more than ten percent of the world's population indulges in this addictive pastime. It would seem a practice as old as India itself, with important social and religious implications, its preparation and presentation formerly attended with ritual and ceremony – a parallel being the tea ceremony of Japan. Ancient Hindu scriptures list its qualities and benefits, and lay down by whom it may be consumed and when it is forbidden. The Muslims adopted it after their arrival in India and under the Moghuls and subsequently the Nawabs of Lucknow, its preparation was developed to a high degree of formality and elegance, both adding their contribution to the art of the utensils required, such as boxes for the materials used, betel nut cutters and serving trays. The best of these are now museum pieces. Today while the bulk of paan making has been converted to the equivalent of a fast-food process, the ubiquitous paan walla, a feature of any street scene over most of the sub-continent, has become a neighbourhood institution and something of a social focal point. Significantly, neither he nor the habit is much in evidence in what were the Old Conquests of Goa – another reflection of changed social customs in this area, especially those with religious connotations.

Reduced to basics, paan is chopped *supari* (nut from the areca palm), with *chunam* (lime paste), folded or rolled inside a betel pepper leaf. But that is only a beginning. Many other ingredients are added in a multitude of combinations. A whole variety of spices are used, such as cinnamon, cardamom, nutmeg and cloves, together with tobacco and, of course in Goa, shredded coconut. For very special occasions crushed pearls are used with hammered silver or even gold foil as decoration. The scope for invention is enormous and, while the general claim is that paan aids the digestion and general good health, all manner of special benefits are attached to specific combinations of ingredients.

Goa grows both the areca palm and the betel leaf in profusion.

The tall, incredibly straight and slender *areca palm* is a pleasure to behold, stately and distinctive with its small crown of fronds and, in season, large bunches of small, bright orange nuts. It graces the landscape over a large part of Goa, though densest in a belt north to south down the centre of the country. Ponda has the largest area under areca and they often provide a distinctive background to its temples. Moisture is all important: it needs water all the year round which means irrigation in the dry months, especially just before the monsoon. So its natural location is on the river flats and in the depths of the narrow valleys of the hills with their natural streams and springs. Shade loving, it is often grown in partnership with other trees, such as the most robust coconut palm, either intermixed or providing a sheltering surround. In addition,

Areca palms covered in Betel Pepper Vines.

where the areca palms are cultivated specifically as a plantation crop, as soon as they are well established, betel leaves are trained to grow up their trunks so that nuts and leaves grow together in a mutually helpful combination.

Harvested between August and December, the nuts are sold outside Goa for processing. They require first to be shelled and the kernels are then sliced in two and cured by boiling in a mixture of the previous season's extract from the vats topped up with fresh water. After drying, the nuts are then finely chopped ready for use. Formerly, when this was carried out in the household, there were strict conventions as to how the nut should be cut and which parts should be used, practices now only followed where old traditions are preserved.

The heart-shaped leaves of the betel pepper bush, botanically the Piper Betel, come in many varieties and, though these are mainly regional, a true connoisseur would have his preferences.

The method of folding or rolling the leaf also varies, a flat triangle being the most common shape, while Lucknow is typified by a cone-shaped paan, and in the south cylinders are traditional, inevitably here sprinkled with coconut.

If offered in an Indian home at the end of a meal, acceptance is a courtesy that will give pleasure to the host apart from being a quite memorable experience if never sampled before. Otherwise the local paan-walla is not difficult to find.

MINES AND FORESTS – THE WEALTH OF THE HILLS

Travelling through some of Goa's pleasantest countryside, north of the Mandovi River in the area of Maem Lake, it is disconcerting to emerge onto the ridge above Bicholim town to be confronted by a scene of total desolation. This is the outward face of one of the largest contributors to Goa's income, the price of economic prosperity, the mining of iron ore. The landscape it produces is not without its fascination, a futuristic scene from another planet, barren and unreal with a theme of red dust.

Economically, the most important of Goa's mineral resources are iron ore, manganese ore and bauxite. These occur in a belt that sweeps down from the eastern part of Pernem, through Bicholim and western Sanguem to the south-east corner of Canacona. The northern section of this belt is mainly iron-based ores, while southwards from about the Ponda-Molem road that cuts across northern Sanguem, the emphasis is on manganese. As manganese and ferro-manganese constitute only about one percent of Goa's mineral output, the visual impact of mining operations is concentrated in the north-eastern part of the country, especially the taluka of Bicholim.

The ore lies on or near the surface, accessible by open-cast mining methods, huge mechanical diggers scooping away the hillsides in great swathes. The ore is taken away by trucks or rope-way conveyor to the banks of the upper reaches of the Mandovi where there are several collection points where barges are loaded to take the ore to the massive, modern ore-handling terminal in Mormugao harbour. The Cumbarjua Waterway between the Mandovi and Zuari Rivers, enables the barges to reach the terminal even during the monsoon when the mouth of the Mandovi is closed to river traffic, although rough seas may then hold up operations. These barges are a familiar sight on the lower reaches of both rivers, low in the water with about 700 tonnes of ore when loaded, often battling against high waves and strong tides, rusty hulls high out of the water when empty, bustling back up-river to the loading points for more. Repair yards are scattered along the river banks to help keep the flow of barges moving.

Although the Portuguese began prospecting mineral resources in 1905, little was done to exploit

Ore barges being loaded at a terminal on the Bicholim bank of the Mandovi.

their findings until 1947. Since then the industry has grown steadily, reaching an output of over 13 million tonnes per year. Little of this ore is used within India, there being no integrated steel plants accessible enough to make it viable and there is the problem of the change of gauge of the railway link. So, although Goa accounts for almost one third of India's iron-ore production – an astonishingly high proportion from such a small area – it is all exported. This increases the industry's vulnerability to changes in world demand and fluctuating prices, which affects the volume of production and profitability. The biggest customer by far is Japan, which takes almost three-quarters of production, with the balance going to South Korea, Taiwan and various European countries.

To make even better use of Goa's iron-ore, the need is for further processing before export. Pelletisation plants have been set up at several places, the one most likely to be encountered being near the Borim Bridge that crosses the Zuari to link Ponda and Salcete, but now a mini-plant is being built, using high technology to produce high-quality foundry pig-iron – a project with international co-operation. This is in the mining area at Amona in Bicholim Taluka.

Inevitably there have been environmental problems with open-cast mining in the midst of agricultural and forest land, the difficulty lying not only with the rehabilitation of the literal mountains of waste left by this process, but also the encroachment of slurry washed onto surrounding paddy fields during the monsoon, and the pollution of rivers affecting fishing. Bunds have been built to contain the waste and some afforestation has taken place, though more is promised.

The halting of deforestation outside, as well as within, the mining areas is a constant battle for the Conservator of Forests. Over a quarter of Goa's land surface is under forest, but, together with mining, a great expansion of construction as well as illegal felling, has led to a reduction that the department aims to counter by controlling such activities and by re-afforestation programmes. Inland, teak and eucalyptus have been planted extensively, with casuarina on sandy soils near the coast.

Glorious natural forests blanket the foothills of the ghats, providing opportunities for delightful walking expeditions or just wanderings. Using one of the wildlife sanctuaries as a base is an excellent way of experiencing this aspect of Goa. Tall evergreens are mixed with many varieties of spice bushes and stands of bamboo, with creepers creating fantastic patterns and ferns and flowers carpeting the forest floor.

FRUITS AND SPICES FROM AROUND THE WORLD

In the kaleidoscope of first impressions on arriving in Goa, a strong element must be that of a land brimming over with exotic tropical vegetation. In this, fruits and spices play a major role, broadened by the fact that they are scattered over a wide area, intermixed with other trees and shrubs in gardens and small plots rather than concentrated in orchards or plantations. The variety of fruits and spices is huge, and a visit to any of the larger bazaars reveals a veritable Aladdin's Cave of riches. As a tropical land it is expected to have many fruits and spices native to its own soil, but, through its history as a focus point for trade from earliest times, Goa has been the gateway to India for many strange and wonderful trees and plants; its own natural riches have multiplied as a result.

The list of fruits to be seen growing in the gardens and fields and on sale in the innumerable markets in towns and villages all over Goa just about covers the entire range of tropical delights and can take you on a journey round the world, the only constraint being the seasons.

Spice stall in the bazaar, Margao.

Vegetable stall, Margao.

Of the most commonly encountered fruits, bananas, oranges, water melons and limes, all have their origins in the myriad of islands beyond the Bay of Bengal that stretch from Sumatra eastwards to New Guinea and came into India many centuries ago, brought by those that ventured across unknown seas. Much later, papaya was brought in by the Portuguese from still further east, the Philippines, followed by pineapples from the West Indies, once they became part of their American colonies. These are all grown widely now in Goa. The distinctive leaves of a banana tree appear in every garden, almost a mandatory item it would seem. Bananas are to be had red, yellow or green and, as you would expect, Goa has its own speciality of even such a common item, the 'Moira' banana – a long fat red fruit only eaten cooked. However, although bananas are grown commercially here, the bulk of demand is met by 'imports' from the plantations of adjoining states. All varieties of melon thrive – water melons, honeydew, musk and canteloupe.

Melon seeds are dried and eaten as a delicacy; they are also used as an ingredient in paan. Pineapples, requiring a considerable amount of moisture, are, more than the other fruits, grown as a plantation crop, often to be seen on the fringes of areca palm plantations whose water they share.

Apart from these, the list of exotic, perhaps less common, fruits is long. Mangosteen, custard apple, chickoo, guava, figs, granadilla (better known as passion fruit) and lichees are all here to be enjoyed, even if some come from across the border.

The breadfruit deserves mention, not as a delicacy but because it is such a common sight in the western parts of Goa, distinctive in its foliage and knobbly round green fruit. It is not really a fruit but a nut, and its starchy pulp resembles potato when cooked. Closely related to the breadfruit is the jack-fruit, a native of southern India, its fruit similar but very much larger. Its massive green and yellow fruits, which can be over 60 centimetres long and weigh up to 30 kilos, are unmistakable. There is one type of jackfruit that is eaten as a fruit and the other cooked. The many large seeds inside can be

Banana plant.

the whole art of painting, the sage Narayana, a manifestation of Vishnu, used mango juice to paint the world's first ever portrait. Naturally, it was of a girl more beautiful than any goddess or earthly woman, but that is another story! It appears often in Hindu, Muslim and Buddhist art from all periods and every part of India.

The Portuguese and British both succumbed to the mango's charms and between them were responsible for its introduction to the Americas. The Portuguese in Goa also made their contribution in the development of cross-breeding and grafting techniques, the magnificent Alfonso being one of their achievements. There are over 1000 varieties now, each suited to conditions in different parts of India. The Malcorada, with the Fernandes later in the season, are Goa's chosen favourites, but to enjoy it at its best, you will have to be here when the weather is at its hottest and wettest, for the mango is a compensation, if compensation is needed, offered for those in Goa between April and July. Its succulent fruit is a delight, as are the juices, jams and the host of pickles and chutneys for which it forms the base. Grown intermixed with other trees and plants, rather than in orchards, it is Goa's largest fruit crop.

As well as fruits, there are many spices that make their contribution to the scenic as well as the gastronomic pleasures of Goa.

One of the most interesting is the chilli, or in fact the whole capsicum family of which it is a member. Indian cuisine, in common with similar climates across the world, had always had a spicy basis, an essential ingredient being black pepper which grew particularly well on the western slopes of the ghats of southern India. In the 16th century, demand for black pepper in Europe escalated

Breadfruit.

roasted and eaten like nuts. The large leaves are good for cooking leaf-wrapped dishes; the wood is prized for furniture making.

Even taller than the jackfruit tree is the tamarind, a rough-barked tree with delicate feathery leaves. Yellow flowers are followed by long pods containing pulpy seeds. Tamarind is used in flavouring several dishes as well as in chutney. Try tamarind water, made from the extract of the pulp, as a pleasant digestif.

The last should perhaps have been first. Another native of this place, the queen of tropical fruits, is the mango. Its fruit and leaves appear as a decorative theme on pottery 4000 years old from the Indus Valley civilisation at Harappa and Mohenjodaro, and has always had great religious significance. Buddha was born in a grove of mango trees and it features frequently in Buddhist mythology, as it does in Hindu puranas and epics. It is used as an offering to the gods, Ganesh in particular having a fondness for it. In the ancient legend that explains rapidly, and reached such a peak that demand exceeded availability and prices soared. Competition for the 'black gold' was fierce, wars were fought over it and it was the dowry for princesses. Happily for Indian palates, the Portuguese, in the nick of time it would seem, brought in an acceptable substitute from their colony of Pernambuco in Brazil. The substitute was the capsicum family which included the chilli and which first Goa, then the whole of the sub-continent, took in, adapting and developing the many varieties that are so important to Indian cooking today. In its many and various shapes and sizes, colours and flavours, it grows much more abundantly and in many more places than black pepper would ever have done. With the subsequent rationalisation of black pepper demand, this too has resumed its proper place in the spice hierarchy of Indian cooking, complementing rather than competing with the now well-entrenched chilli.

One of the key factors in terms of a spice-based cuisine is the freshness of the spices used: here, Goa scores heavily with a bewildering array grown locally, many native to the general area. Cardamom and coriander, cumin and cinnamon, turmeric and ginger, cloves and garlic, nutmeg and sesame are all to be seen on display in the bazaars. A walk through the spice section of the markets of Mapusa or Margao is a test for the nostrils. They will be used in many combinations to produce the great dishes of Goa.

THE RICE BOWL

As in the whole of the southern part of India, rice forms the staple diet of the people of Goa, and paddy-fields cover a greater area than any other crop. When you are in Bardez, Tiswadi or Salcete – only coincidentally the area of the Old Conquests – one third of the entire land surface is paddy. Give thanks that it is so restful on the eye and yet never dull for long. Fields are broken up into small compartments created by low bunds, sometimes filled with stubble and dotted with rice stooks, sometimes sheets of water shining like panes of glass and, for part of the year, shimmering with the richest of greens imaginable. They stretch into the distance, filling a flat landscape or appearing broken up and scattered, terraced into the slopes of a river bank or hillside, making use of all available space. When one or two small patches have been

hard won from an otherwise rocky plateau, they stand out like jewels. The seasonal activities of ploughing, bullocks and ploughmen up to their knees in muddy soil, the lead boy pulling them round in tight turns in the tiny enclosures, the planting of the seedlings by women, bent backs in rows, or the reaping, when the atmosphere is joyous and all play their part, produce an ever-changing pattern of colour and interest.

Two crops are grown wherever conditions allow, the Kharif, or Sorod, which is the monsoon crop, and the Rabi, or Vaingon, the winter crop. Kharif is sown from the first week of June to early July and harvested September–October. Rabi is sown from the first week of November to the second week of December and harvested in March, a three to four month cycle.

Goa does not produce enough rice to meet its own needs, the balance coming from central government stocks obtained from states with a surplus, yet the area under paddy has remained static for many years now, a reflection of the constraints on land available for rice production. So it is essential to keep all the available area under crop and improve its yield. A winter crop is only possible with irrigation and this, together with the continued introduction of higher-yielding varieties, is the key to increased production. At present only about a quarter of the area under paddy is irrigated and this is being slowly expanded by means of some major river projects and many small schemes.

An important project nearing completion is the Salauli Project on the Sanguem River, where a dam will create a substantial reservoir which will feed a 25 km canal, boosting considerably the total irrigated area. There are plans to develop the reservoir as a tourist attraction. Smaller schemes involve the use of natural springs, the storage of monsoon rains in tanks and the tapping of wells in low-lying areas, the water being brought up by pumps or by more picturesque manual methods. The type of water lift using bullocks is not so common in Goa as it is in other parts of India.

Sugar cane is another crop heavily dependent upon irrigation. Cultivation began in about 1970 in association with the establishment of a sugar manufacturing unit at Piliem, just in Sanguem Taluka about 10 km beyond Ponda. So far, only a relatively small area is under sugar cane and the processing plant is meanwhile dependent upon supplies from neighbouring states.

7 THE PEOPLE

Goa's population has increased rapidly since Independence in 1961, mainly as a result of an increased influx of labour from other parts of India, mostly to work in the iron-ore mines or at the port of Mormugao where the shipment of the ore is handled, or as part of the steady trickle of those attracted by the higher standard of living available. In 1961 the population was 590,000, now, only a quarter of a century later, it has risen to over one million, this in spite of the regular and traditional emigration of large numbers of Goans seeking fame and fortune elsewhere.

The shortage of suitable employment opportunities to meet Goan aspirations and abilities has for long led to a steady flow to 'foreign' parts – other parts of India or beyond. Their varying ambitions have been satisfied in places as far apart as Bombay or New York, in Europe or the oil sheikhdoms of the Middle East, as businessmen or artisans, as doctors or musicians, as barmen, cooks or waiters. These latter are the successors of their countrymen who established such a high reputation in this field during the British time in India when their services were eagerly sought on land and sea.

But, wherever they may go, they always remain true Goans (never Goanese) and for all exiles the sense of community while away is strong and the longing to revisit their homeland ever present, with nostalgia for all the things left behind a genuine emotion. Many do pay regular visits and in fact for some this is regarded as a family duty. For others, the sole objective of the move away from Goa will be to make sufficient money as quickly as possible to enable them to move back to their village with a plot of land and a home of their own.

These movements, both inwards and outwards, mostly related closely to recent economic developments, have inevitably altered the traditional population balance and distribution, with rapid growth in the three main urban centres an important feature.

Perhaps this is as good a point as any to mention one other immigrant group, and that is the floating population of hippies for which Goa was once 'famous'. They are now much smaller in numbers and tend to keep very much to themselves. There is certainly not the dominant presence of several years ago, partly a result of their having moved northwards from their earlier base on Calangute Beach which, although the visitor may still find it peaceful enough, has become over-developed from the hippies' point of view. They now favour the isolation of the northern beaches and it was only when they held their weekly market at Anjuna, now banned by the authorities because of drug problems, that a visitor was likely to encounter them in any numbers.

Goa is often thought of as being predominantly Christian, this being the strong impression given in the area most often visited by tourists, and here the difference between the Old and New Conquests comes into the story yet again. Taking Goa as a whole, of the million or so inhabitants only 31 percent are Christian, 64 percent are Hindu and 4 percent are Muslims. However, the Christians are concentrated in the Old Conquests and although even here they are still not a numerical majority, except in Salcete, this is partly due to the massive Hindu influx into Mormugao and Vasco. Salcete with its actual Christian majority is the only taluka where this position has been maintained. In contrast, in the New Territories, 85 percent of the population are Hindu. These statistics are reflected in the character of the different areas.

So, apart from the immediate vicinity of Mormugao and Vasco da Gama, the Old Conquests retain much of the Christian ethos that is part of their attraction as a 'different' corner of India, this being attributable as much to the character of the people as to the physical environment. They have defied and yet also responded to the effects of being ruled by a foreign power for 450 years and the overall effect, like throwing a pebble in a pond, reveals the foreign influence deeper and more long-lasting in the centre with its ripple effect diminishing rapidly with distance. This does not mean that the outer areas are any less fervently Goan than those of the Old, but the differences between the two are quite apparent.

CHRISTIANITY

Factors affecting the degree of Portuguese influence on the area have already been mentioned. The great length and the all-embracing nature of the Portuguese occupation, their fanatical determination to convert all their new subjects to Christianity, were all compounded by the fact that this effort was directed at a small geographically isolated area. Far more than any other occupying nations, the Portuguese stamped their character on the area and the people under their control, this being reflected in religion, language and many other aspects of life, giving a distinctive flavour to the Goan character.

Physically, there is now little Portuguese blood running in Goan veins. Although at the very outset, Albuquerque, in an attempt to establish a stable community, offered some of the remaining Muslim girls as wives to his soldiers and sailors, with offers of land and their right to trade as additional incentives if any were necessary, the overall long term effect was minimal and subsequently there was no interbreeding on any scale. The abundance of Portuguese names derives mainly from their adoption by converts at the time of their baptism, insisted upon by their converters and yet another example of the fanatical approach of the Portuguese. It has already been emphasised that the Portuguese influence was superimposed on an existing culture, itself based on deep-rooted tradition and that in spite of the intensity of Portuguese efforts this was in no way totally submerged.

This is no better illustrated than in the Christianity of Goa. The Portuguese determined to convert every man, woman and child to a pure form of Roman Catholicism and went about their task with implacable zeal. Within the Old Conquests, they achieved their goal, to all outward appearances, with those that had not fled the territory, and yet this was not all that it seemed. The Christianity of Goa was not as Portuguese pure as they would have wished; in fact many of the roots of the past survived and subsequently flourished in their new environment. This came to the surface gradually, so that by the time this was evident, even to the Portuguese, it was not only too late to remedy but their inclination to do so had waned.

In 1623, Pope Gregory gave special dispensation that Brahmins converted to Christianity could continue to wear their sacred thread and caste marks. More important than this, however, the Hindu caste structure itself was perpetuated among the Christian communities and this still survives today. However, castes tend to be a geographically distributed phenomenon rather than stratified, one village being occupied by one caste.

Another outward aspect of the maintenance of these links with the past, much in evidence today, is the often-seen mingling of people of different religions at their various ceremonies, particularly at festival times when, whatever their religion, Goans appear to be prepared not only to join the festivities associated with the occasion but to participate in the spiritual activities as well. This shows itself in one of the most evident aspects of Goan character, a gentle tolerance towards other religious views that contributes towards the relaxed atmosphere that is one of Goa's subtle attractions.

THE KONKANI LANGUAGE

One unifying factor throughout the centuries has been the Konkani language. Spoken over a much wider area than Goa itself, it is in Goa where the determination to establish and preserve its official status is centred and the battle to achieve this is being fought. That it is the mother-tongue of the majority of the people of Goa is not in dispute, but at the core of the problem is the fact that it has no single script of its own; Hindus tend to use the Devnagari script while Christians use the Roman script. There are three others in limited use. This lack of a uniformly employed script has led to the use of Marathi for administrative and commercial purposes, and the output of regional literature has for some time also tended to be mainly in Marathi, although this has been as much with the objective of reaching wider audiences as because of any constraints Konkani may impose on expression. On the contrary, Konkani supporters would argue hotly in its favour on this aspect of the debate.

Most of the problems stem from persistent Portuguese efforts over virtually the full period of their occupation not just to discourage but to stamp out completely the use of Konkani in their territories and to promote Portuguese in its place. Over the years, starting from the moment of the conquest and prompted mainly by the Church, a whole succession of laws were passed to achieve its suppression, such as prohibiting its use in business, forbidding marriage between couples one of whom did not speak Portuguese and, most damaging of all, the destruction of all books and the banning of any written works in Konkani. It was outlawed from education at all levels. These efforts met with little success, causing the Chief Inquisitor, as late as 1731, to bemoan the fact that the diminishing number of conversions was largely due to the failure to enforce the edict 'forbidding the natives of the land to speak their own language'. Nor was the campaign to introduce Portuguese all that successful. By the mid-nineteenth century the Viceroy would comment that 'merely two or three among a hundred' could 'understand' Portuguese and even by 1962 the figure was not high, although of course it was a significant section of the population. Those involved in administration, international commerce and of course the Goan clergy all spoke Portuguese and the mainly church-based education system reinforced this, especially amongst the middle and upper classes.

This is still evident, and independence, now over a quarter of a century in the past, still has not eliminated the fact that there are a number of people to whom Portuguese is still their natural first language after their native Konkani. This will eventually change with even fewer people using it in everyday conversation, although it survives and it seems that there is a sprinkling of words in everyone's vocabulary. The last daily newspaper in Portuguese, *O Heraldo*, survived until 1982.

Although the laws to suppress Konkani failed in their full intention, the damage inflicted on the Konkani language was appalling. That it survived to the extent that it has must reflect on the quality of the language itself as much as on the people.

After Independence, great pressure was exerted to establish Marathi as the official language, originally as part of the efforts to have the territory incorporated into Maharashtra and although Goa has now achieved independent statehood, the conflict is not over. Claims that Konkani is but a dialect of Marathi have been discounted and its official position secured through its recognition under the 1987 Official Languages Bill as the sole official language of the State.

However, in spite of the fact that over 90 percent of Goans speak Konkani, the implementation of the Bill is no simple matter in practical terms, due mainly to the already mentioned diversity of scripts used. The other obstacle is the strongly continued rearguard action from Marathi supporters. With the support given by the Government to Marathi after Independence, this language has become the medium of over 80 percent of the pupils in Government-run primary schools, with only 0.25 percent beginning their education in Konkani. In

privately-run private schools 96 percent of the pupils are taught in English. This situation, together with the fact that most medium and high school education is now in English, compounds the problems facing Konkani as the official language. In official terms the next step is to have Konkani recognised as an official regional language by its inclusion in the 8th Schedule of the Indian Constitution. In practical terms it is the expansion of the use of Konkani within the educational system. The use of English as a language option has increased, and currently three daily newspapers are published locally in English, as well as the English language newspapers from other parts of India which are now available.

LOVE OF MUSIC

Another element in the Goan make-up, their deep and abiding love of music, has again been fashioned by Portuguese influence, but has been redefined by Goans to make it their own. There is music wherever you go in Goa, from the blaring of incredibly violent loud-speaker systems to the strummed guitar floating on the quietness of evening, though with the Old and the New Conquests once more following different paths – the New pursuing traditional ways, with the Old being more Western-based in their approach. It is this latter aspect that is regarded by other Indians as being particularly Goan and that makes its impact on visitors. Western music was introduced as part of the Christianisation process of their colony; in church music that was such an important part of the ritual. As a result, it was also taught in schools and the Western idiom, so far removed from its Indian counterpart, became deeply entrenched.

Throughout Goa, there are endless traditional folk-dances and songs of many varieties, seemingly something special for any of the innumerable festive occasions. There is one form, however, that seems to epitomise everything Goan in music: the *mando*. This dance form, to music in which the words of the song are as important as the melody, originated in the drawing-rooms or ballrooms where Western-style living had been adopted, but, as the upper classes were of the village as well as the town, it broadened its base and is now truly part of the Goan scene, especially at weddings or festivals but also just performed for its own sake. The mando attained its true form in the 19th century and to say that it somewhat resembles the minuet being danced in European drawing-rooms at about that time, while inadequate as a description, is at least a starting point for Europeans. It is danced with men and women in two rows facing each other, the women with fans and the men holding handkerchiefs stretched between both hands. The words normally recount tales of love, certainly emotional or soulful, as is the melody provided by the violin with rhythm from a traditional instrument, the pottery *ghumat*. It is a distillation of Goan folk music and western classical form and it is difficult to draw lines or establish the proportionate contribution from East and West. Either way, it is unique and, happily, being preserved and perpetuated as part of the cultural heritage, another memory that will remain with the visitor when Goa is distant.

While modern western 'pop' music is impinging everywhere in India today, Goa's familiarity with Western music gave them a head start and the talents of Goan musicians are in great demand.

FOOD AND DRINK

A love of food and drink, both of which are taken extremely seriously, offers the opportunity of unique and happy experiences to the traveller. John Fryer, an English doctor visiting Goa in the 17th century, wrote of Goan women as 'cooking deliciously and in such a way that no upset is caused to the stomach which can digest all without trouble.' Nothing has changed, they still do so today.

In food, as much as in any other aspect of life, the end results reveal the influence of outside elements on a traditional base. The introduction by the Portuguese of the chilli to the west coast of India, (see p. 55) subsequently made an enormous impact over the whole sub-continent, but many influences confined themselves to the small enclave of the territory itself, producing an extremely individualistic culinary result. Apart from the positive contribution of basic ingredients, the Portuguese also left their stamp in terms of the names still applied to many Goan dishes.

Rice is the staple cereal but produced in many forms including Saanas, a form of bread in which palm toddy is an essential ingredient! Intoxicating varieties apart, bread in many different forms is an essential part of Goan food and is usually leavened, in contrast with the naans and chapattis of northern India although these are also available. Fish and shellfish are at the heart of the matter, with pork the favourite meat. While fresh fish or shellfish, all out of the sea only hours before, hardly need adornment, even they receive special treatment. A dedication to coconut plus the use of vinegar in cooking, another Portuguese introduction, together with a wide and subtle range of traditional spices, means

that the long list of Goan specialities offer endless new delights, however well versed the traveller may be in other Indian regional cuisines – all joyously prepared and equally joyously shared. Prepare to extol the virtues of *balchao, xacuti, recheiado, vindaloo* and even the humble pork sausage, the *chourico*. All these are in addition to the Goan *seet corri* (rice-curry) which should really be mentioned first rather than last. Concocted with generous use of coconut and other mysteries, it is quite distinctive and brings out the flavour of the fish or shellfish used as the base. Sprinkle on a little *kismur* and you couldn't be anywhere else other than Goa.

Nor must one forget the sweet offerings, of the region. All the tropical fruits are there in season, mangos, papayas, water melons, pineapples and other sweet things culminating in the ultimate delight, the carefully nurtured, many-layered Bebinca.

It is a happy development that, to wash all this down, the local wine industry, based on grapes from the vineyards of Bangalore and Hyderabad, is making great strides forward. After the Portuguese departed, wine virtually disappeared from Goa, but a local industry was established and the range has now been expanded so that everything from 'dry' white wines to port is produced. While the dry white is relatively light while fresh, it matures rapidly in the bottle, assuming heavier, sweeter characteristics, but if drunk well chilled soon after it is bottled, it is eminently appropriate as an accompaniment to Goan sea foods. The local bottled beer, also well chilled of course, will cope with the spicy side of life. The 'national' drink, feni, has already been discussed (p. 49). It is another experience not to be missed.

Although all this talk of food and drink may be wandering somewhat from the theme of the people of Goa, there is ample excuse in the fact that food and drink are a philosophy here, not a question of mere sustenance and something of which Goans will speak at length with great pride and feeling!

This reveals another dominant Goan personality trait. There is little about Goa they do not regard in this way. Their true love for their homeland is infectious and with only a little encouragement a visitor soon finds himself emulating their admiration and love of Goa in all its many aspects.

Perhaps one thing above all else impresses the visitor. It is the generally relaxed attitude of the people wherever you go, an inbred philosophy referred to as *socegado*, a word that embraces everything associated with taking things gently, an example the visitor finds easy to follow, in fact irresistible. This gentle approach to life is not to be confused with idleness or lack of interest – far from it, they are full of enthusiasm and emotions can run high if their traditions or their heritage are threatened. May all this never be submerged by the incursions of today's world.

Arch of the Viceroys. Memorial slab to King John I 'restorer of Portuguese Liberty'.

House with Portuguese soldier on the gable, Betulbatim.

PART TWO

SEEING GOA

8 RAMBLING ROUND PANJIM

The most appealing explanation of the name Panjim is that it is derived from the Konkani *Panch yma afsugari*, 'Five Enchanted Castles', which the Portuguese corrupted to Pongy. Let's settle for that, even though there are several other learned guesses at its source. Today the Marathi form 'Panaji' appears on the sign posts.

For centuries, the site of the present-day capital of Goa housed only a tiny fishing village amongst the swamplands and palm trees bordering the banks of the Mandovi River. The place remained of little consequence until, in about 1500, a fortified palace was built there by Yusuf Adil Shah, or Khan, the first of the Sultans of Bijapur. He had developed a great affection for the banks of the Mandovi and had already built himself a fine palace at the port further upstream which was to become the Portuguese city of Goa.

It was the fortress palace near the mouth of the river, defended by 55 cannon, that the Portuguese first had to overcome when they attacked in 1510. Once established, Afonso Albuquerque recognised the site's strategic value and ordered its defences to be strengthened with additional artillery. It was also organised as the point of entry control at which all vessels had to report.

The Portuguese referred to the Sultan of Bijapur as the *Idalcao*, or *Idalcan*, a corruption of Adil Khan, and the building was known as the Idalcao's Palace. This name persisted throughout the period of Portuguese rule and is even still in use today.

The first Portuguese structure of note was inevitably a church, the original Church of the Immaculate Conception, built sometime around 1541.

Even then the site was an isolated place, virtually accessible only from the sea, but the beauty of its natural surroundings led a few rich noblemen to reclaim the swampland and build country houses along the shore. In 1631, a causeway was built parallel to the river to link it with the higher ground further upstream and this increased its importance as a residential area.

As early as 1684, because of the unhealthy conditions in the city of Goa, the need to find a new site to replace the city as capital was being discussed, with Mormugao then the favourite choice. However, in 1759 it was to Panjim that the Viceroy moved, taking over the Idalcao's Palace as his official residence. After that there was a general flow of population in his wake. Panjim had emerged from its surrounding swamps.

In the 1820s and 1830s, streets, lighting, public buildings and housing were rapidly developed and in 1834 its official status was raised by the govern-

Panjim: The High Court Building and the Mandovi River.

ment in Lisbon to that of a city with the title Nova Goa.

In 1843, it was declared the capital by royal decree and since then it has grown into a bustling little town, at least in the fringe area along its riverfront. Beyond this the less frenetic atmosphere more typical of Goa takes over again.

Panjim is essentially a town to be wandered about rather than toured with dedicated determination. It has many points of interest and the visitor is rewarded with considerable and varying atmosphere in its nooks and crannies.

A good place from which to start is the building on the waterfront already referred to so frequently, the Palace of the Idalcao.

THE IDALCAO PALACE

Built by Yusuf Adil Shah in about 1500 as a riverside pleasure palace, but fortified with as many as 55 guns because of its strategic position, it was further expanded and reinforced when the Portuguese took over in 1510. They added to its artillery strength and maintained a strong garrison. It also acted as the first customs post, the cargo of all ships entering the river being checked here.

For much of the time during Portuguese rule, the Palace was also used to house new Viceroys arriving to take up their post, some of the Viceroys-elect staying here until it was time for them to make a triumphal procession up-river to the city, where they would be installed with great pomp and ceremony. The outgoing Viceroy would then also stay at the Idalcao's Palace, awaiting the ship that would take him home to Portugal. The seminary of St Jerome near to the Fort of Reis Magos on the opposite shore was also used for this purpose. When the Viceroy moved to Panjim from Old Goa in 1759, the building was used as the Viceroy's Official Residence and in 1760 a small chapel was created inside the building for his use.

In 1918, the Viceroy, or by this time the Governor General, moved from here to the Cabo Palace on the headland. The chapel was dismantled, the cross going to the Church of St Sebastian in Fontainhas, the eastern suburb, and the reredos of the altar to Panjim's main church, the Church of the Immaculate Conception on top of the hill. After 1918, the building was used for various government departments including the Attorney General and the Captain of Ports. Since the incorporation of Goa into India in 1961, the building has served as the Secretariat, first for the Union Territory of Goa, Daman & Diu and now for the State. The Legislative Assembly sits here.

Panjim: The Idalcao Palace, now the Secretariat Building.

In the course of the almost 500 years of its existence it has been considerably modified. We know little of the original fortress-palace of Adil Khan, but in 1613 it was recorded that the Portuguese made extensive changes. At that time it was built round a large central courtyard, the river coming right up to the walls of the Palace with steps leading down to a landing stage. The main entrance, as now, was through the arched doorway on the opposite side, away from the river. Above the main doorway was the crest of the Viceroys, now replaced by the Asoka Chakra, the Buddhist Wheel of the Law which appears in the centre of the Indian national flag. The red-tiled roof is particularly interesting, the roof-line following the slope of each separate room, each varying in size and height and producing a most unusual effect.

THE STATUE OF ABBE FARIA

In a small 'square' next to the Idalcao Palace, the Praca Abbé Faria, is an intriguing and dramatic

Panjim. Statue of the Abbé Faria.

statue of a priest hypnotising a woman. Abbé Jose Custodia Faria, one of the most fascinating of Goan exiles, was born in 1756 in Candolim village just behind Calangute Beach near Fort Aguada. Life for him even started eventfully. When he was only eight years old his parents separated, his mother to become a nun, his father to become a priest. In 1777 his father took him to Lisbon where Jose studied for the priesthood, completing his studies in Rome where he was ordained.

Back in Lisbon, rumour was that in 1787 he plotted with the Pinto Conspirators who had gone to Lisbon to enlist support, the Pinto Revolt having been hatched in a neighbour's house in Candolim (p. 9). Soon afterwards he left hurriedly for Paris for discussions with the envoys of Tippu Sultan and the French government as to how they could combine their efforts to overthrow both the Portuguese and the British in India. The Pinto Revolt failed as did the intrigues of the French and Tippu Sultan.

The Abbé Faria stayed on in Paris and became involved in the French Revolution, in 1795 actually leading a battalion of revolutionaries against the National Convention.

It was at this time that he embarked on the stage of his career that would make him famous as the originator of hypnotism through suggestion. It is this achievement that is commemorated in this statue.

He died in Paris in 1819 a pauper, but this was not to be the end of his story. Alexander Dumas, writing his *Count of Monte Cristo* fifty years later, included in his novel a prisoner in the Château d'If known as the Mad Monk. He gave this character the name of Abbé Jose Custodia Faria, obviously based on the real Abbé though hardly on the true facts of his adventurous life.

THE MHAMAI KAMAT HOUSE

Opposite the statue is one of the oldest houses in Panjim. It belongs to a prominent Hindu family, the Mhamai Kamats, who fled from their village of Guirdolim, now part of Chandor, in the mid-16th century in order to escape the Christian crusade of the Jesuits in Salcete. Some members remained to convert and the Christian branch thrived to the extent that at some time in the future a daughter of the family would marry a Portuguese admiral. The Hindu branch also prospered and became involved in many aspects of commerce and finance in Vijaya-nagar, through which channels they established direct links into Portuguese government circles. In the mid-18th century, as a result of this, the family moved into Panjim. Another reason for the move into this particular house related to the close connections the family had with the Rajas of Sawant-wadi. As already described, the Bhonsles had had a torrid relationship with the Portuguese government in Goa, which continued even after the treaty of 1788. The Raja of Sawantwadi thought that the Mhamai Kamats, with their existing connections, would make an ideal diplomatic link with Viceregal circles in Panjim. Hence, the move by the Mhamai Kamats into the house almost next door to the Palace of the Idalcao, into which, in 1759, the Viceroy had just moved as his official residence, having abandoned Old Goa. The family has been there ever since.

Further along the waterfront is the quay where the ships used to arrive from and depart for Bombay. On a ship's arrival the whole place was turned into a seething noisy throng of porters, passengers and baggage. Departing deck-passengers desperately tried to board the ship before arrivals could get off, their objective being to lay claim to the choicest positions. Let us hope that the suspended steamer service is soon re-established. Opposite the quayside, the public buildings continue.

First is the High Court originally built in 1878 when it was moved from Old Goa. This is followed by a bank and hotels including the famous Man-

dovi Hotel whose first-floor balcony is an acknowledged meeting place for refreshment while
watching the world go by, although with the
growth of trees in the park opposite one needs to go
to the top floor to obtain a view across the river. The
white building on the hillside on the other side of
the river is a Sikh Gurudwara, the only one in Goa
with the Sikh population totalling less than 2000.

An intriguing little building onto which the
Mandovi Hotel has attached itself was once a private family chapel. Built in the 18th century, a great
deal is crammed into a small space, with its strange
combination roof of a red tiled pyramid and a white
plastered dome, while inside there are still the
remains of altars together with memorial slabs and
coats of arms of the Noronha family. It is known as
the Chapel of Dom Lourenco.

Forking to the left after passing the Mandovi
Hotel, we come to the Azad Maidan.

THE AZAD MAIDAN

In the centre of the square is a recently renovated
pavilion that was originally built to house the
statue of Afonso Albuquerque. The statue, made of
bronze and an imposing two metres tall, was commissioned soon after the conquest and occupied
various sites in Old Goa, finishing up, in the
middle of the 19th century, in the midst of disintegrating ruins. The monument to house it in Panjim
was built and the statue installed in 1847, soon after
it had been declared Goa's capital city. The columns
were brought from the ruins of Old Goa, including
some from the first great church to be built there,
the Dominican Church of 1550.

After liberation, the statue was for a short time
removed to the headland at Miramar before being
sent back to Old Goa where it stands, magnificent
but forlorn, in the museum. Until recently the

*Panjim: Azad Maidan with Police Headquarters in the
background. A memorial originally to Albuquerque, now to
Dr Tristao de Braganza Cunha.*

pedestal on which it stood, with inscriptions recording his achievements, remained in its decaying pavilion. This too has now been removed, the pavilion renovated and an impressive black marble plinth topped by a brass sculpture has been installed to the memory of Dr. Tristao de Braganza Cunha, one of the foremost of Goa's Freedom Fighters, 'The Valiant Hero of Goan Fight for Freedom'.

Nearby is another monument to those who struggled over many years for liberation from Portuguese rule. A modern pillar, in its simplicity, stands out in contrast to the neo-classical style of architecture that characterises much of Portuguese Panjim's official and public buildings.

The long stretch of buildings on the west side of the square are typical of this style, the former Portuguese army barracks and military headquarters with its huge parade ground behind. Built in 1832, it is now Police Headquarters and it is a sobering thought that most of these buildings are constructed from material taken from a host of grand churches, monasteries and public buildings that once made Old Goa one of the wonders of the Orient, a massive transfer of stone that must be almost unequalled.

Adjoining the Police Headquarters at the corner of the Square nearest the river is **The Menezes Braganza Institute.**

Originally the Vasco da Gama Institute, established in 1871 for the promotion of Literature, Arts and Science, it was re-named in 1953 in honour of Luis de Menezes Braganza (1878–1938), a great crusader for social, religious and political causes even under the repressive Salazar dictatorship.

Panjim: One of the Azulezos in the entrance hall of the Central Library, Menezes Braganza Institute.

Brought up amongst great wealth, he devoted his life to the people of Goa. His family house at Chandor, near Margao, is one of the finest examples of Goan domestic architecture.

The Institute itself, which now also contains the Central Library, is mainly of interest for the blue-tiled panels which line the entrance hall. A uniquely Portuguese art form, *azulezos*, they depict scenes from the great epic poem by Luis de Camoes, *The Lusiads*, which tells the story of the adventure of the Portuguese empire in the East.

On the river bank opposite the Menezes Braganza Institute and near to the ferry terminal is a monument to the victims of an accident to a ferryboat, the *Goa*, which sank in 1901 in the Mandovi between Panjim and Verem on the opposite bank. Eighty-one people lost their lives. Providing yet another example of the dispersal of Goans to many corners of the world, this memorial was erected by Goans living in Aden, who no doubt lost relatives in the tragedy. The memorial is treated as a shrine with flowers draped and candles burnt at its base acknowledging the plea on the inscription for passers-by to say a prayer for their eternal rest.

At the opposite end of the square to the Institute is the Government Printing Press and the rest of the buildings behind forming this huge quadrangle are occupied by other State Government offices.

Leave the Azad Maidan from the corner furthest from the river, on the opposite side of the square from Police Headquarters, and wander until you reach the Municipal Gardens.

THE MUNICIPAL GARDENS

This pleasant square was formerly known as the Garcia da Orta Garden, named in honour of a 16th century physician. He came to Goa in 1534 as private physician to Dom Martim Afonso de Sousa, Admiral of the Fleet. Incidentally, Dom Martim was to return to Goa in 1542 as Governor, a fellow passenger on that occasion being the young missionary Francis Xavier.

Garcia da Orta was to spend the rest of his life in India, devoting himself to a comparative study of European and Indian medicine with particular reference to the use of herbs and herbal remedies. His encyclopaedic work resulting from these studies became a standard textbook in Europe, being translated into several languages. The original work was published and printed in Goa in 1563. The introduction contained a piece of poetry by Luis Vaz de Camoes, the first thing ever printed from the pen of the man who was to produce the great epic *The Lusiads*. It is strange how the lives of many of Goa's

THE CHURCH OF OUR LADY OF THE IMMACULATE CONCEPTION

The church was one of the first to be built in Goa, certainly being there by 1541 and not in any way because of proximity to the centre of a well populated area. Far from it, the hillside on which it stands was surrounded by swampy land and stagnant water interspersed with a few paddy-fields and coconut groves. It was, however, on high ground above the Palace of the Adil Khan, near the narrowing of the river, at which point all vessels arriving in Goa were forced to anchor and register their cargoes before proceeding up-stream to Old Goa. Ships' crews, especially those having made the long and perilous voyage from Europe or the Far East, were anxious to get ashore and give thanks for their safe arrival.

Above the church on the hilltop was the area known as the Bairro Altos de Pilotos as, in these early days before lighthouses, huge beacons were lit here to guide ships into the estuary.

The early church was completely re-built from its foundations in 1619 and that this was even considered, taking account of the still negligible population of the area and the size of the new church, is a striking commentary on the religious climate of the time and the wealth available to the churches.

The church was being re-built at the same time as the Se Cathedral was nearing completion, the Basilica of Bom Jesus having just been consecrated, and, like these two great churches, the Renaissance influence is obvious in its façade, with its twin balustraded towers. At this stage, neither the elaborate pediment with its bell nor the steps in front were there and the church was still isolated in fields and swamps. It was not until long after the Viceroy had moved to Panjim and the town began to expand as a result of the abandoning of Old Goa that anything was done. By 1843 the land between church and river had been reclaimed and in 1855 the Praca de Flores, 'Square of Flowers', was created in front of the church, followed by the adjoining Praca de Comercio.

The great bell of the Augustinian church of Our Lady of Grace in Old Goa, of which only half a tower is today's dramatic monument, was brought to Panjim in 1841 and installed on the hill of Fort Aguada to toll the passing hours. In 1871, it was decided to move the bell to the church in Panjim but, because of its great size and weight, second only to the Golden Bell in the Cathedral, it would

Panjim: Ashoka Pillar in the Municipal Gardens, originally a memorial to Vasco da Gama.

famous characters intertwine.

In the centre of the garden is a monument originally built to commemorate the 400th anniversary of the first ever sea voyage from Europe to India. On 17 May 1498, Vasco da Gama anchored off Calicut having rounded the Cape of Good Hope with his three caravels, the largest of which was only 150 tons. In May 1898 the foundation stone was laid.

The column, again built out of material taken from Old Goa, this time the Convent of San Domingos, is over twelve metres high and was once topped with a bust of the great sailor. This has since been removed and replaced by India's national emblem, the Lion capital of the Ashoka pillar at Sarnath.

At the southern end of the garden is a narrow square, the Praca de Comercio, at the end of which, on the hillside, towers Panjim's main church.

*Panjim: The Church of Our Lady of the Immaculate
Conception, with the great bell, the second largest bell in Goa.*

not fit in the belfry tower and the whole pediment
of the façade had to be remodelled, giving it its
present unusual, though not displeasing, proportions. At the same time, as part of the overall
face-lift, the four-tiered steps leading up to the
church were added, making it one of the most
distinctive church façades in Goa.

The interior of the church is relatively simple by
the standards of the time although the backdrop to
the main altar, dedicated to Mary Immaculate, is
impressive enough. However, it is the two flanking
altars that catch the eye, that on the left dedicated to
Jesus Crucified and that on the right to Our Lady of
the Rosary. Each is a riot of heavily gilded, deeply
carved ornamentation, yet compact and controlled,
a fine example of the period. At the side of each is a
marble statue, one of St Peter and one of St Paul.

In the south transept to the right of the main altar
is a Chapel of St Francis Xavier, whose glass-
encased statue occupies the centre of the reredos.
This retable, with its interesting panels on either

side of the central compartment, was transferred
here when the Chapel of the Viceroys in the Idalcao
Palace was dismantled in 1918.

From the lower terrace in front of the church can
be seen, on a side street to the left, a modern
building that could be mistaken for an office block
if it were not for the symbolic minarets and the
remnants of green paint. This is the Jama Masjid
and also contains a Muslim college. If you go
further along the street containing the Mosque, you
soon come to the most important Hindu temple in
Panjim, the Mahalaxmi Temple. This was the first
temple to be allowed to be built in Panjim since the
arrival of the Portuguese. The deity of this temple
originally came from the village of Taleigao on the
outskirts of Panjim and was moved out to Bicholim
in the 16th century. In the face of stiff opposition
the Viceroy gave permission in 1818 for the construction of a temple in Panjim and this image was
brought back with great rejoicing. The opponents
of the Viceroy's liberalism delayed matters until
official approval arrived from Lisbon the following
year. During the delay the deity was kept in the

Mhamai Kamat house. The temple was rebuilt and enlarged in 1983.

This leaves three further areas for exploration:

THE ALTINHO, the ridge on which Panjim Church stands.

SAN THOME and FONTAINHAS, old residential areas lying at the foot of the ridge on the far side from the church.

THE CAMPAL, the area alongside the river on the western side of the town.

Altar to Jesus Crucified, on the left of the main altar, Panjim Parish Church.

THE ALTINHO

The hill is divided into two parts by the Emidio Gracia Road, climbing the hill to the right of the church and linking the main part of the town with the suburb of Fontainhas on the other side.

The hilltop above the church was the Hill of the Pilots, as already noted, with the first 'lighthouse' being operated from there.

On the other side of the church, the old buildings on the top of the hill are occupied by various colleges and the Avenue P.E. Agnelo leads through what has become a favoured residential area with its wooded slopes and flights of steps providing shady walkways.

The main building of interest in this area is the **Patriarchal Palace**, residence of the Archbishop of Goa.

The diocese of Goa was established in 1533, and raised to an Archdiocese in 1557, its importance growing rapidly as new dioceses were established by the crusading missionaries on the heels of commercial expansion. Eventually, its responsibility covered a vast area from the eastern side of Africa to the Far East including China and Japan! As a result, in 1572, the Pope bestowed on the Archbishop of Goa the title of 'Primate of the East'.

Although the Portuguese were quick enough to accept Goans into the priesthood, the first being ordained as early as 1558, they were firm in their determination not to allow their promotion in the ecclesiastical hierarchy within their territories. This resulted in many of the most energetic and talented priests leaving Goa. In 1637, in Rome, one of these exiles became the first Goan to become a bishop, returning to India to work outside Portuguese territory, in spite of opposition from both the church authorities in Lisbon and in Goa, who were at that time in conflict with the Papacy on the question of control over missionary activities in the sub-continent. This outflow of trained priests continued, and subsequently Goans rose to become cardinals, archbishops and bishops in many parts of India and beyond.

In Goa itself, the discontent with Portuguese discrimination manifested itself in such movements as the Oratorian Congregation of Goa, established in 1685 by Fr. Joseph Vaz, one of the objects of which was to extend the participation of Goan clergy. Even at this time, not one of the religious orders would admit Goans as members. The Oratorians were formally approved by the Pope in 1707 only in the face of severe Portuguese opposition. Also, too, the Pinto Conspiracy at the end of the 18th century had its seeds in the frustration of Goan clerics.

The ability of the church in Goa to finance and administer, or indeed influence, such widespread territories, especially with the political changes that had taken place, rapidly diminished, and progressive reorganisations to meet changed circumstances

Panjim: Patriarchal Palace, home of the Archbishop.

were initiated by Rome. Other areas were given more autonomy.

In 1886, the structure of the Roman Catholic Church in India was reorganised, several Archbishoprics and Bishoprics being created. The Archbishop of Goa was elevated to Honorary Patriarch of the East Indies, entrusted with the exercise of moral influence over this vast area, while reducing the limits of his actual administrative jurisdiction. Eventually, this was confined to the Portuguese territories of Goa, Daman and Diu.

The Portuguese Archbishop left Goa following Portugal's political eviction and in 1962, in his absence, the Holy See appointed Bishop Francisco Rebello, a Goan, as Apostolic Administrator. He was succeeded in this office by Bishop Raul Nicolau Gonsalves. In 1976 after fifteen years' absence, the Portuguese Archbishop resigned and, in 1978, Bishop Gonsalves became Archbishop of Goa, Daman and Diu and Patriarch of the East Indies, the first Goan to hold the office.

The present palace on the Altinho was begun in 1886 following the elevation of the Archbishop to Patriarchal status, and completed in 1894. The impressive coat of arms decorating the entrance is that of the first Patriarch, Dom Antonio Sebastiao Valente. The chapel is given character and individuality by the modern reredos intricately carved in polished wood. The temptation to reproduce a traditional Baroque-style piece has been resisted, keeping the chapel in harmony with the rest of the palace. There are some fine examples of old blackwood furniture, but of particular interest are the richly coloured portraits of several former prelates of Goa, including a particularly impressive one of the first Archbishop, Dom Caspar Leao Pereira,

who, from his first setting foot in India in 1560, coinciding with the arrival of the Inquisition, was involved for many years in the early problems of establishing the church here. He died in Goa in 1576, during his second spell in office.

The towering mast of All India Radio together with the television relay centre dominate the skyline, a budding Goan version of the Qutb Minar (Victory Tower), while nearby on the hill slopes is the colourful Maruti Hindu temple.

SAN THOME AND FONTAINHAS

Situated on the opposite side of the hill to the Church of the Immaculate Conception, between the bottom of the steep slope and the river to the east, a tributary of the Mandovi, this is one of Panjim's most colourful areas, full of character and well deserving of a gentle exploration of its narrow streets and small squares.

Galleried house, Fontainhas.

Like much of Panjim, it was originally marshland and only became important as a residential area in the 19th century. From the early part of the century, after the Viceroy had moved to Panjim, the ponds and swamps began to be filled and houses built. The first chapel on this side of the hill was built in 1818 and dedicated to Saint Sebastian. Even so, the area continued a somewhat disorganised and poorly served collection of crowded alleyways for several years.

It was only towards the end of the 19th century that it assumed its present character, with some degree of planning and improved water supply through the fountains that give it its name. The opening of the Corte de Oitero, now renamed Emidio Gracia Road, cutting through the hill and linking it with the main part of the town, made it more accessible and, at about the same time, in 1879, the road was opened that runs along the banks of the tributary of the Mandovi and by which traffic from the south and the airport, enters Panjim. This, the Rua Nova de Ourem, is named after the Governor who initiated this project.

All this led to it becoming one of Panjim's finest residential areas and today this part, more than anywhere else, still has an atmosphere more Mediterranean than Indian. Amongst the jumble of narrow streets, the houses, all shapes and sizes and highly individualistic, are painted in contrasting colours as elsewhere in Goa, often with windows and door frames picked out in white. Colonnades and balconies, decorated balustrades and ornamental ironwork are much in evidence and, together with the inevitable red-tiled rooftops, all add their contribution to the character of the district.

The Emidio Gracia Road cut into the ridge means that this eastern area can be approached either from the Church of the Immaculate Conception on the other side of the hill, or by skirting the Altinho along the river front beyond the Secretariat building.

The tiny quarter of San Thome is 'centred' on the square of that name containing Panjim's main **Post and Telegraph Office**, known at one time as **'Tobacco Square'** because the building, now the Post Office, occupying its southern side was the

Panjim: Casa Moeda, 'The Mint House', Tobacco Square.

tobacco trading house.

On the right-hand side of the square looking from the Post Office stands what was for a short time the **Casa Moeda**, the 'Mint House'. Originally a private house, it was acquired by the Royal Treasury in 1834 and the mint transferred there from the Arsenal in Old Goa. This followed the report of a commission of inquiry into the unsatisfactory quality standards of the coins being produced in Old Goa. After a short time the Mint was moved back to the Arsenal but only survived until 1870. It was then shut down by the Portuguese government, again because of the poor quality of its performance, but this time arrangements were made for coins for Goa to be supplied by the British Mint in India. There are some interesting samples of Portuguese coins in the museum at Old Goa.

In 1863 the Treasury sold the house in 'Tobacco Square' and two years later its new owner leased it to the British who used it as the British Telegraph Office until 1902. Since then it has been considerably altered.

In front of the 'Mint House' was Panjim's pillory and place of execution. Here died the fifteen of the Pinto Conspiracy condemned to death. The last execution took place here in 1843, after which the pillory was moved to a site on the river bank.

The tiny church of **San Thome**, tucked away in a corner of the square, was built in 1849 and rebuilt again in 1902, still very active and thronged to overflowing, especially on festive occasions.

Behind the church, the streets of San Thome merge into the district of Fontainhas and here, at the top end of a square that is really nothing more than the widening of a road lined with flowering trees and balconied houses, is the attractive and

Panjim: Tobacco Trading House, now the main Post Office, Tobacco Square.

most interesting little church of **Saint Sebastian**.

The original church of 1818 was situated at the opposite end of the square from the new church built in 1888 and for a while, before the old chapel was demolished to build a new through-road, now called Cunha Gonsalves Road, the two churches faced each other at a distance of only a hundred metres. The present church was consecrated by the Archbishop Valente, who had just recently been elevated to the dignity of Patriarch of the East Indies.

The gleaming white uncluttered façade sits comfortably against the wooded slopes of the hillside in its quiet surroundings. Three-doored at its base to accommodate two side aisles, the façade narrows to the width of the nave on the second storey and this is surmounted by a narrow belfry.

Panjim: Chapel of St Sebastian, Fontainhas.

Inside, in the dim light, three elaborate retables seem to fill the tiny church, their heavily carved wooden columns forming alcoves containing statues of their saints. All three were brought from a disused and much larger church in Diu, far to the north. The main altar is dedicated to St Sebastian, that on the right to St Joseph and that on the left to Nossa Senhora de Livramento. There are also altars in each of the aisles, almost a surfeit of altars for so small a church, but that in the left aisle is of particular interest. Dedicated to Nossa Senhora do Bom Despacho, Our Lady of Good Counsel, the statue is believed to have come from the Chapel of the High Court in Old Goa where mass was said each morning when the court was in session.

At the end of the right aisle is a huge crucifix, also very ancient and with a intriguing history, being originally the crucifix in the Palace of the Inquisi-

tion. On the final suppression of this dreaded institution in 1812, the crucifix was installed in the chapel of the Viceroy at the Idalcao's Palace. When this chapel was closed in 1918 the crucifix was transferred here. Perhaps significantly, unlike traditional crucifixes, the head is raised and the eyes open.

THE CAMPAL

The Medical College on the coast road leading out of Panjim, now renamed Dayanand Bandodkar Marg, after the first Chief Minister of Goa following its incorporation into India, marks the beginning of a long stretch of flat land running alongside the river. Known as the Campal, an abbreviation of 'Campo de Dom Manual', Dom Manual de Portugal e Castro being the Viceroy who was responsible for having this area cleared and reclaimed in 1830, this esplanade with its parks and gardens is a pleasant place for an evening stroll or for wandering at any other time of day.

On the river side of the road is a huge old cannon nearly four metres long, one of the first to be cast in the Arsenal at Old Goa and mounted in the fort at Banasterim on the bank of the waterway linking the Mandovi and Zuari Rivers which formed the eastern boundary of the Old Conquests. It was from here that Ismail Adil Khan launched his attempt to re-take Goa in 1512, but in the end it was Albuquerque who captured Banasterim and, reinforcing it with cannon such as this one, turned it into the eastern bulwark of Goa's defences. The fort, remnants of which can still be seen as you cross the river on the road from Old Goa to Ponda, fell into disrepair following the shifting of Goa's borders still further east with the acquisition of the New Conquests. This cannon lay in the ruins until 1840 when it was moved into Old Goa and set up as a memorial to Portuguese victories during these early wars. It was subsequently moved to its present site, still an impressive reminder of the skills of Goa's craftsmen in the Arsenal, whose products remained much in demand by warring factions beyond the Western Ghats long after Golden Goa's glitter had faded.

In the gardens opposite the cannon there is a statue of Francisco Luis Gomes, one of the earliest and most lucid advocates of freedom from foreign rule, not only for Goa but for India as well, this in the mid-19th century. He was one of Goa's earliest representatives in the Cortes, the Lisbon parliament, and became well known in Portuguese intellectual as well as political circles for the breadth and integrity of his opinions. It is interesting that not

Panjim: Detail on the cannon of Banasterim, now at the Campal.

only was his contribution openly acknowledged in Goa, but that it was allowed expression during Portuguese rule in the statue erected here in 1929 to mark the centenary of his birth, an indication of the

high respect in which he was held by the Portuguese, who were not in the habit of allowing the honouring of those advocating their departure from India. The inscription lauds him as 'champion of liberty' and 'patriot' as well as 'orador eloquente'.

Further on, the **Kala Academy** has excellent facilities, especially its auditoriums, both indoor and outdoor, in which are staged a wide range of the performing arts as well as exhibitions.

The wide and pleasant road continues on along the length of the Campal past the **Panjim Gymkhana** and other sports facilities, ending at the **Miramar Circle**. Here, on the point, is a statue to Hindu-Christian Unity, erected on the same base that was the last resting place of the magnificent statue of Afonso Albuquerque before he was consigned to the entrance hall of the museum of Old Goa. He had a fine view from here across the shallow waters of the Mandovi Estuary to the headland of Fort Aguada. The walls of the fort trace dark lines across the red, rocky hillside and along the water's edge past the buildings that are now used as a jail, while the lighthouses and St Lawrence's Church stand proudly on the skyline.

9 OLD GOA – ROME OF THE ORIENT

Cities have risen and declined in a shorter space of time than did Old Goa, but rarely will the traveller find the strange and fascinating situation that exists here. Hundreds of buildings, including literally dozens of huge and magnificent structures, have disappeared without trace, totally submerged by the returning jungle, and yet in the midst of this vanished city, rising above the palm trees, a small number of buildings remain perfectly preserved, some even still in use today.

With the new and considerable wealth that came with Portuguese trading activities, the city grew so rapidly in splendour that, within fifty years of Albuquerque's conquest in 1510, it became one of the wonders of the Orient, 'the Rome of the East'. Even though it lost its trading importance soon after the end of the 16th century, building activity, now mainly ecclesiastical with vast churches and monasteries, went on apace.

However, the city was already doomed. Cholera had first struck in 1543 and, as the population grew, the primitive drainage systems were unable to cope. The problem was compounded by water seepage through the porous soil resulting in a contamination of water supplies. A whole series of epidemics resulted, with malaria adding to the death toll. The city's population was decimated time after time.

By the middle of the 17th century, the citizens of this fabled capital were also beginning to feel the economic pinch, and although vanity and pride resulted in an effort to perpetuate the luxurious life of the early years, so vividly described with some awe by European visitors,[1] private buildings were already falling into ruins through lack of funds to maintain them. Before the end of the century, the population, once well over 200,000, had fallen to less than 20,000. As early as 1684, proposals were made to move the capital, with Mormugao the favoured site. Building even began there and was well advanced before the decision was changed and the project abandoned. In 1695, following yet another epidemic, the Viceroy moved his residence out of the centre of the city into the suburb of Panelim, but it was not until 1759 that the Viceroy moved to Panjim, a healthier site nearer the coast. With his departure, and the co-incidental expulsion of the Jesuits, the population was reduced to less than 2000.

Less than 100 years later almost all the convents, colleges, monasteries and churches had also been allowed to disintegrate or had been deliberately demolished to provide building materials for houses, monuments and barracks elsewhere, particularly in Panjim.

The jungle began to take over and complete the eradication of Old Goa's glorious past. In 1843, royal decree declared Panjim the official capital. In 1846, the Convent of Santa Monica was reported to be the only building inhabited. The ladies were a tougher breed, or more stubborn in their refusal to move.

Today several other of the surviving buildings have been restored to life as theological colleges or training centres and some churches are still in use, if only on special occasions. What is left are some of the most magnificent of the old churches, almost as if survival was determined on merit, which of course to some extent it was, and a unique experience for the visitor to savour the city's great and glorious achievements during that brief span of time so long ago.

THE JOURNEY FROM PANJIM TO OLD GOA

The finest approach is from the river. For over 100 years after the Portuguese arrived this was the only way to reach the city from the coast; it was 1633 before a causeway was built across the swampland that borders the south bank of the River Mandovi eastwards from Panjim. A visit by launch provides a fascinating experience although, at the time of writing, this is not easy to arrange.

By bus or car, leave Panjim by the causeway that starts near the Nehru Bridge at the eastern end of the town. The causeway, nearly three km long, was completed in 1634, built on the orders of the Viceroy Count of Linhares. It was a project that would have considerable influence on the future of Panjim when the time came for the enforced shift of the capital from Old Goa.

On the right, amidst the marshes, are the salt pans. The arches in the causeway allow these to flood with sea water, they are then sealed and natural evaporation leaves salt deposits that are subsequently collected into grey piles for further treatment.

The river flows slowly by on the left with its seemingly endless stream of iron-ore barges hea-

Old Goa: Nossa Senhora de Penha de Franca, seen across the Mandovi River.

vily laden and incredibly low in the water going downstream to the sea, and bows high buffeting their way against the current when returning empty for another load. On the far bank of the river, the white church with its steps at the water's edge is the church of **Nossa Senhora de Penha de Franca**, Our Lady of the Rock of France, one of only few churches in the world with this intriguing dedication. It was here, under the shelter of the far shore, that Albuquerque's ships lay at anchor through the monsoon of 1510, having been driven out of the city by Yusuf Adil Shah.

Beyond is the island of **Chorao**, with its encircling mangroves which include many rare species. As this area is also the home of many migratory birds it is earmarked for protection and development as a nature reserve.

Still further up river on the left is the island of Divar, again with its white church on the hill, this one the famous Piedade.

At the end of the causeway is **Ribander**, the name meaning 'Royal Landing Place', a long rambling village and home of one of Goa's historic hospitals. The Hospital of the Poor here was successor to that first famous Portuguese institution, the Royal Hospital of Old Goa, the old establishment being transferred here in 1851.

Nearby is Ribander's oldest church, **Nossa Senhora da Ajuda**, Our Lady of Help. The church earned its dedication from the rescue by Our Lady of a Portuguese ship that, having almost reached Goa, met with so violent a storm that it went out of control. The Devil himself quickly took the helm but Our Lady appeared beside him, remaining there all night giving instructions on how the ship should be steered. By morning the ship safely reached shore and at the point where it anchored, here in Ribander, the church was built in 1565 to commemorate the vessel's miraculous deliverance. It was rebuilt in 1711, and high on the outside wall of the church, under the eaves on the riverside above Ribander Ferry, there is a delightful illustration of the ship moored at the quayside with Mary and Jesus and a host of angels giving it their protection.

As you leave the village, the solitary half-tower of the church of the **Monastery of St Augustine** appears in silhouette on the hill beyond with, next to it, the squat fortress church of Our Lady of the Rosary. You are nearing what remains of 'Golden Goa'.

After winding through woods, with views across the river on the left, the road suddenly leaves the trees and a cleared space opens up with the great mass of the Convent and **Church of St Francis of**

Assisi together with the **Se Cathedral** seemingly forming one huge building on the left. The dark bulk of the **Bom Jesus Basilica** looms on the right.

Even if you haven't made the journey by river, it is a pleasant fantasy to enter Old Goa as did the Viceroys and Governor Generals on their first arrival. Apart from this, the river-front is an excellent place to pause before starting your exploration of this city of the Viceroys and to contemplate what was once the greatest city east of Constantinople. In addition, what remains can be conveniently seen from this starting point, minimising the to-ing and fro-ing necessary. So, carry on past these huge churches and, turning left at the island with its statue of **Mahatma Gandhi**, continue until the river is reached.

THE RIVER FRONT

The riverside at this point was a bustling dockside area with quays capable of taking alongside the biggest ocean-going ships and dealing with their cargoes of spices and silks, horses from Arabia, porcelain from China and a host of other exotic goods. Where we now stand was once the Quay of the Viceroys, the principal landing stage; now there is only the small jetty from which the ferry plies and the short span of water between here and the island of Divar.

Away to the left, at the far end of the quayside as one stands with one's back to the river, was the impressive Customs House, while adjoining the archway a short distance up the road, again to the left, was the fortress palace of the evicted Sultan of Bijapur. The outer walls of this fort, overlooking the quayside and the river, were rebuilt by Albuquerque as the core of his defences as soon as he gained control of the city. After 1554, Adil Shah's palace in the fort would become the residence of the Viceroys.

To the right from the point where we stand stretched the quays where the great sailing ships docked and the biggest ship-building yard in the Orient was sited. Behind, was another 'biggest in the Orient', the Arsenal with its towering walls and bastions which also contained the Mint.

It is difficult now to conjure in the imagination these fine buildings and ships and the constant bustle of activity, with tangled undergrowth amidst gently waving palms smothering even any heaps of rubble that might remain, most of the stone having been removed for building elsewhere.

Leading from the jetty is what was the main street of the city, the once glorious Rua Direita, 'Straight Street', which, with its tall buildings, red tiles, with oyster shell windows and balconies overhanging on either side, was lined with the shops of jewellers, goldsmiths, carpet makers, money lenders, silk vendors, spice merchants and every other product of the east. Splendidly and fashionably dressed nobles and their ladies, together with the not so noble but equally rich, paraded the streets on horseback, in *machillas* (the local version of a palanquin), even on elephants, surrounded by the normal accompaniment of hangers-on and beggars. This led to more crowded squares and streets with their mansions, public buildings, and, dominating all parts of the city, a great variety of churches and monasteries.

'He who has seen Goa need not see Lisbon' was no idle contemporary boast. In fact, it was bigger than the London or Paris of its day.

Up the hill from the jetty on the approach to all this vanished splendour, today's traveller still encounters, as did all arrivals by this route, the Arch of the Viceroys, which once was the main gateway to the city. This now stands in isolation.

THE ARCH OF THE VICEROYS

Built by Vasco da Gama's great-grandson, who became Viceroy in 1597, it carries the deer crest of

Old Goa: Arch of the Viceroys, viewed from the landing stage.

Old Goa: Arch of the Viceroys, looking back towards the river.

the great seaman along the frieze above the arch. The first to sail to India round the Cape of Good Hope, the man himself, wearing full regalia, gazes out at the Mandovi River from his niche. The arch is built from red laterite, but on the river-side is faced with greenish granite, an effective combination. Originally, the arch had another tier with a niche containing the bronze statue of St Catherine, but the arch collapsed in 1948 and in the restoration in 1954, this was omitted. She can now be seen in a courtyard of the nearby Archaeological Museum.

Inside the archway, there is an inscription recording the building of the arch in memory of Vasco da Gama and another, a later addition, a fittingly decorated memorial slab to the first Portuguese king after the liberation from Spanish rule in 1640. The upper part of the inscription, translated, reads 'The legitimate and true king, Dom Joao IV, restorer of Portuguese liberty'. He died in 1656.

On the back of the archway is a symbolic piece of statuary. A crowned lady in flowing robes stands with both feet firmly set on the back of the reclining figure of a man. Gazing sternly into the distance, she holds an open book in one hand and grasps a long sword in the other, pointing it at the man beneath her. He, obviously a heathen but someone of rank with his equally flowing and decorated robes, slippers and a turban, is propped on one elbow with a lugubrious resigned expression on his face.

On taking office, all Viceroys made their processional entrance with great ceremony through this archway where they were presented with the keys of the city. Beyond, further along the Rua Direita, lay the main square.

Before this, however, on the left, is one of the best preserved of all the churches and monasteries of Old Goa, that known as the Church of St Cajetan.

In the tree-shaded gardens of the church, there is, on the left, a small remnant of pre-Portuguese Goa, a reminder of the existence of a substantial city of considerable wealth before 1510. This is the only surviving fragment of the fortress palace of Yusuf Adil Khan, already referred to, which became the Palace of the Viceroys. Already in a state of decay, it was demolished in 1820 to provide building mat-

Old Goa: Doorway to Yusuf Adil Khan's palace.

Detail on a doorway: all that remains from the fortress palace of Yusuf Adil Khan.

erials for Panjim and all that remains are these pillars and lintel of a gateway with steps leading up to it. Although part of a Muslim ruler's palace, this was obviously the work of Hindu craftsmen. The decoration on the pillars and the remains of screen-work on either side is reminiscent of a Hindu temple. The scrollwork decoration on the lintel would have been added during Portuguese remodelling of the palace, giving us just one more fleeting example of Manueline decoration.

THE CHURCH OF SAN CAJETAN – OUR LADY OF DIVINE PROVIDENCE – built 1656–1661

St Cajetan, an Italian contemporary of Francis Xavier, spent little time in Goa, but this church with its Roman associations is more popularly referred to by his name than its original one, Our Lady of Divine Providence, to whom the main altar is dedicated.

Built by the monks of the Theatine Order, of which St Cajetan was the founder, it is wholly European in concept and is in fact a version of St Peter's in Rome, all combining to produce a most Italian-flavoured end result.

The façade has towering Corinthian columns and pilasters supporting a plain central pediment, above which the twin belfry towers rise in perfect balance. Four niches flanking the triple doors contain statues of Apostles. Above and behind the facade, almost hidden despite the height of its drum, rises the massive yet graceful dome, adding further to its Roman spirit. This is the only surviving domed church in Old Goa; in fact it would seem that few were ever built.

Within the oblong exterior of the building, its interior is converted into a complex Greek cross in plan, with four huge piers creating the aisles and supporting the great drum of the dome in the centre of the church.

These massive supports are made graceful by their facing of classical Corinthian pilasters and above them soar an interplay of beautifully proportioned arches and vaults that carry the eye into the misty light of the dome itself, its airiness and lightness presaging one of the important features of the true Indian Baroque that would later emerge. Around the base of the dome in bold lettering in Latin is a verse from St Matthew's Gospel, 'Seek ye first the kingdom of God and His righteousness and all these things shall be added unto you.'

This all forms an impressive setting for the unrestrained Baroque of the reredos, the backdrops to the seven altars in the church, gleaming with intricately worked gold.

The reredos of the main altar is one of the outstanding examples of the Baroque style. Heavily-carved scroll brackets support the platform on which swirling salomonic columns frame the winged angels on either side of the tabernacle. Above this the elaborate composition soars upwards to its pinnacle where a symbolic sun, bathed in light, is overtopped by a crown of gold. Little of Indian influence is to be seen at this early stage of the development of the reredos in Goa, except for the treatment of decorative details.

One of the six side chapels, the large one on the right side of the church, is dedicated to St Cajetan himself.

The pulpit is a fine example of Indian wood carving and around the upper part of the church at gallery level are shell design niches containing wooden statues of saints.

Directly beneath the dome in the centre of the church, a square raised platform covers a well, or tank, which is alternatively described as being either the tank of a Hindu temple which occupied the site before the church was built, or as a reservoir created as an integral part of the design to draw off water from the porous sub-soil that would otherwise weaken the foundations.

Below the main altar are **catacombs**, entered from the rear of the church, originally the burial place of priests of the Theatine Order and in later years the temporary resting place of the embalmed bodies of Portuguese Governor Generals who died in office, awaiting their last voyage back to Lisbon. It may be that three 19th century Governor Generals still lie there. The wooden coffins have been prised open, but the leaden caskets are still intact.

The monastery to one side of the church has been well restored, its peace and serenity somehow retained. It is one of the few buildings in Old Goa in permanent use, now functioning as a theological college, the Pius X Pastoral Institute, where not only priests but lay preachers and church workers from all over India come for training.,

Back on the Rua Direita and continuing up the hill, the façade of the Se Cathedral rises on the right.

THE SE CATHEDRAL – built 1562–1652

Raised on a massive plinth of laterite, the exterior is

Façade of the Se Cathedral.

Tuscan in style and the severity of the façade, unbalanced by the loss of the north tower which collapsed in 1776, is relieved by the splendid decoration of the framework of the three doorways. The remaining tower houses five bells including the famous 'Golden Bell'. The largest bell in Goa, cast in the village of Cuncolim in the south of Salcete, is so named for the beautiful deep resonance of its sound which can still be appreciated by visitors today.

There is an inscription on the pediment over the main door, recording that in 1562 the King of Portugal ordered the building of the Cathedral at the expense of the Royal Treasury. It was built to replace as Goa's cathedral the small church that grew from that originally built by Afonso Albuquerque in 1510, which he dedicated to St Catherine of Alexandria (on whose feast day he took the city). The new cathedral was also dedicated to her.

The Dominicans took responsibility for its construction but, it seems, made a slow start and it was not until 1597, when Julio Simao, a Goan-born architect, and 'Chief Engineer in this State', returned from a visit to Portugal, that designs were crystallised and work went on apace. Even so, it was not until 1619 that the main building was put into use, still with unfinished altars which were not consecrated until 1652, ninety years after the church was ordered to be built.

Before entering, look back from the entrance to the Cathedral. You are standing at one side of what was once the main square of the city. On the left stood the Senate House and on the right, where now there is a pleasant garden, stood the dreaded Palace of the Inquisition. Originally this was the palace of Yusuf Adil Khan, the Sabaio, and the principal building of the city before the arrival of the Portuguese. Its frontage of black stone and the many exotic rooms and galleries were described with some awe by contemporary visitors. The first Viceroy immediately requisitioned it as his residence. However, its main feature was a long imposing flight of stairs leading to the main reception chamber and in 1554, the 6th Viceroy, Dom Pedro Mascarenhas, old and feeble, found them an insuperable obstacle. He moved into the palace in the fortress and in 1560, the Inquisition, finding it vacant on their arrival, moved in. It was in this square that the autos-da-fé took place, announced by the tolling of the Golden Bell above. No doubt the majesty of its sound was lost on the victims of the Inquisition.

The interior is again a straight import from Europe, a large central nave with a broad aisle on each side, all with barrel-vaulted ceilings resting on plain, square Doric arcades. Within this grand but simple setting we are transported into the luxuriant world of the Baroque.

Entering through the main door at the eastern end of the cathedral, the vast expanse of the nave stretches upwards and away to the glimmering glitter of the main altar in what seems to be the far distance. Over 75 metres long and 50 metres wide, it is the largest building in Goa and the biggest church in Asia. It looks the part.

Immediately inside, under the sheltering choir, two columns have recesses containing basins on marble pedestals, one with a statue of St Francis Xavier and the other of St Ignatius Loyola. In a chapel to the right is the font. It was made by a local craftsman, and tradition has it that it was used by St Francis Xavier for the baptism of his converts, before being moved here from the former cathedral, now the Chapel of St Catherine. Its inscription records its donation to the cathedral by one Jorge Gomez in 1532.

An oil-painting of **St Christopher** that should re-assure all travellers of the capabilities of their patron Saint, hangs beneath the choir.

Internal buttresses have been used to create four chapels on either side of the nave and, in doing so, within what is a rectangular building, have created a cruciform plan with a transept the full width of the building in front of the main altar.

Of the side chapels, two have carved wooden screens. Other than their function as screens, there is little that is owed to Europe in these superb examples of the Indian wood-carver's skills.

The screened chapels include, on the right, the **Chapel of the Cross of Miracles**. The story of this huge wooden cross is that a priest had placed a

A painting of St Christopher in the Se Cathedral.

simple cross on a hillock on the southern edges of Old Goa known as the Monte Belle Vista and, in 1619, in an event witnessed by many people, the figure of Christ appeared on this Cross in a halo of light, wearing a crown of thorns and bleeding from hands and feet. The Archbishop ordered a church built on the spot to house the miraculous cross. Incidentally, this church later became the headquarters of a movement to further the cause of Goan-born priests. Father Joseph Vaz, 'the Apostle of Ceylon', joined this movement in 1685, affiliated it to the Oratorians of St Philip Neri and established the Order of Oratorians of the Holy Cross in Goa. A Brahmin himself, it was initially specified that only Brahmins could join the Order. After the suppression of the religious orders in 1834 the church was abandoned and, like many others at that time, fell into disrepair. The cross was transferred

Old Goa: The Cathedral. Altar in the side-chapel of the Cross of Miracles.

to the cathedral in 1845. The legend goes that the first simple cross was one made by shepherds out of the stalks of palm fronds and that this grew and grew in size, becoming a cross of solid wood. Again, in 1619, having been placed in a nearby church while the new church was being built, it is attested that it again grew in size to the extent that it was impossible to remove it without widening the doorway.

The Chapel of the Blessed Sacrament opposite, also with its carved screen, is a fantasy of golden splendour. Do not pass it by; spend a few moments in contemplation.

The floor of the transept is composed mainly of graveslabs with fascinating inscriptions. Included is the grave of Julio Simao, architect of the Cathedral. The marble-topped table centred in front of the main altar is where the sacred relics of St Francis Xavier have been placed during the expositions of his body since 1952; after 1955 in its glass-casket. The last exposition took place in December 1984, to which record crowds of pilgrims flocked from all over India and the world, packing the great nave while waiting their turn to file past

the body on the pedestal. Between these rare occasions, echoing services are still held to tiny congregations and a small group of canons perform the rituals that keep the cathedral alive. Marriage ceremonies also take place.

The gallery on the right wall of the chancel contains the 18th century organ but this, and the unoccupied marble pedestal, tend to be ignored, with the eye constantly drawn to the reredos of the main altar, diverted only by the subsidiary splendours of the six altars in the transept in front. These altars, each of them an individual work of art, require careful study, their detail being extraordinary and beautiful. The altar to St Anne, on the north (right) wall of the transept, contains the relics of the martyrs of Cuncolim, and to the right of this altar is the tomb of Goa's first Archbishop, Dom Gaspar de Leoa Pereira, who was so strongly active in the introduction of Christianity from his arrival in Goa in 1560 – coinciding with the establishment of the Inquisition – to his death in 1596. He was especially involved in the Christianisation of the newly acquired territories of Salcete and Bardez (1567), initiating the widespread destruction of temples leading to the movement of Hindu deities into areas beyond Portuguese control. There is a fine portrait of him in the Patriarchal Palace.

The setting and composition of the main altar is impressive in every way, its gilded craftsmanship a classic example of the pre-Baroque Mannerist style. Within the main structure of carved and gilded wood, the compartments into which it is divided contain stucco reliefs over-laid with gilt, with the heads and hands of the figures being polychromed, an effective combination of techniques.

There are six main panels, each defined by Corinthian columns. The columns of the lower part are decorated for their full height with a simple geometric pattern with rosettes added. The columns of the middle section are plain below, with typical Mannerist fluting above. The scene within each compartment, contained within an elaborately decorated arched frame, is taken from the life and martyrdom of St Catherine.

St Catherine was martyred in Alexandria and the story is told of how, following torture and beheading for preaching the Christian faith, her body was carried by angels to Mount Sinai. Her corpse was disinterred by monks in the 8th or 9th century and her relics placed in a monastery there. In 1065 the Order of the Knights of Mount Sinai was formed to protect these relics, their emblem being the broken spiked wheel of her martyrdom with which, as here, she is usually portrayed.

High above, in the centre is Jesus on the Cross with the Virgin Mary and St John the Apostle at his feet. Archangels fill the panels on either side. The two central panels show her debating with heathen philosophers, awaiting execution, her beheading while angels offer the martyr's palm, and in the fourth panel they carry her head to heaven while Archangels take her body to Sinai.

Below the panels, on and between the pedestals of the lower columns, is a bas-relief running the full width of the retable, portraying Jesus with apostles, priests, scholars and doctors, each a character in his own right.

The main altar, another masterpiece, sets off the other fourteen altars in the Cathedral, each of which would be the outstanding feature of a church anywhere else.

Leaving the cathedral by the side door from the transept that leads onto the open square, the next building is the original Archbishop's Palace, still occupied by a few resident clergy, and beyond is the Church and Convent of St Francis of Assisi.

CHURCH OF ST FRANCIS OF ASSISI – THE CHURCH OF THE HOLY SPIRIT – built 1661

The first of the religious orders to arrive in Goa, Franciscan monks built the first convent here in 1517, reputedly on the site of a mosque. The church was completed in 1521 and dedicated to the **Holy Spirit**. Of this church, only the main western doorway survives: the rest of the church was completely rebuilt in 1661.

The **doorway** mentioned is of pure Manueline style, a form developed in Portugal at the end of the 15th century in the reign of King Manuel, after whom it was named. Elaborate doorways were characteristic: here the flowing curves and abundant decoration contrast strongly with the severe Tuscan style that was adopted for the rest of the

Old Goa: Espirito Santo, St Francis of Assisi.

Detail on the doorway to the church of St Francis of Assisi.

exterior when the church was rebuilt. This doorway is as fine an example of this art form as can be found, which is perhaps why the rebuilders of the church could not bring themselves to destroy it. Its plain setting serves to highlight its detail. The combination of the slenderness of the columns and the strength of the carving of the narrow moulding create a most elegant yet striking trefoil-arched frame for the wooden panelling of the door. This wooden panelling is finely carved and there were once delicately painted figures in the upper corner panels, now sadly disappearing under layers of whitewash. Above the frame there is a splendidly sculpted heraldic composition in which the Portuguese royal coat of arms, now badly weather-worn, is surmounted by an intricate crown with, above this again, the Cross of the Order of Christ under which Prince Henry the Navigator's captains explored uncharted seas. This royal nautical theme, the essence of Manueline style, is continued with armillary spheres, the model of the celestial sphere used in fixing the position of heavenly bodies, on either side. Above the conventional triple doors, two plain storeys each with three windows are topped by twin towers with a pediment between, in which a niche holds a statue of St Francis. Here, the Manueline spirit steals in again in the slender turret-like design of the octagonal towers. Other than the façade, the rest of the exterior is extremely plain and the belfry is added on to the north-eastern corner seemingly almost as an afterthought.

As in many cases, however, the exterior belies what is to be found inside, without doubt one of the most beautiful church interiors in Goa. As your eyes adjust to the light, the overall effect is breathtaking.

The simplicity of both its plan and its structure enhances the effect of superb decoration. There are no aisles, just the immense nave, which is wider than that of Wren's St Paul's, while above is the Indian planed groin vault at its most effective, the merging of the ribbing into the panelling causing the upper part of the church to appear to be floating in light.

Internal buttresses create six chapels, three on each side, and support the gallery above. The buttresses, pilasters and arches are magnificently decorated with floral designs, and especially impressive is the massive arch that supports the choir at the western end, spanning the full width of the nave.

The floral theme appears again in the exquisitely carved pulpit on the left. It also has a fine painting of St Francis of Assisi feeding the fishes. Beyond, a wooden statue of St Francis stands on a pedestal.

Old Goa: Espirito Santo, St Francis of Assisi, decorated arch spanning the width of the nave.

Much of the floor is composed of memorial slabs.

At the eastern end, an unusually deep and high-vaulted chancel provides a perfect setting for the main altar and its reredos. The tall, narrow windows flood the chancel with light and again the airiness deriving from the planing of the ribs of the vaulting enhances the overall effect of ethereal loftiness.

At the front, two small altars flank the entrance to the chancel like golden sentinels. Inside, the walls are hung with large paintings, in oil on wood, of scenes from the life of St Francis of Assisi. Framed in a repeat of the floral panelling of the ceiling, their glowing colours add to the richness of the setting of the main altar.

The main altar and its reredos fill the whole of the eastern wall with faded gold. Again, the emphasis is on the vertical with the soaring columns, although heavily decorated at their base, being

Detail of pulpit in the church of St Francis of Assisi.

Old Goa: Espirito Santo, St Francis of Assisi, the main altar.

plainly fluted above. Between are two compartments on each side for statues of the Apostles with a large central bay for the tabernacle. High above this, Christ on the Cross has one arm freed to embrace St Francis, who stands on a pedestal on which are inscribed his three vows of Poverty, Humility and Obedience.

A fitting climax to an inspired creation.

Leaving the church by the main entrance, there is, just inside the door, an intriguing cameo, the holy water basin resting on a pedestal which is part of a pillar from a Hindu temple, its decoration of beaded garlands still intact.

The convent building on the right now houses the Archaeological Museum which is well worth a visit (See Appendix I).

Take note of the octagonal piazza cross that stands in front of the church, one of the oldest examples, built in the 1660s at the same time as the church.

Continuing beyond to the road at the end of the

garden in front of the museum, and turning to the right, brings the traveller to the site of what was the first Christian church to be built in Goa, the Church of St Catherine.

THE CHURCH OF ST CATHERINE

To commemorate the taking of Old Goa on St Catherine's Day 1510, Afonso Albuquerque had a mud and palm leaf church built for immediate use and dedicated it to the Saint. The site chosen here, on the slope down to the river, was a key point in the battle for the city. Three years later it was replaced by a stone building. In 1539, the tiny church was raised in status by official decree to become the Cathedral of the Diocese of Goa and was enlarged in 1550. An inscription preserved on the outside wall of the present church translated reads:

Here was the gateway through which Afonso de Albuquerque entered and took the city from the

Moors on the day of St Catherine in the year 1510, in whose honour and memory the Governor, Joao Cabral, had this church built in 1550 at His Majesty's expense.

Renovated in 1952, the chapel has a simple dignified façade with twin towers that goes well with the rich red of the exposed laterite walls, its simplicity making it seem very much at home, rather than incongruously foreign, in its setting of waving palms. It is currently undergoing further restoration.

At this point we are near the site of the famous Royal Hospital, the first hospital in India. Run by the Jesuits, it was reputed to be at least the equal of any in Europe at that time. All traces have disappeared, as have any signs of the great Arsenal whose massive walls once towered to the left of this chapel, filling the space between here and the river.

Returning to the square we now cross to the dark bulk of the church on the far side. On the way, in the centre of the garden, is the pedestal where once stood the splendid statue of the poet Luis Vaz de Camoes. He arrived in Goa in 1553 and wrote the epic *The Lusiads*, describing Vasco da Gama's voyage to India and Portugal's conquest of her eastern empire. His statue was not erected until 1960, just before the Portuguese were evicted, their final contribution to Old Goa. It has now been removed.

Ahead lies Goa's most famous church, the Basilica of Bom Jesus, the Good Jesus.

THE BASILICA OF BOM JESUS – built 1594–1605

Attached to the Basilica is the Professed House of the Jesuits. Completed in 1585, before the church was started, it was from here that the Jesuits sent out their missionaries all over the east. The building is now deserted, but it is appropriate that in the nearby Basilica lies the body of one of the greatest of all Jesuit missionaries, St Francis Xavier.

The plaster has been removed from the outside of the church itself and the dark red laterite shows the effect of weathering. Its bulk is increased by the huge buttresses on the open wall facing the square.

Old Goa: St Catherine's, the first church raised by the Portuguese in 1539.

Old Goa: The Basilica of Bom Jesus.

The three-storeyed façade exhibits three classical orders: Doric, Ionic and Corinthian – the columns and pilasters in light-coloured basalt from Bassein, nearly 300 miles away to the north, contrasting pleasantly with the red of the laterite. There are no towers, but the three storeys are surmounted by an elaborately decorated pediment, the main feature being the Jesuit emblem IHS (the first three letters of 'Jesus' in Greek). This centrepiece is flanked by a classical fan motif.

This is one of the most attractive of the façades of the larger Goan churches to have survived and deserves more than a casual glance, its delicate carving and colours showing to best advantage in the late afternoon.

The squat belfry tower is at the far end of the church.

The church is true cruciform in plan and the simplicity of the nave itself, once barrel-vaulted, now with a new wooden ceiling, contrasts dramatically with the dominating reredos of the main altar.

Immediately to the left as you enter the church is

Old Goa: Bom Jesus, the main altar, with Ignatius Loyola above the diminutive Christ-child.

a statue of St Francis Xavier.

Inscriptions on the two columns, one in Portuguese and one in Latin record the start of building in 1594 and its consecration in 1605. On the right-hand column is another plaque commemorating the elevation to a Basilica Minor in 1946. Otherwise, the spaciousness of the nave is uninterrupted.

The pulpit, to the right, is yet another example of the skills of local craftsmen. On the wall opposite is the memorial to the Captain of Cochin, Dom Jeronimo Mascarenhas, who, when he died in 1593, bequeathed the funds for the building of the church.

The reredos, itself a wall of gold filling the far end of the church with light, soars up into the high panelled vault of the huge arch within which it is framed. The massive spiralling columns represent the Baroque in full flower, as does the large central compartment. Above the pedestal, decorated with elaborately carved panels, the composition is dominated by the huge, heavily moustachioed figure of St Ignatius Loyola, founder of the Jesuit order, who

Old Goa: Bom Jesus, St Francis Xavier.

Old Goa: Bom Jesus, altar dedicated to St Michael, which stands on the right hand at the end of the nave.

towers over the tiny infant Jesus to whom the church is dedicated. This central compartment is flanked by huge salomonic columns, cleverly highlighted by the introduction of a plain fluted pilaster on either side. Ignatius Loyola gazes upwards at a symbolic sun flowing above him with the initials IHS. Above this again in the gloom of the high, panelled, barrel vault is the Holy Trinity.

The end wall of the nave framing the chancel arch is a complementary mass of intricate Baroque splendour with the altar of Mary, as Our Lady of Hope, on the left, and St Michael on the right, completing what is a dazzling spectacle.

This naturally dominates the nave, but in spite of all, this is St Francis Xavier's church and pilgrims and visitors head unerringly for the side-chapel to the right of the main altar.

Sit quietly and rest awhile while reading his story (see Appendix II).

St Francis Xavier

On the arrival of the body in Goa in 1554, it was placed in St Francis's favourite retreat, the Chapel of St Paul's College. In 1613 it was transferred to the Professed House next to Bom Jesus. After his canonisation in 1622, it was moved into the church itself, where it lay in the chapel in the north transept on the left. With the construction of the new Sacristy in 1654, there was more room in the transept on the opposite side and in 1659 the coffin, in a new silver casket, was transferred across the church and put on display on a trestle. Then, nearly 40 years later, the catafalque from Florence was erected.

Here he lies in the elaborate silver casket which rests on top of an equally impressive catafalque.

Old Goa: Bom Jesus, St Francis Xavier in his silver casket on top of the catafalque from Italy.

Death of St Francis – one of the bronze panels on the catafalque.

Although the two were designed at different times and on different continents they complement each other perfectly.

The catafalque came from Italy, given by the Grand Duke of Tuscany in exchange for the pillow on which St Francis's head had rested in his coffin. It is the work of the Florentine sculptor Giovanni Foggini and was sent in pieces to Goa, being assembled in the Bom Jesus in 1698. It has three tiers.

The base is of red and purple jaspar onto which decorative sculptures in white marble have been superimposed.

The second tier is of marble, with bronze plaques on each of the four sides depicting scenes from the life of the Saint in bas-relief. Over each plaque, angels unwind an inscribed scroll:

1. Preaching in the Moluccas – over which is the inscription *Nox Inimica Fugat* (All hostilities are put to flight).

2. Baptising converts – over which is *Ut Vitam Habeant* (That they may have life).

3. Swimming to escape wild savages of Moro –

over which was *Nihil Horum Vereor* (I fear none of these things).

4. His death at Sancian – *Major in Occasu* (Greater in setting).

These bronze panels set into the marble are each flanked by panels containing sculpted lilies, at that time an emblem often associated with St Francis. On the nave side is also hung the coat-of-arms of the Xavier family.

Above this, the third tier is a balustraded plinth in beautiful variegated marble on which the silver casket rests.

The casket was made by Indian silversmiths in 1637, a most exquisite piece of craftsmanship. The sides were divided into sixteen double panels in which scenes of the Saint's life are portrayed. Each panel is framed with intricately fretted patterns. Above, the complex design continues with a row of angels, each one different, interspersed with urn-shaped pinnacles. A curved lid supports a pedestal in which the shape of the casket is repeated and on which a cross completes the beautifully proportioned whole. Originally, inset precious stones added to the richness of the total effect.

Since its arrival in Goa in 1554, the body has been subjected to public or private exposition many times. In the formal exposition of 1952, held over a period of 35 days, 817,000 people kissed the relics of the Saint; following this it was decided that the actual touching of the body by pilgrims was accelerating the deterioration of the sacred relics and a glass casket was ordered from Rome. In 1955, the body was transferred to this from its wooden coffin that had lain inside the silver casket. It is in this glass casket that the body has been shown at all subsequent expositions.

In 1977, it was decided that, to satisfy the growing number of pilgrims to the Basilica, all seven of the upper panels on the nave side should be removed, giving some view, however unclear, of the sacred relics. This also required the removal of a silver statue of St Francis that formerly stood above the Xavier shield and is now in the Sacristy.

Paintings relating to the Saint's life cover the walls of the chapel.

Beyond is a corridor leading to the Sacristy which has a superbly carved wooden door that itself is

Cloisters at the professed house which stand next to the Bom Jesus Basilica.

worthy of attention. Among the many treasures kept in this exceptionally large sacristy are a toe of St Francis in a glass case, the silver statue removed from the tomb when one side was opened, and the Golden Rose, awarded by the Pope to Goa in 1953 for its services to the Church, especially as a missionary centre.

In the corridor are photographs and paintings relating to the state of the Saint's body.

Near to the doors to the Sacristy, stairs lead up to a gallery above containing a collection of unusual paintings by a Goan painter Dom Martin.

To the left, on returning down the staircase, is the entrance to an arcaded courtyard. If a few moments of peace are necessary, this court, linking the Basilica with the Professed House, will provide it. Leave through the Professed House.

While the Basilica receives a constant stream of pilgrims and other visitors, there is one day each year when the great church is full to overflowing, with crowds surging outside. This is on 3 December, the anniversary of St Francis's death in far-away China.

From the Basilica, return along the road to Panjim and at the end of the gardens of the Basilica take a road that forks left up the hill through the trees. This is the Monte Santo, the 'Holy Hill'.

THE MONTE SANTO

The first building on the left at a fork in the road is the **Monastery of St John of God**. Built at the beginning of the 18th century, it has had various occupants and is now a home for old people.

Much more impressive is the three-storeyed building on the right with the road running under its huge flying buttresses, the **Convent of St Monica**. Built in 1606, this was the first nunnery in the east, and soon became the largest and the richest. With the banning of the religious orders it was not closed down, but recruiting was forbidden and numbers dwindled. Eventually it fell into decay, but was only abandoned when the last sister died in 1885, a poignant piece of history. From 1954 the building was taken over by the Portuguese army as a barracks and by Indian troops from 1962. Handed back to the church in 1968, it is now happily well restored, the ladies have taken over again and it serves as a Mae de Deus Institute, a college for nuns from all over India. Built round a courtyard with rooms opening off its cloisters, it has eleven chapels.

The road to the left leads to the dramatic remnant of the Augustinian Monastery. All that is left of what was once one of the largest buildings in Goa is

Old Goa: Convent of St Monica.

Old Goa: Tower of N.S. da Graca, with a statue of St Augustine.

half of one of the towers of the **Church of Our Lady of Grace**. Completed in 1602, it was one of the great churches built at the same time as the Cathedral and the Basilica. Its façade was five-storeyed with twin towers 40 metres high, the highest of any in the city. Remarkably, the remaining half tower is its full original height.

With the final suppression and eviction of the Orders, the monastery was abandoned in 1835. Within seven years the huge barrel-vaulted ceiling had collapsed and in 1846 the Monastery and College buildings were pulled down, leaving only the shell of the church. The façade survived until 1931, when this too collapsed, leaving only the half tower that still remains.

The largest bell in the church, the second largest in Goa giving precedence only to the great Golden Bell in the Cathedral, was removed and now rings from the Church of Our Lady of the Immaculate Conception on the hill in Panjim.

On the other side of the road is the **Royal Chapel of St Anthony**, dedicated to Portugal's national saint and the patron saint of the army and navy. Because of this connection, St Anthony was actually gazetted as an officer and an annual 'salary' was included in the state budget. Each year, on his feast day, his statue was taken in procession to collect his dues. In 1838, the Governor, Baron de Sabroso, decided that this practice should be stopped. On 13 June, the Saint's feast day, he fell from his carriage and was almost killed. St Anthony's pay was restored! In 1894, Governor Vila Nova de Ourem was considering cancelling the traditional holiday on St Anthony's feast day. He fell from his horse, took the hint and abandoned the idea.

One of the earliest of Goa's chapels, built at the direction of Afonso Albuquerque to celebrate a particularly critical encounter during the taking of the city, it was abandoned in 1835 on the departure of the Augustinians. Brought back into use at the end of the 19th century, the last governor, Vassalo da Silva, an army general himself, had the chapel rebuilt just before the Portuguese left in 1961. It is of particular interest for the semi-circular apse superimposed on a plain façade. Following the road that runs in front of Santa Monica we come to the high western bluff of the Monte Santo. Here, dramatically sited on the edge of a steep cliff, stands another of the earliest Goan churches, the **Church of Our Lady of the Rosary**, built to fulfil a vow made by Albuquerque while watching the progress of the attack from this vantage point. There is an inscription referring to the victory:

Old Goa: Royal Chapel of St Anthony, Monte Santo.

Old Goa: Our Lady of the Rosary: simple interior of the church.

From here on 25th November 1510 Afonso Albuquerque watched the battle that was to lead to his conquest of Goa.

The first simple church, built on this site soon after the conquest, is recorded as being used by St Francis to teach the catechism to children in the first year of his arrival in Goa, 1542. He also preached to huge crowds on this hill-top and one can easily imagine these inspiring scenes. It was raised to the status of a parish church in 1544 and the present church was built not long afterwards, being consecrated early in 1549. It would have been in the process of completion when St Francis returned to Goa in November 1548 for six months and in full use during his last fleeting visit in 1552. It is not only the oldest of Old Goa's monuments but 'the only surviving edifice in the city whose pavement was trodden by Xavier's feet.'[2] It is worthy of careful preservation if only for this, but there are other reasons.

The exterior is of interest as the only real example of Manueline style architecture surviving in Goa. This particular style, dominant in Portugal at the beginning of the 16th century when King Manuel was on the throne, hence its name, never took root here, partly because its characteristic arrangement of windows, high under the roofline, was impractical for the west coast of India but also because its decorative themes, derived as they were from Portuguese sea-faring links, strangely held little appeal for Indian craftsmen. It reflected Portuguese pride in their dominance at sea at that time, with ships, ropework, waves and sea shells much in evidence.

At its western end is a square, three-storeyed bell tower with twin rounded corner buttresses and stair turrets to the belfry giving it its oft commented-on fortress-like air. There is little exterior decoration, apart from the typical twisted ropework moulding on the towers.

The church is now disused, opened only on special occasions, but its interior demonstrates a complex mix of influences. The whole of this small church is a delight. The unadorned tiled roof over the high wooden beamed nave contributes to the atmosphere, and the delicate simplicity of the main reredos, set in its Gothic-ceilinged chapel which is itself a reminder of earlier times, is restful after the gilded extravagance of other churches. An impressive reredos in the side chapel with its many small niches, each with an intricately carved wooden figure, is a treasure that demands time to appreciate its details. This is certainly the oldest surviving reredos in Goa.

Old Goa: The church of Our Lady of the Rosary.

Old Goa: Our Lady of the Rosary.

The church contains the grave of Governor Garcia de Sa, who died in 1549 and was in office when this church was consecrated earlier that year. He lies beneath a memorial slab in front of the chancel. His wife, Caterina a Piro, who was the first Portuguese lady to set foot in Goa, is also buried here, her marriage to the Governor sanctified only on her deathbed, legend has it by Francis Xavier himself. She has a marble tomb in the chancel: it is one of the earliest examples of local craftsmen exercising their influence on decorative motifs, the designs here showing distinctive Gujarati characteristics. Around a doorway on the opposite side are intriguing signs of graffito-style decoration.

From the hill-top there are fine views across the Mandovi River to the islands of Divar and Chorao and westwards across the swamps to Panjim.

The remaining monuments of interest in Old Goa are to the east of the Basilica of Bom Jesus.

The **Archway of the Church of St Paul and the Ruins of the College** lie about a kilometre from the Basilica on the road to Ponda and the important group of Hindu temples only about ten km further away. The college was founded in 1541, the first western-style university in Asia, originally as the Seminario da Santa Fe, the Seminary of the Holy Faith. The object was to train local youths so that they could work as missionaries amongst their own people, and the Jesuits became involved immediately upon their arrival.

The first grammar of any of India's modern Aryan languages, in this case Konkani, was largely produced here. The huge archway of the entrance to the church known as 'St Paul of the Arches', built 1560–72, is all that remains, although the work started here still continues at Rachol Seminary today.

It was in the small chapel attached to the seminary that St Francis retired at nights for solitude and prayer and it was here that his body was placed when it first arrived in Goa in 1554. The chapel, first built in 1575, is near to the Portal of the College, the present chapel being built in 1884 and known quite naturally as the **Chapel of St Francis Xavier**.

If you really want to get away from the madding crowd, and if you have a little time and energy to spare, then visit the **Church of Our Lady of the Mount** – well worth both the time and the effort. After the splendours of the great churches below, it and the main road to Ponda (see map 2). This route is motorable to within a short walking distance of the church. Fork right at the Palm Grove Bar and when, further on, another fork is reached with a cross at the junction, again take the right fork. From here it is a short pleasant walk through bamboo, cashew and fish-tail palms with their cascades of hanging fruit, together with an abundance of bird life.

The church is deserted and decaying, but the atmosphere reaches out to you as you approach. Vegetation encroaches on the red laterite stairway, a cashew tree standing guard in the middle. Once a huge banyan tree spreading its tentacles at the top of the steps threatened the church and this has sadly had to be destroyed.

A simple church with a tiled roof and, all across its front, a tiled porchway, it signals its desertion, but any feeling you will have that, for centuries, no-one else has trodden these steps is shattered by a multitude of graffiti, of the modern not the decorative variety. No matter, there is a feeling of deep calm and remoteness here.

Old Goa: Central doorway of S. Paolo dos Arcos, St Paul of the Arches, 1560–72, within the college of St Paul.

has little to offer by way of gilt and glitter but everything in terms of peace and atmosphere.

The church can be approached from two directions. Almost another kilometre beyond the Chapel of St Francis Xavier on the main road to Ponda, is a painted stone cross on the left-hand side. At this point a rough track, motorable for only part of the way, climbs up the hillside. Make sure to fork left about 250 metres from the cross. Here, you are in the land of the bamboo-cutters with evidence of their activities all around. Soon, the red-tiled roof can be glimpsed on the hill to the right and the track soon brings you to the long shallow flight of steps leading up to the church.

The alternative and better approach, especially with transport, is from the roundabout in Old Goa to take the road between that leading to the river

Old Goa: The church of Our Lady of the Mount (the mango tree, sadly, is no more.)

View of Old Goa and beyond, from the steps of the church of Our Lady of the Mount.

From the steps and the terrace of the church, through tangled bushes, there is a splendid view over Old Goa and the river. In the foreground, St Cajetan, the Cathedral and St Francis of Assisi rise above the groves of palm. Beyond, on Monte Santo, the finger of the solitary tower of St Augustine has, on its right, the Church of Our Lady of the Rosary, from whose hill Albuquerque directed his battle.

Here, where we now stand, Yusuf Adil Khan posted his artillery, first in May 1510 when he retook the city following its first capture by Albuquerque, as is recorded on a plaque on the side wall near the front entrance, and again during his unsuccessful defence against Albuquerque's second attack in November, after which the triumphant general ordered this built as one of his votive churches.

The church façade with its sprouting tufts of grass is simple, dignified and different from most other small chapels. All seems to be locked and barred, but at the far end on the left-hand side, a friendly door gives access.

Darkly quiet, the nave is plain and barrel-vaulted, the decoration of the walls peeling, the pulpit gone. A few dusty plain wooden benches remain. The main altar is dedicated to Our Lady, a compartmented reredos, above an elegantly simple altar-piece, containing paintings that still retain hints of their rich colourings as do those on the walls and ceilings of the chancel. The niche in the centre is now empty, as is that in the flanking altar to the left. These side altars are dedicated to St Anthony and St Andrew.

There are several memorial slabs in the dusty floor, the one in front of the main altar marking the burial place of the architect of the church, Antonio Alvares Pereira, one of the early Portuguese arrivals in Goa. The slab bears a rough skull and cross bones and a plea to say an Ave Maria for him.

One further monument remains to be mentioned – **The Pillory**. Unimposing and standing in a corner near modern houses, this stone pillar on a raised

platform is made up of two separate sections of pillars taken from an ancient Hindu temple, almost certainly the original Saptakoteshwar Temple on the island of Divar. The upper section is round with a plain circular capital, while the lower part is octagonal resting on a square base. In the centre, where the two sections are joined together by means of iron brackets, there is a band of sculpted decoration. This was used by the Portuguese as a pillory where law-breakers were tortured, flogged and put on display. More striking than the pillar itself is the realisation that this was at the centre of one of the main market squares of the Golden City. Thinking back to our starting point, on what used to be the massive quaysides on the river-front more than two km distant, drives home the concept of the great city that once thrived here.

Old Goa: The Pillory, built of two sections of pillars of a Hindu temple, probably Saptakoteshwar on the island of Divar.

10 THE OLDEST CONQUEST – EXPLORING TISWADI

Cabo Raj Niwas – Dona Paula – Goa Velha – Agasaim – Pilar Monastery – The Church of San- tana – The Island of Divar – St. Estevam.

This tiny area, one of the smallest of the talu- kas, encapsulates much of the spirit of Goa. Less than 20 km across in any direction, this was the core of Portuguese India. Known to them as the *Ilhas*, the Islands, it consists of the main 'Island of Goa' created by the Mandovi and Zuari Rivers, together with the Cumbarjua waterway linking them in the east, and, in addition, there are the smaller islands in the channel of the Mandovi itself, Chorao, Divar, Vanxim and Jua (map 3). Even today there are only three ways to cross by road from the mainland to the main island and, at two of these three, ferries have been replaced by bridges only relatively recently. The exception is the long-established bridge over the much narrower water- way at Banasterim. The Jawarhalal Nehru Bridge over the Mandovi, linking Panjim with Bardez, was only opened in 1970 and the bridge over the Zuari in 1983.

This was the first area conquered by the Portu- guese and, for the first thirty years or so, their only foothold. But it was the key to the whole of this west coast territory and has been so for many centuries, long before the Portuguese had ever heard of Gowapuri. From the 8th century, Goa's future as an international trading centre was being established from here and, as a result, it was to the banks of the Zuari that Kadamba kings transferred their capital. Some of the holiest of Hindu places of pilgrimage, with temples of high renown, were here and, when the Konkan fell to the Muslim Yusuf Adil Khan, the city port, by this time transferred across the island to the Mandovi, came near to usurping Bijapur as the capital of his kingdom.

Interest naturally tends to focus on the city of Old Goa or on Panjim, the modern capital, and both of these have been dealt with separately, but there is much else of interest to be seen.

CABO RAJ NIWAS

The headland known simply as the Cabo, the Cape, has a special place in the scenery of this, the busiest stretch of Goa's coastline. It reaches out to divide and overlook the estuaries of the Mandovi and Zuari Rivers, the area focal to the history of the territory. Between Fort Aguada to the north and Mormugao to the south, the Cabo stands sentinel to the gateway to the Ilhas, the heart of Goa. It rests there quietly with its heavily wooded slopes broken by cliffs falling steeply to the rocks and sand encircling its base.

From the sea it imposes its presence as a land- mark as soon as the steamer from Bombay rounds Fort Aguada and is in distant view almost all the way across on the ferry from Mormugao to Dona Paula. Framing one end of Caranzalem Beach, it is a noble promontory with distinction added by the crown of buildings clustering on its crest above the Arabian Sea. Almost inevitably these include the white-washed façade of an ancient church, but today its claim to fame is as the site of the residence of the Governor of the State of Goa, causing it also to be known as the Cabo Raj Niwas. Unfortunately, this also means that most visitors will have little opportunity of exploring the tip of the promontory where the grounds occupy over 35 hectares.

From the arrival of the Portuguese, so fine a place has seen a succession of churches, fortresses and grand houses and at one point was even considered as the site for a new capital once the abandonment of Old Goa had been accepted as inevitable.

The first building was a small chapel, one of a group of six religious houses for which funds were approved for maintenance in 1541, which also included the churches of Panjim and Divar. On such a site, this first Cabo church would seem to have been built as much as a welcoming landmark for approaching ships as a church to serve a parish. It was dedicated to Our Lady of the Cape. In 1594, the original church was replaced by Viceroy Albuquerque with the church that survives today. He built it for the Franciscans and added a small monastery. Built at a time when architects were experimenting with new ideas, it has an unusual, pleasantly severe façade owing more to Mannerist and Manueline Portugal than to true Baroque.

In the chapel is a memorial to Dona Paula Menezes who died on 21 December 1682. The wife of Antonio de Souto Maior, she was a lady-in-waiting to the Viceroy's wife and reputedly mistress of the Viceroy. She bequeathed the land she owned to the church, including the nearby village now named after her.

The Cabo had obvious strategic significance and it had a key role in the defence of the Portuguese colony, a role acknowledged as early as 1540. Early in the 17th century, with huge fortresses being built on the headlands of Aguada and Mormugao, the Cabo was reconstructed to provide supporting crossfire for these two, although it was always designed mainly as an artillery platform rather than a stronghold to resist direct attacks.

All Goa's forts had drifted into decline by the end of the 18th century but the Cabo experienced what was then an unwelcome, though brief, return to a military life-style. British troops made it one of their bases during their 'occupation' of Goa during the Napoleonic Wars and apart from their withdrawal for a few months during 1804, they encamped here from 1798 to 1813 (p. 10). All traces of the barracks and hospital they built have long since disappeared, but there is a poignant reminder in the **British cemetery** which lies just outside the

The British cemetery, Cabo Raj Niwas.

gates of the Governor's residence. After the departure of the troops, the cemetery continued in use for the handful of British families living in or near Goa, mainly military personnel or railway employees. The last burial was in 1912, an employee of the Madras Southern Maratha Railway. Little remains of the fort itself except for a few ruined walls.

In 1844, ten years after the abolition of the religious orders and the departure of the Franciscans, the monastery and chapel were handed over to the Diocese of Goa for use as the Archbishop's residence. Conversion, including the cells and cloisters, turned it into a splendid mansion; perhaps too splendid, for in 1866 the Viceroy took it over for use as his country house and in 1918 moved in permanently, leaving the Idalcao Palace free for other civic duties. Several further changes were made including the long glassed-in verandahs supported by slender iron pillars that are now such a feature of the house.

In 1961, defying the orders of Prime Minister Salazar to destroy everything before leaving, the last Governor General handed over the house intact, with all its treasures, mirrors and chandeliers, china and glass, paintings and superb old black rosewood furniture. It must be the best preserved of Goa's great houses, yet stands apart because of its complex origins and the way it has evolved rather than being built to a single masterplan.

On the cape, behind the Governor's residence, the National Institute of Oceanography has taken over the landscape.

DONA PAULA

Just beyond and below the Cabo, another finger of land points out into the sea. This is Dona Paula, made up of delightful rocky bays and inlets with a fishing village nestling on the sheltered side of the point. This is the land bequeathed to the church in the 17th century by the lady of the Cabo chapel inscription. There are no other memorials to Dona Paula here, only her name and the many legends that surround her, mainly revolving around her lovers and her emerging from moonlit waves wearing only a pearl necklace. However, there is an intriguing white sculpture on the rocks near the point. *Image of India* by Baroness Yrsa von Leistner, portrays a man and a woman together – he, older, looks back over his shoulder contemplating the past, she gazes thoughtfully ahead into the future and what it may hold. The inscription reads, 'Lead me from untruth to truth, from darkness to light and from death to immortality.' Such sombre

Images of India: Dona Paula.

thoughts contrast with the almost festive air that usually prevails at the very tip of the promontory. Several circumstances combine to produce the bustle that concentrates on an otherwise peaceful bit of Goan landscape. The ferry to Mormugao, linking Tiswadi with the south, has its terminal here. The ferry takes no cars, no buses, only people, and is an experience in itself, worth going if only just for the ride there and back. In fact, there is little in Mormugao or Vasco to attract a visitor counting precious hours. As a practical way to travel, the ferry is to be recommended, although it is almost a sea voyage, crossing right at the mouth of the estuary, and rough weather should be avoided. It does not operate during the monsoon.

A bus service completes the link with Panjim only seven km away. The bus system of Goa not only gets you to almost anywhere, it does so in flamboyant if crowded style. An expanded, modern version of the *caminhao*, the old country bus now part of folklore, it is still a country bus in spirit and

inherits much from its ancestors. These buses, with drivers under the protection of a judicious mix of Christian and Hindu fairy-lit garlanded benefactors, and controlled by whistle-blowing conductors, reincarnated magicians in confining so many reluctantly willing victims in such a small space, hurtle backwards and forwards bringing the capital within easy reach.

Apart from being a staging post on this particular route from north to south, Dona Paula has other attractions that bring the tourist buses on their whistle-stop tours. Here, you are on the edge of the open sea, and the rocky platform on the highest part of the point gives one of Goa's finest sea views. To meet the needs of all these travellers and tourists, stalls crowd along the jetty, offering straw hats, sunglasses and T-shirts as well as refreshment.

From the viewpoint, a wide sea horizon sweeps round from Cabo to Mormugao, with the estuary of the Zuari River in between. This is usually a hive of subdued activity with ore barges shuttling round from the Mandovi and fishing boats of all shapes and sizes coming and going together with the ferries. In the distance below the skyline lie the ore-carriers and an assortment of cargo ships from many different parts of the world, all against the background of Mormugao harbour, currently India's fourth largest port in terms of volume handled. The cranes and derricks of the massive ore-handling terminal stretch low along the river front.

Looking down on all this modern activity are the battlements of the old fort of Mormugao. On rare occasions such as Republic Day, the dull boom of guns firing ceremonial salutes from there, with smoke drifting above the ramparts, chases the

'Feri Bôt': Dona Paula to Mormugao.

imagination back four centuries to times of galleons, cannon balls and grapeshot. More recent battle scenes took place here in World War II, ending in the sinking of three German ships and one Italian vessel in these waters in 1943 (p. 11). Another war-time incident was the choice of neutral Goa by the American and Japanese governments for the exchange of prisoners-of-war and civilians. The Americans chartered a Swedish vessel, the Japanese used one of their own merchant fleet, and in October 1943 these two ships anchored here in Mormugao harbour and about 1500 POWs were exchanged between the two vessels.[1]

Nearer at hand, the water-scooters buzz busily and, apart from joy-riding, can be used to reach the main sweep of Dona Paula beach. Further upstream the silhouetted outline of the distant road bridge over the Zuari marks where the first great port of Goa once stood nearly 1000 years ago.

GOA VELHA

To have two Old Goas seems unnecessarily confusing, but both can lay claim to the title and both are abandoned capitals. Velha Goa, the city of churches, is old, Goa Velha, which once was a city of temples, is much older and perhaps its Konkani name was more appropriate: Voddlem Goa – Great Goa.

Now that traffic from the airport rushes across the new bridge from Cortalim to the north bank of the Zuari River, the village of Agasaim has come and gone almost before the traveller is aware of it and Goa Velha which follows is dispersed over such a wide area, straggling along either side of the road, that this too passes without making any great impact. When there was an enforced pause to cross by ferry, there was more time to contemplate the far shore but, even so, there is little left to indicate that here was the real birthplace of Goa's international future. Even the shoreline has undergone physical change with the heavy silting that has taken place in the 1200 years since it began its emergence as the greatest sea-port on India's western shores and the point on which trade routes would converge, first from all round the Indian Ocean and later from all around the world.

The peoples of those western seas, the Persian Gulf and the Red Sea, were great sailors and efficient traders. Before the sea-route round the Cape of Good Hope was conquered, their land connections with the Mediterranean made them the natural link between Europe and the East. Traders from Mesopotamia and Egypt had long been travelling to many ports on India's west coast but, from the 8th century onwards, Goa's importance slowly but steadily increased, eventually, for a time, to supersede all others. The Zuari River became a focal point and Arab traders began to settle on its banks.

Under the Kadamba kings, the volume of trade and, as importantly, the size and power of their own naval fleet increased to the point where, in 1052, the capital was transferred here. By this time, the names by which the port was known at various times, Gopakpuri, Gopakapattana, Gowapuri, or simply Gove, had become familiar to many traders across many seas.

The waters of the Zuari ran deep in those days and sheltered inland waterways provided safe anchorage. Ocean-going vessels could anchor, unload and refit far up the Siridao creek, much beyond the point where today the single-file bridge, about to be replaced, crosses the present narrow stream. Around this point there grew a fine city. Palaces, gardens and fountains spread out around the busy landing stages and shipyards. Above, looking down from high on a hilltop, was a Shiva temple, with at its foot the temple to their favourite goddess Chamunda, one of the fiercest aspects of Kali.

Success and fame attended the city for 300 years until, in 1312, its glory was literally shattered. Malik Kafur, general of the Sultan of Delhi's raiding troops, razed the city to the ground. The Kadambas fled south across the river back to Chandrapur, incidentally taking with them Chamunda's emaciated image. She would eventually be reinstated in a temple at Piligao in Bicholim taluka, to which people of Goa Velha still make pilgrimage. (See p. 3).

Although life trickled back into Gowapuri, and the subsequent peace of Vijayanagar rule revived trade, especially in horses, the city had lost its aura of success. In any case, as a port it was already condemned to slow extinction, the silting-up process already beginning to stifle its creeks and, for ocean-going vessels, threaten its access to the sea. By the time another Muslim incursion under Mahmud Gawan and his Bahmani regiments swept across the country, in 1470, knocking over what was left of Gowapuri, a successor city had already emerged. Across the island, on the banks of the Mandovi, a new Gove, Velha Goa of today, had been born, taking over from its parent, Goa Velha, its functions as port and capital as well as its name.

Nothing now remains of the parent city, or rather grand-parent, as Velha Goa subsequently spawned Nova Goa, now more affectionately known as Panjim. The more ancient capital's existence is recorded on a sad noticeboard, which you would need to be quick to spot amongst the palms at the side of the main road, but it still has something more than a history lesson to offer. Agasaim has an 18th-century church of especial interest. Shiva's hilltop houses one of Goa's two remaining seminaries, and Goa Velha itself celebrates a Christian festival unique in Goa, almost in the world.

Approaching Goa Velha from Panjim, an important part of the village lies at its northern end, centring on the **Church of St Andrew** in its dusty square set back from the main road. The church itself, a good example of a solid parish church with few embellishments, is the scene of a festival during Easter celebrations that is unique in Goa. On the first Monday of Passion Week, the annual *Procession of Saints* takes place.

The procession dates back to the 17th century when it was started by Franciscans, typifying the colourful ceremony and pomp of the times. Dozens of life-sized statues of saints, richly robed and bejewelled, were taken out on palanquins, their paraded virtues being an example for the people to follow. After the banning of the religious orders in 1835, the procession lapsed and many of the statues disappeared or fell into a state of disrepair. When the Franciscans began to filter back into Goa half a century later, the members of the Reformed Franciscan Order were attached to the Church of St

San Lourenco, St Lawrence, Agasaim.

Andrew and, in 1895, a subscription was raised to enable new statues to be made and the procession revived.

There are now twenty-six statues altogether, all beautifully garmented and decorated. The procession used to visit all the surrounding villages but now, starting from in front of the church, it winds its way along the four principal roads of Goa Velha before returning to the square. Here the floats are arranged for display, bedecked with flowers and candles, and a service is held. It is a memorable event attended by large crowds. The statues are on show in the church for two days before being put into store for another year.

At the opposite end of the village, not far from the end of the road bridge over the Zuari, Goa Velha merges into Agasaim, in older days right on the river and the original Arab settlement. Here is the **Church of St Lawrence**.

ST LAWRENCE'S CHURCH
– SAN LOURENCO –
AGASAIM

It is eminently appropriate that this church should be dedicated to the patron saint of sailors, even though by the time even the earliest church had been built on this site, its significance as a port had long vanished. Built in the 18th century, today's small church provides one of the outstanding examples of Rococo art in Goa. It is part of a small group of buildings which includes a school and a large cross at the top of the slope up from the road.

The church exterior follows the pattern of many churches built at this time, being severely plain almost as if to counter-balance its exotic interior. In particular, it contains one of the finest examples of a reredos, the backdrop to the altar, that demonstrates to the full the spirit and techniques of true Rococo. There is a side entrance, the porch forming one arm of the cruciform plan, while opposite is a side chapel to Our Lady of Carmel. However, it is the backdrop to the main altar that claims attention.

The movement and intense detail is almost overwhelming in its humble setting, the gilded mass swirling against the blue background. The central section is projected forwards, giving great depth to the whole composition, an impression amplified by the high relief of the carving and the superimposition of a multitude of elaborate candelabra, together with features such as the figures framed in scroll-work at the front corners. Above and behind the tabernacle, the shadows of the central space, dramatically flanked by triple salomonic columns,

San Lourenco, Agasaim: main altar.

contain a statue of St Lawrence haloed by a sun-burst. The design gains in substance as it rises through several tiers into the shadows of the vault, reaching its peak in yet another aureole under a crowning canopy.

The chancel ceiling and walls complement the reredos, providing an effective frame. The ceiling is of bold square compartments in blue and white, with a simple theme of crosses, rosettes and stars. The two flanking altars in front of the chancel, although themselves elaborate, in no way compete with the main altar.

PILAR MONASTERY

Overlooking the city of Gowapuri or Gopakapat-tana rose a hill on which the Kadambas built their temple to Shiva, here worshipped as Govesvara and referred to in inscriptions of Kadamba kings as the city's presiding deity. Several remnants of the old temple have been found on the hilltop including a headless Nandi, Shiva's bull. The hilltop is in view for some considerable distance along the road through Goa Velha and Agasaim, but it is a church

and seminary that now occupies this lofty site, the Monastery of Pilar, its identity proclaimed in large letters on the white gable-end of one of the church buildings.

In 1613, Capuchin monks built this church here on the ruins of the temple, together with what they themselves described at the time as a 'University of Arts, Sciences and Technology'. They had brought with them from Spain a statue of Our Lady of Pilar and the church was dedicated to Our Lady under this name. The name derives from the time when St James was working in Spain and experiencing great difficulties in his evangelical work. Our Lady appeared there, transported by angels and standing on a pillar or column, giving him encouragement and strength to continue.

In 1835, following the expulsion of the religious orders, Pilar was abandoned and the property fell into disrepair. However, unlike many of its counterparts in Old Goa, it was not subjected to the ravages of builders seeking raw materials, only the depredations of cows in the chancel. In 1858, the Carmelites, although subject to severe restrictions, were allowed by the Government to move into the buildings and the work of restoration began. Some time later, the Archdiocese of Goa assumed responsibility for their maintenance.

With the departure of the religious orders, a heavy burden had fallen on the Diocesan priests, and while work in the parishes was maintained, the reduced numbers did not permit missionary work in new areas and there was still much to be done, especially in the New Conquests where Christianity had hardly penetrated. In 1887, in an effort to remedy the situation, Father Bento Martins with three assistants and the full support of Archbishop Valente founded the Missionary Society of St Francis Xavier and from Agonda, far to the south in Canacona, revived missionary work in Goa. In 1890, the Archbishop transferred the Missionary Society to Pilar from where they could more easily reach other areas and hopefully recruit more support.

Sadly, over the years, loss of members again reduced missionary activity and by the time Father Bento's successor died in 1936, the Society was down to only two members and on the verge of extinction. However, before this, in 1931, young seminarists at Rachol had seen the need to do more in the missionary field and had formed the Xaverian League there. In 1936, the Society having virtually ceased to function, Pilar was handed over to the League and the reformation began. The newly reformed Missionary Society of St Francis Xavier at Pilar officially came into existence in 1940 and since then has steadily grown in numbers and in its sphere of activities.

A revered member of the original society was Father Agnelo de Souza, born in 1869 in Anjuna, Bardez. After completing his schooling he went to Rachol to further his theological studies. He joined the Missionary Society in 1897 and two years later was ordained in the Cathedral at Old Goa. The next ten years were spent in meditation and prayer in seclusion at Pilar and then as missionary vicar in several places until, in 1918, he was appointed Spiritual Director at Rachol Seminary, where he worked until his death in 1927. Always the victim of ill-health, he drove himself to the utmost limits. On 19 November 1927, he collapsed while preaching in the pulpit at Rachol church and died that night. In 1939, because of his earlier connections, his body was transferred to Pilar. His followers impatiently await the completion of the long processes of beatification (and ultimate canonisation), begun over 40 years ago.

Pilar: Church of Our Lady of Pilar.

Modern Seminary Chapel, Pilar.

The site of Pilar is superb, reached by a narrow winding road that threads its way up the hill from the plains below. On arrival at the top, the fading yellow buildings of the seminary are something of a disappointment, although, once inside, the newer wing has a modern **chapel** with an impressive circular Italian marble platform and altar and stained-glass windows – created in Germany from the paintings of a Goan artist, the centrepiece of which depicts Our Lady of Pilar.

In the high, narrow, barrel-vaulted church, typical of its period, the compartmented reredos of the main altar also has as its centrepiece **Our Lady of Pilar**, this the original statue brought by the Capuchins from Spain, showing Our Lady standing on a column borne by angels. The ornate, heavily carved and gilded pulpit is a feature of the church. In the shallow alcove of the altar at the back of the church, to the right of the entrance, there are traces of delicately painted wall decoration that may once have been more widely used in the church. They deserve to be better preserved if only as a memory of what once was there. There are other frescoes here that are worthy of attention, especially in the cloisters of the courtyard.

To the right of the front of the church is the chapel containing the tomb of Father Agnelo, the object of pilgrimage for thousands of people each year. Beyond this is a **shaded courtyard**, cloistered and galleried, with frescos that give an excuse to linger, if excuse is needed, in this haven of peace. For, while the monastery is secluded, high above the busy world below and not casually accessible,

Our Lady of Pilar, brought from Spain by the Capuchins in the sixteenth century.

Pilar Seminary, Courtyard.

this is no cloistered retreat inhabited only by silent seminarists. The narrow road is lively with pilgrims drawn by Father Agnelo's presence and there seems to be a constant bustle outside the church, with stalls selling mementoes doing a thriving trade and even a shaded 'Father Agnelo's Canteen' catering to more earthly needs. Several well attended masses are held each day, but on Thursday, which is Father Agnelo's special day, they continue with hardly a break in order to cope with the stream of worshippers.

The view from the hilltop is magnificent. Once surrounded by a great city and a port full of ships and bustling trade, there is now a typically gentle Goan landscape of palms and paddy, low hillsides and waterways. To the west in the distance is the Arabian Sea, to the north there is the inevitable scattering of white churches – **St Andrews** down to

the left just visible above the palm trees in **Goa Velha**, the Curca parish church of **Our Lady of the Rosary** on the hillside opposite and immediately below, the church of the village of **Batim**. Still further away to the north-east, now isolated and almost deserted but still one of the great churches of Goa in every respect, is the Santana.

THE SANTANA AT TALAULIM

One of the largest of Goa's churches as well as one of the finest, the **Church of St Anne**, more often referred to simply as Santana, now stands in isolation, the village of Talaulim whose parish church it was, now hardly a village at all. Once a thriving community, its proximity to Old Goa, to which it was once linked directly, led to its demise for similar reasons as the nearby city, pestilence and epidemics reducing its population to practically nothing.

The first small church here was built in the 16th century and was dedicated to St Anne, the Mother of the Virgin Mary, after she had appeared to parishioners in visions as an old lady carrying a cane and wearing a hat. The present church dates from 1681, when the parish priest, Fr Francisco do Rego, started its construction. He did not live to see the completion of the building he inspired; it took until 1695, but he would surely have been well content, for it is one of the greatest of the churches that can be classed as true Indian Baroque, earning, from those well qualified to judge, the description of being 'the most sumptuous', 'an architectural jewel', 'a true masterpiece' and 'the most perfect'. It embodies all the features that characterise this peculiarly Indian development and on a scale that cannot fail to impress. Cracked and peeling plaster and encroaching vegetation cannot detract from its

dignified and imposing presence and it is happily at last receiving the attention it requires to ensure that it will survive for future generations to appreciate and delight in.

Based on the Augustinian church of Our Lady of Grace at Old Goa, of which only half a tower still remains, the façade of the Santana is without doubt the most imposing of this outstanding group of

Detail of the façade of Santana.

churches. Its five generous storeys enable it to counter the broadness of the towers with their flattened balustrades of such unusual design, each spindle having its own small pinnacle, and the central section is emphasised by the use of coupled fluted Corinthian pilasters decreasing in size on each successive storey, until the elaborate gable provides a fitting climax that focuses the attention.

The gable is a complex but effective mixture of designs. The shell motif, already seen in a much earlier façade, that of the Bom Jesus Basilica, is used to great effect, not only in the gable but to decorate the compartments of the occuli below. In the centre a traditional St Anne looks out from her niche.

The now crumbling piazza cross in front of the church once handsomely complemented the composition of the façade.

The church is built on a cruciform plan. The nave, without aisles, gives a feeling of great spaciousness beyond the broad arch that supports the choir, the same form as used in other churches of this period, that in the Church of St Francis of Assisi being particularly dramatic. This was a feature that would be adopted later in many smaller churches. This impression of great height and space is not in any way diminished by the fact that here in Santana, two instead of the normal single tier of windows have been fitted in above the entablature that

The Church of Santana, Talaulim.

marks the level of the choir and galleries. The second entablature embraces the whole nave at the same level and above this the barrel-vaulted ceiling is pierced by groins to permit the insertion of the upper tier of windows which throw their light into the upper reaches. Emphasising the height of the nave is the fact that the chancel, while lofty enough in itself, reaches to little more than half the nave's full height.

All along each side of the nave, shallow, semi-circular, shell-headed alcoves are defined by sturdy coupled pilasters, with flattened capitals barely approximating to Corinthian in design. This free adaptation of classical orders in terms of design and decorative themes, the assertion of local influences, is more powerfully in evidence here in Santana than in any of the other Indian Baroque churches.

Above the lower level, abundant stucco work continues to cover every surface with the same flamboyant intermingling of eastern and western

St Anne, as seen in parishioners' dreams in the 17th century, wearing a hat and carrying a cane. (This wooden picture had fallen from the chancel arch, but is due to be repaired and restored to its former position.)

Interior Santana, with painting high above on the chancel arch.

themes. In the second tier, windows are framed by rounded arches topped by triangular pediments and flanked by spiralling columns, a favourite format of the day and one to be repeated here in the reredos of the main altar. The ribs of the huge vaulted ceiling are decorated with the same type of intricate patterns to be seen in close-up on the arch supporting the choir.

Above the great central bay of the main reredos, a panel in bas-relief shows Our Lady with the Infant Jesus on her lap reaching out towards his grandmother, St Anne. This is repeated in the side chapel under the choir containing the font, while in the nave above the arch of the chancel St Anne is depicted, as seen in the parishioner's visions in the 16th century, as an elderly lady wearing a hat and carrying a cane in one hand.[2] She can be found elsewhere in the church portrayed in this way, unique to Talaulim.

A gilded panel on the underside of the choir arch, Santana.

There is much to reward time spent here and on most occasions it can be enjoyed in solitude, provided you can find the sacristan! The feast day of St Anne is on 26 July.

THE ISLAND OF DIVAR

Leaving Panjim on the road to Old Goa, the island of **Chorao** comes into view almost immediately. The mangrove forests that cling to its shore contain some species not found anywhere else in India and these are being replanted and protected in order to preserve these rare examples of estuarine vegetation. Perhaps encouraged by this revival of the environment, more and more birds are flocking to the island. With its special situation where the river water meets the tidal sea, it has a combination of fresh and salt water that attracts a wide range of water birds, some of them migrants from distant parts of the world. It is hoped that this can be developed as one of India's important bird sanctuaries.

Immediately beyond Chorao is the smaller island of **Divar**. This can only be reached by ferry, either from the north bank at Naroa or from Old Goa, where it leaves from the small jetty just beyond the Arch of the Viceroys.

The island was one of the holiest of Hindu places and the object of pilgrimage for the whole of the Konkan. Even the Portuguese gave it special mention, 'Divar was as much venerated by the Hindus as the Holy Land is by us.' There were many temples on the island but two were of particular importance, especially that at the northern tip of the island in the village of Naroa. This was the temple built for the family deity of the Kadamba kings, Saptakoteshwar, a manifestation of Shiva. The other was a temple to Ganesh, or Ganapathi, high

on the hill that rises steeply from surrounding paddy-fields in the centre of the island.

The Ganesh image of this temple has had a chequered career, starting off during the period of Kadamba kingship as the main deity of the village of Ela on the banks of the Mandovi, the village that was later to become the city of Golden Goa. His was to be a story of constant upheaval and secret flights to safety. Under the Kadamba rulers, Ela was at the centre of the kingdom, fertile and wealthy and near the hub of trade, although at this stage the port of Gowapuri on the Zuari was still supreme. Ela was an important religious centre, however, with a Brahmapuri, a Brahmin centre of learning and prayer, and several famous temples. Shiva was worshipped here as Goveshwar and there was a rare temple to Saraswati, the Goddess of Knowledge.

The Muslim raids of the early 14th century saw the destruction of Ela's temples and Ganesh went into hiding for the first time. Only with the return of Hindu rule under Vijayanagar in 1378 was he able to come out of hiding and his image was installed on the superb hilltop site of Navelim here on the island of Divar. From the fragments that survive it must have been a magnificent edifice but, with the return of the Muslims in the shape of Mahmud Gawan and the Bahmani troops nearly a century later, Ganesh went into hiding again and the temple was certainly desecrated, if not totally destroyed. It is clear that in the first few years after the Portuguese conquest, while Albuquerque was in command, there was no policy of temple destruction in order to build churches. One writer records, however, that on his return to Goa in 1515

Divar Island: Piedade seen from the opposite bank of the Mandovi.

Nossa Senhora da Piedade, Divar.

When the Church of Our Lady of Divar was rebuilt in 1625 it was as **Our Lady of Compassion, Nossa Senhora da Piedade**, and it is the successor to this second church on the site of the Ganesh temple that is one of the main attractions of a visit to this pleasant island. Its situation is magnificent, the church itself being visible for miles around and, once there, offering a splendid vantage point from the shady belvedere that has been built to the south of the Church. There are especially fine views of Old Goa across the river, and to the west Panjim is bracketed between Ribander on the left and the white dot of the church of Nossa Senhora de Penha de Franca on the right – with Chorao and wide stretches of the Mandovi River in the foreground.

The present church is one of the great Indian Baroque churches that grace Goa. Started in about 1700, it was completed in 1724, its architect being the parish priest Fr. Antonio Joao de Frias, a converted Brahmin. The church he built is on a slightly smaller scale compared with others in this group, but no less impressive.

The façade is of three storeys giving an impression of great solidity and strength, the relatively wide towers and the gable design reinforcing this. The central section stands well forward from the towers, its round arched windows repeating the outline of the doors below them. This is continued in the large niche containing the Pietà with the dove of the Holy Spirit in the pediment above.

Inside, the theme of solidity continues with deep bays along the nave created by broad arches, repeated in the galleried alcoves above, and in the massive columns of the arches that frame the chancel and transepts. The stucco work, however, is delicate and restrained, picked out effectively in subdued colours. The ceiling of the nave does not have the height of the other Indian Baroque churches and, with the second tier windows set back in their alcoves, cannot produce the ethereal lightness so characteristic – even though the planed groined vaulting dissolves any gloom. It also serves to draw the eye to the chancel where shallow, shell-headed niches frame windows on either side and light also floods in from behind through the central bay of the reredos.

The reredos of the main altar is controlled and uncomplicated in design, the essence of dignified uncluttered Baroque art, while the same design effectively repeated in the two smaller side altars imparts a sense of symmetry. The altar on the left has a statue of the boy Jesus seated in the temple and that on the right St Agatha with the symbol of her martyrdom. The figures of the four evangelists in front of the tabernacle are finely carved, as are all

Albuquerque struggled from his bed, on board his ship anchored in the river, in order to see the new church on the hill, **Our Lady of Divar**. In this case there would have been no need for the destruction of the temple; this had already been done by the Muslims and Our Lady of Divar must have been one of the first churches to be built.

It also meant that Ganesh was on the move again, long before the real wave of Portuguese temple destruction began with the first law of 1541. He was one of the forerunners of refugee deities and in fact it was to him, already established in Bicholim across the river, that the people of the island of Divar decided to appeal for guidance when, in 1560, they were under enormous pressure to convert to Christianity. The boatload of young men they sent to Ganesh for guidance was captured and they were taken into custody. As a result, parents and fellow villagers capitulated and agreed to become Christians, leading to one of the first mass baptisms in Goa. As for Ganesh, his stay in Bicholim was temporary and he soon moved to Candola in Ponda.

Interior, Nossa Senhora da Piedade.

the individual statues on all the altars.

This fine church is in the process of restoration and one looks forward to being able to appreciate its beauty to the full when all is completed.

In the walled cemetery to the south of the church is a tiny, plain, square, white plastered chapel with a tiled roof. Unimpressive from the outside, it has a surprise within. This must have been a standing remnant of the Temple of Ganesh that once occupied the hilltop, as the **ceiling** consists of a heavily sculpted stone slab with a striking resemblance in style and design to the ceiling over the mandapa in the 13th century temple at Tambdi Surla. Here there are still traces of the strong colouring of the Hindu temple that contrasts with the fresco over the small altar framed by its Corinthian pilasters. Another fragment, also reminiscent of Tambdi Surla, is a piece of carved stone lattice-work inserted as a window in the chapel.

Right at the other end of the scale, in terms of size as far as churches are concerned, is the **Chapel of Our Lady of Candelaria** which, hidden amongst the trees above the river, occupies the site of the other great temple on the island, the former Saptakoteshwar Temple in the village of Naroa. This chapel is not to be confused with the newer church below the hill on the road leading to the ferry. It is a curious and fascinating structure, originally consisting only of the central circular chamber with its tiny chancel to one side. The extensions on either side are recent additions. It is thought that this was adapted directly from part of the temple still left standing when the Portuguese arrived, possibly even the garbha-griha, the temple sanctuary itself, an intriguing possibility. On the slopes of the hill just below can be seen what could have been the huge rectangular tank of the temple.

Saptakoteshwar, another form of Shiva, became the family deity of the royal family and has a history similar in many ways to that of Ganesh. The first Saptakoteshwar temple was built at Naroa in about the middle of the 12th century and was also destroyed in the early Muslim raids. However, the linga was saved and, somewhat ignominiously, buried in a paddy-field for safety. During Vijayanagar rule the temple was rebuilt by the conquering general and governor Madhav Mantri in 1391. This was its golden period, becoming the centre of pilgrimage for thousands of worshippers, especially on the day of the main festival of the temple, Gokul Ashtami, something which again demonstrates the intertwining of Shaivite and Vishnaivite worship here, this being the day on which Krishna's birth is celebrated.

Piedade: Cemetery chapel, Navelim, Divar.

Piedade: Ceiling of cemetery chapel, taken from Temple of Ganesh that was formerly on this site.

Pillory, which is made up of two sections of pillars probably from the Saptakoteshwar Temple, and the pillar supporting the font in the Church of St Francis of Assisi. There are many other items in the museum at Old Goa that give some indication of the splendour of the temples on this island of Divar.

The bank of the river below the hilltop of Our Lady of Candelaria is an interesting place either just to rest or to wait for the ferry across to the Bicholim shore. Near here, thousands of pilgrims bathed on festival days for so many centuries, and it was here that the boatload of young men attempting to cross the river to consult Ganesh were captured by the Portuguese, resulting in the mass conversion of the island's inhabitants. The Portuguese certainly knew how to turn the screw, selecting 15 August, the day of the great festival of Saptakoteshwar, for one of the first mass baptisms in Goa. On that day, amidst great pomp and

Piedade: Cemetery Chapel window. Fragment of 14th-century tracery from the Ganesh Temple on this site.

It became one of the most famed temples in the Konkan, but again, like Ganesh, it would not be left in peace for long, being the object of Mahmud Gawan's fury only seventy years after being rebuilt. The linga this time was abandoned amongst the ruins; some say it was even used as a pulley in a well. The practice of smuggling deities out across the river was becoming widespread and the linga was eventually rescued by the Hindu ruler of the north bank, where it was installed in a make-shift temple on a site renamed New Naroa, where in time its fame would be re-established.

In the case of both Ganesh and Saptakoteshwar, parts of the ancient temples are still there to be seen, incorporated into the fabric of the churches built on their sites. In addition, the Portuguese took away stone for use in their own buildings, some of it going to Old Goa to become parts of churches and monasteries. Three hundred years later, when Old Goa itself was being pillaged for building materials, some perhaps made the onward journey to Panjim. Noteworthy surviving examples in Old Goa are the

Divar: Our Lady of Candelaria

ceremony, with the Viceroy and all his entourage present, over 1500 new Christians were baptised.

Looking at this quiet stretch of the river at Naroa Ferry, so narrow that the reflections in the water of the palm trees on the opposite shore reach like beckoning fingers almost halfway across, it strikes home how near was 'the other bank' and freedom to worship traditional gods.

Here, too, we are at the very scene of a legend that is the theme of a song that was extremely popular in Goa for some years and still is at the core of any medley of Goan songs that a visitor is likely to encounter. *Hanv Saiba Polthandi Vaitan*, 'Sir, take

Remains of tank of Saptakoteshwar Temple, formerly on the site of the Chapel of Our Lady of Candelaria

me across the river', relates the story of a former devidasi of the temple here at Naroa who had converted to Christianity and remained on the island. Invited to sing at a wedding ceremony on the other side of the river, she arrives dressed for the occasion bedecked with jewellery and asks the boatman to take her across. Their negotiations constitute the words of the song, with the boatman refusing her offers of jewels and she becoming more and more desperate. The song leaves us in suspense as to the outcome, though, through innuendo and the repeated refrain, *Maka Naka Go*, 'Please no, I don't want it', it would seem that his intentions were not entirely honourable.

ST STEVENS – SANTO ESTEVAM – JUA

On the small island of Jua, lying next to the island of Divar, is the church of **St Stevens** which is one of the last of the large churches to be built (1759). The principal feature of the exterior is a false dome with a lantern which is flanked by twin towers with lanterns and squat domes. The interior of this fine church is in the rococo style. The main altar is somewhat ponderous, culminating in a four-pillared canopy where St Steven stands. There are double-niched canopied side-altars and a restrained but elegant pulpit. Broad bands sweep across the nave ceiling between each groined vault, ending in strong pilasters in the Corinthian style. There are arches along the sides of the nave where the ceilings are decorated with floral stucco.

From the village **The fort of Jua** can be approached by means of a fairly formidable flight of rough steps. The climb is well worth the effort and at the top is a modern but impressive shrine to Christ the King. Here was a sailor who was visiting the shrine on the day before he left Goa to rejoin his ship. He said that he always came to this spot to say his prayers and farewells and perhaps even to view once more, from this excellent vantage point, his beloved Goa.

To the east the view is again dramatic looking onto the giant red scar of the iron-ore workings and to the terminal where barges are loaded before journeying down river and thence to Mormugao. Little remains of the fort but there is a pleasant atmosphere and it is not difficult to conjure up something of its original state when it was built as an outpost to protect the Ilhas from attack by muslim armies.

11 TWO SIDES OF A RIVER: 'THE OTHER BANK' – HINDU PONDA

As we have seen, there are no Hindu temples in the Old Conquests older than the 19th century. Even in the New Conquests, few of the structures themselves were built before the 17th century as, although there was little temple destruction here, these were mainly economically poor areas and great stone temples that would survive the centuries were not part of the culture – much cheaper, less durable buildings being more characteristic. So most of the 'old' temples we see in Goa date from the 17th century at the earliest and the majority from the 18th. By then, even Goa's fringe areas had come under strong Muslim and Christian architectural influences and this resulted in Goa being distinguished from the surrounding areas of India by a distinctive style of temple construction (see p. 22).

There are two major distinguishing features. The first is the widespread substitution of the traditional pyramid shikara, the temple tower over the sanctuary, by a dome rising from an octagonal base, which must be the result of a combination of Muslim and Christian influence, the degree varying depending on the date of the building of the temple and local factors. The second distinctive feature is the existence at almost every temple of a lamp tower, a *deepastambha*, which evolved from the Maratha lamp tower into the more elegant version, seen with many variations all over Goa. A very small group of temples are additionally distinguished by a still further refinement of the design of the lamp tower, this a later development with a distinct Christian Baroque basis (Fig C). Temples in this latter category are clustered in an area between Old Goa and the town of Ponda (map 4).

Five km after leaving Old Goa on the road to Ponda, the road crosses a wide slow-flowing water-

way. This links the Mandovi and Zuari Rivers, creating the island of Tiswadi and marking its boundary with the Ponda taluka. In crossing the waterway we have also passed from the area of the Old to that of the New Conquests. Here at Banasterim on the far bank was a fort of which there are still signs at the roadside. At first this was the bridgehead of Muslim attacks in their efforts to drive out the invaders and subsequently, after its capture by the Portuguese, a key point in the defence of the Old Conquests and in particular the city of Old Goa.

Beyond here was an area that escaped Portuguese rule until late into the 18th century, more than 250 years after the first conquests, and it was here that conquered Goans referred to when they spoke of going to 'the other bank'. In spite of Muslim overlords, the Hindu faith remained strong and, as we have seen, this was the main refuge for deities evacuated from the Old Conquests to escape destruction, resulting in a concentration of important temples all within a short distance of each other.

From Banasterim, the road now takes us first into flat, well-watered countryside with its paddy-fields, but soon begins to climb and twist steeply into attractive wooded hills. Deep valleys are filled with groves of palms, both coconut and the stately slender areca (the source of the betel-nut), together with cashew, whose dark green leaves set off the white and pink flowers in January, to be followed a few weeks later by the red and yellow apples from which the nuts grow. There are also patches of pineapple plantations to be seen from the road.

Another six km sees the road drop steeply into a heavily wooded valley in which, on a small hillock, lies one of the most important and famous Hindu temples in Goa.

THE MANGESH TEMPLE – PRIOL

Like many others, the temple has its origins in this area as a 'refugee' temple. Salcete was added to Portuguese territory in 1543, but it was not until the arrival of the Inquisition in 1560, followed in 1567 by orders for a new wave of temple destruction, that images were smuggled across the river.

At that time, on the south bank of the Zuari River, in the village of Kushastali, was the ancient and famous temple of Mangesh – Mangesh being an aspect of Shiva peculiar to Goa. Under the Portuguese, the village came to be known as Cortalim and, until recent times when the new road bridge was built, was well known as one end of the ferry route across the river on the road from the airport, or Margao to Panjim. The conquistadors, following their usual practice, were to destroy the temple and build a church on its ruins, but, before this could happen, the linga was removed and secretly carried across the river to safety here in the village of Priol where the present temple now stands. Mangesh could continue to be worshipped, although for his devotees this now meant surreptitious river crossings.

There is of course a legend to explain how Shiva came to be worshipped in Goa as 'Mangesh', first in Cortalim and then at Priol. There are several variations on the story but, broadly, it is told that Shiva lost a game of dice with his wife Parvati, on which he had staked everything he possessed, including his home on Mount Kailasa in the Himalayas. Forced to leave, his wanderings took him to the south to what is now Goa where he decided to stay and meditate. The place he chose was Kushastali. Parvati, heartbroken and lonely, left Kailasa to search for Shiva and, while wandering through the forests of Goa, was suddenly confronted by a fierce tiger. Almost speechless with fright, she managed to cry out *'Trahi Mam Girisha'* an understandably jumbled version of what she meant to say, which meant 'Oh Lord of the Mountains protect me', a call to Shiva for help. The ferocious beast was immediately transformed into who else but Shiva, who had assumed the form of a tiger only to frighten her!

Shiva and Parvati were, of course, reunited and to mark the occasion he agreed to adopt *Mam Girish*, the last two words of Parvati's cry for help, as another of his innumerable names. When they eventually left Goa, Shiva left a linga in the forest to mark his eternal presence there. 'Eons' later a cowherd noticed that one of his cows went to the same spot every day and sprinkled it with milk

from her udder. On investigating, he discovered the linga and the villagers of Kushastali built a temple in which it could be housed. The name Mam Girish became shortened to Mangesh and so it was under this name that he came to be worshipped here.

So the linga has been on its new site in Priol for little more than four centuries. On its arrival in Priol it was set in a simple shrine hidden among the palm groves of the valley. More than 150 years later, in the middle of the 18th century, a Goan in exile, Ramchandra Sukhtankar, took a hand in the fortunes of the linga in exile. He had achieved high rank in the Maratha court at Poona and because of this was able to persuade the Rajah of Sonda, who ruled the area as a vassal of the Marathas, to donate sufficient land to provide funds for the temple's upkeep. The new temple was built and the estate survives today as a self-sufficient unit, with a highly organised administration and numerous retainers ranging from a whole array of priests responsible for various rituals, together with appropriate musicians and dancers, to teams of maintenance men, farm managers and workers. All this comes under the direction of a management committee elected every three years from the trustees of the temple. The trustees, or Mahajans, are the successors of the original founders and, in the case of Mangesh, these were twenty-four families of Gaud Saraswat Brahmin community from the deity's original home in Salcete.[1]

But to return to Mangesh. When in 1764, not so long after the building of the new temple, the Raja of Sonda put Ponda into Portuguese hands, this was one of the estates he stipulated should continue as the endowment of the temple. The Portuguese, less intolerant in their attitude by this time, accepted and honoured the condition.

The buildings have been added to and renovated many times since the reconstruction in the 18th century but superbly demonstrate all the features of the temples of this period and this type.

The main approach to the temple from the road is through an arch and along a walkway paved with huge slabs of laterite, although this formal approach on foot can be, and often is, by-passed along an alternative motor road.

Even before the temple is reached, the visitor's attention is seized by the dominant gleaming white *deepastambha*, the lamp tower that evolved from Baroque church towers. However, having arrived at the temple, the first thing deserving attention is the splendid **water tank**, reputedly the oldest part of the temple. This is approached by twin ramps that lead down to an arch in the central gate tower in the

Priol: The tank of Mangesh Temple, believed to be the oldest part of the temple.

front wall. At the top of the tower, under the pyramid red-tiled roof, is the *naubat khana*, the place where drums are beaten and music played. The ramp is paved with laterite blocks worn smooth by the feet of countless pilgrims. The mirror-like waters of the tank, surrounded by waving palms and always filled with contrasting light and shade, reflect the ancient walls with their changing alcoves as well as the temple gateways and the tip of the lamp tower, creating an altogether delightful picture.

The temple is reached through one of two gateways symmetrically sited at the front corners of the courtyard. It is not one of the largest of the temples, but is beautifully designed and proportioned. The spacious courtyard is bounded by buildings which are the *agarshalas*, living quarters for pilgrims, rooms for wedding and thread ceremony parties, together with the offices and workshops of the administration. There is a well in the far corner.

Outside the walls are the village and the farmlands of the estate.

The **lamp tower** rises immediately inside the entrance gate, the seven-storeyed octagonal tower being a classic example of the adaptation from the Baroque. To provide the maximum number of niches for lamps and to give the required massed effect within a practical height, each layer has been severely compressed and yet the whole still retains an overall elegance. On the bottom storey, each of the eight sides contains a panel with painted bas-reliefs illustrating various religious figures and themes.

In the design of the temple itself, all the characteristics are there. Not only is the shikara over the inner sanctum an octagonal tower topped by a dome, but there are domes over the entrance hall, where the octagonal format is repeated yet again, and the two side entrances that create the cruciform ground plan are domed as well. A steeply pitched tiled roof over the *mandapa*, the main hall, links the entrance hall with the tower over the inner sanctum. The dome of the tower rests on an octagonal

Lamp Tower, Mangesh Temple

within the temple complex. There can be a considerable number of these: here is no exception. Outside the main temple in the courtyard there is a small shrine inset into the central gateway dedicated to Bhairava – Shiva in one of his most violent forms. This is a particularly fine image in black basalt shown with Shiva's four traditional accoutrements, trident, sword, kettle-drum and cup, and accompanied by a dog. Bhairava was a form adopted by Shiva during an altercation with Brahma in which he cut off one of Brahma's heads, leaving him with only four. Here he is shown holding the severed head in his left hand.

Immediately behind the main temple, sandwiched between the agarshalas, is a small temple where one named Mukto who, according to legend, was responsible for smuggling the deity across the river to Priol and safety in the 16th century, is honoured as Mulkeshwar. Mukto belonged to the Kundbi community of Cortalim and Kundbis from this village still have special privileges here in the Mangesh temple. To some, Mulkeshwar is also associated with Mullo, the god of the Kundbis.

Outside the walls of the courtyard at the side of the tank is a small, domed, plain building, a temple to Shanteri, the village Goddess of Peace, here traditionally represented as an anthill-shaped mound of earth.

Of those inside the temple, the most obvious of the parivar devatas are Ganesh and Bhagavati whose shrines flank the main sanctuary and who will be mentioned again later.

Near the lamp tower to one side of the main entrance to the temple, is the tulsi vrindavan, in this case elaborately and colourfully decorated with tiles.

Above the main entrance at the top of the steps is

drum in which blind windows replace the niches seen in the lamp tower. The drum, instead of being compressed, is extended to give height. The dome itself supports a cylindrical lantern with a gleaming golden finial representing a water pot. The domes over the side entrances are elegantly ribbed. The whole is linked by balustrades that appear everywhere at each level, all being given an almost festive air by a profusion of distinctive pinnacles based on the *amalaka*, a flattened globe vertically grooved all round which symbolises fruit and fertility. This design is also used as finials on all but the main dome.

Although Shiva in the form of Mangesh is the principal deity and everything centres on his shrine, there is, as in almost every other temple, a supporting cast of affiliated gods, the *parivar devatas*, who either have shrines within the main temple itself or have separate buildings or shrines

Mangesh Temple

the symbol of the Supreme Being, Brahman,[2] pronounced as 'OM', the most powerful word-symbol used in meditation. This symbol will be found frequently in most temples. Beyond the octagonal entrance hall, the mandapa is divided by two rows of four huge round columns into a central space with an aisle on either side.

The decorated ceiling has two areas of stuccoed geometric pattern either side of an elaborate and impressively composed centrepiece, the whole being clustered with an impressive array of chandeliers and lamps of different designs. Temple bells hang between and the whole effect is worth a second look.

But it is to the far end of the hall that attention is drawn, where all the pilgrims wait to attend on the deity. A small *Nandi*, the bull and Shiva's mount, lies before the screen that secludes the main shrine and a carved wooden rail extends further protection on either side. The screen itself is deeply and heavily carved and overlaid with silver in much the same way that reredos in churches are embellished. The same craftsmen or their inheritors were no doubt involved. The intricate designs, while basically traditional in origin, draw on many sources for their inspiration. In the centre of the screen, two massive doors lead to the shrine itself with the deity deep within, accessible only to the attendant priests. On either side of the doorway, niches in the screen contain silver statues of *dvarapalas*, the guardians of the shrine.

On either side of the screen, at the end of each aisle, are small shrines – that on the right to Bhagavati, a form of Parvati, Shiva's consort; that on the left to Ganesh, known more often in South India as Ganapathi. There may be only two temples in the whole of Goa dedicated to Ganesh as the principal deity, but he is one of the best-loved of the gods and appears as an important affiliate in many temples, as well as his image decorating lamp towers, doorways and tulsi vrindavans. Ganesh, with the head of an elephant, the God of Wisdom and Prudence, is also the remover of obstacles, and his help is sought at the start of any undertaking, from a business enterprise to, for instance, making a journey. He is very fond of fruit and sweet things and is always depicted with a fat belly. There are many different legends to account for his acquiring the head of an elephant. His vehicle, which always accompanies him, is a rat.

In one of the aisles is kept the *palki*, the palanquin, in which the deity is taken out in procession on certain festivals. On such special occasions, the linga is adorned with a mask and dressed in rich clothes and jewels.

Some time has been spent describing the Mangesh Temple, as often this is the only one visitors see, but there are several other temples concentrated in a small area nearby, each with their own distinctive character and well worth a visit.

In Mardol village, only a kilometre further along the road from Priol, is the next of the temples of Ponda.

THE MAHALASA TEMPLE – MARDOL

Another 'migrant' deity from Salcete, this temple originated at Verna only about ten km south of Cortalim, the original home of Mangesh. Goan individualism seems to extend to their gods and, in so many cases, although the 'parent' gods themselves are from the traditional Hindu pantheon, in Goa they have been adopted not only in a form peculiar to this area but also in one which makes them adaptable and acceptable, for different reasons, to a wide range of devotees. Mahalasa is a good example. Here Vishnu is worshipped in female form – Mahalasa representing either Vishnu's consort Lakshmi or one of Vishnu's female appearances, Mohini, which he adopted on one occasion to tempt Shiva and on another to resolve a crisis in the saga of 'The Churning of the Ocean of Milk'. This legend is one of the best-known in Indian mythology, which also accounts for the rebirth of Lakshmi and the beginning of her connection with Vishnu as his consort – an association that was to continue henceforth, just as Parvati is linked with Shiva and Saraswati with Brahma. The 'Churning' legend is the subject of frescos and wood-carved illustrations in many of Goa's temples.

During one of the frequent periods of turmoil

which afflicted the Three Worlds, usually caused by conflict between Gods and Demons, all was plunged into chaos because the Gods were weakening rapidly and losing their power due to the shortage of *amrita*, the ambrosia or nectar which ensured their superiority over the Demons. On Vishnu's advice, the enfeebled Gods enlisted the aid of the Demons to churn the Ocean of Milk to produce supplies of the much-needed nectar, promising them a share of the precious liquid.

In rural India, milk is churned by winding a cord round a stick which is swished around in the vessel by pulling on the cord. Here, a mountain was used as the churning stick and Vishnu appeared in his second incarnation as Kurma the Tortoise so that his shell could be used as a pivot to support the enormous weight of the mountain on the ocean floor. Vasuki, the great serpent, was enlisted as the rope to be wound round the churning stick.

When, after being pulled backwards and forwards for some time by teams of Gods and Demons, the serpent not surprisingly vomited up his poison, Shiva leaped forward and caught the poison in his mouth before it could contaminate the Ocean of Milk. Parvati prevented him from swallowing it by clutching his throat but the poison turned his throat blue, which is how he is often depicted. Eventually the amrita was produced and was gathered in a bowl. The Demons immediately made off with it but then started to quarrel as to who should drink first. Vishnu again came to the rescue, appearing as the most beautiful girl they had ever seen. The girl, Mohini, was so entrancing that eventually she persuaded the Demons to allow her to distribute the nectar. She arranged the Gods and Demons in two long rows and passed first down the line of Gods giving each a sip. When all the Gods had drunk from the bowl, Mohini and the bowl suddenly vanished. The Demons, enraged at being cheated, attacked the Gods, but the Gods, strengthened already by the amrita, achieved a crushing victory and order was restored to the Worlds. During the churning process, the ocean not only provided the nectar but also many precious objects previously lost when, during the time of the great flood, the ocean had covered the earth. Chandra, the Moon, emerged together with a dozen other things. Most important for our story, however, was Lakshmi, Goddess of Fortune and Beauty, who rose from the ocean seated on a lotus leaf and was given as consort to Vishnu. Here, at Mardol, Mahalasa is Lakshmi, or Mohini, but – and here it becomes very Goan – to Shaivites, Mahalasa is Bhairavi the consort of Khandoba, a folk-god and predecessor of Shiva, so everyone is satisfied. She is

held in such high regard by all castes and all sects that a wide range of oaths taken under the bell of the temple were built into local law and were regarded as inviolable.

In any case, to all she is a Goddess of Peace, Harmony and the provision of wealth, not necessarily material. Links with folk-gods and the appeal of female deities is emphasised by the fact that amongst the *parivar devatas* (the retinue of associated gods), Shanteri, the local folk Goddess of Peace worshipped in almost every village and hamlet throughout Goa, is given pride of place, with a separate temple, in one corner of the courtyard.

The deity was brought to Mardol from Salcete at almost the same time as Mangesh was making the journey to Priol and again there was a long delay before the present temple was built in the mid-18th century. Although showing many of the same general characteristics, these produce a quite distinctive end result with interesting individual features.

The temple is approached by a short, narrow and congested lane off the main road through the village and the courtyard entered through a triple-arched gateway with its naubat khana above the central arch. Immediately inside the entrance is the lamp tower, but there is also a newer addition, a **brass lamp pillar** symbolically resting on the shell of a tortoise and with the figure of Garuda on top. Garuda, half man, half eagle, is Vishnu's vehicle just as Nandi, the bull, is Shiva's. Cast in Mangalore in Kerala, this was a donation to the temple erected in 1978. A ringed stone column nearby denotes the **Cosmic Pillar** which represents Mount Meru whose summit is Brahma's heaven, the centre of the Universe on which the main axis of this and every other temple is aligned.

A modern extension is under construction in front of the original mandapa, a huge concrete structure. No doubt practical considerations make this necessary in terms of providing space for the music, dance and other celebrations associated with festival occasions and it has become fashionable at several of the larger, richer temples – though with unhappy results in terms of the effect on the appearance of the temple. Here, it seems that thought has been put into the design and attempts have been made to blend the new with the old. The columns are being traditionally sculpted out of huge blocks of stone. Three panels in bas-relief decorate the tower over the new entrance.

On the left-hand side of the new extension is one of the most unusual and impressive tulsi vrindavans to be seen in Goa. Of noble proportion and Baroque inspiration, the architect (and although

Mahalasa Temple, Mardol, with the huge gothic tulsi vrindavan before its demolition

one doesn't often refer to creators of this art form as architect it seems appropriate in this case) must have hugely enjoyed designing this piece with its pedestals, columns, brackets and balustrading and even shell- headed niches. Its somewhat dilapidated appearance seems appropriate. Let us hope that the renovation that must come does not destroy the mood.[3]

The courtyard is surrounded by the usual accommodation and office buildings. In one corner is a separate temple for the parivar devatas, which, with its turrets and domes, has a doll's house appearance. This is the abode of Shanteri. In the opposite corner, near the well, is the shelter for the huge rath, the wooden chariot in which the image is hauled by dozens of willing helpers along the processional route decreed for special occasions.

The tank is situated behind the temple through a

The new tulsi vrindavan

gated archway, a pleasant oasis surrounded by areca and coconut palms with wide views across paddy-fields.

The old buildings of the temple itself are a harmonious blend, pyramid red-tiled roofs replacing the domes seen in the Mangesh Temple, except of course for the main tower whose sectioned dome, an inverted lotus, overhangs the balustrades to provide a balcony, a unique design, which is crowned by a finial of water pots.

External decoration is also both most unusual

Gateway to tank, Mahalasa Temple

and highly effective, a pleasing design of stone and wooden railings combined with carved and decorated wooden brackets and panels.

Inside, the original hall in front of the garbhagriha has a particularly intimate air with its half-light filtering through the wooden rails that form the side walls. Immediately striking are the carved wooden pillars, their solidity contrasting with the delicacy of the workmanship. Makaras, those mythical beasts with the heads of crocodiles, form brackets to the roof beams. Above, a colourful frieze of panels runs around the central raised section of the ceiling. Paintings and carved wooden door-

Design detail from Mahalasa Temple, Mardol

keepers flank the silver-framed doorway that leads to the sanctuary where the deity can be seen deep inside. Two peacocks drape their tail-feathers down each side of the door-frame, while in the centre there is a Gaja Lakshmi panel below the *kirti mukha*, or face of glory. This is a grotesque face, all that remains of a demon created by Shiva as his supreme destructive force in the Cosmos, who possessed an annihilating hunger so powerful that he even consumed his own body – only his head is left. A common symbol that appears frequently in Hindu temples – a guarantee of protection to the devotee, but a dire warning to the impious.

Leaving the village of Mardol and travelling towards Ponda, the first road to the right, after no great distance, leads along the side of a hill into a valley and the village of Velinga. Not far from the turn-off and before the village is reached, a path up the hillside on the left leads to one of the few temples in Goa dedicated to Vishnu in one of his *avatars* or incarnations – this the only one to him as Narasimha, the Man-Lion.

LAKSHMI NARASIMHA TEMPLE – VELINGA

Vishnu took the form of Narasimha, half man, half lion, to deal with a powerful demon who had obtained from Brahma a boon which gave him complete immunity against attack by man or beast, by day or night, inside or outside his palace. Arrogant with the protection this gave him, he ordered that no other god should be worshipped except himself. However, the demon's son was a staunch devotee of Vishnu and resisted all the terrible things his father inflicted on him to break his faith. Finally, frustrated, the demon challenged Vishnu, if he were as omnipresent as his son claimed, to emerge at once from a pillar at the door of the palace. Vishnu did so, appearing as Narsimha, and tore the demon to pieces, the protection of Brahma's boon being circumvented by Vishnu being half man, half lion, therefore neither man nor beast, the time being evening, therefore neither day nor night, and the place being the palace threshold, neither inside nor outside.

The original temple was in Sancoale on the south bank of the Zuari River in what was then Salcete and the image transferred here after the temple's destruction in 1567. The present buildings are mainly 18th century. Other than the tower with its dome, the exterior of the buildings within the main courtyard are unremarkable, with tiled pyramids over the side porchways and the original entrance. A newer extension has been added that blends in with the old. The dome is unusually straight-sided, another example of the many possible variations on this particular theme. Note the painted wall decoration on either side of the entrance to the mandapa.

Lakshmi Narasimha Temple, Velinga

Tank at Lakshmi Narasimha Temple

Inside, there are fine examples of heavily-carved, dark wooden pillars. The silver-framed doorways from the mandapa to the *antaralaya*, the vestibule, and then to the sanctuary are exceptionally beautiful in their decoration and design, as is the canopied shrine for the small Narasimha image. There are no subsidiary shrines inside the main temple.

Outside again and beyond the wall of the courtyard lies one of the finest of tanks amongst the many outstanding examples provided by the Ponda temples. The deeply sunken tank, fed by a constant stream of fresh water from a spring on the hillside above, is surrounded by tiers of steep stone steps, above which there is a walk-way in front of arched changing alcoves, alternating with wall niches and separated by pilasters, that enclose the whole area. In line with the entrance archway of the tank, set into the hillside on the opposite side, steps continue upwards through twin arches to the balconied tower of a naubat khana.

Between these archways is a niched, lamp tower-like shrine, two storeys high and topped with a balustrade, with behind it the Cosmic Pillar on which the temple is aligned. Altogether unique and pleasing.

With its backdrop of dense palms on the hillside, the whole setting of the temple is delightful, offering unusual and interesting cameos rather than a spectacular overall effect.

Four km from Mardol along the road to Ponda is a traffic island marking the village of Farmagudi and from here a fork to the right leads to the villages of Bandora and Quela and the important temples of Naguesh, Mahalaxmi, Shantadurga and Ramnath. However, just beyond the island, on the left, is an equestrian statue and, opposite, a small temple. The statue is of Shivaji the Maratha leader who brandishes his sword in a garden set within the walls of a miniature fort. The temple on the other side of the road is dedicated to **Gopal Ganapathi**, Ganesh, whose image was discovered by cow-herds on the nearby hill and put into a wayside shrine here. This temple, a new one, was built by the first Chief Minister of Goa following Independence, Dayanand Bandodkar, who came from this place. The

Gopal Ganapathi Temple, Farmagudi

temple, designed on traditional lines, with a particularly colourful interior, was consecrated in 1966.

THE NAGUESH TEMPLE – BANDORA

Now taking the road to Bandora, or Bandode, the temple of Naguesh is reached in less than a kilometre, set in a high-walled enclosure on the right of the road.

This is not a migrant deity, but one that has been well established here for many centuries. A 15th century inscription is preserved in the temple, although the present buildings date, like most other temples here, to the 18th century, and conform to the same general design. Yet it has its own atmosphere, being particularly attractive in this respect.

Naguesh Temple, Bandora

One of the smaller temples, it somehow seems less busy, with a solemn peaceful air about it.

The exterior of the temple is a happy blend of pyramid tile roofs and low rounded domes, presenting an uncluttered appearance. The quiet grassy courtyard is surrounded by low agarshalas and the lamp tower has only five storeys. However, the tower has more elaborate bas-reliefs on the lower storey, and other deities set in some of the niches on the level above, with Ganesh prominent. The main entrance to the temple itself is at the back

Detail on Lamp Tower

of the enclosure away from the road and facing the archway leading to the tank. Set in the wall to the left of this passageway is the inscription already referred to, carved in a slab of black basalt. Dated 24 December 1413, it is in Marathi mixed with Sanscrit and refers to the provision of funds for the worship of Naguesh and Mahalaxmi in this village.

The tank itself is large and well designed in a palm setting. It has the feeling of having been here for a long time and witnessed many things. With fish swimming among the reflections in its green waters, it makes a pleasant place to rest and contemplate or gently wander.

This is a shrine to Shiva and in the open porch at the top of the steps, even before entering the temple itself, a polished black Nandi lies on guard. Temple bells hang low just beyond the entrance to the mandapa with another rank of three in the centre of the hall. To accommodate the small size of the mandapa, two of the eight pillars are incorporated into the screen in front of the inner shrine. The carved and painted wooden ceiling has a raised central portion decorated with well-executed panels depicting a number of deities in subdued colours, but one of the features for which this temple is famous is the frieze of small carved and painted wooden panels fringing the mandapa below the ceiling on either side. The subject on the left is the Ramayana, the story of Vishnu's *avatar*, or incarnation, as Rama and his rescue of his wife Sita, an incarnation of Lakshmi, from the demon Ravana. Those on the right include scenes from the other great epic, the Mahabaratha. So, Vishnu is not left out entirely and in the porch of the side entrance beyond the pillars, on the left side, is a shrine to Lakshminarayana, the form in which, in conjunction with his consort, he is most commonly worshipped in Goa. Here, carved in white marble, they are shown standing side by side.

The shrine in the right-hand porch is almost inevitably Ganesh, here benevolent in black stone.

Out in the courtyard once more, in the buildings opposite Ganesh's porch, are set four small shrines each with a linga. One is of the rare variety, a mukhalinga, with a face carved on it.

THE MAHALAXMI TEMPLE – BANDORA

Leaving the Naguesh Temple and continuing towards Quela, there is a turning to the right after only a short distance that leads down to the Mahalaxmi Temple buried deep in the valley.

Mahalaxmi is the female energy of the Supreme Being, the Mother of the World created by all three members of the Trinity – Brahma, Shiva and Vishnu. In this part of India, she has been worshipped for many centuries and by the 8th century had been adopted by some of the earlier Hindu rulers. The main Mahalaxmi Temple in this part of India, is at Kolhapur, about 150 km to the north, in what is now the state of Maharashtra. The notable thing about the deity at both Kolhapur and here in Bandora is that Mahalaxmi wears a linga in her headdress, thus establishing her connection with Shiva. However, inside the temple, apart from the deity itself, Vishnu's presence is also strongly felt.

Following the pattern of other female deities here, she is regarded as a peaceful form of the goddess. It is Mahalaxmi that was chosen as the principal deity in the first temple to be built in Panjim following the greater tolerance shown by the Portuguese towards Hindus early in the 19th century.

The image here was originally established in a temple in Colva on the coast near Margao and was brought here at about the same time as the other 'migrant' deities in about 1565. However, although this particular image is 'new' to the village, the inscription of 1413 in the Naguesh Temple refers to funds being granted for the worship of Mahalaxmi as well as Naguesh, quite possibly on the same spot as this present temple.

Here the layout of the enclosure is less formalised. The offices and rest houses cluster along one side and at one end there is a small arched entrance with the naubat khana above, beyond which is the village. The other two sides are open. The parivar devatas are housed in a miscellany of individual shrines, plainly plastered shelters with red-tiled roofs, scattered in the courtyard. The tank is some distance away down a lane that runs between the dharmasalas. In this lane is the house built for the Raja of Sonda when he gave his territory into the hands of the Portuguese and sought asylum here in 1764. The house, newly renovated and extended, is still occupied by the Raja's descendents.

The main temple building has its domed octagonal temple tower and most unusual double domes over the two side entrances, but it all has a somewhat flattened look about it – this impression heightened by the truncated dome of the main tower being topped by an over-large lantern.

There is no lamp tower, but a black stone column, the Cosmic Pillar, stands in front of a large extension that further accentuates the horizontal element in the elevation. The floor of this new hall is sunken with a stepped surround, providing a setting for the dance and musical performances associated with some festivals. On each side of the entrance to the mandapa are paintings of Hanuman, the Monkey God, Vishnu's devoted ally in the Ramayana, and Garuda, Vishnu's Vehicle, half eagle, half man, while the doors themselves are beautifully carved in wood with Ganesh presiding over them.

A splendid arched silver doorway in the screen leads from the pillared hall to the sanctuary, but the main item of interest is the series of twenty-four carved and brightly painted wooden panels ranged along each side below the ceiling. These show scenes from the Bhagvata Purana which includes the story of Lord Krishna, Vishnu's eighth incarnation.

Returning from the Mahalaxmi Temple to the 'main' road from Farmagudi to Quela and turning to the right, the road winds through pleasant country and here a white church stands out high on a hilltop, the first to be seen since crossing into Ponda and a reminder of the difference the crossing of the river makes. In the village of Quela, or Kavalem as it is sometimes written, is the biggest of Ponda's temples.

THE SHANTADURGA TEMPLE – QUELA

Unlike the valley temples, this stands on the slopes of the hillside, its striking white towers and red roofs standing out against the green of its backdrop.

When Shiva and Parvati were reunited, Shiva wished to remain in Goa to meditate, so Parvati settled down nearby, just a little way along the banks of the Zuari River at Kelosi, now called Quelossim or Quela. Subsequently a temple to her was established there, but she was not worshipped as Parvati, but as Shantadurga. The name Shantadurga is in itself a contradiction in terms, Shanta meaning peace and Durga being the very embodiment of violence. Shiva's consort, like Shiva himself, has many roles and adopts many forms, Parvati being only one of them. Durga is one of her fiercest aspects, created by Brahma, Shiva and Vishnu and given great powers to restore order when the Worlds were under threat. In this form she took on many difficult tasks, on one occasion slaying a fierce demon called Durga whose name she adopted. At the time of a fierce quarrel between Shiva and Vishnu, which turned into a full-scale battle so violent that the very existence of the Universe was threatened, Brahma, the third member of the triad, approached Durga, as the most powerful of the ladies, to intervene, this time without violence. This she did, restoring peace and harmony amongst the gods. From this time, one of her names was Shantadurga, indicating a peaceful aspect of Durga. Goa has elected her as Goddess of Peace and associates her with their favourite folk-goddess Shanteri. It is no wonder that this temple has more pilgrims in a year than any other in Goa.

The image was moved from her home near Mangesh to safety in Quela and, in the first half of the 18th century, like her consort, she also benefited from the efforts of powerful Goans in the Maratha Court, in this case Naro Ram Mantri who himself was a devotee of Shantadurga. As the board outside the temple announces, it was 'Built by Shahurajt, Satara ruler, 1738'. Grandson of the great Shivaji, he

was actually named after him, but was always known as Shahu Raja instead of Shivaji II. He maintained his Court at Satara south of Pune and it was Naro Ram, one of his ministers, who himself funded the building of the temple and persuaded vassal Sonda to contribute the lands of the village of Quela for its estate. So two of the most important temples in Goa have inscriptions attributing their construction to a Shivaji for, as we shall see later, Shahu's grandfather had rebuilt the Saptakoteshwar Temple in Bicholim on the 'other bank' of the Mandovi River 70 years earlier. This was a time of Maratha supremacy in the region, resulting in a bold site being chosen on a prominent hillside instead of a secluded location tucked away in a valley, as were other refugee temples when they were rebuilt over the same hidden shrine established on their arrival nearly 200 years earlier.

A wide flight of steps leads up to the high gateway with the tank cut into the hillside on the left. The vast courtyard is surrounded by a comprehensive range of offices, agarshalas and meeting rooms and such are the numbers of pilgrims and visitors that there is even a branch of the local bank included in the facilities provided.

The design of the gleaming white, six-storeyed lamp tower and the tower over the temple itself, is emphasised by the contrast with the terracotta colours of the remainder of the buildings and the fact that these two towers are topped by the only readily visible domes in the total concept, the rest being a whole series of steeply pitched pyramids of red tiles. The octagonal tower over the inner shrine is one of the most effective examples of its type, the size of the temple making possible a much higher drum with two storeys, giving the whole tower

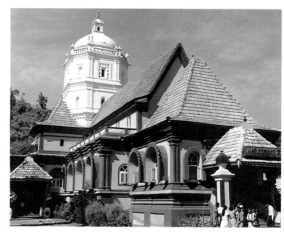

Quela-Ponda: Shantadurga Temple

Shantadurga Temple, Bhagavati. Shrine on platform under Aravali Tree

doorway from here to the main hall. Hanuman, the Monkey God and faithful servant of Rama, together with Garuda, the mount of Vishnu, make their appearance in paintings in the entrance hall. The silver-studded doors lead to a well-appointed mandapa with all the usual features – four huge pillars on each side, decorated ceiling with chandeliers and temple bells and a splendid three-part silver screen in front of the shrine. The chandeliers form a shimmering layer of light after dusk, reflecting in the marble all round, an outstanding collection of different designs. The small garbhagriha is itself something special, heavily worked in silver, a canopied alcove with a sitting image of Shantadurga in white marble. The deity is flanked on one side by Shiva and on the other by Vishnu, a reminder of her origins as the peace-maker between these two gods and the circumstances in which she took her name.

This is a temple that has had frequent additions over the years. The main affiliate is Lakshminarayana, whose shrine is in an extension to the right of the mandapa and there are others here as well.

Only a few hundred metres away to the left after descending the steps and along the lane of busy shops is the last of the major temples in this group.

THE RAMNATH TEMPLE – BANDORA

Ramnath and Shantadurga, near-neighbours in their original 16th century settings in Salcete, are now again only a short distance apart. The linga of Ramnath – for it is basically a Shiva shrine at least in this respect – came from the temple at Loutolim. However, although the linga takes pride of place, Vishnu's presence is strong throughout the temple, there even being an image of Lakshminarayana within the sanctuary itself. The relationship is complex. Even the name can be interpreted as meaning Lord Rama the incarnation of Vishnu, though with the linga as the principal image, Ramnath is Shiva, Lord of Rama.

The main temple building was completely renovated in 1905, resulting in its original proportions being badly distorted by a huge unsympathetic additional hall that overpowers all else.

However, all is compensated for in the original small mandapa. The glowing green and red of the floor and huge round pillars and the profuse, yet orderly array of chandeliers and lanterns, make a fitting setting for the exceptional wall of silver, a magnificent composition, that shields the inner sanctum. An archway is flanked by columns on

greater prominence, with its dome topped by an elegant small square lantern, a further small dome and then a soaring finial of a whole series of spheres representing water pots. The total effect is dramatic.

The huge wooden **rath**, the chariot of the goddess, elegant in black and gold, is often to be seen in the courtyard, there being many festivals here, but it should in any case be sought out in its shelter. Reminiscent in its design of the lamp tower, octagonal and with windows on each of its four storeys, it has symbolic horses at the front, although its great weight is actually drawn by teams of devotees. Also to note in the courtyard is the great aravali tree with its platform, on which there are twin pointed arched shrines. One contains the tiny image of **Bhagavati** (one of the fierce forms of Shiva's consort) who, elsewhere in Goa, has large and important temples dedicated to her.

The main entrance hall to the temple has carved wooden doors studded with silver, as does the which, in fine detail, monkeys, deer and birds mingle between interwoven vines and bunches of grapes. A row of naga heads forms the first level of a many-tiered exotic capital, as complex and eloquent as any Rococo artist could have conceived. The archway itself has a border of roundels, each with a different theme deeply carved, all linked by a delicate floral pattern. Rosettes fill the space between arch and columns, which rest on pedestals decorated with rectangular panels of bas-relief, an array of gods with Garuda and Hanuman, vigilant as usual in their positions on either side of the inside of the archway.

Above, in the pediment of the arch, are two more panels. In the lower one the kneeling figures of Sita, Rama and his brother Lakshman worship a linga, while Hanuman, Rama's devoted helper, stands behind. Shiva, carrying his trident, looks on with Parvati from the clouds above. The upper panel shows Vishnu reclining on the coils of Ananta, the serpent, floating on the Cosmic Ocean, sheltered by the serpent's hoods and with Lakshmi kneeling at his feet.

At either side, each in their own silver arched niche, are the *dvarapalas*, the guardians, the panels below them showing elephants with garlands in their trunks. The carved and painted black background sets off what is altogether a fine piece of art, the craftsmanship as well as the design of each component being of the highest order.

Beyond the screen is the sanctuary with Lakshminarayana set above the Ramnath image, accompanied by Shanteri.

Outside in the courtyard, there is a temple to one side, the same building containing adjacent shrines, one to Betal and one to Kalbhairava. This Kalbhairava image came from Raia, the next village to Loutolim from where Ramnath originated. Betal is the only god in Goa that appears naked (see Fig. A).

Apart from the tightly concentrated group of temples just described, Ponda taluka as a whole is a high-density temple area. Those of the refugee deities add considerably to the numbers but, as typified by Naguesh, there are many more which have been long-established here even though the buildings themselves may be relatively recent. Not many of these are on the scale of the 'Ponda' temples already mentioned. When rebuilding these other temples to deities of local origin, they were specifically to serve the immediate local community, and there was no need for provision to be made for marriage ceremonies and accommodation for pilgrims from across the river. In the case of other migrant deities, not all had wealthy benefac-tors. Many are built with distinctive Goan characteristics, with domed temple towers and with a lamp tower, although the lamp tower is always of the more usual type, rather than the Baroque extravagances seen at Priol, Mardol, Bandora and Quela. Many of these temples are much simpler still, with tiled pyramids for towers. There are particularly large numbers in northern Ponda in the pleasant countryside on the circuit enclosed by the Mandovi River, from Savoi Verem through Candola and Marcela to Banasterim (see map 4).

Not all require description but two can be mentioned, one because of its special atmosphere and the other because of the interest attached to its deity.

THE ANANTA TEMPLE – SAVOI VEREM

In Savoi Verem there is a temple where a feeling of timelessness descends as soon as the gateway is entered, a feeling that, it would seem, is quite independent of this being a specifically Hindu place of worship and difficult to analyse. Its remoteness, some way away from the village, and its soft green setting both contribute. From one end, the gateway is at the top of a flight of steps so that the temple, its courtyard and surroundings are all spread out below. Beyond the low walls of the small courtyard stretch wide areas of low-lying, well-watered paddy, rich green for most of the year, while fringing the edges are stands of upright areca palms, some with only their neat crowns emerging from masses of tumbling pepper vines. Banana and

Ananta Temple, Savoi Verem

bread-fruit trees provide contrasting outlines. Perhaps history too has left its mark on the atmosphere here, for Savoi Verem is an ancient settlement, for centuries a centre of both spiritual and secular learning. An 11th century inscription records the granting of the village to the teacher and mentor of Shasta Deva, one of the early Kadamba rulers, as a token of respect for his wisdom.

Vishnu has been worshipped here for at least 1000 years, evidence for this being provided by the magnificent image showing all his avatars, now on display in the museum at Old Goa, which was found in this village (p. 193). This temple is also dedicated to Vishnu, here as Ananta, the serpent. Nara is the Cosmic Ocean that floods the Universe in between different stages of the World's existence and, during these times of flood, Vishnu takes the form of Narayana, who floats on the waters asleep on the coils of Ananta the serpent, sheltered by his hoods and with Lakshmi kneeling at his feet. When the time comes to re-create the world, a lotus stalk rises from Vishnu's navel and from its flower, Brahma, the Creator, emerges to perform his task. The image of this temple is a carved black stone panel on which Narayana is shown floating on Ananta on the surface of the Cosmic Ocean.

The outside of the temple itself, with its completely plain plastered walls, does nothing to disrupt the quiet atmosphere and there is no dome, only tiled pyramids. Inside, however, the change in mood on entering the small mandapa is startling. Strong colour is everywhere, every detail of the intricately carved wooden columns, picked out it would seem in every different hue. Decorative panels maintain the effect. It is amidst this

rainbow-like setting in the tiny sanctuary that Ananta lies peacefully on the surface of the waters.

THE GANESH TEMPLE – CANDOLA

The road northwards roughly follows the course of the Mandovi, sometimes low on its banks, sometimes climbing above the wide green stretches of paddy with views across the river where mining activity makes its presence felt on the opposite bank.

Candola, the next village to Savoi Verem, houses what was until very recently the only temple in Goa where Ganesh, or Ganapathi, is the principal deity.[4] This particular image has had an eventful life. Starting more than 700 years ago as the principal deity of the village of Ela, the village that was to become the city of Golden Goa, he was moved to the hilltop on Divar, then to Bicholim and finally here to Candola. The story of his travels has already been told (p. 108).

Ganesh Temple, Candola: Old well-travelled Ganesh, who now sits on the right hand of the new image

Ganesh Temple, Candola

Ganesh Temple, Candola

His temple here is not elaborate – part of a group of relatively modern buildings topped by a segmented dome. The ancient image has not long ago been retired, literally moved to one side in the garbhagriha – a fine and impressive sculpture with a benevolent air, seemingly not at all distressed by this young successor now taking centre stage, perhaps mellowed and made philosophical by the vagaries of his adventurous past.

KADAMBA TEMPLES – OPA & KHANDEPAR

Ponda can also boast of some pre-Portuguese temple remains of considerable interest, if not on a grand scale. At **Opa**,[5] a structural Kadamba temple to Shiva, originating from the 13th century, has been well restored and is still in use. In a quiet beautiful setting on a platform cut into the sloping rock of the river bank, this simple but attractive temple, consisting only of an entrance hall and sanctuary, is built of laterite, with basalt for its pillars, ceiling and door-frames. The unusual two-

tiered tower over the sanctuary, topped by an almost lantern-shaped structure with its small dome, settles comfortably into its surroundings. In front of the tower, the now sloping tiled roof covers a plain entrance hall that has trefoil niches either side of a door with a well-carved frame that leads to the sanctuary. The low metallic linga gleams here in the darkness.

Nearby, in the village of **Khandepar**, are four rock-cut sanctuaries. These are attributed to the 10th or 11th century, the time of transition from rock-cut to structural temples.[6] Here the slope of the hillside overlooking the river has been excavated, leaving only the solid blocks of rock from which the sanctuaries have been sculpted, a formidable task. Three have two cells and have low platforms in front, the fourth is a simple single cell. Outside they are completely plain, except for the pyramid-shaped shikaras added by building up horizontal layers of slabs. Entered by square-framed doorways, the interiors have been given some attention in terms of comfort, and even decoration. The door-frames have sockets for wooden doors to be fitted, there are carved hanging brackets and a variety of storage niches. The carved lotus ceiling

Shiva Temple, Opa

decoration is inevitably roughly executed, fine work in laterite being impossible. The fact that they are rock-cut, obviously living quarters associated with shrines, has led to the suggestion that they are Buddhist in origin. This is possible in that, at the time they were built, written accounts show that there was still a surviving handful of followers of Buddha, mainly associated with and tolerated by the court. It is possible that the shikara additions, a Hindu feature, could have been made later.

The town of Ponda itself has changed considerably in recent years. What was just a bustling, busy little market town of only about 3500 inhabitants at the time of Independence is now five times that size and still growing, mainly because of the development of hotel and tourist infrastructure, associated with the rapid increase in the number of pilgrims and tourists visiting the temples. It is, however, a town with a long history. After the arrival of the Portuguese and the retreat of the forces of Bijapur beyond the river, the town of Ponda became the centre of Muslim influence in these territories that would later become part of Goa. In the 16th century, twenty-seven mosques flourished here in the Ponda area and it was, of course, the spearhead of Muslim attacks against Portuguese-held territory and the scene of much conflict.

In the town there are the ruins of an old fort,

Rock-cut sanctuary, Khandepar

Carved ceiling of rock-cut sanctuary

Safa Shahouri Mosque, Ponda

Mardanghad, on the site of an original 15th-century Muslim stronghold. This was destroyed by the Portuguese not long after their arrival, rebuilt by Shivaji the Maratha leader a hundred years later, destroyed and rebuilt by Sambhaji (his son) in about 1685. Within the walls, and surviving all the vicissitudes of fortune of the fort itself, is the Dargah, the tomb and shrine of a Muslim saint, Hazrat Abdullah Khan. The great Urs, the festival and fair celebrating the death anniversary of the holy man, is held each year in February and attracts huge crowds.

On the outskirts of town at the side of the road back to Panjim is what remains of one of only two really ancient mosques left in Goa.

THE SAFA SHAHOURI MOSQUE

Built by Ali Adil Shah in 1560, this bears little resemblance to traditional mosque architecture, even allowing for the fact that many of its surroundings have been destroyed and that repairs carried out over the centuries have had little regard for the original. The essence of what now remains is a most unusual prayer-hall standing on a high plinth. The square building, with its arched recesses, some framing doors and windows, some blind, on its high platform pierced with arched cells, is more like a Muslim tomb than a mosque. The tiled roof is certainly a fairly new addition. There are remnants of columned arcades round the mosque, but no minarets. The picturesque tank, with its arched changing alcoves, bears closer resemblance to a Hindu temple tank, at least those in this immediate area, rather than those normally found in mosques.

Altogether, it is a most interesting structure with considerable atmosphere, unfortunately usually locked and barred as it is only opened on special occasions. Happily, work is being started to keep this rare sample of Muslim architecture in existence and the building is now receiving some attention from the Archaeological Survey. The upper part has been repainted and the collapsed steps to the tank are being repaired.

THE KAMAKSHI TEMPLE – SIRODA

Away to the south of Ponda taluka, far from the main concentration of temples, is one of the most distinctive. Shiva's consort is worshipped here as Kamakshi, a form of Shantadurga and, like her, popular as the Goddess of Peace, even though she embodies violence as well as gentleness in her make-up – a fact acknowledged by her image here being that of Mahisasurmardini, a violent image commonly used to represent many of the different names under which Durga is worshipped. This deity was originally in the village of Raia, directly opposite Siroda on the Salcete bank of the Zuari, only being transferred here when the temples of Raia were destroyed by the Portuguese. There are still close links between the two villages (see p. 150). The Linga of Rayeshivar, the principal affiliate deity here, and the image of Lakshmina-rayana came from other temples in Raia.

The temple, set in a busy, almost congested courtyard, has no domes and the design of the main tower is intriguing, its tiled roof having the concave profile of a Buddhist pagoda, projecting beyond a two-storeyed octagonal tower. With low, decorative wrought-iron balconies running all round the tower on each floor, it is a very unusual and distinctive concept for Goa. Elephants kneel at the corners of the square base on which the tower rests, while hooded nagas rear from the projecting corners of the pagoda roof. Above all this soars a golden finial. Tiled pyramids top the entrances to the main temple, the octagonal lamp tower and the gateways to the courtyard.

Inside, there are conventionally carved pillars in the Mandapa with shrines to Dattaraya and Maruti (Hanuman). Beyond the silver-encrusted screen to the sanctuary, images of Kalbhairava on the left and Betal on the right flank the Goddess on her pedestal.

The Kirti Mukha – face of glory.

12 TWO SIDES OF A RIVER: THE WEST BANK – CHRISTIAN SALCETE

In contrast with Hindu Ponda, with its predominance of temples, Salcete became a stronghold of Christianity and today is the only taluka of Goa where Christians are still in the majority, making up nearly seventy percent of the population. This remains true 'Old Conquest' country in every respect.

The area acquired its name long before its Christianity, in fact, as part of the legend of the creation of Goa itself. When Parashurama shot his arrow from the peaks of the Sahyadri mountains and commanded the sea to withdraw beyond where it fell, virgin land was created on which the god could perform his purification sacrifice (see p. 17). Bannali (Benaulim) a village on the coast is 'where the arrow fell'. But, to perform the *yajna*, the fire sacrifice, he also needed the assistance of a host of highly qualified priests and so he summoned the Gaud Saraswat Brahmins. They were Saraswati because they originated on the banks of the holy river of that name far to the northwest in Kashmir, and Gaud because on their way south they deviated by way of Gaud, near Bengal in the north-east. Ninety-six families arrived in Parashurama's new land to perform the ceremony, sixty-six settling to the south of the Zuari River, leading to the area becoming known as Sassast or Sashtti, Konkani for sixty-six, which was later corrupted to Salcete. Thirty families settled on the island to the north of the river and, Tissis being thirty, this became Tiswadi, land of thirty villages.

The area that is now Mormugao taluka was for centuries part of Salcete, only separated in 1917 for administrative purposes, so this is included here.

Salcete, together with Mormugao, can best be described by taking four distinctively separate elements: the town of Margao, the Salcete coastline, a group of inland villages, and the stretch of countryside between Dabolim airport and Cortalim village, the latter providing the glimpses of Mormugao experienced by almost every visitor travelling by air (see map 3).[1]

MARGAO

Using population statistics as a measure, the relationship of the towns of Goa in terms of size and rate of growth are in a constant state of flux as a result of economic development and the movement of labour. But whatever the figures may say, Margao will always be Goa's second 'city' after the capital Panjim. It has a long history, with its origins as the principal market town for the south. While in the early centuries it left the job of capital to the river port of Chandrapur, modern Chandor, only a few kilometres away, it was even then famous for its many outstanding and beautifully built temples and, long before the Portuguese came, had its university with a library of over 10,000 books – something to wonder at in those times. Its early importance was acknowledged by the Portuguese when the Jesuits chose it as the site for the establishment of their college for the south, although defensive considerations soon caused the college to be moved to Rachol, where it would have the fort's protection from Muslim raiders.

The town grew as a commercial centre, and attracted further attention centuries later when Goa's rail link was built to pass through the town, adding to its already significant economic status. The centenary of the railway era in Goa was celebrated some years ago, the first track being opened in 1881. The single line runs from Mormugao Harbour through Margao to beyond the state border in the east, where it links with the Indian Railway's network in Karnatika.[2]

Margao today is a bustling, happy place to be, its hub being the main square with the **Jorge Barreto Park** at its centre (see map 6). There are few old civic buildings left, but the municipal building built in 1905, which includes the library, adds a touch of colonial formality to the atmosphere. Occupying the southern end of this considerable open space, its colour-washed, arched arcades and verandahs look out across the constantly hooting parade of circling traffic, fencing with pedestrians attempting to reach the colourful safety and relative peace of the gardens in the centre.

Almost next to the municipal building is the **Bazaar**. Margao's position as market centre for a large area is reflected in the scope and level of activity in this part of the town – except in the early afternoon of course! Here you can buy almost anything. The outer lines of modern shops provide a conventional, somewhat ordinary range of wares, but for real interest, penetrate the dim light of the maze of covered alleyways, where a bewildering assortment of stalls are jumbled together. Catching the eye, and the nostrils, are great heaps of dried chillies and fresh spices of every sort, huge brown slabs of sweet jaggery and fruits in abundance. Piles of freshly baked Goan breads add their contribution to the sights and smells, while, in between all these are arrays of terracotta pots and coir ropes, bright bedcovers and colourful cloth while, now and then, rows of gleaming bottles offer cool temptation. There is much much more besides – more than an excellent substitute if you cannot find time to visit the market of Mapusa.

Leading from the north end of the square, the

In the bazaar, Margao

opposite end to the Municipal Building, is the **Rua Abade Faria**, Margao's tribute to a famous Goan, our old friend of the hypnotic statue next to the Secretariat in Panjim. Fifteen minutes wandering along here presents a kaleidoscope of some of the oldest, most notable town houses in Goa, typifying Goan domestic architecture of the 18th and 19th centuries and demonstrating a whole range of styles. Along the length of the street no two houses are alike, from the overflowing wooden decoration of the splendid 'Vista da Avenida' to the severe graciousness of the house that is now a convent. Even where the design of the whole may not be

Nandi in Damodar Temple, Margao

particularly impressive, there are countless examples of design details on display in individual windows, doors and balconies.

At the end of the street on the left, a low, single-storeyed building of little distinction can easily be ignored, but in fact this contains a Hindu temple of great interest. This simple building now houses the Temple of Damodar, worship taking place in a small room adapted for the purpose from part of an ordinary house – a sad replacement for the great 'pagoda' of Damodar described by early Portuguese arrivals in Salcete, before the temple was destroyed a few hundred years ago. The Rua Abade Faria, rewarding in itself, leads us to the nearby site of the original Damodar Temple and the great church that was built in its place. Here, in this delightful corner of the old town, Salcete's

Church Square, Margao

Portuguese heritage, suitably adapted to Goan tastes of course, is encapsulated in **Church Square**.

The square is full of character with the fine old church at the top end and one of the best examples of a piazza cross at its centre. Old houses fill the other three sides, and a variety of trees draw everything together in a picturesque whole – an ideal place for a browsing visit.

The first church here was consecrated in 1565, on record as being deliberately built on the site of the most important of the many Hindu temples in this place. Indeed, it was the first Archbishop of Goa himself, Dom Caspar Leao Pereira, who, in that year, personally visited Margao to choose the site. After inspecting several places, he dismayed local people by casting an arrow into the ground in front of their most revered temple to indicate where the church should be. Diogo Rodrigues, Captain of Rachol, who was to become a famous – or infamous – wrecker of temples, was called in. He soon razed it to the ground along with six other temples there. This particular temple was of great significance locally as it was here that they worshipped the equivalent of their own patron saint, special only to them. The story is one of jealousy and hired assassins. Macaji Damodar, son of a local Dessai, was returning from his wedding in Quelossim when he and his bride were attacked and murdered by the henchmen of a frustrated suitor from a nearby village. A temple was built by the people of Margao on the spot where Macaji was murdered, honouring him amongst their gods. Before Diogo Rodrigues arrived to destroy the temple, the image was taken away to Zambaulim in southern Sanguem where it is now established in a fine temple (see p. 184). In recent years, a new Damodar Temple has been established in Margao in the Rua Abade Faria,

though, as has been seen, not the imposing structure of its destroyed ancestor.

So, standing in Church Square, we are on ground that has seen great drama and violence that was not to end with the building of the church. The 1565 church was burned to the ground by Muslim raiders soon after it was built and its replacement suffered the same fate in 1579 along with the seminary that had been established alongside. As a result, the seminary was moved to Rachol under the protection of the walls of the fort.

The present church was built in 1675 and is one of the finest examples of genuine Indian Baroque architecture. This is the Espirito Santo, the Church of the Holy Spirit, well maintained and in constant use today. The white-painted façade and the walls of the transepts contrast with the bare red laterite of the rest of the church exterior. The central part of the façade is projected forward from the line of the towers, enabling the gable to extend downwards to the top of the second storey, with its line of windows each surmounted by an oculus, the circular window intrinsic to many Baroque façades. An impressive arrangement, the design of the scrolled

Church Square, Margao: Church of the Holy Spirit

gable makes the most of the prominence it is given. In the centre, framed within a balcony topped by an elaborate tented canopy, is a relief of **Our Lady surrounded by the Apostles**. Above is a dove, again in deepest relief, symbolising the Holy Spirit. Emphasis on the central section is further subtly accentuated by the use of blind windows in the towers on each side. A signficant addition to these towers is a low dome, topped by a cylindrical lantern, itself with a small dome, all extending only just above the upper balustrading – an addition elegantly slender columns soaring to support an intricately traceried arch across the vaulting – an arrangement that, together with the tiered pedestal, would subsequently be used in many smaller churches, especially in Salcete.

The panelling of the ceiling of the chancel and the nave is finely decorated, well able to withstand the scrutiny directed at them through the illuminating effect of the planing of the groins of the vault so characteristic of the Indian Baroque.

The length of the nave is lined on each side with deep shell-headed alcoves. Even in basic features such as these alcoves and the panelling of the vaulting, the decorative work is delicately conceived and carried out, fine workmanship being characteristic of the whole church.

The heavily decorated altars in the transepts are dedicated to St Peter and St Michael, while under the arch of the choir there is an altar worth seeking out dedicated to the marriage of Joseph and Mary, charmingly depicted.

Church of the Holy Spirit, Margao: Our Lady surrounded by the Apostles

unique amongst Indian Baroque churches of this period, but one which would be further developed in later churches and can be seen in the designs of Hindu temples and lamp towers.

To the left of the church, an archway leads to a small restful courtyard of houses originally built for the clergy, and here too is the side entrance to the church.

The interior is magnificent, the first impression a striking loftiness, the eye being everywhere carried upwards into the light. Inside the chancel the effect is the same, the design of the reredos building up to the crucifix at its apex. This upward movement is especially heightened by the four-tiered pedestal rising to a most beautiful panel depicting Our Lady and the Apostles, the Dove of the Holy Spirit above, repeating the theme of the panel on the façade. Adding to this, a splendid frame is created by two

Main Altar, Church of the Holy Spirit

Sat Burnzam Gr (the seven-towered house) Margao

In the centre of the square outside, is a grand **piazza cross**. There are hundreds of crosses in Goa but it is seen here in its most advanced and sophisticated form, equalled only by the cross of St Alex in Curtorim. These are both about a hundred years older than the church here.

In this piazza cross, many classical features in their adapted form are compressed into a small space. Salomonic columns, heavily scrolled pilasters and pedestals, while above, in the four pinnacles as well as the central spire that supports the cross itself, rich baluster curves are combined with the flattened grooved spheres of the amalakas of Hindu temple architecture. The decoration on all the curved surfaces, and there is barely a flat surface anywhere, are the Indian whim of the moment rather than western traditional patterns. The individual components are worthy of attention as well as the overall effect produced. The detail, in stuccowork, has survived many coats of whitewash remarkably well, although the sharpness of their outline is a little blunted. Note the etching on the

face of the cross itself. There is even shade provided by the adjacent solitary tree.

There is one other house in Margao of outstanding interest. Not too far from Church Square is the famous house belonging to the Silva family, the **Sat Burnzam Gor**, the Seven-Towered House, also referred to locally, and understandably, as the Casa Grande. Sadly, only three of the seven high-pitched roofs survive but it is still a large and elegant house. Built at the end of the 18th century by Inacio Silva, who was Secretary to the Viceroy in the 1790s, much of its elegance derives from the very simplicity of its design. Everything about it has a graceful air, except of course for the corrugated iron protective canopy attached just below the pediments of the upper line of windows. Although this has been added as neatly and unobtrusively as possible, it still obscures the beautiful proportions of the tall windows behind their neat wrought-iron balconies. The vertical nacre-filled slats show up particularly effectively when used in such a long row of tall windows and make an important contribution to the overall distinction of the building.

Descendants of the builder of this superb house still live here.

Two small chapels here in Margao are typical products of the late 18th century and, in particular, both illustrate the neat slim façades achieved by Rococo architects. That of the **San Joaquim Chapel**, built in 1789, is especially attractive, or was before the unsightly porch was added to disguise its appeal. As in the case of some of the extensions to Hindu temples, all the original architect's skills have been sacrificed to practical needs. Here the inclusion of two towers with balustrades and domes has been achieved while still maintaining a slender, narrow frontage. The vaulting of this chapel should be noted. The **Chapel of Our Lady of the Rosary**, 1767, on the outskirts of the town in Fatorda is another good example of the period.

The remaining church worthy of mention is known as **Mount Church**. Nossa Senhora da Piedade was rebuilt in 1820 and a visit is recommended mainly for its situation on the hilltop overlooking Margao, giving extensive views of the town below and the surrounding countryside to the coastline and the sea.

THE SALCETE COASTLINE

As far as Salcete's beaches are concerned, it could almost be said that, as in the case of towns, there is only one, for although the twenty km of its shoreline has half-a-dozen differently named beaches, there are no rivers or headlands to break the long stretch of sand usually collectively referred to as Colva Beach. Local names are given, taken from the villages that sit behind the fringe of palm groves which helps to identify a particular point – and so we have from north to south, **Majorda, Colva, Benaulim, Varca, Cavelossim** and **Mabor** beaches. However, it would be difficult to say where one ends and the next one starts (map 5). On this long, unbroken line of sand, there is, for much of its length, the impression of it stretching away forever on either side, there being so few landmarks, but it still offers great variety and changes in character – depending on developments that have taken place in the immediate hinterland.

Increasingly, there has been hotel development with its associated attractions, but in between there are still long stretches of beach, palm-fringed, wide and golden, where sand and sea will only have to be shared with the fisher-folk and the palm groves with toddy tappers. As is to be expected, facilities for visitors diminish proportionately with the increase in solitude, but the choice is there.

Amongst and behind the palm groves are the coastal villages that give the beaches their names. They have always been more closely associated with the sea, the beaches and the palms rather than the countryside inland. It is the shoreline that provides the fish, nurtures the coconut products and attracts the tourists, all of which form the basis of their livelihood. This links them with a common atmosphere, although there are many points of special interest. One feature common to all is of course the village church. Here all are of later 18th or early 19th century vintage, all offering glimpses of the Rococo style in vogue at the time they were built.

The Rococo developed from the Baroque in an atmosphere of lighter mood. In Goa, as well as in Europe, it fitted in with the times, the stern conversion process with its purposeful need to impress having relaxed its grip; the weight and power and the discipline of the Baroque gave way to the delicacy and elegance – almost light-heartedness – of the Rococo. It was fortuitous that the need for

Church of Our Lady of the Rosary, Fatorda

churches on an epic scale was past; the Rococo spirit as it reached Goa needed to roam more freely and was well suited to the small churches now being built.

These were churches conceived and designed by local architects and priests and, while it gave great scope for individual expression, there was some regional supervision by the church and a tendency to follow the same general pattern as one's neighbours. Here, the façades, with variations on the theme, are all basically simplified versions of the greatest church in the locality, the Espirito Santo in Margao. There are many permutations. All have a verandah or courtyard attached to one side where the huge symbolic wooden cross hangs. There is almost always a school connected with the church.

The same principle of conforming to a general theme common to the area applies to interiors as well as façades and, although there are exceptions reflected in the degree of Rococo feeling, such as at Benaulim and Carmona, main altars also show the influence of the Espirito Santo. Columns inside the chancel supporting an arch frame a reredos dominated by a pedestal, made up of diminishing tiers on which stands a statue or panel appropriate to the dedication of the church. Most are decorated with additional niches for other figures. By the second half of the 18th century, the vaulting of the chancel had become the object for more elaborate decoration, the ceilings in Majorda and Cavelossim typifying the abandonment of the regular panelling characteristic of the Baroque in favour of the swirling patterns of the Rococo. There is much to be seen and enjoyed in all of them.

Majorda

This northernmost village is the site of a five-star hotel development and alone amongst the Salcete beach villages can boast its own railway station. Admittedly, it is as basic a station as can be conceived, but it is possible to travel either leisurely northwards to Vasco, a journey of about 45 minutes, or south-east to Margao and beyond, even to Dudhsagar almost on Goa's border, a journey of 50 km and a long day's expedition.

The church, near the railway station, was built as usual on the site of a Hindu temple – in this case one dedicated to Mahamai, the Great Mother. It is appropriate that the church should be dedicated to **Nossa Senhora Mae de Deus**, Our Lady Mother of God. The old church was burned down during the Maratha raids of 1738 and rebuilt soon afterwards with additions over the next half-century. Inside and out it demonstrates many of the features

Majorda Railway Station

already mentioned. The vaulting of its chancel, a graceful pattern of rosettes, leaves, fleurs-de-lis and scrolls.

Betalbatim

The next village takes its name from the fiercest of Goan gods, Betal or Vetal, and who was once worshipped here (see p. 197). One of the most dramatic pieces of sculpture in the Museum at Old Goa was found here – a figure of Betal, fearsome in its strength even though it is without its head.

Colva

The effect of having Margao only five km inland has been the development of a busy stretch of beach here with 'all the fun of the fair' in a modest way, centring on where the road from the town meets the beach. Stalls and shops cover a growing area, offering their wares to musical accompaniment from strategically placed loudspeakers. Potential trade has even attracted the gypsies spreading their colourful offerings at the side of the road leading to Margao. Two bridges have been built across the creek running behind the sands to give easy access and stalls have appeared on the beach. Incidentally, for no apparent reason, some of the best coconut water is to be had here. Perhaps Colva palms are special. There has also been a rapid growth of small hotels and restaurants to cope with the increased volume of visitors, including touring coach parties. These supplement the small thatched eating places and tavernas that have long been there, first encouraged into existence by local residents and which will offer fish as fresh as can be imagined. It is a popular spot for local people, strolling and picnicking, especially at weekends, with families from Margao taking advantage of their nearness to the sea. However, quiet areas can still be found by walking only a short distance in either direction from this hub of activity. There is a heavy concentration of fishermen near here, refusing to give way to this invasion of their territory.

A road runs north to south all down this coast, winding just behind the palms and, like most of these coastal villages, Colva centres on this road. This is where the church is to be found. **Nossa Senhora das Merces**, Our Lady of Mercy, is not one of the old-established churches, the first church here being built in 1630 and rebuilt in the 18th century with its simple façade and single low tower. Almost as though seeking to give it some distinction, an extra narrow tier containing three shell-headed niches has been added below the gable; instead of the usual round window, it has a round panel simply inscribed with the symbol IHS

Church of Our Lady of Mercy, Colva

(the Greek abbreviation for Jesus) which is the Jesuit emblem. All this underlines the individuality of these churches when it comes down to detail. The large platform in front of the church, shaded by an ancient tree, makes this a pleasant place to watch the passing show.

The principle of conforming to a general theme, common to a geographical area, applies to interiors as well as façades (see p. 15). Here, slender columns and a tracery arch frame a heavily gilded, four-tiered pedestal on which stands a large statue of Our Lady in a dramatic aureole, a sunburst of light, all overtopped by two angels supporting a splendid crown. Four niches decorate the wall behind, the rest being covered in painted cherubs that now overflow onto the ceiling of the chancel within the

frame. The decoration of the two canopied altars flanking the chancel illustrate a restrained use of the elegance and lightness of the Rococo, the restraint here being typified by the well-organised swirling floral decoration of the canopies themselves. Rococo luxuriance can be seen in less controlled abundance in the nearby church at Benaulim.

The carved wooden altar in the nave, somewhat Gothic, and in total contrast with the gilded splendour of the other altars, represents a popular later style, special to this area. The main altar in the chapel of the Patriarchal Palace in Panjim would follow similar basic concepts.

On one wall of the nave is a special altar with the small figure of the Menino (Boy) Jesus. The **Menino Jesus** has a special place in Colva's story.

Menino Jesus, Colva

October in Colva offers an opportunity to witness an unusual event, when the Fama of Menino Jesus is celebrated at the church. This involves a religious procession of great pomp, followed by the exposition of the miraculous statue attracting thousands of pilgrims. A fair is held over the several days of the festival. The original object of veneration, a statue of the young Boy Jesus, was found on the east coast of Africa by a Jesuit missionary who subsequently, in 1648, became Vicar of Colva. The statue that he brought with him soon attracted wide attention by its miraculous response to appeals for help, especially in curing ailments. A special altar was built in the nave and jewels and donations flowed in. However, when in 1834 the religious orders were banned and the vicar of that time was forced to leave Goa, the miraculous image together with its jewellery was removed by the Rector of Rachol and installed in the seminary church. Every effort on the part of the parishioners of Colva to retrieve their statue failed, even the support of the King of Portugal failing to move the Rector of Rachol. So the villagers subscribed for the purchase of a new statue. The only thing remaining in Colva connected with the original statute was a diamond ring, overlooked and left behind when the statue was removed. The new statue was installed in 1836, wearing the ring and, remarkably, while the statue at Rachol ceased to perform miracles, the new Menino Jesus at Colva took up where his predecessor had left off and even today favours his supplicants.

On the second Monday of October each year his Fama is celebrated, the image being taken in procession round the church, richly robed and covered in gold and jewels, before being ceremonially bathed and displayed for special veneration and then returned to its special altar where it can be seen for the rest of the year. At the time of the Fama, the offerings and thanks for favours take the form of wax limbs, arms, legs, hands, whatever is appropriate, all manufactured specially for the occasion and sold at a stall by the church, the takings going to the Menino's charity fund. Also sold are *Medidas*, cords the length of the statue which have been blessed by being touched against it. The fair with stalls and attractions of all descriptions goes on for several days.

Benaulim

The next village is also known as Bannali, its pre-Portuguese name, which means 'the place where the arrow fell', referring to the arrow shot by Parashurama from the top of the Sahyadri Moun-

tains into the sea to mark the shoreline of the new land that would become Goa.

In 1596, the church here (originally built nearer the shore) was moved to its present site on Monte Benaulim – only a low hill, and some distance from the village, although offering a fine site. The **Church of St John the Baptist** that now stands here is one of the most impressive on the coast. Low domes top four-storeyed towers that flank a well-decorated gable, distinguished by an unusually prominent fringe of crosses outlining its side scrolls. Inside, the Rococo flourishes, its gilded surfaces glowing in this small church. On the main reredos and side altars almost every inch of space is covered in decoration. Plain panelling in the vault of the chancel in this case enhances the impact of the main altar. Much attention is given to detail in this church, as illustrated by the reproduction of the attractive cornice design in the 'gallery' with its fine tracery that defines the first storey. The pulpit is a superb example of Rococo art, flowing upwards from the lowest pendant in a triumphant sweep up to the scrolls above the canopy, with the Lamb of the Apocalypse on the Book of the Seven Seals at its summit. Providing stark contrast, the wooden altar triptych makes it appearance here also.

In the chapel under the choir **Father Joseph Vaz** was baptised. Born here in the village of Benaulim in 1651, he was prominent in the struggle to gain acceptance for Goan clergy, establishing the Goan branch of St Philip Neri's Oratorians, a congregation of secular priests. He subsequently earned fame as the 'Apostle of Ceylon' and soon after his death in 1711, proceedings for his canonisation were initiated, so far without success.

On no account neglect the delightful **St Christo-**

St Christopher, Church of St John the Baptist, Benaulim

pher on the wall of the nave opposite the baptismal chapel, crossing a river full of crabs and fishes with cheerful assurance.

The villages continue down the coast, the scattered cottages of one almost merging with the next in this still-quiet countryside, and there are many interesting, some distinguished, houses here, with an assortment of terracotta figures – Portuguese soldiers and cockerels being favourites – adorning the gables of their roofs.

Varca

The church offers a fine façade. On its towers, the concept of the shallow dome topped by a cylindrical lantern, both balustraded, is based directly on the Espirito Santo. They are also virtual twins to the main dome of the Mangesh Temple far away in Ponda. Its gable design, the most complex among any of this group, contributes to the appealing effect.

Carmona

Nossa Senhora de Socorro, Our Lady of Help, has an imposing presence in the centre of the village and behind its prominent porch is another exuberant and sophisticated interior. This contrasts with its immediate neighbour to the south and underlines the variety that can be seen within a basic framework.

Cavelossim

The **Santa Cruz**, the Holy Cross, built in 1763, is not sophisticated. It is in fact somewhat fussy, yet full of charm. Its neat and compact façade is simple, but inside the architect shows his determination to fit

Church of Santa Cruz, Cavelossim

in as much as possible, using all the features of its grander neighbours though in simpler style. This can be seen in the straightforward design of the altars and the flat, detached canopies over the side altars. The nave is lined with shell-headed niches, although space does not allow for Margao's elegance and the swirls of the vault of the chancel, which are bold rather than delicate, even without the emphasis given by subsequent choice of colour. Nothing about the workmanship is crude, however, and it is a joyful little church. Beyond Cavelossim, the narrowing peninsula formed by the approach to the sea of the Sal River, is the site of extensive hotel development which will provide a wide range of first-class hotel facilities to this southern stretch of Salcete's coastline.

INLAND VILLAGES OF SALCETE

Between the Salcete shoreline and the taluka's eastern boundary, for most of its length defined by the Zuari River, the countryside and villages offer so much of what is typically 'Old Conquests'. However, there is a small area along the river bank into which something of everything has been concentrated. The four villages of **Chandor, Curtorim, Raia** and **Loutolim** together contain the essence of this aspect of Goa[4] (map 5). Here are some of the finest examples of the typically Goan house, from great mansions to the smallest cottage, and the same is true of its churches. There is more than a hint of history in the air at **Chandor**, formerly Chandrapur the first Goan capital, and there is one of Goa's two remaining seminaries, historic **Rachol**, all of these set amidst the lushest of Goa's countryside.

Chandor

About ten km inland from Margao is the village of Chandor. Chandor has two aspects to present to a visitor, one ancient and one modern – or relatively so. The newer Chandor is represented by the main square of the village on to which all roads now converge, its ancient aspect by a wedge of undistinguished countryside that was once of fame across India and even beyond the Arabian Sea, as a great capital and, even more difficult to believe, a port of international repute.[5] This is difficult to conceive now, standing by the signpost announcing this as the location of **Chandrapur**, the capital and a temple that once stood here in the citadel of the fort, the hub of this seat of kings. In addition, it is difficult, on this flat low-lying ground, now well wooded, to appreciate the geography of the place, a natural defensive site in a loop of the Kushavati River and with another tributary of the Zuari to the west. The old moat linking the two natural waterways still creates almost an island when it floods. But Chandrapur is a vital cornerstone of Goa's historic past, gradually revealing itself through sparse documentation in the form of copper-plate inscription and the treasure of spasmodic excavation. Through these early centuries, Goa itself was generally overshadowed by its neighbours, a pawn in the chessboard moves of the great dynasties of south India. Yet Chandrapur is a constant factor in this haze of history, with repeated references to it as a seat of local kingship. The antiquity of the place is attested to by the fact that its name honours the first Mauryan emperor **Chandragupta**, who established his power in India with the defeat of the Macedonians soon after the death of Alexander the Great in 323 BC and whose empire spread over much of the sub-continent including Goa. From Chandrapur, a Bhoja king would issue his writ on a copper-plate inscription in the 3rd or 4th century AD. The earliest written piece of evidence we have of Goa's past, the 'Siroda' plate, was found in the village of that name on the far banks of the river. The brick-built foundations of the Shiva temple a few paces from the signpost, assignable to the same date, together with traces of fortress walls, constitute the oldest structural remains in Goa. But even this does not mark Chandrapur's origins, for digging along the river bank revealed pottery of the Satavahanas, their dynasty older even than the Bhojes, ruling as far back as 200 BC.

At the time of his original discovery of the site in 1929, Father Heras also came across a **Nandi**, Shiva's bull, battered and headless, up-ended in a ditch, a victim of 13th-century Muslim raids. Colossal and splendid, this has been dated to about the 7th century and so would have been placed here in front of the temple, at about the time when Pulakesim II, the great Chalukyan emperor, installed his son – coincidentally named Chandraditya – to rule the Konkan from Chandrapur on his behalf. The kingdom's status grew as did its sea links and trade, using the then deep-flowing Zuari's access to the Arabian Sea. By this time, stimulated mainly by adventurous Arab traders, the whole area of the Arabian Sea, the Persian Gulf, the east coast of Africa and the length of the west coast of India to Ceylon was abuzz with trading activity in which Chandrapur played an important role.

Its fame continued to spread, but it was 400 years later, during the first half of the 11th century, that, as capital of the Kadamba kings, it reached its zenith. A contemporary description refers to 'when white plastered houses, alleys, horse stables, flower gardens, agreeably connected bazaars, harlots' quarters and tanks were charming to the eye'. This was during the reign of Shastadeva I who expanded his territories by conquest, including the port of the Silaharas at the mouth of the Zuari on its north bank, Gopakapattana or Gowapuri. Chandrapur's access to the sea was assured, but the acquisition also signalled its demise. For a kingdom now based on naval power and sea trade, the attractions of Gowapuri were irresistible. Chandrapur was too far from the sea and commercially vulnerable, limited in the volume of trade and ships it could handle. By mid-century, soon after Shastadeva's death, his son had transferred the capital to Gopakapattana, known to foreign seamen as Gove.

The Kadambas returned briefly to Chandrapur in defeat nearly three centuries later, after Malik Kafur, the Delhi Sultan's general, had destroyed Gopakapattana in the raids of 1312. But a few years later it too suffered at the hands of marauding Delhi Sultanate troops, razed to the ground in 1327 – an event evidenced by the discovery of a coin of Sultan Muhammed Tughluq in the very sanctuary of the Shiva temple here, no doubt dropped by one of his soldiers during the act of destruction. It was the end of a long chapter.

Until the mid-19th century, the river continued to remain navigable as far as Chandor by quite sizeable vessels, but now only by country craft. The railway has replaced the river as an important line of communication, with a station in the village, whose real centre has now shifted to the large square two km away from the old fort.

At one end sits the church, built on the site of the main Hindu temple in this part of the village. The temple, destroyed by the Portuguese in 1567, was

Nandi: Shiva's bull at Chandrapur

dedicated to the Saptamatrikas, the Seven Mothers, who are worshipped as a group representing the female energies of seven principal gods. Although the church was not built until 1645, the Jesuits still followed their frequent practice of making the dedication of the church relevant to the Hindus of the area and chose the Mother of God as Our Lady of Bethlehem. The façade has been rebuilt after its collapse in 1949. There is a cluster of memorials to one side of the church, one being particularly ornate. Above the church on the hillside is the walled cemetery. Some distance away, in the centre of the huge elongated space in front of the church, a simple piazza cross looks a little lost, but on one occasion in particular during the year the square comes vigorously to life. On 6 January, Chandor is one of only three places in Goa[6] to celebrate the Epiphany. The offering of gifts of gold, frankincense and myrrh to the Infant Jesus by the three Magi is commemorated in the special festival of Reis Magos and the Feira dos Reis, the Fair of Kings. The centrepiece is a procession with three boys representing the three kings. After a special Mass, the three, one chosen from each of the three hamlets that make up Chandor, mounted on horses and richly dressed in regal robes, are led, colourful parasols held above their splendid crowns, along the traditional route, all to the usual cacophony of trumpets and drums, finally returning to the church. The event is the occasion for a fair and even a special football match.

On days other than festival days such as this, the size of the square gives it a quiet, almost deserted appearance and the eye is invitingly drawn to one of Goa's most impressive private houses, a veritable mansion, that fills one side of the square. In

Main Square at Chandor, with the Menezes Braganza House and piazza cross

fact the 'square' is only as long as it is to accommodate this frontage. This is the house of one of Goa's great families, the **Menezes Braganzas**.

The most famous member of the family, Luis de Menezes Braganza, born in 1878, became a leading protagonist for Goan political rights in the first part of this century. Born with a wealthy background, he certainly did not spurn the lifestyle it allowed but enjoyed it to the full. However, he used his money and position not only to fight a ceaseless political crusade, but campaigned for social rights as well. His heart was with the people and he was one of their heroes. Educated at Rachol Seminary, his main career was as a journalist. Owning his own newspaper, *O Debate,* he also wrote prolifically and forcefully in other publications and was an eloquent public speaker. He died in 1938 and is buried in the cemetery on the hillside in Chandor within sight of the family home. To mark the 25th anniversary of his death, the Instituto Vasco da Gama in Panjim, founded in 1871 for the promotion of literature, art and science, was re-named after Menezes Braganza.

Towards the end of the 19th century, another famous freedom fighter, also now honoured in Panjim, was born in Chandor village. Tristao Braganza Cunha was born in 1891 and his memorial now occupies the monument in the centre of the Azad Maidan, originally built for Afonso Albuquerque's statue. So, two sons of this small village have displaced two of the principal figures in the history of the discovery and conquest of Goa by the Portuguese.

Yet another connection between Chandor and Panjim is that the Mhamai Kamat family originate here in the hamlet of Guirdolim (Giddhli). As a notable Hindu family they were victims of the first religious purges in Salcete and, taking their family deities with them or sending them away for safe keeping, most crossed into Ponda. Some remained behind and converted to the Christian faith. By the 18th century the Hindu branch of the family had developed trading links with the Portuguese and as the Christian branch were also well connected by this time, they were able to return to Goa. The family house in Panjim near the Secretariat building is one of the oldest in Goa (see p. 66).

The son of Menezes Braganza continued the political struggle, supporting the movement for freedom from colonial rule to the point where, in 1950, the family had to flee to India. In 1963, following liberation, the family returned to find their home intact.

The house embodies the spirit of elegance and culture that characterised high society in the late

Balconied windows on the Menezes Braganza House, Chandor

18th and early 19th centuries, which is when most of it was built, although, like many grand houses here, the original dates back much further – in this case perhaps to the end of the 16th century. The façade extends a huge distance either side of the central entrance, 24 windows gracing each of its two storeys. The exterior is, typically, without many frills, the seemingly endless rows of windows defined by simple pilasters and characterised each with its own tiny but intricately worked wrought-iron balcony. The trefoil upper sections of the tall windows have curved wooden tracery filled with stained glass. Above, the overhanging red tiled roof rests on a projecting tile cornice typical of Goan houses. In fact the whole house, inside and out, demonstrates virtually every characteristic of the period.

Its length requires a double courtyard arrangement behind the facade, ensuring light everywhere instead of the gloom that can afflict a house with so many rooms. The whole of the first floor across the front of the house consists of formal rooms for entertaining. Several drawing rooms, a splendid dining room fit for banquets, the library, with one of the finest private collections in Goa (very much a memorial to Luis de Menezes Braganza) and the salon, long and gracious with chairs set along the walls – as though at any moment the strings of the orchestra will surge above the murmured conversation of colourful and fashionably attired guests with the strains of the mando. As with all these front rooms, the arrangement by which windows open on one side onto the small balconies overlooking the square and on the other to the long open verandah that runs around the inner courtyards, enhances the feeling of spaciousness – as do the reflections in heavily gilded Venetian mirrors. The doorways as well as the windows are decorated with a variety of wooden tracery, while the plaster mouldings round their arched openings add stylish detail. Windows in the salon are set in openings inspired, it would seem, by the shell-headed niche, contriving to let in even more light, while a stuccoed ceiling is reminiscent of the Rococo vault-

Santo Aleixo, Curtorim

ing of the chancel of some of Salcete's churches that are contemporary with the house. Here, the chandeliers almost reflect in the gleaming marble floor, all these linked entertaining rooms being distinguished by the varying patterns of the marble used.

At the heart of the house is the private chapel rich in Baroque gilt, while bedrooms open off the verandahs on the other sides of the courtyard. The ground floor was occupied by servants, kitchens and storage.

In this setting, an abundance of old furniture, much of it traditional black wood submerged in carving – rich comfort often being sacrificed for rich decoration – is seen in its original habitat. Together with white-and-blue porcelain reminders of Macao, stern family portraits and nostalgic fading sepia photographs ensure that the spirit of Goa's past is kept alive.

The countryside around Chandor is noticeably green in winter, the result of many natural lakes and springs that no doubt attracted original settlement here, many indeed being associated with the past in local legend and history. In one such lake, a princely shepherd drowned with his flock and still holds court on its bed; another is assuredly the tank used by Kadamba war elephants and horses. Two famous springs in the village have wondrous healing properties. Now, these natural waters are utilised for extensive irrigation, the Paroda Canal being a prominent feature, especially along the road northwards to Curtorim.

Curtorim (Kurhtori)

This is another widely spread village consisting of several hamlets and, like Chandor, with a heavily predominant Christian population. Its main interest centres on the **Church of St Alex**, Santo Aleixo, of some renown. Its builders certainly had an eye for location and, refusing to accept the obvious, built the church with its back to the centre of the village, allowing the front of the church and its square to face across the serene waters of a palm-fringed lake to wooded slopes, an enviable setting. Although there has been a church on this site since 1597, built (it is said) on the ruins of a temple to the widely popular deity Ravalnath, it was rebuilt in 1647. The present building is dominated by late 18th-century refurbishment. The façade is unremarkable in that it has three storeys with a gable between twin towers, but the upper section of the towers is octagonal, not frequently encountered, topped with a dome and a balustraded round lantern with its own small dome. The decoration is much livelier than usual – more complex balustrades, more elaborate, certainly imaginative, capitals to the pilasters, scrolled pediments over the windows and pinnacles that bear a strong resemblance to the amalaka design of those that bedeck the temple of Mangesh. In fact, the whole of the upper part of the towers of St Alex has much in common with the tower over the sanctuary at Mangesh. The octagon form may not be often seen in church towers in Goa apart from St Cajetan in Old Goa and, while some piazza crosses are octagonal, it is of course a well-established feature of Goan Hindu temple towers and the small specific group of 'Ponda style' lamp towers that evolved in the 18th century. Eighteenth-century Goan architectural experience saw a greater merging of Hindu and Christian ideas once the evolution of the Indian Baroque had established a genuine independent Indian style during the previous century. Even before the formal political union of the areas of the Old and New Conquests, there had developed a freer exchange of people and ideas.

St Alex is an example of Goan-style Rococo exuberance spreading to the outside, joyous but without excess. The slimness of the façade has been retained, noticeable in a distant view from the far side of the square, or even better looking across the lake from the road leading to Raia and Rachol. In fact the towers extend either side beyond the width of the nave. Only the towers, the façade and the porch are plastered and painted white, the rest of the walls being left as exposed red laterite, a feature of several Salcete churches. At the end of the narrow nave, five altars gleam and glisten. The main altar is full of drama and elegance, the triple salomonic columns framing the three central niches – a reminder in miniature of the reredos of the seminary church at nearby Rachol, here slender though heavy with foliage. To each side, the design breaks free with scrolled pilasters supporting complex balustraded pedestals for guardian angels in all their splendour. The whole is framed by twin columns and an unusually elaborate tracery arch across the chancel vault, the basic design taken

from the Espirito Santo in Margao. As in the whole of this altar, the concept of detail even of the columns is outstanding, from the curving freedom of the capitals to the most delicate fluting of their upper section. This is carried into the decoration of the deeply panelled ceiling of the chancel and the notable stuccowork of the chancel arch itself. This is a reredos to spend time with.

The four side-altars, all canopied, retain the same triple column frame for their two niches, together providing an impressive setting for the chancel, all in turn complemented by the delicacy of the pulpit.

From the front steps of the church, the considerable size of the square, its spaciousness augmented by the open country beyond, diminishes the apparent size of the piazza cross, but this is another fine example, equalling the Margao cross and having much in common in terms of design and detail (see p. 136). On the square base the arched openings are flanked by salomonic columns and fluted pilasters each with their complex capitals, framed above and below by prominent heavily-grooved entablatures. Above this, curves are of the essence and Indian elements are introduced. Separating the baluster curves and the mouldings that build up the four pinnacles and the central column for the cross, are flattened groated spheres of the amalaka, as in the pinnacles of the church towers. There is no repetition of decorative pattern on any of its many layers. All this detail is still clear in spite of many coats of whitewash but it underlines the problem of preserving stucco, especially as fine as this, outdoors. Incidentally, the actual cross on top is not the original, which accounts for its lack of proportion, the replacement being much too small for the pedestal.

Rachol

Not far along the banks of the Zuari River is Rachol. In a long bend of the Zuari River, here wide and slow-flowing, there are many byways turning off from the road between Margao and Borim Bridge that crosses into Ponda. One such road winds its way between paddy-fields, palm trees standing sentinel along their boundary banks, to a low hillock rising from the valley floor at the river's edge. Here, set away from the slightest disturbance, in tangible solitude, is the **Seminary of Rachol.** Inside, there is nothing superficial about the atmosphere of hushed calm; it sits naturally. There is also a strong sense of history. Rachol is a very special place.

Seminaries became an important part of the Goan scene soon after the arrival of the Portuguese and have made a vital contribution to Goan development. Initially established as a weapon in the armoury of the soldiers of Christ, their original purpose was to provide secular priests able to communicate with the local people. Their role as communicators and educators was to result in much more broadly based benefits than the spread of Christian doctrine alone.

The first seminary was established in Old Goa in 1541. Originally the Seminary of the Holy Faith, its development lacked real drive until Francis Xavier, pressured to involve himself with its activities, persuaded the Society of Jesus to give it its full support. The college was formally handed over to the Jesuits in 1551, becoming the College of St Paul, and results were immediate and dramatic. It became one of the greatest seats of learning in the East and it was the birthplace of Goan priesthood that would, after a long struggle, emerge to make a massive contribution, not only in the Indian subcontinent but across the world, a contribution out of all proportion to the size and Christian population of this minute territory. Inspired by the success of this enterprise, other religious orders established seminaries and colleges of their own. Amongst the most important of these were the Dominicans' College of St Thomas Aquinas at Panelim and the Franciscans' two establishments, St Bonaventure, also in Old Goa, and St Jerome across the river near Reis Magos. On the Monte Santo was the Augustinians' 'People's College', while the Capuchins established their 'University of Arts, Sciences and Technology' at Pilar.

The youthful King Sebastian of Portugal agreed to sponsor the foundation of a second Jesuit seminary in Salcete, an area for which the Jesuits had been given spiritual responsibility, and in 1574 the College of All Saints was opened in Margao. Within five years it had been razed to the ground by Muslim raiders, but in the following year, 1580, it was re-established, this time on its present site under the protection of the guns of the fortress of Rachol, one of Goa's strongest defensive points at that time. It was renamed the college of Ignatius Loyola, and the church, when rebuilt and enlarged to accord with its new status, was also dedicated to the founder of the order.

Rachol is associated with a long line of famous names. Among the earliest was Father Thomas Stephens, the first Englishman known to have set foot in India, who arrived in Goa in 1579. He set to work studying Konkani and Marathi and by 1616 he had produced a 'bible'. Written in verse, in Marathi mixed with some Konkani, it was printed in Roman script on one of the three printing presses brought by the Jesuits to Goa, the first of these being the first printing press in India. Not in any way attempting a literal translation, its title, *Christa Purana*, the 'Mythology of Christians', sums up his intentions of putting the Christian story into a form familiar to the local people, that they could also put into song, in this way relating to the chanting of Mantras which was at the core of Hindu worship. He also revised Francis Xavier's catechism, putting it into pure Konkani, and produced a Konkani grammar based on work already started at St Paul's. Published in 1640, twenty years after his death, it was the first grammar of any of India's modern languages. Another of Rachol's early scholarly priests, Father Diogo Ribeiro, published a Konkani–Portuguese dictionary in 1626, which was to be only the first of many such linguistic studies to come out of Rachol. Throughout the 17th century, the press here produced a cavalcade of learned works.

After the expulsion of the Jesuits in 1759, Archbishop da Silveira decreed Rachol a diocesan

Rachol Seminary: main doorway

seminary with the title 'The Good Shepherd', Bom Pastor. Other religious orders rallied round and, with others, Dominicans and Oratorians played their part in maintaining the education and training standards established over the years. In 1835, with the expulsion of all religious orders, it became more and more difficult to staff the seminary, but the work continued, especially encouraged towards the end of the century by the Archbishop and first Patriarch of the East Indies, Dom Antonio Valente, who even prompted the addition of a new wing.

In 1899, in the Cathedral at Old Goa, the Archbishop had ordained a young priest, Father Agnelo de Souza, who, after working in remote areas of Goa and then spending several years at Pilar Monastery, was appointed Spiritual Director of Rachol. He was to become famed for his work and dedication in spite of ill-health and, in 1927, he died after collapsing while preaching in the pulpit here. His body now lies at Pilar and his canonisation as St Agnelo is eagerly awaited (p. 104).

The seminary has had fluctuating fortunes in terms of the numbers of students it has been able to recruit. It is a long, hard training and requires dedication to stay the course. Boys are first educated in the minor seminary at Saligao in Bardez, before starting their seven-year stay here at Rachol. Over recent years, the number of students in residence at any one time has varied between 50 and 100. There are students here not only from Goa but from many other parts of India.

Rebuilding the church and seminary started in 1606 and this includes most of the buildings we see today, with the exception of the new wing added in 1890. The church is, therefore, contemporary with the cathedral in Old Goa which was then under construction, and the Bom Jesus Basilica which had just been completed. Dedicated to St Ignatius Loyola, as already mentioned, its interior has been superbly restored and contains much of interest. It has the immediate feeling of a live and active church, no mere monument, and this not just because of its physical well-being.

The well-proportioned, compartmented reredos, Mannerist in style and reminiscent of the cathedral retable, gleams dully at the end of the high narrow nave. Gold is the main impression, enhanced by flashes of deep rich colouring. The walls of the chancel are most unusually decorated with elaborately and deeply carved panels, bas-reliefs in wood, subsequently enamelled.

Immediately within the main entrance doors, under the choir, there are altars on either side. The altar on the left as you enter is dedicated to St Constantine. Bone relics of the Saint which,

together with a vial that once contained his blood, were brought from Rome in 1782, are kept in the altar, where St Constantine is depicted wearing military uniform as a Soldier of Christ.

Concealed beneath the altar on the opposite side of the nave is a statue of Christ that is only revealed on Good Friday.

Another point of interest is the once-miraculous statue of the Boy Jesus on a side-altar. This statue, with its origins on the rocky coast of Africa, was acquired by a Rector of Rachol from the Church of Our Lady of Mercy at Colva in 1834, the time of the expulsion of religious orders in Goa. The story is told on p. 139, where the church at Colva is described.

Looking back up at the choir, the elderly pipe organ presents its decorated pipes to the church. Brought out from Lisbon early in the seminary's history, it is the oldest pipe organ in the East. It has a formidable pedal that must require great energy to operate, but it is apparently still in good tune although now requiring a great deal of maintenance.

Outside the entrance to the choir, a first-floor corridor, known as the Corredor des Patriarcas, runs the length of the church. It is lined with mural portraits of the founders of many of the religious orders, fine pieces of art, that of St Francis of Assisi being particularly dramatic. Below St Ignatius Loyola are exquisitely painted small doors in a stuccoed plaster frame that lead to the tiny Archbishop's Gallery.

Beyond are the Archbishop's private quarters, kept for occasions when he visits the seminary, and the corridor continues round the **main courtyard**, the upper walls here also being covered with delicately coloured murals.

Below this corner of the church end of the buildings is the Sacristy, the highlight here being two carved wooden pyramids of niches containing a magnificent collection of small sculpted figures. There are 24 niches in each.

The entrance hall to the seminary itself sets the atmosphere for the place. Architecturally it is highly original, an impressive concept with the ceiling arching down to each corner from a single massive column in the centre of the hall. Here too are further examples of the murals that are a feature of the seminary. Some are beginning to deteriorate, but they still glow with their soft and delicate colours. Appropriately among the paintings here is one of St Philip Neri, founder of the Oratorians, who in Goa have struggled to achieve the recognition and acceptance of Goan priests denied by other religious orders.

Rachol Seminary: main courtyard

The main buildings are ranged round a large courtyard of which the church forms one side. Columns in the courtyard once supported a trellis-work of vines, now replaced by masses of colourful bougainvillaea together with chickoo and ashoka trees. An unusual sundial graces one wall.

Below the pavement in the centre of the quadrangle are huge water cisterns. After one has squeezed down the narrow steps, these tanks, impressive in their emptiness, echo eerily – but even so are not the most curious of Rachol's underground mysteries, as we shall see. It has been suggested that the seminary may have been built on the site of a Shiva temple and that the cisterns were in fact its underground holy tank, a feature not uncommon in pre-Portuguese temples. Supporting the temple theory, a Nandi bull, headless of course, was found here. It sits at the top of the staircase leading from the entrance hall.

The corridors on the two floors around the courtyard contain more soft murals, nothing clashing, nothing harsh, nothing to grate on the senses, this being the case with everything from even the old wooden doors to the splendid furniture, paintings and other works of art encountered everywhere. In a quiet corner, the room in which Father Agnelo lived and worked remains a memorial and a place of pilgrimage.

In the main hall on the first floor hangs a large portrait of the founder, **King Sebastian of Portugal**, the boy-king adventurer, only fourteen when he came to the throne in 1568. Ten years later he led an impetuous, ill-fated crusade against the Moors in North Africa and was killed at the disaster of El Ksar el Kebir. He is portrayed in eminently appropriate style on prancing horseback.

There are also portraits of **Archbishops of Goa**,

including the present incumbent, Raul Nicolau Gonsalves, the first Goan to hold this office.

A room which makes a great impact is the library, full of many rare books in a seeming multitude of languages.

Like some of the Hindu temples, Rachol is virtually a self-contained unit and behind the refectory and extensive kitchens is a veritable farmyard, with buffaloes (for milk), hens, pigs, and orchards stretching down to the river. And in the cellar is a doorway, usually locked, the entrance to a tunnel, narrow and dark and leading no-one knows where. Perhaps an escape route, perhaps to a hide-away. Strange tales surround the tunnel, of searchers lost in its darkness trying to unravel its secrets. The most favoured solution is that it was a link with part of the fort in early years, but no-one knows for sure.

The fort is now in ruins, hardly anything to be seen except for a few shattered walls or lonely blocks of stone – but these remnants reek of history. This was a real outpost of empire, standing isolated and alone, even before Salcete formally came under Portuguese control in 1543, right on the front line between opposing forces. Built as a Muslim fort, it was captured from the Sultan of Bijapur, Ismail Adil Khan, by the Emperor of Vijayanagar in 1520 and

Gateway remains of ancient fort at Rachol

handed over by the Hindu ruler to the Portuguese to encourage their assistance against the Muslim foe. It was a vital point in Portuguese defences, at its peak mounted with 100 cannon. After the Muslims came the Marathas and it saw frequent action until their final withdrawal in 1740, often being isolated and besieged but never being taken throughout its history from 1520. At the end of the 18th century, no longer on a disputed frontier, Goa having expanded to the east with the New conquests, and no longer on guard against raiders seeking tribute, it lost any significance and was finally abandoned in 1842, then allowed to fall into decay. However, like all else here it leaves a lasting impression.

Rachol Parish Church

A fort had seen action here before the arrival of the Portuguese and it would be more than another half-century before the first church would be built. The Jesuits had performed services here as early as 1566, but this was a frontier post in troublesome times and it was another ten years before even a mud-and-thatch church was built, just outside the walls of the fort on the site of what is today Rachol parish church. On the river bank, only a short distance from where the seminary now stands, it was dedicated to Nossa Senhora das Neves, Our Lady of Snows. Today, there could hardly be a more peaceful place, quiet, almost isolated, yet it has close associations with the terrible violence of those conversion years of the late 16th century.

Buried here is the infamous temple destroyer, Diogo Rodrigues, his memorial slab, translated, recording that

Our Lady of Snows: Rachol Parish Church

> Here lies Diogo Rodrigues 'O do Forte' Captain of this Fortress, who destroyed the pagodas of these territories. He died on 21 April of the year 1577.

Known widely as 'O do Forte', the 'Man of the Fort', it was said of him that, after a particularly violent bout of temple wrecking, 'he was so pleased with the destruction of the Temples that he used to deface the images with the butt of his sword.'

Persecution and temple destruction in the area did not end with his death and another memorial slab, resting on the steps of the chancel, marks the original burial place of five Jesuits who died in a clash with the villagers of Concolim in southern Salcete in 1583 (see p. 188). Translated, the inscription reads as follows:

> Under this large slab were deposited the bodies of five members of the Society of Jesus, Rodolfo Aquaviva, Affonso Pacheco, Antonio Francisco and Perno Berno, Priests, and Francisco Aranha, a Lay Brother, whom the idolators put to death in Cuncolim on 15 July 1583 and whose relics were removed to the College of St Paul, of Goa, in July 1597.

In 1907, the relics of the Martyrs were transferred again, this time to the cathedral, where they now rest on the altar dedicated to St Anne.

The incident of the death of the Cuncolim Martyrs is graphically illustrated in a fascinating old primitive, but effective, painting on the wall above an archway just beyond the side entrance to the chancel.

Raia

Between Rachol and Loutolim lies the village of Raia. This was the original home of the goddess Kamakshi, whose temple now adds to the celebrity of Siroda village on the opposite bank of the Zuari River in Ponda. Before the take-over of Salcete by the Jesuits, the temple here was held in high esteem in the area, Kamakshi being a form of Shantadurga and, like her, worshipped as the Goddess of Peace (see p. 130). At the time of the destruction of the temple in Raia by the Captain of Rachol, Diogo Rodrigues, it was a potter of the village who smuggled the deity across the river to safety, an event still acknowledged by a potter from Raia having the hereditary right to light the first lamp of the Kamakshi festival in Siroda. More practically, the potters of Raia also have the right to supply the clay lamps used for the festival, which are numerous as there is a huge procession of lamp-carrying devotees.

Wall painting depicting the death of the Cuncolim Martyrs: Chancel of Our Lady of Snows Church – Rachol

When the Portuguese eventually built a church in Raia, they dedicated it, like the parish church of Rachol, to Our Lady of Snows.

Loutolim

The countryside along this river flatland continues at its lush greenest, with the many typically Goan houses dotting the wooded landscape a principal ingredient. Fresh and colourful samples appear around almost every corner and the village of Loutolim and the surrounding area has somehow produced a concentration of so many examples from mansions to small cottages, a treasury of Goan domestic architecture, with every component on display. In their gardens, bright with flowers, shrubs and trees, red-tiled roofs above a tile cornice overhang colour-washed walls and the curves of Baroque windows grace modest as well as grand houses, some with well-preserved examples of the shell windows of old. Above all there are the balcaos, porches, that together with wide verandahs of all features seem the essence of Goan village life. These characteristics, in some degree common to all, somehow produce a unity and harmony with the natural setting that could be nowhere in India other than Goa.

The village square itself contains the right ingredients, a white church with Baroque façade, with priest's house and school to one side, and opposite a shaded walled cemetery. Even modern accretions such as ugly clusters of wires on stark standards cannot spoil the atmosphere or offend the façade's dignity.

From here the whole route northwards along the river between hills that form this wide valley, is gently pleasing, wooded slopes on one side, paddy merging with the river's waters on the other. Through Quelossim, where Parvati waited for Shiva to end his meditation and where, in ancient times, her temple as Shantadurga was first built; her image now, on the other bank of the river beyond the hills that form the skyline to the east. Then to Cortalim, where Shiva left his linga to be found by cowherds and worshipped as Mangesh and where, just beyond the ferry station, the route now joins the Panjim–Margao road, almost at the road bridge across the Zuari.

GLIMPSES OF MORMUGAO

The taluka of Mormugao is a relatively recent creation, established in 1917 for administrative reasons. Part of Salcete for most of its history and, in terms of physical features imperceptibly merging, its modern prominence derives mainly from the recent, rapid growth of the Vasco-Mormugao urban area and especially the importance of Mormugao as a port.

Up until the later part of the 19th century, the Mormugao headland was distinguished mainly for the presence of its great fortress, and towards the end of this period even that had been abandoned and was slowly disintegrating. Started in 1624 to complement Fort Aguada, it was built on the same architectural principles and, like its companion, spread over the whole of its promontory. Its future seemed assured when, at the end of the 17th century, it was selected by the Viceroy as successor, as capital, to Old Goa. New building actually started and in 1703 Viceroy Caetano de Melo e Castro even transferred residence for a few months. However, the project was abandoned on orders from Portugal and Mormugao fort reverted to its role as a military base. At the end of the 19th century, the opening of the railway led to increased activity in Mormugao port and the population grew until, in 1917, Mormugao taluka was created out of part of Salcete. It was also decreed that a new town should be built. Named Vasco da Gama, this has since grown into one of the greatest concentrations of population in Goa, the port area retaining the old name of Mormugao, one of the three villages on the site of which the new town was established. When the airport was built on Vasco's outskirts, its role as transport centre of the state was confirmed and its attractiveness for industrial development resulted in yet further growth.

But for visitors the area has special significance for other reasons. For anyone arriving at Dabolim airport, the first sights and sounds of Goa are experienced along the road that follows the south bank of the Zuari River estuary before joining the main north-south road leading either to Panjim or Margao.

Even at the airport itself, we are already treading in the footsteps of somewhat earlier arrivals, Dabolim being one of the sites from which stone-age man hunted and fished many thousands of years ago, leaving behind in his camps tiny implements such as arrow-heads and scrapers.[7] A short distance after leaving the airport, with only the briefest glimpse of the outskirts of Vasco, the road drops down the hill to Chicolim. To the right of the road on the hillside is another site selected by Goa's early inhabitants as being a pleasant place to live, this about 5000 years ago, leaving traces of Goa's earliest dwellings, holes cut into the laterite hillside and broken pieces of the earliest local pottery. More recent inhabitants of the neighbourhood are the Carmelite nuns whose convent, which can be seen through the trees, was founded in 1947.

Meanwhile, travelling along the road, this already has the feel of Goa, quite unique and, once encountered, unmistakable. The roadside walls of large blocks of rough, pitted red laterite introduce the material that forms Goa's land surface and of which much of Goa is built – mostly plastered over but there at the core. All along the road its red dust is raised in clouds by gaudily painted trucks, not in any way unique to Goa, as they drive along the verges, manoeuvring to overtake, all happily accepting the invitation 'Horn Please' inscribed on the backs of competitors. This stretch of road seems

St Jacinta Island with the church of St Jacinta (St Hyacinth)

to inspire competition, though ignored by slow plodding bullock carts on which even the drivers doze gently.

Behind the low walls, palms, bananas, mangos, bougainvillaea and many others provide colour and lush greenery to surround red-tiled roofs above long verandahs, while in gaps on the slopes, away from the rocky shore of the estuary, glossy green cashew appear.

Further along the road is a tiny islet only a short distance off-shore and recently linked by a causeway. Thick with trees and with the still-visible remnants of defensive walls, it has only a few fishermen's cottages and the tiny chapel at the water's edge with landing steps nearby. The island is named after its chapel, **St Jacinta**.

Just after the road leaves the shoreline, a signpost to the left proclaims the 'Rua Escravo de Maria', which turns out to be only a track through the palms and the 'Slaves of Mary' only slaves in the sense of devotees. This road leads to an open space in front of what was the church of the village of Sancoale, Nossa Senhora de Saude, **Our Lady of Health**. Hidden from the road, all that is left of the church built in 1606 is the central section of the façade, its towers and everything behind gone, destroyed by fire in 1834. But what is left is well worthy of its designation as a National Monument. It is elegantly proportioned and much attention was given to its fine decorative detail, especially interesting being the panels above the arched side entrances which somehow strengthen its wistful air. It would once have ranked with Goa's finest.

The views open out beyond this, across the estuary to the Tiswadi shore and, at a distance, across paddy fields to the right and set in wooded slopes, is a white church amongst the greenery, a typical Goan scene. This church is built on the spot where Jesuit priests said their first mass on setting foot in Salcete for the first time on 1 May 1560. The foundation stone was laid on that day and on the same day in 1566 the complete church was dedicated to San Filipe e San Tiago Apostolos, **St Philip and St James**, whose feast day this is. It is the village church of **Cortalim**, site of the original Mangesh temple, history determining its siting rather than its relationship with the main part of the village – which is some distance away on the other side of the main road.[8]

Not far from Cortalim church is **the sanctuary dedicated to St Philip Neri** which was built in memory of Fr. Joseph Vaz. Fr. Vaz was born in Benaulim in 1651 and baptised in the church there, but his father came from Sancoale and it was here that a sanctuary chapel was planned to celebrate the 200th anniversary of the death of this famous son of Goa.

All that remains of the church of Nossa Senhora de Saude (Our Lady of Health), Sancoale, Mormugao

Educated in the seminaries of both Jesuits and Dominicans in Old Goa, he was one who spoke out strongly against the dismissive attitude of the Portuguese clergy to native priests, discriminating against them by preventing appointments to the church hierarchy, denying higher religious education and the refusal by all the religious orders to accept Goan priests as members, in spite of being responsible for their education and ordination. He joined a small group of priests, then based at the Church of the Cross of Miracles in Old Goa, and they formed themselves into the Congregation of the Oratorians in India, attaching themselves to St Philip Neri's congregation of secular priests in Lisbon in spite of the opposition of Goa's archbishop. So, Goan priests had their own order, one of the rules being that only Brahmins could join. This was an important milestone in gaining recognition for Goan priests, but Fr. Vaz, claiming inspiration from the Cross of Miracles, was soon to leave Goa.

He went to Sri Lanka, by this time lost by Portugal to the hostile Dutch, and spent the next 24 years, until his death in 1711, earning widespread admiration for his missionary work there in desperately difficult circumstances. The first moves towards the canonisation of Fr. Joseph Vaz were taken by the Bishop of Cochin in 1713, an objective pursued by his followers though still without success. Special prayers are offered at both the Sanctuary and at the Church of the Cross of Miracles for the beatification of the 'Venerable Apostle of Ceylon'.

This short stretch of road from the airport ends at its junction with the main road from Panjim to Margao at Cortalim, until not long ago best known as one terminus of the busiest ferry in Goa. The opening of the road bridge over the Zuari made the ferry redundant in 1983 although the ferry station is still in operation, a less frequent service now connecting with Marcaim (Morhkoi) on the Ponda shore.

From the road bridge there are sweeping views to the mouth of the Zuari. On the left, the façade of the old Sancoale church, with St Jacinta Island beyond, are followed by the Mormugao headland with its port. On the right, another tiny islet forms the most distant landport where the promontory of Dona Paula extends into the sea. It is between these two most distant points that a launch service provides what is almost a sea trip across the mouth of the river.

13 BEACHES, BASTIONS & BAZAARS – BARDEZ

With so much of the population, both resident and visiting, concentrated along the stretch of country behind Calangute Beach, Bardez has grown rapidly in significance in the Goan scene, especially since efforts have been directed towards developing tourism. With some of the finest beaches, more forts than anywhere else, including the best-preserved, Goa's most famous market and several outstanding churches, there is something here for everyone. In scenic terms, broad sweeping palm-fringed beaches bracketed by rocky headlands typify the coastline and its hinterland – rich, gentle and restful, characterised by paddy-fields laced with coconut groves, interspersed with slow waterways and colourful villages – creates an atmosphere very Goan.

Its attraction beckons from across the Mandovi. Low tree-covered hills rise from the river bank opposite Panjim, deep inlets hiding a string of fishing villages and boatyards with several features outstanding. At present, attention is caught by the turmoil surrounding the rebuilding of the collapsed road bridge, prompting the intense ferry activity to Betim and on either side of the new bridges. To the left of the ferries that shuttle backwards and forwards from near the Secretariat, the white marble building, with its collection of domes, is the Gurudwara, one of the few Sikh temples in Goa – the small Sikh population making these a rarity. Further towards the river mouth the façade of a large white church with steps just above the water-line is Reis Magos, with the towering black walls of the fort above it. Beyond this, Nerul Creek cuts deeply inland, defining the headland of Fort Aguada clustered with its fortress, lighthouses and church. In the other direction inland from the bridge, the Bardez shoreline soon curves away

behind the island of Chorao, but not before another riverside Baroque church makes its presence felt – this is the fine church with its unusual dedication of Nossa Senhora de Penha de Franca, Our Lady of the Rock of France.

With three churches and two fortresses visible on the far shore before even crossing the Mandovi, it is obvious that these are a vital part of the general scene. Bardez has many fine and attractive churches with a variety of styles and dates. The Franciscans built widely when the province became part of Goa in the mid-16th century but all have now been rebuilt and modified, some several times at different dates and in different styles. As elsewhere, the architects tended to take inspiration from other churches in the area as well as the general style of the period, giving a sense of unity amongst the diversity.

One such group of 18th-century churches is of specific interest for the adoption, on the façade, of a false dome. There are few domed churches in Goa but, no doubt inspired by the major example of St Cajetan in Old Goa, several 18th-century architects in this area developed this theme, replacing the more usual gable, or pediment between the towers, with a false dome on an octagonal drum complete with balustrades and lanterns. Examples of this can be seen at St Alex, Calangute, St Cajetan, Assanora and Our Lady of the Immaculate Conception at Moira. Beyond Bardez on the island of Jua in the Mandovi, it is a feature of the great church of St Estevam. The towers have flattened cupolas and, together with the domes, are adorned with a profusion of pinnacles, lanterns, balustrades and arched windows, all of which offered great scope for invention.

It so happens that the churches mentioned as

illustrating false domed façades also provide examples in their interiors of the move away from the Baroque towards the lighter, freer atmosphere of the Rococo that took place in the 18th century. This can be followed readily here from the older Baroque churches such as Reis Magos, to the Rococo at its peak, where the exquisite church at Pomburpa cannot be bettered.

While in Bardez look out for the elaborate mortuary chapels attached to church cemeteries. They came especially into vogue during the first half of the 18th century, when the province was ravaged by the Maratha invasions as well as a long series of famines. Grottoes are another speciality here. Relatively recent additions, they add considerable interest to church squares.

But, to return to our landing on the Bardez shore from Panjim, these river banks are worth exploring. The side roads that follow them run through gentle Goan countryside, offering meandering alternatives to the new main road that carves its way straight through the hillside at the end of the bridge on its direct route to Mapusa and the north (see map 7).

PANJIM TO CALANGUTE

Calangute beach is now most frequently reached along the main road to Mapusa, turning off at Porvorem to pass through the pleasant village of Saligao, where there is the minor seminary – from which the pupils move on to Rachol – and an abundance of cottages illustrating typical Goan domestic architecture. However, a sharp contrast is provided by its church, Nossa Senhora Mai de Deus, Our Lady Mother of God, with its spikey Gothic design, whose shrine with its miraculous image of the Virgin was brought from the ruin of the Convent in Daugim, Old Goa, in 1873 for installation in this new church.

The long straight road from Saligao ends at Calangute's church of St Alex, one of the churches already mentioned, its false domed façade intriguing. The interior is much remodelled, a stately composition of white and gold where all the elements of the Rococo decoration, its flattened pilasters, swirling brackets and widespread sunbursts of the altars have been ordered and controlled. The deeply groined, almost severely plain, vaulting of the chancel complements the design of the reredos perfectly. The end result is impressive and the elegance of the pulpit would be difficult to match, building up from the lowest pendant to the tassels and flowers of the exotic canopy without losing any of its slenderness and lightness.

St Alex, Calangute

Rococo pulpit in the church of St Alex, Calangute

The alternative route to Calangute beach from the bridge or Betim ferry is to take the road along the river seawards which leads through a string of boat-builders' yards and fishermen's cottages to the village of Verem where, at the crossroads marked by a Hindu shrine sheltered by a sprawling banyan tree, a side road down to the river leads to the area known as Reis Magos.

Reis Magos fort and church

This little headland, reaching out into the nar-rowest point of the river at the northern end of the sandbar, has obvious strategic significance. Albu-querque had to put troops ashore here to subdue a Muslim outpost during his attacks of 1510, and once Bardez was added to Portuguese territory a fort was built in 1551 that would remain a key position. An inscription in the fort records that it was completely rebuilt in 1703, soon able to prove its worth in 1739, when the Marathas occupied the whole of Bardez with only the forts of Aguada, and here at Reis Magos, holding out on the north bank of the Mandovi.

Dramatically high sloping walls on the side over-looking the river are necessitated by its position on the steep slope and, typically, there is a walled corridor linking the main fortress with the river anchorage. It has many underground passageways and rooms and its own water supply from a fresh-water spring. Cylindrical look-out turrets decorate the bastions, a distinctive feature of this period of Portuguese fort building.

It is now in use as a prison and remains a prominent landmark from the river and from many places on the opposite shore. The white façade of the church, next to the fort, is especially prominent from a distance. It is the church that has given the fort, and subsequently this part of the village, the name by which it is known today – Reis Magos, the Magi Kings, the Three Wise Men who followed the star to Bethlehem to offer their gifts to the Infant Jesus.

The first **church** was built here in 1555 not long after the fort. The Franciscans, who had been given missionary responsibility for the new province, set about converting the people of Bardez with enthu-siasm – first a school and later a seminary were attached to the church. Named after **St Jerome** it quickly became a centre of learning rivalling the Jesuits' efforts at St Paul's in Old Goa and that at Rachol. Like the Adil Khan's palace across the river, some Viceroys stayed here while awaiting their great moment when they sailed up-stream to the city to assume office, or between handing over to

Reis Magos Fort: in the foreground is the piazza cross

Gable on the church at Reis Magos

their successor and their departure for Portugal. Some went no further, three Viceroys being buried here. There are no traces of the great college now but the church is very much with us. A bold uncluttered façade is given added distinction by its position at the top of a fine flight of steps, the full width of the church, running up from the river bank. Five doorways, one blind, give breadth while the pairs of slender Corinthian columns that divide the compartments add grace to simplicity, an impression strengthened by the high scroll-decorated gable with its insignia of the crown and the Portuguese coat-of-arms. A royal church indeed and one of Goa's most dignified.

There is a local tradition and several historical references to the church having been built on the site of a Hindu temple. This was common Portuguese practice, but here there is interesting and unusual supporting evidence in the inclusion, at the lower end of the stone balustrades on each side of the church steps, of figures of lions in bas-relief. Such 'Viyala' figures were commonly used as decoration on balustrades of Hindu temples in South India and this was especially a feature of Vijayanagar architecture in the 14th and 15th centuries.

The small shrine near the foot of the steps was erected in 1916. Dedicated to 'Our Lady of Health' it is said to be on the site where Albuquerque landed to take a Muslim outpost in 1510.

Inside the church, which was restored in 1771, interest centres on the reredos. Above the large central space containing the tabernacle flanked by the four evangelists, the dominant feature is the **polychromed wooden panel** of the three gifts of gold, frankincense and myrrh to the Infant Jesus seated on Mary's knee.

In the corridor along the side of the church to the right of the altar is a large and impressive carved slab marking the burial place of one of the greatest of the Viceroys, Dom Luis de Ataide. In 1568, one of the first acts of the young King Sebastiao was the appointment of Dom Luis as Viceroy. The young king's confidence was not misplaced. In 1570, three Muslim states plotted together to evict the Portuguese: their formidable coalition army of 100,000 troops and 2000 elephants descended on Goa. Besieged on all sides and with a military strength of only 700, Ataide inspired the defence of the city for ten long months until the enemy withdrew. If it had not been for Ataide, Golden Goa's glory would have been short-lived. Acknowledging his administrative ability as well as his military skills, the king sent him out for another term – a most unusual occurrence – but sadly he died in office in March

Lions: Viyala figures at the foot of steps to the Church, Reis Magos

1581; some say his heart broke at the news of the death of his young king fighting the Moors at the Battle of El Ksar el Kebir in North Africa.

Above the church on the steep hillside is the walled cemetery near to what are now the prison gates.

The feast of Reis Magos, celebrating the Epiphany, the offering of gifts to the Infant Jesus by the Magi, is held here on 6 January each year – one of the only three places in Goa where this takes place. The Festival of Reis Magos is also celebrated at Chandor, Salcete taluka (see p. 141) and at Cansaulim in Mormugao taluka. The colourful procession and attendant ceremonies make this one of the highlights of the festival calendar.

After leaving Verem the road follows the river bank, turning inland to circle the Nerul River and its many creeks before crossing wide paddy-fields to reach the landmark of Candolim church, **Our Lady of Hope**. The towers for this church were only added in 1764, about 100 years after the rest of the church was built and their builders were obviously determined to make them a distinguishing feature. The village beyond, spreading along the coast road, is being much rebuilt and places of interest, such as the birthplace of Abade Faria and the Pluto House where the conspiracy of 1787 was hatched, are disappearing. To the south rises the headland of Aguada and the spread of the Fort Aguada hotel complexes.

The Three Magi, Melchior, Balthazar and Gaspar, presenting gifts of gold, frankincense and myrrh in church at Reis Magos

Church of Our Lady of Hope, Candolim

FORT AGUADA

Fort Aguada, the largest and amongst the best-preserved of Goa's forts, is one of its best-known landmarks, prominent in the scene from many directions. The headland on which it is built offered its military architects an ideal site, superbly located for both seaward and landward defence, shielding the most vital sea access to the heart of Portuguese territory. It retained its importance right up to the end of the 18th century when the Maratha threat was finally eliminated and the acquisition of the New Conquests had established Goa's future borders. Its impregnability is demonstrated by the fact that it was never taken by any enemy attacking by land or sea, or even both at the same time as often happened.

The Portuguese mostly feared attack from the sea, especially by their European rivals in the East, and in 1604 their fears were realised, a Dutch squadron appearing in the Mandovi. The forts of Reis Magos, Gaspar Dias and the Cabo proved inadequate to keep them out and, although eventually driven off, the Dutch entered the harbour and burned several Portuguese ships at anchor. Soon afterwards, in 1606, the Dutch naval force returned, this time to sit at the entrance to the river, blockading the harbour and preventing the entry or departure of all vessels. Their naval strength by now inadequate to take on the Dutch in open sea-battle, the Portuguese were driven to take defensive action to keep the Dutch at a respectful distance and work on the fort on the headland was started.

All was finished in 1612, the cost of building being met by a special levy on shipping. An inscription inside reads:

> In the reign of the Most Catholic King Dom Filippe of Portugal, the Municipality ordered the construction of this fortress with the one percent duty for the protection and defence of ships coming to this fort, which fortress was completed by the Members of the Municipality of the year 1612, Ruy Tavara being Viceroy.

The whole of the headland was used and the Nerul River, which now dissolves into creeks behind the peninsula, was extended to complete the water-link with the sea on the north side, creating a huge defensible 'island'. Its design was based on the principles, by now well established, laid down by the Italian military architects employed by the Portuguese government in Lisbon (see p. 38). The fort consists of a citadel on the highest point of the headland, linked by a defended passageway to the riverside and anchorage. Stout walls with occasional bastions surround the entire area at sea-level and along the riverside. Most of this outer wall has now disappeared, although there are still fragments to be seen, especially along the river.

At the heart of the fort was the citadel on the highest point, happily for the architect situated at the western tip of the headland and commanding every possible seaward approach. The citadel area can still be visited as it is outside the area used as a jail. As in all Goa's forts built by the Portuguese, the plan conforms to the configuration of the ground, but it is roughly in the form of a square with bastions for artillery at three corners, the fourth being occupied by the main gate (see fig). The three approachable sides are heavily defended with a dry moat and extremely thick walls. The fourth faces onto the steep slope to the river. The bastions are basically arrow-shaped but with rounded corners. The embrasures are wide and low to allow a broad field of fire for the cannon. At one time Aguada carried 200 cannon, a massive armoury.

It is an extremely solid, workmanlike fort with no frills. None of the usual delicate cylindrical turrets are here and no towers break the line of the battlements. The only gateway to the citadel is high and narrow and would have been sealed with

Fort Aguada: View from Old Lighthouse. Calangute Beach beyond; Candolim Church on the right

heavy, iron studded doors. Access across the narrow bridge over the ditch would have been fearfully difficult and, immediately inside the gateway, the ramp into the fort leads off at a sharp angle, as do the steep steps up to the battlements where the first lighthouse was built two-and-a-half centuries later. There is a magazine adjacent to the main gate, its half-round roofing designed to deflect enemy shot.

Lighthouses are a feature of the Aguada headland, as ideal a site for them as for a fortress. The oldest, one of the first lighthouses built in Asia, was commissioned in 1864. In earlier times ships were guided in by bonfire beacons lit on the Hill of the Pilots above Panjim Church. The first lighthouse, with several modifications to its workings, continued in service up to 1976 when it was replaced by the square, modern lighthouse situated nearby just outside the walls of the citadel. The new lighthouse is open to visitors. A climb up the spiral staircase followed by a short metal-runged ladder is rewarded with superb views.[1] The old model is a splendid structure, and from a distance dominates the skyline. The Viceroy, together with the architect and engineer, is suitably commemorated on a copper plaque in the 'turret' of the tower. Somewhat squat and with a solid appearance relieved by a balustrade around the platform and a curving staircase up to the lamp housing, it is a most satisfying building. This is where the great bell from the Augustinian church in Old Goa was brought before being transferred to Panjim church. Wherever it was hung it must have deafened the lighthouse keeper. There is a third and smaller lighthouse, the Aguada Beacon, at the foot of the slopes near the buildings on the river bank. Built in 1890, it marks the entrance to the river.

There is no need to climb the lighthouse to enjoy the splendid views all around. To the east along the river is Panjim, with Miramar and Caranzalem beaches leading round to the Cabo, with the Governor's house on its point. Beyond is the estuary of the Zuari River and the port of Mormugao with, offshore, the small islands of St Jorge and Cambariem. Westward, the Arabian Sea sweeps round to the northern beaches of Calangute and Baga, sealed off by its own headland on the horizon. Inland from the beaches, a sea of green palms is broken by the white dot of Candolim's church.

In the centre of the courtyard of the citadel, steps lead down to the gloom of a massive underground cistern for the storage of water. Its arched caverns, now dry, can hold more than ten million litres, or over two-and-a-quarter million gallons. Such vast storage facilities imply remarkable sources of supply and one of the advantages of the headland was the presence of several abundant springs of clear, sweet water giving the fort its name, 'Aguada' meaning 'a place for watering'. Ships would hasten to anchor at the fort after a long voyage and restock before leaving. No wonder the small chapel at the water's edge was dedicated to 'Our Lady of Good Voyage'. Apart from the river anchorage, there is also a jetty extending out into the sea on the northern side at the point where the Taj Group's hotel nestles just within the outer walls. The cannon on its round bastion, far out in the waves, also provide fire cover in the blind spot at the foot of the steep slopes, hidden from the guns of the citadel above. The excavation of the water cistern in the courtyard provided the stone for the building of the fortress walls. In fact, the hill is honeycombed with passages and rooms. There are many places where

Water cistern below fort courtyard – Aguada Fort

narrow steps lead down into the damp darkness of passages to long-lost magazines and storerooms.

Typically, there is a defensible passageway of parallel walls connecting the citadel with the anchorage below where, at river level, there are still some of the old buildings, including the first chapel already referred to. Also in this area is the one remaining spring, the largest of them all, Mae de Agua, Mother of Water. This part of the fort is now out of bounds to visitors, being in use as a jail. At the new gates to the prison area are the statues of a man holding the body of a child in his arms and a young woman, arms raised to show the chains that bound her are broken, standing in front of India's national emblem, the Ashoka Pillar. The inscription reads:

> Dedicated to the memory of those
> known and unknown, dead and alive,
> who have given their all in the cause
> of freedom from foreign domination.

At this point, a ceremony is held on 18 June each year to commemorate the beginning of the struggle for freedom on that day in 1946 when the first *satyagraha*, peaceful demonstration, was held in Margao. The role of prison is no new experience for the fort, having been used to hold those accused of taking part in the 19th-century revolts. Subsequently all through the fight for independence, there was a constant stream of nationalist supporters imprisoned here.

Incidentally, there are now no signs whatsoever of the barracks built by the British forces during their brief stay in the fort at the beginning of the 19th century at the time of the Napoleonic wars (see p. 10).

The Church of St Lawrence

Soon after the fort was completed, it was decided that another church should be built, and in 1630 Viceroy Dom Miguel de Noronha, Count of Linhares, founded the **Church of St Lawrence**. A great builder, he also built the causeway from Panjim to Ribander, anticipating the importance of the site of the future capital by 150 years! True to the principle of not building near to the walls in order to avoid giving the enemy a close-by outpost, the church was sited a considerable distance away from the citadel. With the huge size of Aguada, this could still be within the outer defences, its exact location being determined by the site on the headland of a long-destroyed Hindu temple. It was completed in 1643 and both founding and completion are recorded in contemporary inscriptions above the arch of the porch. A new panel commemorates the raising of the church to parish status in 1688.

There is a substantial group of buildings that includes an enclosed courtyard and residence. A large cloistered porch offers cool shade and conceals most of the simple façade which has a plain triangular gable with a single round window in the centre. Two narrow towers complete the design. The church behind is tiny and, to make up for the limited seating inside, benches are placed in the porch, surely the pleasantest conceivable place to worship. White plaster bas-reliefs of incidents in the Saint's life, including his martyrdom by fire, decorate the pillars.

Inside, the church consists only of a small nave, one end filled by the chancel with its altar dedicated to St Lawrence. It is the only altar. As patron saint of sailors, he is shown holding a boat in one hand and his statue also lies in a glass case beneath this typically Baroque reredos. The especially delicate decoration of the panelled vaulting is outstanding and there are attractive blue-and-white tiles on the risers of the steps of the altar. The tinkling of wind-chimes adds to the restful atmosphere of this out-of-the-way little church that yet can be seen from all along the opposite shore of the Mandovi estuary. The nearby walled cemetery with its new cross on a modern concrete pedestal, is given a place on the skyline by its position on the very crest of the hill.

The festival of St Lawrence is held here at the end of the monsoon and celebrates the clearing of the sand bar which makes the river navigable for large vessels for another season. In former times the ceremonial of the festival included the actual severing of a rope stretched across the river to symbolise its opening.

When Albuquerque stood on his pedestal at Miramar gazing across the Mandovi he would have approved of the view.

Northwards from Aguada the Bardez beaches stretch away to the hazy distance, wide and unbroken until the headland of Baga and followed quickly by the small rockier bays of Anjuna and Vagator, ending finally in the massive heap of Chapora's rock faces crowned by the remains of its fort. Behind this magnificent stretch of sand, a host of accommodation has sprung up, from the cheapest to the most expensive. Yet these beaches are unspoiled still, almost deserted at times. Calangute, Goa's 'Queen of Beaches', was the home of the first hippy population but, reduced in numbers, they have long since transferred to the relative seclusion of Anjuna and may well be on the move

again before long. These Bardez beaches offer all that tropical beaches should, even being oriented westwards, as are most Goan beaches, to give spectacular sunsets over the Arabian Sea.

What is left of the fort at Chapora is not as impressive a fortress compared with Aguada's citadel, but its wide empty space and sky, with tremendous views, make it worth the climb. Chapora Fort is most easily approached from the rough road leading from the far north end of Chapora bazaar. It is motorable for about half-way.

CHAPORA FORT

Almost inevitably, in view of its site, there had been a fort here long before the present one was built by the Portuguese, in fact long before they even arrived. Towering above the wide Chapora River, an important waterway, and commanding distant approaches in every direction, it was much sought after and changed hands several times even after the Portuguese acquired Bardez and this became the northern outpost of the Old Conquests.

View from Chapora Fort, looking northwards

Chapora Fort from Vagator Beach

When Prince Akbar, in revolt against his father Aurangzeb, sought refuge with his father's bitter enemy, the Marathas, and joined forces with Sambhaji in 1683 to try to end Portugal's hold on Goa, he made this his base camp. It was only after their recovery from this scare that the Portuguese decided that their northern defences needed strengthening and, following the Maratha experience, that they needed to provide shelter for the people of the region. Even so it was not until 1717 that the present fort was begun.

It is an excellent site with steep slopes on all sides. The fort sprawls over the whole upland area with its irregular outer plan following the outline of the higher slopes, using the natural contours to add defensive height as much as possible instead of dry ditches being dug. The main gate, at the top of the steep approach track, is small and unpretentious for so large a fort, but narrow and deep. The bastions, with their enormous embrasures for cannon, are irregularly spaced, their position depending on defence requirements, each having the cylindrical turret that gives a special character.

Inside there are few signs left of the barracks and housing that once filled this vast area; even the church that was dedicated to St Anthony has disappeared. Now there is only a tumble of stones in a wide expanse of open space with a few cashew bushes and herds of goats. There is excellent natural access to the sea down a natural valley to the beach, which itself is protected by rocky promontories.

At its first real test the fort fell to the Marathas in 1739, being held for two years after this by the old enemy of the Portuguese, the Maharajah of Sawantwadi, the Hindu ruler of Pernem across the river. Towards the end of the century it lost its military

significance when Goa's border moved northwards, with the acquisition of Pernem as part of the New Conquests.

The views in all directions are superb, south over Vagator, north across the Chapora River to Pernem and of course far far out to the Arabian Sea in the West. A pleasant place to wander.

PANJIM TO MAPUSA

Another option offered by the river bank routes is to travel to Mapusa along the banks of the Mapusa River, a tributary of the Mandovi, instead of by the direct route along the main road. Turning right and moving upstream from the bridge is the village of Britona, where there is the important church of Nossa Senhora de Penha de Franca, Our Lady of the Rock of France, a most unusual dedication.

Nossa Senhora de Penha de Franca

There is a high peak in Spain that became known as the Rock of France when a band of Frenchmen took refuge there during the Moorish invasion. Subsequently, a French monk received divine guidance that a statue of Our Lady had been left buried on its summit and, recovering the statue, the monk built a chapel there. Our Lady of the Rock of France became famous for the miracles performed for those who made the pilgrimage and on the monk's death the chapel was replaced, by the Dominicans, by a great church.

Devotees flocked here, especially from Portugal, and when a gilder from Lisbon, as a vow of thanks for being spared at the battle of El Ksar el Kebir, against the Moors, made nine images of Our Lady under different invocations, he dedicated one to Our Lady of Penha de Franca. He also built a chapel in Lisbon which was completed in 1598 and the statue was soon famed for answering pleas, especially in removing plagues and scourges.

In 1599, a fleet of ships to India was attacked by plague and the captain and crew made a written vow that if they were saved they would make a mass pilgrimage to the Lisbon church. The plague vanished and thereafter it became the practice of many Portuguese ships to carry the Penha de Franca image of Our Lady with the added title of 'The Protector of Ships'. So it was that in Goa in 1626 when a church, for use especially by seamen, was being built down on the banks of the Mandovi this dedication was chosen. The choice may have been further inspired by the fact that in the 17th century this was a rocky outcrop, now less evident beneath the silting-up that has taken place. Later a tiny

Church of Our Lady of the Rock of France, Britona

At the turn of the year pink and white blossom appears and soon its heady perfume fills the air. From the end of February the first nuts and fruits begin to ripen and the people gather for the picking and crushing of the apples, for their juice, together with the high-value nuts. Distilling takes place in the multitude of tiny country stills that cover the area and soon the year's rich harvest of clear soft arrak and feni reaches the pots (see p. 49). In the end they are racing to beat the monsoon. Coconut feni is also made in this area, but it is caju that reigns supreme.

Pomburpa

Steep steps lead from the road to the platform cut into the hillock where the church and school enjoy a lofty site worthy of the delightful **Nossa Senhora Mae de Deus, Our Lady Mother of God**. This is Goan Rococo at its most elegant with loftiness and freedom and a balance of space in combination with an abundance of exotic decoration. The main reredos follows the design of that supreme example

chapel in the village of Ponolem on the Island of Colvale, further to the north in the Mapusa River, was also honoured in this way, not knowing that they were to join a privileged few.

In 1754, in response to pleas to preserve the eminence of the church in Lisbon, Pope Clement decreed that no other church should be so dedicated. There were only two such churches in Spain, one in Madeira and one in the Azores, apart from those in Goa – so this dedication remains rare and interesting.

This old church is distinguished by the upper section of its tower being octagonal, similar to the more famous Franciscan church, that of St Francis of Assisi in Old Goa, just about visible as part of the wide view from the high standing porch. The road moves from the hillside onto the area of river flats created by the silting process.

The pleasant Goan countryside continues as the Mandovi swirls gently with the island of Chorao opposite, the church in view being St Bartholomew. Paddy, coconut and moored canoes line the riverbanks. The slopes above are covered in dense tangled bark and evergreen glossy leaves of cashew.

Church of Our Lady Mother of God, Pomburpa

The Altar of Our Lady Mother of God, Pomburpa

Pomburpa even has its own hot springs. A ferry runs from here across to Chorao, which is further linked now by bridge and causeway to the southern shores of Bicholim or by the Ribander ferry back to the end of the causeway.

Beyond Pomburpa the road continues to Aldona with its ferry link to the little island of Corjuem set in the middle of the Mapusa river and where its tiny fort is still standing.

Moira

This is a village of some fame in Goa, even having developed its own speciality of bananas. The Moira banana is the largest of all varieties, growing to over 30 cm long and 8 cm in diameter. A dark reddish brown when ripe, it is eaten cooked and cannot be overlooked in the market place.

Moira's inhabitants too are a household word. All communities have a group that becomes the butt of tall stories and the Moidekkars[2] provide Goa's. Tales of the 'wise fools of Moira' are legion but one will suffice.

A problem arose because there was too little space behind the church and too much at the front. Invited to suggest a remedy, the Sacristan from Aldona, the next village, proposed pushing the whole church forwards just as they would a large rock. This was accepted with enthusiasm and to

at St Cajetan in Old Goa, a strong upward movement emphasised by the start from the weightier lower section with its fantastic candelabra and elaborate panelling amongst the shadows, between which the tabernacle, another beautiful individual piece, is strongly highlighted. Above, the eye is carried through the image of Our Lady to the area of light created by the high windows and groined vaulting, spilling onto the crucifix with cherubs supporting the crown that, high above all, forms the canopy. The delicate tracery of the stuccowork of the high vault is superb, itself further enhanced by the theme of gold and white.

The rest of the church lives up to the mood and standards set by the main reredos, but you would see little of this if you visit on festival day, 4 February each year. That day is for a different experience, with the church packed to overflowing with a constant flow of worshippers even between the formal masses, great coming and going with processions climaxing in the candlelight procession of the evening. The road below is busy with stalls and a lively bustle is everywhere.

Church of Our Lady of the Immaculate Conception, Moira

Altar of Our Lady of the Immaculate Conception, Moira

tance. Another of the group of churches with its façade centred on a false dome, the Moira architects gave it touches of its own to give it distinction. Originally built in 1636, it was modified in several stages at the end of the 18th century and the beginning of the 19th. Its façade has been given additional width by the extension of its balustrade across the full width of the building and around its towers, and the central windows given trefoil arches.

Even before the expulsion of the remaining religious orders in 1835 there had been considerable ravaging of the buildings of Old Goa, but happily, as in the case of the much earlier salvaging of Hindu deities in the 16th century, steps were taken to save some of the art treasures before they disappeared along with the churches themselves. Bardez was near enough to benefit.

The appearance of treasures rescued from Old Goa, and in particular the statue of Our Lady Mother of God in the church at Saligao, shows a happy development that began to take place in Bardez even before the eviction of the religious orders and the subsequent accelerated destruction of Old Goa's buildings, mainly for the provision of materials for the new capital at Panjim, which by this time was going ahead at a great pace. The churches of Bardez not only took the opportunity of improving their buildings but also to add to their treasure trove. Moira is a good example. The bell from the seminary church at the Jesuit College of St Solhe on the Monte Santo was purchased and installed even though it was larger than their own original bell and required the rebuilding of the belfry. Another art treasure, a beautiful crucifix now in the mortuary chapel, is of unusual interest because its feet are secured with separate nails.

Continue, through the scattered area that is Moira, toward Mapusa.

ensure that the position was absolutely right it was decided that blankets should be laid to mark the area, at the front, over which the church was to be pushed, so that when the blankets were all covered it would be exactly where they wanted it. After laying the blankets the villagers began to push and, while they were so occupied, the Sacristan rolled up the first line of blankets and hid them. When the villagers were nearing the end of their strength the Sacristan called for them to stop and to see that all the blankets were now covered by the church! It was in just the right position and the villagers were full of praise for the wisdom of the Sacristan from Aldona.

The villagers of Moira were certainly right when they said that they had sufficient space at the front of their church, even after pushing it further forwards! The church of **Our Lady of the Immaculate Conception** is set on a great open platform providing an ideal setting for village occasions.[3] It also enables the church to be appreciated from a dis-

Milagres church, Mapusa

The little side road we have followed to reach the market town of Mapusa runs alongside the river, and about two km from the market stands the principal church of the town. Not huge, this church was originally dedicated to St Jerome, the statue of St Jerome coming from the Choras Seminary of St Jerome, but he has been displaced by **Our Lady of Miracles** who now stands on the central altar. The favoured position of Nossa Senhora Mae de Deus is the result of her festival's prominence during the 18th century.

This church, built on the site of a Hindu temple, contains a store of treasures salvaged from Old Goa.

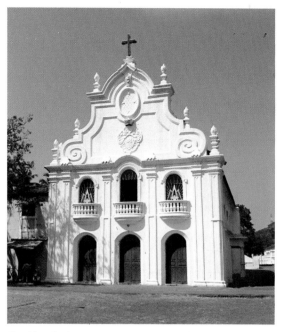

The Church of St Jerome, more commonly known as the Milagres Church (Our Lady of Miracles), Mapusa

Mapusa market

Twelve km from Panjim ferry there occurs each Friday the phenomenon known as Mapusa Market, when the permanent market in the town bulges at the seams, with seemingly every square inch of space occupied by sellers with only just enough room for the prospective buyers, the alleys between the regular stalls being occupied with temporary mats and boards.

Overflowing ferries and buses from every direction lead to Mapusa from early morning. But in spite of the almost frenetic activity even Mapusa stops for siesta.

Although there seems to be total confusion, there are in fact specific sections for different products. Every now and again the maze-like alley-ways bring you back to the point from which you started.

From lottery tickets displayed in great swathes to barbers' shops, the bazaar caters for almost every requirement imaginable. There is the 'fish-street', dried fish of all possible variety and whole fresh fish from baby shark and squid to the ubiquitous

The three retables coming from Our Lady Mother of God in Daugin, Old Goa, are perhaps the most picturesque and colourful in Goa, being painted boldly in almost primitive colours and style. Built in 1594, it was rebuilt in 1674, then partly destroyed by fire in 1838, but has been restored.

St John the Baptist is on the right-hand altar in the transept and St Jerome on the left-hand altar. There is another striking altar dedicated to the Holy Family opposite the font.

A typical grotto to Our Lady of Lourdes is in the large forecourt built in 1920. The mortuary chapel and cemetery are situated some distance away.

There is a gentle atmosphere in this much-used church, affectionately known as Milagres, and the main feast, the Monday in the third week after Easter, is one of the important Mapusa events.

During Operation Vijaya in 1961 – to liberate Goa – the Portuguese, in attempting to blow up the Marby bridge, blew off most of the roof of the church.

Returning to the town the road opens out into the long square in front of the permanent market, which is the main objective for most visitors and for which it has achieved fame and fortune. The market is open every day to some extent, but Friday is the allocated market day.

Mapusa Market: Terracotta pots

Mapusa Market: Bread stall

Mapusa Market: Selling fish

intervals you will find a bar offering suitable refreshment or chai stalls and the sugar cane crushers. Return to the Panjim ferry by bus, three-wheeler or motor-bike taxi.

bhangra (mackerel). Oysters, mussels, clams, live crabs and prawns are there in profusion, the fish-'wives' creating a colourful picture, holding up their umbrellas with one hand to ward off the sun and with the other holding up samples of their wares.

Fresh fruit and vegetables are gathered together and beautifully displayed, from huge sweet pota-toes, and pumpkins and the local shiny red-brown Moira banana to the tiny fresh beans and other pulses. Of the fruits, the usual oranges, bananas, water melon, honeydew and cantiloupe, limes, chi-coos, grapes and pineapple are to be found, depending on the season. Here are also the aroma-tic spice 'streets' and the bakery section with mouth-watering loaves of the many types of bread made in Goa.

In the section selling terracotta items there are pots and other artefacts of many shapes and sizes. There are the sizal baskets, ropes and mats made from coconut coir. Clothes, cloth stalls, glass ban-gles. Piles of stainless steel. Goan sausage stalls, aromatic channa baskets, cashew nuts, chickens and even goats. The outer part of the market is a colonial-style colonnaded walkway. At frequent

14 BEAUTY AND THE BEAST

BICHOLIM

Bicholim is a land of contrasts. On the one hand it contains two of Goa's most advertised and visited natural attractions – the waterfalls at Arvalem and the Maem Lake. More to the point it possesses some of the most glorious countryside, particularly in the southern valleys that are carpeted with cashew bushes. At Saptakoteshwar it can boast one of the most delectable and historic temple sites and it also has the simplest but most dramatic mosque in Goa. The contrast, in other words 'the beast', is provided by the vast areas that have been desolated by the open-cast iron ore mines – so that seeing this area makes for an interesting experience and shows a very different, exciting and vital face of Goa and the real world in which it has to survive. Here, across the river from the oldest conquests, Hindu elements prevail.

Visiting Bicholim needs to be a reasonably well planned expedition. One way is to take the ferry from Ribander to Chorao, Madel being the landing place. Travel across the island to where the river has become so silted up there is a causeway and a short bridge connecting Chorao with Bicholim. Once ashore, the road leads along the river bank and then forks to the right to Naroa, where you come upon the delightful and historic temple of Saptakoteshwar sitting down in its almost hidden valley, with still green waters nearby.

Sri Saptakoteshwar Temple

The Hindus of Goa suffered the destruction of their temples long before the arrival of the Portuguese. In the 14th century Goa was subjected to raiding parties first by the Delhi Sultanates and then by the Bahmani Kingdom, which eventually occupied the area of the Konkan in 1352.

The Saptakoteshwar Temple in the village of Naroa was on the northern tip of the island of Divar and during Muslim incursions the linga was removed from the temple and buried in a paddy-field to save it from destruction, being only restored to its temple during the peaceful years of Vijaynagar rule.

Soon after their conquest of the islands the Portuguese destroyed the temple itself, using some of the stone for the building of the church there. Identifiable remnants of the temple are still visible in the chapel in the cemetery attached to the hilltop church of Nossa Senhora da Piedade (see p. 108).

The linga was without a home and lay abandoned near a well on Divar Island where it was later used as a pulley for the ropes at the well – the marks of the rope being left on the stone. At this time the far bank of the river was held by a vassal chieftain of the Sultan of Bijapur. He organised the rescue of the linga and its re-establishment on the river bank that lay half-hidden in a narrow wooded valley. This village became known as Nae Naroa, which has now become Naroa (Bicholim).

In 1664 Shivaji had occupied Bicholim and in 1668 he returned to spend some time there. The story goes that he went to offer prayers to Shiva, the linga by this time being housed in a building of mud and thatch. While at prayer a straw from the thatch fell onto his shoulder; this he took to be an omen and immediately ordered a new temple to be built.

This temple is typical of the temple architecture of Goa, being one of the earlier examples – however the lamp tower is of a different and unusual style (see Fig C). The linga itself is of the faceted type of daralinga and is of a polished stone.

There is a small entrance hall with bells. In the main five-pillared hall, which is arched and painted, there are few chandeliers and the covering

Sri Saptakoteshwar Temple, Naroa, Bicholim

Remains of aggarshalas, Saptakoteshwar Temple

of the ceiling and the sanctuary wall is of plain wood. To the rear of the temple is a crumbling structure of arches which could be the remains of ancient aggarshalas.

On 15 August each year the festival of Gokul Ashtami is celebrated here. It is not a huge temple, but with its wonderful setting and pleasant atmosphere it is very well worth the detour.

Taking the same road back to the fork one can decide to visit Divar Island, the site of the original Saptakoteshwar Temple and the church of Nossa Senhora da Piedade (this visit is described in the chapter 'Exploring Tiswadi'), or to take the fork in the road to Maem Lake.

Maem Lake

Before going on to Maem Lake, turning to the right at Piligao leads to the famous **Chamundi Temple**.

The Chamundi image in this temple originally

The tank at the Chamundi Temple, Piligao

Maem Lake

came from a temple in Goa Velha which was sacked in 1312 by Malik Kafur. Devotees from Goa Velha still visit this temple at Piligao. The present temple is very old although it has probably been rebuilt several times. The tank here is large and in the middle is an interesting platform stone with some carvings.

From here return to the crossroads and proceed towards Maem Lake. The road rises quite steeply and then winds through quite delightful countryside with innumerable cashew trees covering the hills and valleys, areca palms with their entwined betal leaves and pineapple plantations. Looking back towards the coast one can catch occasional glimpses of the Mandovi River and of Panjim in the distance.

About 7 km from Saptakoteshwar is Maem Lake, a very pleasant and popular picnic spot. By the side of the road there is a handful of stalls selling mostly Goan handicrafts and soft drinks (incidentally we tasted excellent coconut water here).

Mining and the Namazgah Mosque

One of the buildings of the Namazgah Mosque, with iron ore mining operations in the background

One continues through the attractive country previously described for a further 2 or 3 km. This idyll comes to an abrupt end when one suddenly comes upon the bare mountainside where the mining activity is vast and somewhat overwhelming, a great scar of dark red-brown earth. This is one of the areas of great natural wealth to the Goan economy. A large number of the heavily laden ore-barges, seen chugging down-river on their way to Vasco, are filled with ore from here. More detail of the wealth of the hills is to be found in the chapter on 'Scenery and Natural Wealth'. Viewed from this height, the town of Bicholim is spread out below and in the distance are the Sivalik mountains with the mines to the left, and behind. A short distance to the right there is a small structure set on the crest of a bleak hillside. This is Namazgah Mosque, an interesting diversion to see a tiny remnant of Muslim history. This mosque was built by Prince Akbar, son of Aurangzeb, to commemorate a battle which he and the Marathas, led by

Sambjhi, fought against the Portuguese in 1683. It was an unlikely alliance which came about after Prince Akbar had rebelled against his father the Emperor. High above Bicholim on this bare hillside with extensive views to the east, the mosque is of most unusual design and interesting layout.

Returning to the main road one drops rapidly over about one km to reach the bustling town of Bicholim.

Leaving Bicholim take the road to Sanquelim (Sankhali). On the left is the temple of **Datta Mandir**. This temple, only built in the 19th century, is at the side of a river in wooded surroundings. Built on fairly traditional lines, there is however still a dome. It is a temple dedicated to the Trimurthi – the three-headed deity, claimed to have cured many people who were of unsound mind.

The festival of this temple, that of Datta Jayanti, is held each year in December and attracts devotees from all over Goa. Just before crossing the river into Sanquelim is the temple of **Vithal Mandir**, an old 14th-century temple recently rebuilt. There are three black images installed here, dressed in fine clothing and head-dresses, representing Vital flanked by Lakshmi and Saraswati. Vital is the ancestral god of the Ranes of Satari. Satari was originally a province of seventy villages, a wild corner of Goan territory spreading into the forests and foothills of the north east with very scattered and thinly populated communities.

The area was ruled by a group of powerful families, the most powerful being the Sardessais of Rane who were of Rajput descent. Up to 1745 the Ranes were feudatories of the Bhonsles of Sawantwadi; then, following the Conquest of Satari by the Viceroy, the Marquis of Castelo Novo, they swore allegiance to the Portuguese. The Bhonsles, not

Datta Mandir, Sanquelim. A late 19th-century temple

unhappy to hand over, ceded by treaty in 1755. But treaties and sworn allegiances – as with the Bhonsles – were flexible arrangements as far as the Ranes were concerned. They were constantly breaking the terms of agreement, demanding more and more rights, and their guerrilla raids into surrounding territories, after which they would disappear into the jungles, required from the Portuguese constant military expeditions of various size and intensity. Between 1782 and 1822 there were 14 rebellions. Then from 1833 through to 1912 there were many more, culminating in a final flurry of discontent against increased taxes which was efficiently suppressed and the leaders either imprisoned or deported to the African colonies.

The Ranes family house is in Sanquelim near the Vithal temple.

Arvalem caves

The town of Sanquelim is passed and, not far beyond, is sign-posted a turn-off – Arvalem Caves.

These 6th-century caves are quite small with no art, sculpture or paintings. They have long been thought to be of Buddhist origin, with the lingas installed in the four shrines after the decline of Buddhism – but this is not altogether certain and they may have been Brahminical from the start. Locally known as Pandava caves, the legendary home at one time of the Pandava brothers at one of the stages in their wanderings described in the *Mahabaratha*. Inside the caves are four carved lingas

set into square rock-cut bases, the shafts being similar to those found at Elephanta and Ellora.

Carved into the laterite rock, they follow the general pattern of Buddhist caves with, at the northern end, the *chaitya* (sanctuary) and at the southern end the *vihara*, or living quarters. To add to the theory that these were of Buddhist origin, there have been several Buddhist finds nearby, including a large Buddha at Colvale and a large 4th-century Buddha's head found in the Mhamai Kamat house and now housed in the Goa Museum.

Arvalem waterfalls

A little further on, the road ends at Arvalem Waterfalls, a popular picnic spot although, except during the monsoon, the volume of water flowing is small. It is a pleasant place laid out amidst rocks and greenery with areca and coconut palms, bread fruit, bananas and a host of other trees. By the side of the falls is the Sri Rudreshwar temple.

Sri Rudreshwar temple

This is a new building on the site of a very much older temple. The festival here is that of Mahashivrata, celebrated at the end of February when the temple is thrown open to all Hindus irrespective of their caste. A palanquin procession is taken out, at night, followed by the staging of a drama. The following day there is a *rat* (chariot) procession during the dawn hours.

Unless travelling further east (a visit to the Brahma Temple at Carmoli is covered in the chapter on 'Fringe Benefits'), from here return to Bicholim.

Lamgau caves

The caves at Lamgau can be approached in two ways, either through Lamgau village and a fairly complicated walk along the base of the hill, or by driving through Bicholim on the road towards Mapusa, when fairly soon you come upon a new building that has a row of shops on the ground floor. Here it is wise to ask for directions to the Pandava Caves. After following a path through the paddy-fields at the foot of the hill, you come upon two rock-cut caves of Buddhist origin. The one nearest to the village of Lamgau is small but of elegant design. It is, unfortunately, not possible to get a distant view because of the areca palms which have grown up in front of the caves, where there is a small fast-running stream, all combining to give an air of almost domestic tranquillity. A stone linga has been installed and there is a very simple clay

Rock-cut Buddhist caves at Arvalem, Bicholim

Lamgau Caves, Bicholim

tulsi vrindavan and a small nandi in the modest courtyard. The other cave is larger but is much more of a dwelling place; possibly used as a monsoon shelter, it does go quite deeply into the hillside and there is a rather complicated passage system. Above the caves, but not in very obvious evidence from the site, are the huge open-cast iron-ore mines where the odd distant rumble is a reminder of the 'other side' of Bicholim.

Returning along the road to Mapusa is a most pleasant journey with many temples and villages along the way.

There is an interesting temple dedicated to **Ravalnath** at Mulgao. At Assanora, where you cross from Bicholim taluka into that of Bardez, it is interesting to note that the final sight on leaving Bicholim is of two temples and on entering Bardez it is of two churches. At Advalpali, a village along the road – with a short diversion to the right – is a

Maruti temple which has exceptional examples of graffito art both inside and out in a temple which is itself small but beautifully proportioned.[1] Here we have lions, a fine Hindu figure, flower patterns and of course Hanuman himself, with friezes of pipal leaves.

Graffito decoration: Maruti Temple, Advalpali, Bicholim

15 FRINGE BENEFITS

Terekhol Fort – Pernem; Brahma Temple – Cormoli, Satari; Mahadeva Temple – Tambdi Surle, Sanguem; Wildlife Sanctuaries; Dudhsagar Falls and Goa's Railway; Chandranath Hill and beyond Quepem; Cabo de Rama – Canacona

On the outer fringes of Goa, to the far north, in the deep south and beyond to the east, the country changes, everywhere becoming hillier, sometimes mountainous. Rivers run faster through forests and the scenery is altogether different from the country that borders the sea. The mood changes. These are areas not often used as a base by travellers but there is much to be discovered and appreciated. In fact some of the jewels in Goa's crown are here, easily accessible by expeditions from the heartland. There is a tiny coastal fort, with an intriguing history, some of Goa's finest and rarest carved images, fascinating temple frescoes, the only substantial and intact Kadamba temple left in Goa and the most dramatic temple site of all. Add to this Goa's highest waterfall, three wildlife sanctuaries and some of the last secluded beaches, and it can be seen that this outer area has much to offer.

Goa is blessed in that more than a quarter of its land surface is forested and the Forestry Commission is fighting to maintain this by the control of indiscriminate cutting and by replanting programmes – especially eucalyptus and teak, both commercially valuable and suited to the terrain. Rows of young eucalyptus saplings planted along the roadside are a common sight and experiments with growing rubber are also in progress. In the north and east, iron-ore mining threatens to encroach on the forest and recently evoked a 'Save the Western Ghats March' along the mountains aimed at drawing attention to the problem. Soon after Independence in 1961, Goa's first wildlife sanctuary was established and there are now three protected areas which will hopefully be expanded in the future.

Several destinations of particular interest have been selected to cover the attractions of the fringe area and, in addition to the particular objective of the expedition, a visit to any of these will give an opportunity of seeing the many aspects of Goa's countryside in its different regions, its villages and its cultural life.

TEREKHOL FORT – PERNEM

Visitors to Pernem are usually headed for its northwestern corner, either to the long stretch of sand that is Arambol beach or beyond to the most northerly tip of Goa's territory, the outpost fortress of Terekhol. Terekhol, evocative of border encounters, political intrigue and confrontation, is a Goan toe-hold beyond its natural boundaries. The northern boundary is naturally defined by a wide east-to-west flowing river, a neat and tidy arrangement with Maharashtra beyond on the north bank. Almost inevitably, however, there is one small anomaly to disturb this orderly situation. It just happens that the only point from which the river mouth can be controlled and defended is the rocky headland running high above the river on the north bank. So, in the 18th century when Pernem became part of Goa, the Portuguese made sure that the headland and its fort came with it. This spur of ground is literally only big enough to hold the fort with its accompanying village.[1]

Pernem was the last of the New Conquests to be added to Portuguese territory and completed the boundaries of Goa as we know them today. A narrow strip of rolling hilly country stretching inland between the Chapora and Terekhol rivers, Pernem was the fringe territory of the Rajas of Sawantwadi and only formally became part of Portuguese India in 1788 when ceded by treaty in exchange for assistance against an even more predatory northern neighbour.

Until recently, with wide rivers flowing east to west across the country, accessibility has been a problem as far as Pernem is concerned, but this has been eased by the building of a bridge over the Chapora at Colvale. However, speed is not everything in Goa, and one of the pleasantest ways into or out of Pernem is the long ferry ride from **Siolim** across to **Chopdem** on the north bank near the mouth of the Chapora, which deposits the traveller at the beginning of the coast road that runs from Agarvada behind the beaches of Morgim, Mandrem and Arambol, finally passing through Paliem to reach the banks of the Terekhol River.

Morgim beach, across from Chapora Fort, and Mandrem beyond with its lagoons, and islands of clean swept sand, are still quiet and peaceful, left to the fisher-folk. Their main traffic is still patient bullock carts taking the catch to market. But motorcycles parked along the track down to Arambol, with latter-day tavernas among the trees, prepare the visitor for the thatched cafés and bars that have appeared in the fringe of palms, even competing with the fishing boats on the beach itself.

PERNEM TO TEREKHOL

Using the Colvale bridge already referred to, the more usual route follows the main road north from Mapusa and quickly reaches the 'capital' town of Pernem only 18 km away.

Dominating the central square is the ancient **Bhagavati Temple**, the entrance to its colourful new extension flanked by two gaudy life-sized elephants balancing light fittings on their trunks. The tall Bhagavati image, a fierce form of Shiva's consort Parvati, is an extremely fine one, carved in black stone and framed in brass fretwork. It is a temple

Mulvir Temple, Malpem

with a long history and at the autumn festival of Dussehra more than 20,000 people pack this small square.

Two small temples offer worthwhile detours to the outskirts of the town, both only a short distance from the main road to Terekhol.

To the south of the town, just opposite the fork that takes the main road north to Sawantwadi and Bombay, there is a rough track, currently being resurfaced, which ends at steps leading to a footpath through the quiet filtered shade of areca palms. Deep in the plantation in a clearing is the **Mulvir Temple of Malpem**. A small, plain temple, its charm lies in its setting, with its fascinating frescoes the main attraction.

The convolutions of a gnarled banyan tree guarding its gate contrast strikingly with the slender elegance of the arecas. A plain lamp-tower and tulsi vrindavan occupy the courtyard in front of the temple, and the small domed pavilion by the green waters of the tank is presently unoccupied. But it is the frieze of frescoes all round the mandapa and the *pradakshina*, the passageway around the sanctuary, that is worthy of close study. Framed in graffito, these worn but beautifully executed panels include a reasonably well preserved illustration of the legend 'The Churning of the Ocean of Milk', with Vishnu in his avatar as Kurma the Tortoise supporting the mountain, while gods and demons pull away at Vasuki the serpent, who is being used as the rope around the churning stick (see p. 118). In another, Krishna is shown as Arjun's charioteer in the great battle of the *Mahabharata* in which the Pandava brothers were victorious. Krishna's discourse to Arjun before the battle is the basis for the great gospel, the *Bhagavad Gita*. Also illustrated

Pernem Town: Bhagavati Temple

Mulvir Temple, Malpem, frieze

here is the departure into exile of Rama and Sita. A whole galaxy of gods and goddesses are there, with calvalcades of kings and armies parading with horses, camels and elephants. In the spandrels formed by the frieze above the arches in the mandapa are preening parrots. There is urgent need to stop the peeling and flaking process that is causing these beautiful pieces to gradually disappear.

North of the town of Pernem, about one kilometre along the road to Arambol and Terekhol, a road to the left climbs up to the **Mauli Temple of Sarmalem**. Not particularly impressive from the outside, though pleasing in its very simplicity, its setting is idyllic and it has an intriguing interior design with examples of extensive graffito decoration (see p. 25).

Surrounded by coconut, areca and flowering shrubs, it sits on a high plinth set into the steep hillside. It is a simple structure – no domes or towers, no lamp tower. The temple tree has been uprooted from the middle of its surrounding platform. In front of the temple, a low cinquefoil

archway leads to the spring of Sarmal amongst a tangle of boulders on the steep hillside, washed clean by its waters which run down through rocky pools past steps that lead to a shallow pond below.

Behind the main temple is a separate building of red unplastered laterite for the affiliate deities.

At the top of the front steps in a narrowed, almost chapel-like façade, an archway leads to an entrance hall from which there are three entrances to the mandapa beyond. A wide central rounded arch is flanked by low Muslim-style arches similar to those in the 17th-century Safa Shahouri Mosque in Ponda. These lead onto the aisles on each side of the mandapa created by two rows of solid round pillars. There are no shrines at the end of the aisles: they lead straight into the passageway round the sanctuary where the open arches of the outer wall of the temple are continued, making for a light airy atmosphere.

At the end of the main hall is the shrine to Mauli, its vivid green wall stucco decorated with niches for the painted guardians. There are columns on either side of the entrance to the gated sanctuary, a leering kirti mukha above. Higher still are two more delicately etched figures. Mauli's tall image is carved in black stone.

Heavy wooden beams support a sharply pointed, high-vaulted ceiling which is entirely covered in graffito decoration in the form of traditional roundels. Pillars are decorated with inverted pipal leaves. Temple bells hang from the beams just inside the entrance, reflecting in the fine highly-polished floor, its different marbles arranged in rectangular patterns.

Just outside the town is one of the grandest of Goa's houses (or rather mansions), the home of one of Goa's most important Hindu families, the Desh-prabhus. Highly influential in this northern area, they were hosts to Viceroys and Governor Generals and were then known as the Viscounts of Pernem. The house covers a vast area, a seemingly endless succession of courtyards, part of which is now a richly endowed family museum. It has its own temple and the drums of its naubat khana can be heard from some distance away.

Beyond Pernem town the road reveals all aspects of the scenery of northern Goa, at first following a deep valley carpeted with dense areca palm groves, many almost inundated with betel pepper vines. These plantations are some of the richest in Goa, but soon the road climbs up through cashew-covered slopes on to the high ground, parched dry in winter with monsoon paddy-fields waiting for June rains to bring them to life. The countryside here is scattered with haystacks, monsoon feed for the cattle when they are kept inside. An occasional church appears in this land of temples.

At **Paliem village** where the coastal road from Agarvada in the south joins the road to Terekhol, the elaborate, graffitoed 'Tree of Life' pattern

Graffitoed Tree of Life on the Vetal Temple, Paliem

embellishes the outside walls of the Vetal Temple at the roadside. The road then drops down to the Terekhol valley, the scenic way along the river bank leading on to Keri.

The road ends on the banks of the Terekhol River at the ferry crossing and here the enforced benefits of browsing around while waiting for the next ferry can be fully appreciated. It is a place of quiet delights. To the left beyond the casuarina-backed sandbanks, is the open sea; to the right, curving away into the hills, the wide river is busy with small fishing craft that in themselves make for restful contemplation. On the far bank, high on its headland is the tiny **Terekhol Fort**, the small church inside overtopping its battlements. But it was not always so peaceful. For centuries this estuary was a haven for pirates and a focus for military adventurers and those with political ambitions. This was the territory of the buccaneering Rajas of Sawant-wadi, the Bhonsle family, who for long were an irritant on Goa's northern border. Though of only minor significance in their own right in the context of the struggle for power in the Konkan, they were for much of the time vassals at the bidding of greater powers, or would ally with anyone who would help expand the territory from which loot could be extracted, making Pernem a useful spring-board for those with designs on Portuguese Goa. The Bhonsles dotted their territory with small forts from which they could exert local control, and Terekhol was built by them as one of these command posts, probably in the 17th century.

When the Portuguese were driven back to the Mandovi during the Maratha incursions of 1739, with only Fort Aguada and Reis Margos holding firm on this side of the river, the Bhonsles took the opportunity of occupying Bardez, even moving into the fort at Chapora. However, in 1741 with the arrival of the new Viceroy, the Marquis of Lourical, with reinforcements, and the withdrawal of the Marathas, they retired back into Pernem and sued for peace. True to form, however, they lost little time in breaking the resulting treaty and, deciding that enough was enough, the next Viceroy, Dom Pedro Miguel de Almeida, Marquis of Castelo Novo, led his troops on a punitive expedition into Bhonsle territory capturing fort after fort. To celebrate, he added to his titles that of Marquis of Alorna – Alorna being the strongest of the Pernem forts.

Terekhol fell to him in 1746, the fort was remodelled and the chapel inside was built, although it would be the subject of much diplomatic haggling and several attempts to retake it by force of arms before it became legally part of Goa forty-two years later. With the final establishment of her frontiers and the absence of any threats to her existence, there was little more military activity to be written into Goa's story and her forts tended to drift into disuse. However, although small and remote, Terekhol refused to be left out of the spotlight of history.

In 1819, Sawantwadi acknowledged British sovereignty over its part of India and, before long, Terekhol's position on the north bank gave rise to diplomatic exchanges between Bombay and Panjim over its actual boundaries. The magnitude of the problem is illustrated by the fact that a point at issue was British refusal to accept Portuguese calculations as to how far a cannon-ball fired from the fort would travel – one of the factors used to establishing the exact position of the border! But a few years later it was the scene of a much more serious and bloody incident.

In the early 19th century, Portugal was wracked by conflict arising from the emerging liberalism in Europe. In Portugal the liberals prevailed and as a result, a new Governor was sent out in 1835 with instructions to initiate radical reforms. The man selected for the task was a Goan. Bernado Peres da Silva was born near Old Goa and after being educated at Rachol Seminary went to Portugal and became involved in politics. A supporter of the liberal faction, he ended up on the winning side and was appointed as Prefect with powers of Governor, the first Goan to hold such rank. But there were factions in Goa, too, and only seventeen days after he took office on 14 January 1735 he was deposed in a military revolt and deported to Bombay. Counter-revolution followed and da Silva was encouraged to return to Goa. Storms drove his ship back to Bombay and he failed to arrive. A band of his supporters had occupied the fort at Terekhol but soon surrendered to forces sent by the Military Governor. The commander of these troops ordered the execution of all those assembled in the fort, soldiers and civilians alike. The orders were carried out and the heads of the leaders were put on display on stakes in front of their homes to teach others a gory lesson.

During the freedom struggle, Terekhol's position made it an obvious target for Indians supporting the campaign for the hand-over of Goa by the Portuguese and several bands of *satyagrahis*, unarmed demonstrators, crossed the border here. On two such occasions in 1955 the tragic deaths of demonstrators occurred as a result of Portuguese military reaction.

So, these are the ghosts you will meet on the ramparts of the fort – from its 17th-century builder Khem Sawant Bhonsle, to the dashing, all conquering Portuguese Viceroy, the Marquis of Alorna, or the victims of the 1835 massacre and the 20th-century satyagrahis.

The road from the ferry winds up the hill through a straggle of cottages that is Terekhol village, with its more recent chapel dedicated to St Anthony. There is a cross out on a rock in the river that must have welcomed ships to the fort. On reaching the main gate, the fort seems even smaller. There are no towering battlements, though the deep dry moat and the thick walls would still have enabled stout resistance. It has all the classic features of 17th and 18th-century forts, though in miniature (see p. 37). There is protected access down the hillside to the river anchorage defended by bastions for cannon, while on the upper battlements the triangular bastions are decorated with characteristic cylindrical turrets. These make excellent look-out posts, but it is difficult to imagine the effective wielding of long-barrelled, muzzle-loading muskets in such a confined space.

Magnificent views from the upper battlements underline the superb siting of the fort. Even though built with a view to controlling the river mouth and seaward approaches rather than landward attack, the field of observation into dusty Maharashtra is extensive. Westward, the Arabian Sea stretches to distant horizons and, below, the full width of the river mouth would have been well within the range of its guns. Beyond, on the other bank, there is a temptingly deserted sweep of golden sand, the most northerly beach in Goa, enclosed to the south by the bare, red rocky headland that divides it from Arambol beach.

From Terekhol Fort, looking back up the river

Church of St Anthony, inside Terekhol Fort

Brahma: 7th-century image at Bhagavati Temple, Parshem

In the inner courtyard, the church dominates. Also dedicated to **St Anthony**, the patron saint of the army and navy and Portugal's national saint, it was squeezed into the courtyard rather than built just outside the walls, which would have affected the efficiency of the fort's defences and given an attacking enemy a vantage point.

The quarters of the garrison have been converted into accommodation for visitors and, since 1976, it has been run as a Tourist Hostel. It is a delightful place to relax, a swashbuckling little fort that doesn't take itself too seriously, though one can imagine its indignation at the crude attempt to outline with whitewash the laterite blocks of its walls, unfairly making it seem more frivolous than it deserves. Perhaps a monsoon or two will remedy the situation.

Deep in the forest in the middle of Pernem, villagers stumbled across an ancient image of Brahma, the elder statesman of the Hindu Trinity. Carved in the 7th century, the four-headed deity was rescued from the undergrowth and is today worshipped as a parivar devata, along with Vishnu, Ganesh and others in a side temple of the **Temple to Bhagavati** in the village of **Parshem**, near to where it was found. In India it is considered that, as Creator, Brahma's work is already completed,

Bhagavati Temple, Parshem

whereas the Destroyer, Shiva, and the Preserver, Vishnu, are gods of on-going power. As a result, there are few images of Brahma in worship. There are even fewer – only three or four in the whole of India – where the main temple is dedicated to Brahma himself. Goa has one of these, too, the subject of the next expedition, at Carambolim (Cormoli), Satari. The Bhagavati Temple in Parshem, probably rebuilt in the 19th century, has a unique façade into which is incorporated two 'Ponda' style lamp towers! The village also boasts the biggest banyan tree in Goa.

The biggest banyan tree in Goa in Parshem village, Pernem

THE TEMPLE OF BRAHMA – CARAMBOLIM (CORMOLI), SATARI

The cult of Brahma, Creator of the Universe and Mankind and the God of Wisdom, does not have a large following in India today, allegiance being concentrated on the other two members of the Triad, Shiva and Vishnu. This is true to the point where, in the whole of India, there is only a handful of temples dedicated to Brahma himself, that is, where he is the principal deity. That Goa has a Brahma temple at all is therefore remarkable and that the image is one of his finest, an added bonus. Other reminders that once he was more popular here are the 7th-century image mentioned above and, at the opposite end of the state, there is a Brahma image in the Shantadurga Temple at Colomba in Sanguem, not far from Chandranath Hill.

There is something of a mystery surrounding the Brahma of Carambolim. The first thirty years of

Portuguese rule had not been particularly harsh in terms of their efforts to convert Hindus to Christianity, but with the arrival of more and more religious orders seeking converts and the lack of success of persuasive methods, policy was changed. In June 1541, the first royal decree was issued ordering all temples on the Ilhas to be destroyed and no time was lost smuggling deities across the river for safety. In that year, the Brahma image from the village of Carambolim, right on the doorstep of the city of Old Goa itself, was also hurriedly carried away by its devotees. But, whereas most of the gods and goddesses saved in this way were installed nearby, only just across the border, even at some risk, in order to be within reach of their followers, the Brahma image made the long journey far, far to the east into the foothills of the ghats.

It must have been an eventful and difficult journey for the rescue party and it is intriguing to contemplate how the decision was taken to end their trek here. In any event, they must have been driven by an unswerving resolve to ensure total safety for their god's magnificent image.

Even now, Satari is a sparsely populated area, much of it forest and open mountainside. Settlements are widely scattered and Valpoi, its main centre, little more than a large village. For centuries, it was out of the main stream of Konkan history, ruled by militant landowning families that exacted their dues from peasant farmers attempting to scratch a living from difficult soil and sparse grazing. There was little to spare for the building of great temples and, even today, they are few and modest, it being more a land of a multitude of humble shrines sprinkled across the landscape. So it is here that we find the great god Brahma housed in unpretentious surroundings near a village sometimes called Carambolim after his original home, but known locally as Cormoli or Karmali.[2]

Out in the open countryside, the setting is one of great peace and charm, on the edge of an oasis of gently terraced irrigated paddy-fields backed by groves of palm trees with the hills rising beyond. Papaya and banana-trees cluster round the temple and, down steep steps, a small tank in an irrigation channel provides the solitary priest with water for ritual needs.

The temple is a small, plain building, hardly recognisable as a temple apart from the pyramid-tiled roof over the sanctuary, with its amalaka finial seeming almost a concession to extravagance. The square sanctuary occupies one end of the unadorned rectangular building, the whole not more than four metres wide, with, in front of it, an open-sided mandapa and at the opposite end a low

Brahma image: Carambolim, Satari

Beneath the tall ornate crowns, all the heads are different but attention is first focused on the central imperious face despite the fact that the tall standing image is set into a complex, carved framework. The figure of the deity is subtly distinguished from its background by the fineness and delicacy of the carving of the headdress, earrings, arm bands, sacred thread and, especially, his girdle.

In his four hands Brahma carries the holy utensils with which he is usually associated: the spoon that is used in the performance of sacred ceremonies (in his upper left hand facing the image), the book of Vedas, the Hindu holy scriptures (upper right) and the pot or vessel to hold the water for ritual ablution so essential to any Hindu religious ceremony (lower right). The fourth hand holds a rosary of beads, common to many religions in assisting concentration, in this case on the recitation of the innumerable names of God, and here the hand is offered in the Varamudra gesture, palm facing with fingers pointing downwards, showing Brahma as being prepared to grant boons or favours. Brahma's vehicle, *hanasa*, the swan or goose, is not depicted here. It rarely appears accompanying its master, unlike the vahanas of other deities. The image is truly magnificent.

Brahma may not have been given the grand edifice that his image may seem to deserve, but perhaps, after all, that is appropriate. He requires nothing more. He is an exception to yet another rule: no other gods share his simple dwelling.

MAHADEVA TEMPLE – TAMBDI SURLA – SANGUEM

The Mahadeva Temple at Tambdi Surla is the only structural temple of the Kadamba period to survive not only the destructive violence of religious intolerance during Muslim and Portuguese occupations, but also several centuries of the tropic's fierce elements. Thankfully, it provides something more than the sculptured fragments and ruins that are otherwise almost all that is left to show what a glorious period of temple building occurred in Goa during the 11th to 14th centuries. Its survival is largely due to its situation, far to the east, almost on Goa's border, deep in forested countryside and even some distance from any village. It must have been the site itself that was deemed to be holy, for it does not seem to have been built to serve a community in its immediate vicinity. Until recently, the temple was still relatively inaccessible, the road only reaching as far as Sancordem, leaving an 8 km

platform on which a simple lamp tower has been later added in an enclosed space. There is little by way of decoration apart from the beams in the mandapa from which the temple bells hang. A single row of palely stencilled peepul leaves lines the outside wall.

But within the garbhagriha is the fine piece of sculpture that is Brahma's image. It is a large piece, nearly two metres high including its base, and it is intact. Its weight is considerable and it must have been transported with the greatest care and devotion across the wild country between Old Goa and its present home. It is carved from a single slab of black basalt including the many layered *pitha*, the pedestal on which it stands, his four heads gazing in every direction enabling him to be all-knowing. It is said that he once had five heads but that in one of his many altercations with Shiva, the Lord of Destruction appeared in the form of Kalbhairava and cut one off, leaving him with only four.

trek through streams and jungle. Sixty years ago even the determined Fr. Heras admitted defeat, 'I reached Surla, but I could not continue forward for want of road and conveyance.' Now, however, a road journey of less than two hours from Panjim leads to within a few hundred metres of the Temple.[3]

It occasionally happens that, although knowing what to expect to see, having seen photographs or read descriptions of a place, expectations are confounded by the reality, the first sighting striking so forcibly as to leave an indelible impression. If this feeling is sustained on closer acquaintance, it assumes the mantle of a special place as an experience. For me the Mahadeva Temple is such a place.

From where the road ends, a winding track leads through the trees until, suddenly, a large clearing opens up with, in its centre, the surprisingly minute temple. Its small size in its setting focuses attention on its elegant proportions and intriguing design. The setting and the temple complement each other. The isolation is tangible. Beyond the trees, the eastern mountains rise blue in the distance and in that direction, at the bottom of the clearing, the ground slopes down to a stream where troops of monkeys crowding the branches raise screeches of protest against encroachment on their territory.

The temple was built in the 13th century, but it has been suggested that the few monoliths scattered nearby are an indication that it may have been a religious site for much longer. As with many of the Kadamba temples of which we have some knowledge, such as the ancient Ganesh and Saptakoteshwar Temples on the island of Divar, this is

built of black basalt, although there is none available in the immediate vicinity. It would have had to have been brought in from a considerable distance, even perhaps from beyond the ghats.

There does exist a rugged, rocky track across the mountain side near here, making this a breathtaking possibility, a concept made even more awesome by the fact that it is the enormous size and weight of the blocks and slabs of basalt used that has enabled the temple to be built without mortar. The temple certainly has links with the other side of the mountains apart from the possibility that it was a source for building materials. At Tambdi Surla, style and design features, together with construction techniques, have much in common with the temples of kingdoms of the Deccan to the east, contemporary with the Kadamba rulers of Goa. These construction methods permit the particularly striking slab roof design over the main hall and behind this a typical Dravidian-style shikara rises in a pyramid over the sanctuary. Sadly, part of the top level and the finial of the tower seem to be missing but, even without this, the structure has balance, with vertical lines emphasised to give height above the strongly etched low plinth on which the temple stands.

There is little external decoration in terms of sculpture, only a band of chiselled lozenge motif around the low wall of the mandapa and at each of the side entrances, together with a narrow band of rosettes on the projections. On the tower, however, are six small panels each delicately carved within a powerful frame, with its kirti mukha at the top. All three members of the Hindu Trinity are depicted in the lower panels and their consorts in the smaller upper ones. On the south side, the side furthest from the entrance to the clearing, Brahma is in the lower panel with Saraswati in the smaller one above. On the west side, the rear of the temple, is Shiva, part of his frame for some reason being unfinished, and again above in an Uma Mahish, seated in an embrace with his consort (see p. 196). On the north side is Vishnu with a Lakshminarayan above. Lakshminarayan depicts Lakshmi together with her consort Vishnu, in this case seated on his knee.

The interior plan is simple in terms of space arrangements, a main hall (*mandapa*) leading to a vestibule (*antaralaya*) in front of the sanctuary (*garbhagriha*).

Projecting steps lead up to the mandapa from three sides. The ancient temple bell is above the central, eastern, entrance and its sound seems carried so clearly on the air to the distant hills that one waits for the echo. The low walls around the

Mahadeva Temple, Tambdi Surla

Central ceiling panel of the Mandapa, Tambdi Surla

open-sided mandapa still show the sockets that enabled a low rail to be fitted to the outside so that they could be used for seating, which was a usual arrangement in this type of temple.

Four main pillars support a massive rectangular slab over the centre of the ceiling, from above which the great stone roof panels slope down beyond the edges of the hall. This central ceiling panel is beautifully and extraordinarily deeply carved in an eight-petalled lotus pattern with rosettes, a superb example of this typical feature. There are two other panels in the mandapa, and the vestibule and sanctuary ceilings are also decorated in this way, though not so complex or as finely executed. The central panel here is of even finer workmanship than the panel that today forms the cemetery chapel at the Piedade on Divar, which was formerly part of the Ganesh Temple there, beautiful though that is. Below the central ceiling panel, the perpetually garlanded Nandi crouches low on his rimmed pedestal.

The four central columns supporting the roof are heavily worked from single blocks of basalt. The work involved is incredible with great quantities of stone first being removed to give the complex profile onto which the great variety of finely carved decoration has been superimposed. A most interesting item of decoration – a craftsman's tour de force, full of life and vigour – is the small panel at the bottom of the right-hand front pillar showing an accoutred fighting elephant urged on by his mahout, attacking what looks like a horse.

At the rear of the mandapa are four niches with a fascinating framework incorporating the design of the four main columns, topped by a replica of the temple's shikara, here shown complete with finial which indicates how it must have looked in its original form. The two niches either side of the doorway contain *Naga*, images of the serpent gods. There are also loose panels on the floor, one to the left of the doorway to the vestibule being Uma, Shiva's consort in her gentlest form. On the right is a two-headed Naga.

Carved latticework screens surround the doorway to the vestibule. These convey an air of lightness despite their thickness and strength, and their decoration is in fine detail. This screenwork around entrances is characteristic of the period, the only other examples to be seen now in Goa being the piece used as a window insert in the cemetery chapel at Piedade, Divar, and the fragment left clinging to the doorway that once formed part of the Adil Khan's palace in Old Goa, this doorway itself having been salvaged from a destroyed temple for use in the construction of the palace.

Beyond the antaralaya, a narrow step up through a low doorway, undecorated except for a small panel on the lintel, leads to the gloom of the garbhagriha. On a *pitha*, the pedestal, sits the principal linga, unusually squat and low, its size on its substantial pedestal, with brass oil lamps hanging low on either side, focusing attention on the deity. The supporting lingas in the sanctuary do nothing to distract the worshipper.

The delights of Tambdi Surla are tempered only by the realisation of how much else from Kadamba times has been lost, though in turn appreciation is enhanced by its uniqueness in Goa.

WILDLIFE SANCTUARIES

In the hills and valleys between Tambdi Surla and Dudhsagar Falls lie two of Goa's three designated wildlife sanctuaries. At this stage in their development, these are modest by the standards of some of India's more famous game reserves. It is only since 1961 that any development has even been attempted but there has been a tremendous effort to push these projects forward which, apart from their attraction to tourists, is something more than welcome in terms of the environmental needs of such a tiny and rapidly developing state. The preservation of Goa's natural blessings is a constant battle to be fought, and the sanctuaries, though small, can make a vital contribution. Three areas have been designated sanctuaries with the fullest possible protection, under which no forestry or agricultural activities are allowed, avoiding a conflict which has led to serious problems elsewhere in India's reserve.

The Bondla Sanctuary, covering only 8 square km of the Bondla Forest in the southern corner of

Bicholim Taluka, is the nearest to Panjim. Filling a narrow, tree-filled valley, it is reached by a road that beyond Usgao winds steadily upwards into the clear crisp air of the hills, with a growing impression of leaving behind the hustle and bustle of the towns.

The animals here are kept in large enclosures and include bison, sambhar, cheethal, leopard and monkeys. In the central area, gardens have been landscaped around the restaurant, there is a snake-house (the 'Serpentarium') and a hot-house with even more exotic plants than grow naturally here. A 'Wilderness Trail' through the woods leads out to pleasant picnic places.

It makes an ideal expedition for young children and there are cottages which provide simple accommodation in peaceful surroundings.[4]

The Bhagwan Mahavir Sanctuary at Molem, in Sanguem taluka, right on Goa's eastern boundaries, impinges onto the slopes of the Sahyadri Mountains that form the border with Karnataka, giving a wide range of terrain and habitat for the animals. Covering an area of 208 square km, Goa Tourist Development Corporation have established a small resort here with cottages and a canteen catering for basic needs.

Tracks are being developed to give access to the more remote areas of the sanctuary and up into the hills. The Range Forest Office nearby organise daily jeep expeditions each morning and evening and there is plenty of scope for walks. There is especially abundant bird life here, and the most recent animal census included large herds of bison and a great variety of deer, as well as two tigers and eighteen panther. In order to have any chance of seeing anything of the animals, an overnight stay is really necessary – but this has the advantage that it can be combined with visits to Tambdi Surla, only 16 km away by road, or to Dudhsagar Falls, Colem, or Kulem Railway Station, being only 7 km from Molem.[5] It is the last 21 km from Colem to the Falls that is the most entertaining.

The third of the sanctuaries at **Cotigao** deep in Canacona in the south-east, covering approximately 105 square km, is still under development.[6]

DUDHSAGAR FALLS AND GOA'S RAILWAY

The only way, at the present time, to see Dudhsagar Waterfalls, is by train. In this case, this is no great hardship and in fact adds to the whole experience. Goa's one railway line that runs from Mormugao harbour, leaving the State just beyond Caranzol on the eastern border, is itself of interest, and to reach Dudhsagar, the journey along almost its full length of just 82 km of track, enables the traveller to see many different aspects of Goa.

In the middle of the 19th century, while the British, well and truly stricken with railway fever, were criss-crossing India with track, the Portuguese watched with detached interest. In these early days the railways of the sub-continent were being developed on almost a local basis, the princely states, at least the larger ones, having their own. Names from that period conjure up images of smoky grandeur and gleaming delights.

With the growth in Goa's economy and with many goods coming in from British India, Portuguese interest in railways gradually awakened and in 1878 a treaty was signed enabling the link-up of the Goan railway with the rest of the system. The main engineering problem was crossing the Western Ghats and the eventual route chosen took what was thought to be the most practicable route for this section which would link up with the developing port of Mormugao while avoiding the widest rivers. Building began in 1882 and in 1887 the first section, Mormugao to Sanvordem, was opened. The only major obstacles on this part of the line were the Kushavati and Sanguem rivers. The following year, the critical stretch across the ghats was completed and the link with the South Maratha railway was made at Londa Junction, 29 km beyond the border on the Bombay–Pune–Bangalore line. There are many stretches, especially in the mountains, where the track is still single-line. There are fourteen stations.

The Portuguese authorities decided upon metre gauge for the track, a decision no more and no less logical than that being taken elsewhere on gauges at that time by many other small railways, without overall coordination – decisions that would bequeath a root problem to the Indian Railways system that is still unresolved today. In Goa's case, the resulting problem in transferring freight from one type of rolling stock to another sets limits on the volume of traffic that can be handled and adds to costs.

Although some diesel locomotives have been introduced, steam trains are still in use and a check with the main station at Vasco, or even the local station, will hopefully enable steam enthusiasts to select their preferred transport.

Happily for travellers interested in Goa's countryside, the eventual route chosen to meet engineering and economic requirements takes the track over a bridge literally across the face of Dudhsagar Falls. Dudhsagar, the Sea of Milk, are India's highest falls, though not in a straight drop, the water cascading for 603 metres across boulders and down rock faces, dividing and re-uniting in foaming white cataracts before reaching the valley below. The railway crosses about halfway up so that from the train the lower part of the falls is hidden. However, for those alighting here steps lead down to a viewing platform under the bridge. The volume of water varies with the seasons, being at its most spectacular during the monsoon and soon afterwards. When at its peak, trains sometimes have to wait to cross, so near is the bridge to the falls and its spray.

An expedition from Vasco to Dudhsagar and back can be made in a rather long day. The train journey is just under four hours each way and the time to spend at Dudhsagar varies with the train timetable.[7]

An alternative is to do only the last part of the journey by train, the section from Colem to Dudhsagar taking about 1½ hours. Colem is only 7 km from Molem and the Bhagwan Mahavir Wildlife Sanctuary. Molem is approximately 60 km by road from Panjim and 51 from Margao. This is the most scenic, mountainous stretch of the railway, where two locomotives are attached to cope with the gradients, the train whistling its way into and out of tunnels and in places clinging to the sides of the steep slopes. If the train doesn't stop at the falls themselves, then you have to walk back along the track through the tunnel to reach the bridge, but this is closely monitored single-line track and no trains will thunder past without warning.

There are plans for Goa to have another railway, part of the long-hoped-for coastal link between Bombay and Mangalore, the 900 km Konkan railway. A broad-gauge track, the Goan stretch would run north to south the length of the State and enormously improve access to the main railway system.

CHANDRANATH HILL AND BEYOND QUEPEM

Eastwards from Margao, sudden changes in the countryside coincide almost exactly with the boundary of Salcete and Quepem talukas. Here, hills rise steeply from the flat land and on the highest of these, Chandranath Hill (370 m) is the spectacularly sited ancient temple of **Chandreshwar Bhutnath**, the final climb required to reach the summit being well rewarded. Beyond this, the road continues into the valley country of south-eastern Goa, here following the Kushavati River from Chandor back

towards its source in the mountains. Pleasant, relaxing scenery, the rich greens of the irrigated valley floor are backed by the silhouettes of the ghats in the east, with, amongst the tree-covered red rock, the occasional reminder of previous mining activity, together with stands of eucalyptus and teak newly introduced by the Forestry Commission.

From the village of Paroda lying at the foot of Chandranath Hill, the road goes through Quepem Town and, beyond the village of Sirvoi with its rare temple to Chamunda, comes first Zambaulim, the home of Damodar, the refugee god from Margao, and then Rivona, where Buddhist monks carved rock-cut sanctuaries in the red laterite of the hillside 1400 years ago. These are amongst the oldest of Goa's surviving residences. Still further to the east, at Curdi, the remnants of a 12th-century Kadamba temple stood until only recently, now intriguingly dismantled for its own safety.

Chandreshwar Bhutnath Temple

Situated magnificently on top of a high peak, the white temple dome can just be glimpsed occasionally from the valley floor. A road winds up through wooded slopes, heavy with cashew at first, then changing to scrubby jungle, lively with chattering monkeys and scuttling mongoose. At the point where the twisting road ends, a small cluster of cottages marks the hamlet of Parvath, surrounded by encroaching trees that have almost overrun the ruins of ancient temples. This is a hill full of sacred

Chandreshwar Bhutnath Temple, Chandranath Hill, Quepem

Chandreshwar Bhutnath Temple: steps to the temple

hilltop, or even that it was the god that gave his name to the city. Nothing can be certain, but when the moon is full its rays strike directly on to the linga within its sanctuary, and it is Shiva as Chandreshwar or Chandranath, Lord of the Moon, that is worshipped here. Another aspect of Shiva, Bhutnath, Lord of the Spirits, has his separate shrine here which gives the temple its full name.

The plain white buildings that occupy the centre of the clearing on the summit fit perfectly into the space and sky that is their setting. The only discordant note is struck by the corrugated iron structure that houses the *rath*, the processional chariot of the gods. For the rest, the 17th-century temple that we see today is a fine example of the period and illustrates many of the features common to the more famous Saptakoteshwar Temple and others that were built all over the areas beyond the fringes of Portuguese control at about this time, marking especially the beginning of the rebuilding of temples to house deities smuggled across the borders to safety more than a century earlier. Here at Chandranath, this was no refugee god, but the style of the temple, rebuilt around its ancient sanctuary, is similar.

By this time a dome on an octagonal drum had already been introduced to replace the conventional shikara over the sanctuary (see p. 22). There are three domes here, all different in profile but all with a distinctly Muslim flavour. Uncluttered by excessive exterior ornamentation, the buildings are well proportioned, the extended height of the tower and its high straight-sided dome giving it a slender appearance. The neat entrance porch is in nicely judged proportion. The red-tiled roofs provide a striking colour contrast, resting on the traditional, and here substantial, cornice built up of cantilevered tiles. The split roof-line is a common feature.

A single tree grows in the clearing around the temple surrounded by its shady platform, with a simple older type lamp tower nearby. The small temple to one side of the front entrance is that to Bhutnath.

The theme of simplicity is carried into the interior of Chandranath temple, where there is a feeling of age and permanence. Square pillars supporting rounded arches define the central part of the mandapa, these pillars being decorated with unusual frescos with silhouetted figures on sepia backgrounds, worn but delicately attractive, while round the ceiling is a narrow frieze of carved, painted panels of deities and religious themes that preserve the mood. There are no chandeliers but the traditional bells are there at the entrance.

places. A rough, rocky stairway leads upwards for the last part of the journey to the summit and for four of these steps, carved slabs from now vanished 12th-century temples have been used. Their discovery will give good reason for pause in the climb.

Stepping through the gateway into the temple courtyard is to emerge onto an enclosure seemingly suspended in space, detached from the world below. There could hardly be a more dramatic or secluded site for a temple. One of the oldest in Goa, it was perhaps founded by Bhoja rulers who made reference to it in copper-plate inscriptions as early as the 4th and 5th centuries AD. There have been many Chandras in Goa's history from Emperor Chandragupta Maurya, through to the Chandraditya put on the throne by his father Pulekesin, another great ruler, to rule Goa on his behalf in the 7th century. All these have had the name of the nearby city of Chandrapur attributed to their honour. It has also been suggested that Chandra may have given his name to this linga on the

In the centre of the floor in front of the sanctuary lies a fine Nandi, but here there is no elaborate screen. The sanctuary itself has been created out of and around an outcrop of natural rock. The passageway around the garbhagriha contains ancient basalt images including Ganesh, Lakshmi and several lingas.

The principal deity is represented by a linga also carved out of and part of the natural outcrop of rock, a mukhalinga with a sculpted face. Water seeps from the linga at the time of the full moon, the design of the temple allowing the moon's rays to fall on the sanctuary at this time. There is also a more recent image of the deity.

There is only one side entrance, this being on the west side where, near the deepastambha and the tree in its platform, is the entrance to the small temple to Bhutnath, here represented by a finger of unsculpted natural rock more than a metre high. Outside the door, as in the case of the main temple, is a small pen for sacrificial animals.

Some distance in front of the buildings lies a damaged Nandi, while beyond are the sheds of the *raths*, the wooden chariots in which the gods are taken out in procession around the compound at festival times. One rath, the older one, is of traditional design, and of some renown for the quality of the bands of carving on the pedestal that builds up to the platform on which the image is enthroned. The other of sleeker, more recent design has wooden horses prancing in front.

The slopes from the summit are steep but the fringe of trees and bushes surrounding the clearing means that views are fleeting and only of distant countryside, strengthening the feeling of being isolated. **Margao** lies to the west with the **Arabian Sea** beyond and there is an impression of being able to see to the limits of Goa itself. The walk back down the steps seems much shorter than the ascent.

The views open up on the way back down the road as it constantly changes direction, the patches on the valley floor emerging as the source of raw materials for the numerous brickworks scattered on the valley floor below. This is a pale grey clay, very different from Goa's more familiar red earth, and the grey theme continues in the granite quarries that eat into the hillocks.

At the bottom of the hill, the road left leads back to **Margao**, to the right to **Quepem**, the main town of the taluka, only 4 km to the east. Shortly after leaving Quepem, taking the road to **Ponda** and the north-east via the bridge at **Sancordem**, a road to the right eventually picks up the **Kushavati River** and follows it upstream into the hills.

Before this, however, the first village after the turn-off is **Sirvoi**, the temple there being of interest because it is only one of two in the whole of Goa dedicated to that most violent and horrific of Goa's goddesses, Chamunda, the Kadamba royal family's favourite and principal goddess in their capital of Gopakapattana, or Goa Velha. From the middle of the 11th century until the city's destruction more than 150 years later, her temple at the foot of Pilar Hill rivalled in importance the Shiva temple on its summit. The deity from Goa Velha ended up at Piligao in Bicholim Taluka (see p. 169); this image at Sirvoi came here from Margao and the Kadamba connection is maintained by Saptakoteshwar, another royal family favourite, being an affiliate deity in this temple.

The road now leads on to Zambaulim.

The Damodar Temple – Zambaulim

This is an area with ancient Buddhist connections. The monk Punna, who is traditionally credited with the introduction of Buddhism to Goa in the 3rd century BC, based himself in a place called Sunaparant, which is believed to be present-day Zambaulim. More positive Buddhist links will be found in the neighbouring village of Rivona, Zambaulim now earning its fame as the home of **Damodar Macaji**, one of the most important gods of Margao at the time of the Portuguese conquest (see p. 132). The image, along with others from Margao, was brought here in 1567 but almost every part of the present temple is new, originally for safety reasons having been re-built in stages between 1951 and 1972. It is now a substantial complex, a fascinating and successfully conceived modern interpretation of traditional architectural elements.

Situated in pleasant surroundings on the banks of the river, an ancient tree spreads itself above its platform in the centre of a huge cleared space in front of the temple. Itself much older than the new temple buildings, the tree is on the axis on which all else is aligned. A triple-arched gateway with its naubat khana in the tower above leads to the courtyard created by the surrounding well-appointed *agarshalas*, the living and office accommodation. Just inside the gates, simply designed tulsi vrindavans are set against each of the pillars of the archway, the maintenance of symmetry seeming to be the main factor in determining their position. Opposite these, impressive *dvarapalas*, guardians, in their niches flank the entrance to the *sabhamandapa*, the spacious, wide-galleried hall in which musical and dance performances take place on festivals. An impressive carved wooden frame in

Damodar Temple: Zambaulim, Sanguem

the gallery marks the god's throne of honour on these occasions.

The hall beyond has all the standard features of older temples but its modern architecture gives it a very different 'feel', just as there is between old churches and new. In this high airy space, also galleried, richly coloured and varied marbles have been used for the floor and the unusually slender, faceted pillars, six on each side, while in contrast the walls and ceiling are decorated with painted plaster stuccowork. There are small silver panels in bas-relief between the arches.

A low platform defines the central space within the columns, allowing the aisles below the gallery to lead unobstructed into the starkly plain passageway, the *pradakshina*, around the sanctuary. There are no distractions here. The full width of the central platform is filled with a carved wooden screen, with, in front of its central opening, a crouching Nandi. To its right is a silver railed enclosure for a brass linga. Although the lighting is modern, the temple bells just beyond the door revert to traditional design.

Beyond the screen, different coloured marbles have again been used in striking fashion to face the front wall of the garbhagriha. Set into this wall,

with guardians either side, are twin, silver-framed gates for the two deities that are contained in the sanctuary here. The door frames and the shrines, also in finely worked silver, each elaborate canopied design different from the next, demonstrate that this ancient art has not been lost. The raised deity to the left is the linga of Damodar, the shrine on the right contains a black stone Lakshminarayana.

Outside, the architects have reverted to more conventional shikara design for the towers rather than using domes, the huge flat-sided central tower, somewhat northern Indian in outline, being duplicated in smaller towers over the two side entrances.

Outside and to the right of the main temple courtyard, are two subsidiary shrines, older buildings retained from the 1885 temple. Side by side, these quaintly attractive twins with their onion domes, each with its tulsi vrindavan in front, contrast in mood completely with the modern temple. In front stands a somewhat ungainly lamp tower. Perhaps the next building stage will provide something more approaching the elegance of the original inspiration.

The Buddhist Caves – Rivona

About 3 km after leaving the Damodar Temple, and after passing through a straggle of houses and shops that is Rivona bazaar, a water pump stands on the right of the road. Only a short distance along the lane opposite this pump is the first of two rock-cut caves. If the description 'Buddhist Caves' conjures up images of the glories of Ajanta, please be forewarned, the Rivona caves bear no resemblance in size or artistic attraction. Even so, these small, roughly excavated caves in the hillside, with certainly no paintings and precious little sculpture, are exciting and strangely enchanting. Their inhabitants, the monks themselves, are somehow more real. They are inevitably known locally as the Pandava caves. It was here, some time in about the 6th or 7th century AD, that Buddhist monks established a retreat in what was then a remote and deserted corner of Goa, earning for itself its original name **Rishi Vana**, the Forest of Saints, which became Rivona. Much of the forest has been cleared and now-abandoned mining activity has left some scars, but the irrigation of the valley floor has added a new depth of greenness to the scene. Looking across the river to the hills in the distance, the original choice of site by a small band of monks can still be appreciated. It is fine countryside. It must have been a small band, judging by the accommo-

Rivona, Sanguem

Second Buddhist Cave, Rivona

dation available but, of course, real shelter was only required during the brief weeks of the monsoon.

A headless statue of Buddha seated on the lion throne, dating to about the 7th century,[8] was found here and the first cave is less than 100 m from the road along the lane. An interesting dwelling, it is set in its own fold in the hillside, originally almost completely excavated directly from the laterite of the slopes but now with some structural work around the entrance and added to the walling round the level open space in front. This low entrance doorway leads into a staircase that tunnels down through the rock to a small chamber, not much more than 3 m across, with a funnel-shaped ventilation hole above that also provides dim light. In this chamber, a well has been created from a natural spring. Another room was cut yet further into the rock at this level through a neatly formed doorway, but this has now been sealed off. It would have been a cosy, if claustrophobic arrangement, although there is an additional, less enclosed shelter and another way in. To the left of the upper entrance, steps lead down on the outside of the rock face to where an overhanging shelter has been hewn out at floor level in this hidden little valley. From here, a low hole provides crawling access to the first chamber.

Outside the overhanging shelter, another spring feeds a tiny but well-constructed tank with a stepped surround. There was no shortage of water. It is interesting to contemplate the planning of this complicated layout by those confronted with a bare rock face.

As with almost all Buddhist caves in Goa, it was taken into use by the ever-present Hindus following the departure of the monks who had created it. Under the overhang, a carved panel of Hanuman

remains and is still honoured, no doubt by the villagers tending the garden that still occupies the space in front of the cave. The style of this piece relates it to the Vijayanagar period.

The building work on the upper entrance is no doubt connected with an even more recent role assigned to the cave. According to local accounts, a Swami appears before every eclipse of the moon and waits in the cave. At the time of the eclipse he remains submerged up to his neck in the inside wall, leaving after performing certain rituals. He returns just before the next eclipse.

The second cave is down the hill on the other side of the main road, a rough track leading down towards the paddy along the river-ending after about 400 m amongst the trees, just above the level of the valley floor. A large open-fronted cave follows the curve of the hill; a low wall built across the front is now much collapsed. It is light even in its

Lower porch and entrance first Buddhist Cave, Rivona

deepest recesses and although the ceiling has been left rough-hewn, the floor is even, with a platform at the rear. This could once have held the Buddha's image or perhaps acted as a teacher's dais. In any case, it is not difficult to imagine saffron-robed, soft-chanting monks gathered here.

To the right of the cave's mouth is a dark hole in the hillside, the beginnings of a tunnel to which are attached the inevitable local sagas of lost explorers and a far-off destination, in this case Curdi, 8 km to the east.

Water runs plentifully nearby and steps cut into the rock on the left of the cave lead from the cleared space in front onto the hillside above, where a water channel, dry in winter, runs down the slope. This may have been of later construction, possibly cut at the time of the mining of the area.

As has been said, for rough caves in the hillside with little or no artistic attraction other than being well situated, there is considerable atmosphere here.

From Rivona, the road to Curdi passes through Colomba, where it can yet again be proudly announced that the village is of interest as one of only two places in Goa with a particular attribute. In this case, the Shantadurga Temple here is only one of two temples where Brahma is worshipped as an affiliate deity, the other being at Parshem in Pernem Taluka (see p. 178).

Until recently, the onward journey to Curdi would have been worthwhile for the rare sight of a Kadamba structural temple built in about the 12th century. However, the Salauli irrigation project on the Sanguem River threatened the temple site and, with great enterprise, the Goan Directorate of Archaeology took on the daunting task of dismantling the temple stone by stone and re-erecting it in a safe place, the site chosen being at Verna in Salcete. This shrine to Shiva is built of laterite and basalt, the remains consisting of a small hall in front of a sanctuary with a pyramid shikara built up of horizontal slabs. The use of basalt for the ceiling, the doorway to the sanctuary and the pillars at the entrance has enabled them to be decorated with finely carved floral designs.

Celebrating Shigmo, Rivona

It should be noted that the Zambaulim–Rivona area has traditionally celebrated the Shigmo festival of spring in real earnest. The equivalent of Holi elsewhere in India, it is marked here by a week-long programme of colourful processions, folk dances and plays – a great attraction.

CABO DE RAMA – CANACONA

In terms of the fort itself, there is now not so much left to see and perhaps, as the sole objective of an expedition, it may not be considered worthwhile in view of the distance to be travelled if starting from beyond Margao. At least there is now a road leading to the main gate, whereas until not so long ago a two-hour walk each way was necessary from the nearest motorable point. One day soon it will be possible to go by bus. From the landward side of the fort there are no forbidding fortifications. Low walls with a dry moat seal off the peninsula of the Cape enclosing a huge area. Within the walls there is a chapel, but otherwise few of its buildings remain and it is only from its most westerly bastion, perched high above the rocks and waves, that its dramatic situation becomes apparent, giving spectacular views. But a visit to the Cape provides a splendid opportunity to see something of the southern Goan countryside and enjoy the solitude of some of its most unspoiled beaches.

Cuncolim

Although in Salcete, right on its southern border, mention is made here of this small village, the gateway to the south on the main road and almost certain to be passed through if visiting Cabo de Rama, or indeed anywhere in southern Quepem or Canacona.

Cuncolim achieved notoriety during the Portuguese crusade to Christianise the area of Salcete in a bitter conflict that led to the deaths of the Jesuit 'Martyrs of Cuncolim', buried first at Rachol, whose relics are now kept on the Altar to St Anne in the transept of the Se Cathedral in Old Goa. As the 'Golden Bell' in the Cathedral (the largest and most famous bell in Goa) was cast here in the village in 1652, there are close links between Cuncolim and Goa's principal church. If you add that here can be found one of only two *dargahs*, the shrines of Muslim holy men, in the whole of Goa, it can be seen that tiny Cuncolim has some claim to fame and is at least worthy of a thought for its past as you pass through.

By 1583, the Jesuits, who had been given Salcete as their missionary responsibility, had already made good progress in the conversion process, but the villagers of Cuncolim were offering particularly stiff resistance to the efforts of the priests and adopting belligerent attitudes to the tax collectors. Before long, ships of the fleet of the Captain of the Malabar Coast were sailing up the tributary of the Sal River from the coast at Betul. Supported by Diogo Rodrigues, the Captain of Rachol Fort, and his troops, this formidable combination destroyed as many temples and as much property in the area as possible in order to persuade the villagers of the errors of their ways. The priests accompanying the expedition joined enthusiastically in the burning of the temples.

The people fled, but returned later to rebuild their temples and houses, showing little sign of the submissive behaviour expected of them. Yet another Portuguese attack laid waste the area, this time ravaging crops and cutting down palms as well as defiling holy water tanks with slaughtered cows. This resulted in sullen acquiescence to Portuguese authority by the villagers, a reluctant payment of taxes, but few conversions.

It was decided that what was needed now was a church at Cuncolim, but the arrival of a mission, led by Fr. Rodolfo Aquaviva of Verna and several other priests, to arrange for its construction resulted in an attack by a mob in which five Portuguese and six Goan Christians were killed with spears and arrows. The other fled. The Captain of Rachol arrested the ringleaders and had them put to death. The five Jesuits were buried in Rachol parish church, where there is still a memorial slab on the chancel steps, though their relics were soon moved to St Paul's College in Old Goa and subsequently to the Cathedral.

The Chapel of the Sacred Heart was eventually built on the site of the Temple of Shantadurga, the deity having by that time been taken over the border to Fatorpa in Quepem where her temple grows in grandeur even today. The image is still brought back in procession to Cuncolim every year, a festival known as the Feast of Umbrellas (*Sontreos*). Held each year on Panchami in the month of Phalguna, which usually falls in the month of March, it commemorates the day the Shantadurga deity was smuggled away to Fatorpa to save the goddess from the Portuguese. The image is brought in procession back to its original home at Tollebhat in Cuncolim, the twelve umbrellas carried representing the twelve families by whom the temple was originally established. Banned by the Portuguese in earlier years, the procession was reinstated in 1910, after the establishment of a republic in Portugal led to a more liberal approach to Hindus in Goa. Accompanied by musicians it is a most colourful and noisy occasion enjoyed by both Hindus and Christians alike. As already mentioned, the Chapel of the Sacred Heart now occupies the site of the original temple of the goddess.

There is poignancy in the fact that not so many years after the bitter encounter leading up to the massacre, the foundry in the village would be manufacturing such an important Christian symbol as the great 'Golden Bell' for the Cathedral, Goa's largest bell. Even more ironic was that the bell became famous for its use in tolling the autos-da-fé of the Inquisition at which public punishment was meted out to wayward converts.

Wayward the villagers of Cuncolim certainly were, and reluctant to accept Portuguese authority. When in 1683 the Marathas took Salcete, the people of Cuncolim immediately declared themselves Maratha subjects and offered to pay their taxes to Sambhaji instead of the Portuguese. Unfortunately for them, Hindu control of Salcete was short-lived, although there was some attempt to placate them in 1726, when it was decreed by the Viceroy that Cuncolim would be the only village in Salcete where the thread ceremony could be performed.

But, as already mentioned, the village has Muslim links too and is the home of the dargah of Madal Shah, a Muslim saint who is buried here. The mosque connected with the shrine is one of the most important in Goa.

Five km to the south beyond Cuncolim is the little town of Bali.

Cabo de Rama

There are two ways to reach Cabo de Rama from Bali, but there is a damaged bridge on the more direct route. Although a long-standing problem, this is no hardship from the traveller's point of view, as the alternative route leads through the hills and valleys of Quepem until in Canacona it turns back along the coast past some of Goa's most secluded stretches of sand and pleasant deep-wooded valleys.

Beyond Bali, the main road to the south winds through tree-covered hills, with glossy green cashews predominant, but with evidence of the efforts being put in by the Forestry Commission to preserve the high percentage of forest cover with which Goa is blessed. Any spaces are filled with stands of eucalyptus and teak while, as everywhere else, eucalyptus saplings line the roads.

After turning off towards the coast at the village of Canacona, the quiet beaches of **Palolem** and **Agonda** are within easy reach, and now the country is one of steep-sided valleys with occasional flashes of bright green paddy in the depths, amidst some of the densest plantations of areca, coconut and bananas.

A new road turns off and climbs up onto the headland of Cabo de Rama, where Rama and Sita are reputed to have spent time during their wanderings in exile. Across these uplands, under wide skies, the scene is one of bare, red outcrops of rock with hard-won paddy crops only in tiny patches of soil in shallow terraces held together by rows of stones. Scattered farms and cottages dot the landscape, each in their tiny plots.

At the far end of the peninsula is the fort. It covers a huge area, sealed off by a landward wall linking with cliffs on either side. The wall still presents an intact though overgrown frontage with battlements and bastions, complete with downward sloping embrasures and missile shutes, stretching either side of the derelict main gate with its bridge across a dry moat. Enemies would hardly have been overawed by it even when intact. This eventually formed the most southerly bastion of Goa's defences, discounting Portuguese-held Anjediva Island about 20 km to the south, but it was not until 1763 that the fort was extracted from the possession of the Raja of Sonda and saw little action after that, being abandoned 70 years later.

Just inside the main gate is a small chapel still in use, and beyond to the cliff's edge few signs remain of the barracks and other buildings that must once have been scattered all about this huge windswept area. But it is a superb site for a fortress and from its westernmost bastion, overlooking the sea far below, its true character can be appreciated. The cliffs drop steeply to the waves foaming on the rocks beneath and every aspect of a sea approach is covered. Coves cut into either side of a rocky palm-covered promontory and protected steps give access to a landing stage. Most communication must have been by sea, with men and supplies coming in by ship.

The views are superb, south to the beaches and headlands that mark the southern point of Goa, while to the north, beyond an enticing-looking sandy cove, the long golden line of Colva beach stretches into the distance with Margao behind. To the north-east can even be seen the white dot that is the temple on Chandranth Hill, far away in Quepem.

The road to the north to rejoin the National Highway at Bali is much shorter and saves returning by the same route, but there is a local dispute

View to the north from the fort at Cabo De Rama

over the narrow concrete bridge across the stream in the village of Canaquim which, though only a small bridge over a small stream, is a big obstacle. On the last visit it was just negotiable by our intrepid driver in an Ambassador, and motorcycles and scooters would have had little problem, but the situation could change for better or worse and needs to be checked.

This road leads through the outskirts of the village of Fatorpa and only a short diversion is required to reach the Shantadurga Temple, the home of the goddess from Cuncolim, from where she was evacuated in 1583 at the time of the troubles there. The deity, within her elegant silver-screened sanctuary, now finds herself surrounded by reinforced concrete as the temple rises completely restructured around her.

NEVER SAY GOODBYE

No-one, at least no-one that I have yet encountered, leaves Goa happily or at least without a tinge of regret. On one occasion, after a visit of more than a month and having reached the airport for our 1.00 pm flight to Bombay, I was gently chided by my wife when she discovered that there was a second flight that day at 4.00 pm, whereupon she said, 'We could have had three more hours here.' Over the period of the ten years we have been visiting Goa it has never been otherwise . . . a place to come to rather than to leave.

All this is borne out by the fact that the Konkani language doesn't allow Goans ever to say goodbye. They say *'Barem, hanur yeta'* meaning 'All right, I'm coming.' The response to this is *'Yo Yo'* – 'Come come'.

APPENDIX I

THE MUSEUM AT OLD GOA – A PLAIN GUIDE

A visit to this museum is no taxing expedition to be performed with grim determination, but a cool interlude amidst the other attractions of Old Goa and an opportunity to sit down occasionally. Housed in the old convent of the Franciscans attached to the Church of St Francis of Assisi, the museum was completely refurbished and reorganised in 1983, making fullest effective use of the new space then available. It is a gracious building, well suited as the home of this particular collection, ideal for contemplating Goa's past extending over many thousands of years.

Apart from the reception hall, there are three main sections intended to be visited in the sequence followed here.

The Key Gallery – this section acts as an introduction and provides a background to the rest of the exhibits. It lies immediately to the left of the entrance.

The Portrait Gallery – occupies the whole of the first floor and at its heart is the collection of more than fifty portraits of some of the Viceroys and Governors ruling Goa since 1510. There are also stamps, coins and banknotes of the period.

The Sculpture Gallery – is ranged round the quiet courtyard away to the right of the entrance but can be reached by a flight of stairs down from the Portrait Gallery. This contains some ancient inscriptions, one of the finest collections of hero and sati stones and several sculptures of Hindu deities from this area.

Dominating the entrance hall is the magnificent statue of Afonso Alburquerque. It has travelled a long road since it was first erected in Old Goa early in the 16th century. Four hundred and fifty years later it is now back within 200 m of where it started! Originally erected near the gate to the city where

his troops broke through the Muslim defences and near to where the first Church of St Catherine was built, it was moved as the city grew, ending up in front of the Church of Nossa Senhora de Serra at the end of the famous Rua Direita, not far from where the old pillory now stands. At his own request, Afonso Albuquerque was buried in this church, although his body was later taken back to Portugal. After the city was abandoned, the statue stood amongst the ruins until, in 1847, it was taken to Panjim to be installed in a new monument specially designed for it. This is the monument in what is now the Azad Maidan. The statue has been replaced under the pillared dome by a memorial to Dr T. B. Cunha and it now stands here, somewhat lost in its dark corner.

There are also several maps and photographs on display in the entrance hall.

The Key Gallery

This is divided into two parts, the first devoted to exhibits illustrating Goa's history up to the arrival of the Portuguese, the far section covers the Portuguese period.

Goa has attracted man from prehistoric times and although there is still much archaeological work to be done to establish the full story, it is already certain that early man came over the mountains and along the coast to settle over wide areas of this land, especially on sites overlooking the sea where the concentration of settlements was densest. A map shows the sites where stone-age tools have been found. Many visitors pass through one important prehistoric settlement when they go through Chicolim village next to Dabolim Airport on the road from Vasco to Panjim, where stone-age man was enjoying living thousands of years ago. The small pieces of stone on display may not look much, but think for a moment: it was with flakes like these, or rather with the actual lumps and flakes of stone that are displayed here, that early man roaming Goa fashioned a living, hunting, hewing and shaping wood, cutting meat and cleaning hides.

The early history of Goa has been revealed in archaeological digs at Chandor, ancient Chandrapur, the first capital of the Kadamba kings in the 10th century. But this was not the first time it was occupied. Pottery dug from the lowest levels so far excavated dates back to the 3rd century, as do the remains of a brick-built temple there.

Soon after these early days, historical records, though only glimpses through inscriptions, begin to throw more light on what was happening. We know that Buddhism became accepted here and held tentative sway for several hundred years before eventually dying away. Hindu gods reasserted themselves and the other exhibits in this gallery represent the Hindu period from the 9th century up to as recently as the 17th century.

There are many interesting pieces, but it is rewarding to choose one or two to study more carefully:

Vishnu (Exhibit 320). An outstanding piece that is given pride of place in the centre of the gallery. About 1000 years old, probably carved in the 9th century, it comes from the village of Savoi Verem on the inland banks of the Mandovi River in Ponda taluka. It is carved from basalt, as are nearly all Goan sculptures where detail is essential, and is not too badly damaged considering its age. The central figure of Vishnu is traditionally represented and although all four hands are missing, the rest demonstrates an exceptionally high quality of craftsmanship.

The main figure is superbly carved, with intricate detail of the headdress and the hair, the necklace and the anklets and the filmy garments all beautifully executed. The same is true of the two figures flanking him at the base. That on the right as you look at it is his consort, Lakshmi; that on the left a form of his *vahana*, or vehicle, Garuda.

According to some legends, Vishnu, as we have seen, not only created Goa but also gave it its name (see p. 17). He operates as the Protector: whenever cataclysmic problems arose he has appeared in the world in an appropriate form to deal with the situation. Here, as framework to the main figure, is a fascinating depiction of all his *avatars* or incarnations. Apart from their relevance to this particular piece, these are the subjects of carved panels or frescos in many of Goa's temples, even those dedicated to Shiva, so it may be of interest to list them here:

Matsya the Fish, who saved Vaivatswata, the sage, by towing his boat to safety at the time of the Great Flood so that when the water subsided he was left on dry land.

Kurma the Tortoise, who came to act as the pivot for the mountain in the legend of the Churning of the Ocean of Milk to produce nectar for the gods, and Mohini, the beautiful girl whose form Vishnu also took in the same legend in order to prevent the demons stealing the nectar (see p. 117). Mohini is shown here sitting on Kurma's back.

Varaha the huge Boar, 4000 miles tall, who rescued the Earth from a demon who had dragged her down to his palace below the waters.

Narasimha. A demon was threatening the world and could be killed by neither man nor beast, neither by day nor by night, nor inside nor outside his palace. So Vishnu took the form of half-man/half-lion and attacked the demon on the threshold of his house, in the evening, thus circumventing all the conditions that made him invulnerable.

control of the universe, so Vishnu appeared as a dwarf and asked him for a grant of three paces of land. On being granted the request he grew to enormous size and with the first pace he covered the Earth and with the second the Heavens. He didn't bother to take the third step, leaving the Underworld to the demon.

Parashurama the mighty warrior who with his fearful axe released the world from the tyranny of the Kshatriya caste.

Rama who freed the world from the demon king of Lanka and whose story is told in the *Ramayana*.

Krishna whose story requires volumes to relate and who is worshipped in his own right. Here he is shown, minutely, as Arjun's charioteer in the great battle of the *Mahabharata*. His discourse to Arjun before the battle forms the basis of the great gospel the *Bhagavad Gita*.

Buddha who is regarded by Hindus as an incarnation of Vishnu.

Kalki the last of Vishnu's avatars has yet to appear on earth. His coming will mark the end of the present stage of the world's existence and he will appear riding on a white horse. 'Behold a pale horse and the name that sat on him was death.'

On top of the columns on either side of the central figure are *makaras*, mythical beasts with elephant bodies and crocodile mouths from which a winding creeper divides the frame into compartments. Vishnu's incarnations are illustrated in these compartments (see p. 200). In the centre at the top is a *kirti mukha*, the Face of Glory.

There are other stone carved Hindu deities here, mainly of the Kadamba period:

Mahish Mardini (Exhibit 13). This dates from the 11th century. When the gods were defeated by Mahisasura, a demon of enormous power who assumed the form of a huge buffalo, Shiva and Vishnu created a goddess of great beauty and all the gods provided her with different weapons: Shiva a trident, Agni a spear, Kala a sword and shield and so on. She was also given a lion to ride. The goddess attacked the demon and killed him by putting her foot on his neck, thrusting the trident into his body and cutting off his head, which is how she is depicted here. There are famous examples in many other parts of India such as Mahabalipuram and the Kailasa Temple at Ellora. She is shown with a varying number of arms, sometimes as many as twenty, carrying an assortment of weapons. Here she has only four. There are others in the Sculpture Gallery. This form is adopted as the image in many temples to Shiva's consort, although under different names. For example, the image worshipped at the famous Kamakshi Temple at Siroda is in the form of Mahisasurmardini.

Gaja-Lakshmi (Exhibit 241). Although damaged, this is one of Goa's favourite forms of Lakshmi, the consort of Vishnu. In a Gaja-Lakshmi she is shown amongst lotus flowers with elephants anointing her with water. Lotus and water are symbols of fertility and the source of life.

Uma Mahesha (Exhibit 9). Dating from the 7th century this is a typical representation of Shiva seated in an embrace with Uma, the gentlest form of his consort.

Hero Stones. Although the main collection is in the Sculpture Gallery, there are included in the Key Gallery, as an appetiser, three fine examples of hero stones and sati stone.

At one time it was common practice to worship heroes killed in battle, or who had offered themselves as sacrifices to the gods. This also included wives who had proved themselves faithful by sacrificing themselves on their husbands' funeral pyres. These deeds were recorded on slabs of sculpted stone which themselves became objects of worship. The earliest of these date from the beginning of the Kadamba period, in the 10th century, the latest to when Vijayanagar ruled Goa in the 14th and 15th centuries.

The story of the hero is told in a set of panels, usually three, one above the other. There is an accepted pattern, with the bottom panel illustrating the circumstances of the hero's death, the centre panel his journey to heaven and, at the top, the hero in heaven. Sometimes, there are only two panels, the journey being left out. Usually the scenes are framed by pilasters with a 'roof' or pediment to provide a frame above the upper panel.

Some of the Goan panels are particularly interesting because of Kadamban links with the sea and the deaths of heroes in naval battles. Heroes were also those who sacrificed themselves to the gods either by self immolation by fire or by offering their heads to a particular deity, quite literally as it was cut off. Only rarely is there an inscription on the stone to give an indication of the personage concerned or the date. When people are depicted with parasols held above their heads, it usually indicates that it is someone of royal or at the least high-ranking status.

There are some excellent examples in the Key Gallery.

Exhibit 21c. The sea-battle theme is well illustrated in this *century viragal* or hero stone. The hero is shown both on land with a sword and above this at sea, firing arrows at the enemy. In the panel above, he is shown accompanied by his wife, being attended by *apsaras*, heavenly maidens, on their way to heaven. The fact that he is accompanied by his wife indicates that she performed sati to accompany him, so this is a combined hero and sati stone commemorating both events. These stones were intended to stand upright and a tenon can be seen which could be fitted into a slot in a base stone.

The degree of detail and the quality and depth of carving varies considerably from stone to stone. This is one of the finest examples in all respects.

Exhibit 23 A two-panelled stone, again with the hero killed in hand to hand fighting in a sea battle, this time from a spear thrust. The ship with its oars is very well portrayed. The figure beating the gong in the 'cabin' below is probably the oarsmaster keeping the rowers in time. In the panel above, our hero sits on his throne attended by a host of heavenly maidens bearing parasols and fly-whisks. Like the first stone, this also comes from Malcornem in Quepem taluka in the south and also dates from the 12th century. The carving is deeply and beautifully executed with considerable detail, such as the beard of the hero and the handle of his dagger in the battle scene. The decoration of the panels is extremely delicately worked.

Exhibit 37. A typical example of a sati stone is this one from Sancode in Bardez taluka. Often a sati is depicted with arms raised and palms forward and the single arm is symbolic. On this stone, both husband and wife are shown below and a linga also appears on this particular stone to show that they were followers of Shiva.

There is another hero stone but it is badly worn

and there are eleven more stones in the Sculpture Gallery covering a wide range of subjects and styles that make for fascinating study.

Examples of Hindu architectural sculpture include a lintel from the doorway of an 11th-century temple in Old Goa itself (Exhibit 10) that would most probably have been destroyed during early Muslim invasions. There are also two stone inscriptions.

The Key Gallery is divided into two by a projecting display cabinet and beyond is a section devoted to the Portuguese period. There is a particularly well carved life-sized figure in wood of St John the Baptist, probably from a church in Old Goa.

There are also two portraits in oil, one of Dom Pedro de Lencastre, Governor in 1662, and the other Dom Fernando Martins Mascarenhas de Lencastre, a member of the ruling council in 1690. Dom Pedro would have seen the building in which we now stand and the Church of St Francis of Assisi under construction, Dom Fernando would have seen it in its completed state. Both were in charge during the period of Goa's declining (virtually declined) trade and moral decadence.

The stone carvings are illustrative of the way in which local craftsmen turned their hand to less familiar work, such as the burial stone of the first Captain of Daman, who died in 1560, and a coat of arms of a Bishop of Goa.

The stairs at the far end of the room lead up to the Portrait Gallery.

Portrait Gallery

The major part of this section consists of the full-length portraits of some of the men who ruled Goa between the arrival of the Portuguese in 1510 and their hurried departure in 1961. It is an impressive collection, effectively displayed. As explained in a notice at the top of the staircase, Governor Dom Joao de Castro, in 1547, ordered his portrait painted together with portraits of his twelve predecessors, presumably from other paintings, and the practice was continued afterwards and those remaining have now been collected here. In the gallery there is a full list of these rulers of Portuguese India with their dates. There were a considerable number.

Whether you came as a Viceroy or a Governor depended upon your standing with the king in Portugal. On two occasions a Governor was raised to Viceroy while still in office for outstanding performances. In 1774, the titles of Viceroy and Governor were abolished and that of Governor and Captain General substituted, but in 1807 the title of Viceroy was restored and continued to 1835 when the 51st, and last, Viceroy left. After that it was 'Governor General' until 1961. Whatever the title, the appointment was usually for no more than three years and rarely extended, as the absolute power enjoyed, not to mention the potential financial rewards, was considerable, especially in the earlier years of Portuguese rule, which made it advisable to limit the time in office.

The appointment also had its drawbacks, many succumbing to climate and disease after only a very brief time in office. The need for a system to cover this eventuality was soon realised and a Patent of Succession was established. The names of three Captains of Forts in India were placed in a sealed envelope in order of preference and the first on the list still living would take over as interim governor until a replacement could be sent out from Portugal. In later years an interim council of two or three members was often appointed.

This gallery provides a fascinating pageant of the men who ruled here for 450 years and the splendour of their costumes over that period. They certainly dressed in style, with no concessions to the tropical climate. Their coats-of-arms are also a point of interest.

It is diverting to pick out a few outstanding characters and put a face to the events of their Goan interlude, although sadly some of the more exciting contributors to Goa's history are missing:

Diogo Lopes de Sequeira, 1518–22. His is the earliest portrait. All through his time in Goa he was busy fighting battles to hold on to and expand Portuguese territory in the face of strong Muslim opposition. Under him the first expansion outside the Ilhas into Bardez and Salcete took place with help from Vijayanagar. Especially important was the acquisition of the fortress at Rachol.

Dom Joao de Castro, 1545–48. Looking particularly dashing in his splendid red coat and gold doublet and in commanding pose, you can see why he would be one to initiate the idea of the portraits. He came out as Governor, but after saving Salcete by defeating the army of Ismail Adil Khan and then sailing to Diu and achieving a great victory to save the city, he returned to Goa to a hero's welcome and elevation by the king to the rank of Viceroy. Part of the wall of the city was knocked down to create a triumphal archway of suitable size for his return. On his requesting a substantial loan from the Senate of Goa for the reconstruction of the city of Diu, it was granted against the pledge of the hairs of Dom Joao's beard! He was also given a second term of office but died shortly afterwards, reputedly in the arms of Francis Xavier. At the time of his death he was penniless, astonishing in itself for a Viceroy and especially for one with his achievements. A public subscription was raised to cover the cost of his funeral.

Dom Vasco de Gama, Count of Vidiguera, 1524. The first to make the sea-route round the Cape of Good Hope, he landed near Calicut on 17 May, 1498. Twenty-six years later, as an old man long retired, he returned as Viceroy. He died only three months after taking office but it was perhaps an appropriate end to an eventful life.

Dom Pedro Mascarenhas, 1554–55. Another Viceroy who died in office only a few months after his arrival. His portrait gives the impression that he is doing his best to look impressive. He moved out of the Palace of the Sabaio, Yusuf Adil Khan's palace, that earlier Viceroys had occupied, into the other palace in the Fort, because he was too feeble to climb the great staircase that was one of its main features. Looking at his feet one can understand his problem. The main palace was subsequently taken over by the Inquisition.

Antonio de Melo e Castro, 1662–66. He came out as Governor and was later raised to the rank of Viceroy. Soon after his arrival Cochin was lost to the Dutch who proceeded to take over the whole of the Malabar coast. He had a trying time altogether, as he was also sent out with instructions to hand over Bombay to the British as part of the dowry of Princess Catherine on her marriage to Charles II, even being sent out on a British ship. When the British refused military support against the Dutch, which was part of the agreement, the Viceroy refused to hand over Bombay and contended the transfer with great determination even in the face of further orders from Portugal. In the end he had to give in and the transfer formally took place in 1665.

Caetano de Melo e Castro, 1702–07. Under Khem Sawant Bhonsle, this period marked the beginning of real aggression by the Bhonsles of Sawantwadi on the northern border. They took the fort of Amona not far from Old Goa and the Viceroy personally led the army and threw the enemy out, marching on into Bicholim and razing all the Bhonsle forts to the ground. This was the beginning of the long struggle with the rulers of Sawantwadi that 80 years later would end in the completion of the New Conquests. In 1684, it had been decided to move the capital to Mormugao but after many delays little had been accomplished. Dom Caetano pushed ahead and completed the palace and hospital and actually moved there himself before he was ordered to abandon the project.

Dom Luis Mascarenhas, Conde d'Alva, 1754–56. This was not a happy time for Viceroys. His predecessor,

the Marquis of Tavorna, 45th Viceroy, was executed on his return to Portugal. In 1756, the Count of Alva ordered a misguided skirmish against what he thought were the troops of the Raja of Sonda, only to discover that it was the Marathas occupying the Mardanghad, the fortress at Ponda – a very different kettle of fish. Regrouping and about to attack again, he was 'shot in the back and killed while inspecting his troops. No charges were brought in connection with his assassination!

Bernado Peres da Silva, 1835. Beyond the staircase to the left, we are now in more recent times and a less imposing portrait than the others records the only Goan appointed to govern the territories. Born not far from Old Goa, he was educated at Rachol, after which he went to Portugal and became involved in politics. In Portugal there were several factions, and coups followed by counter-coups resulted in a series of rapid changes of sovereign. In 1834, ending up on the right side, Bernado Peres da Silva was sent out as Prefect with the powers of Governor. He arrived in Goa and took up his position on 14 January 1835. His term of office lasted seventeen days. On 1 February he was arrested by the military and the previous Viceroy, Manuel de Portugal e Castro, 51st and last Viceroy and creator of the Campo de Dom Manual, the Campal, was reinstated. Da Silva was deported to Bombay and the army took over. When an attempt to invite him back failed, the massacre of his supporters in Terekhol Fort was a tragic end to the affair and he never returned to Goa.

Jose Ferreira de Pestano, 1844–51 and 1864–70. Goa's longest-serving Governor, 12 years all told in two terms of office, he was a most able administrator. A professor of mathematics, he did much to further the interest of Goa and Panjim in particular, 'Nova Goa' having just been declared a city. He introduced improvements to the newly established Medical College there and the first graduates, eight of them, received their degrees in 1846. Under his direction, the monument to Afonso Albuquerque in the Azad Maidan was built and the statue from Old Goa, now downstairs in the entrance hall of the museum, was installed in 1847. During his second term, a reorganisation of the army, with several companies being disbanded, led to a mutiny at Volvoi and de Pestano gave way and rescinded the order. As a result, he was ordered back to Portugal and replaced.

Jose Ricardo Pereira Cabral, 1938–45. He had the difficult job of governing Goa during the Second World War when Portugal remained neutral, posing difficulties for the tiny enclave of Goa. The incident of the scuttling of German and Italian ships in Mormugao harbour was only one of many problems with which he was confronted.

In one dim corner, there is even a portrait of Prime Minister Salazar. On the opposite side of the gallery are some unusual paintings by Goan artists of incidents of Franciscan martyrdom.

The staircase leads down to the Sculpture Gallery.

The Sculpture Gallery

This is a pleasant courtyard preserving the atmosphere of the old convent. The figure in the centre of the garden is the statue of St Catherine that originally stood in the niche on top of the Arch of the Viceroy. The top compartment was omitted when the arch was rebuilt after its collapse in 1948.

Stone Inscriptions. Turning to the left as you enter there are several stone carved inscriptions, of interest to the casual visitor mainly for the beauty of the different scripts and the workmanship.

At the end on the left in a glassed alcove is a small shrine 'made in 1630 AD'. It contains a stone pillar brought from San Thome in Madras, the site of the martyrdom of St Thomas the Apostle. 'A piece of iron out of the lance with which St Thomas was supposed to have been killed was preserved in the small niche at the top of the pillar.'

Hero and Sati Stones. Along the next side of the cloister is the remainder of the fine collection of hero and sati stones, some examples of which have already been seen in the Key Gallery. All follow the same general pattern, with the circumstances of the hero's death in the bottom panel, the journey to heaven in the middle and the hero in heaven at the top.

Exhibit 27. This is the remnant of what was almost certainly a three-panel stone, the top being missing as well as the pilasters forming the right-hand side. A 12th-century stone from Cuncolim in the south, it is carved in great detail, the panels being filled with figures in extremely high relief. Its theme is unusual in that it shows a battle on horseback. The fighting appears to be continuing around our hero on his way to heaven in the second panel.

Exhibit 3. This three-panelled stone from Betgi in Ponda is set in a plain undecorated frame, but the carving of the panels makes up for this. This is a good example of a hero offering himself to the gods in self-immolation by fire. The tiny figure of the hero is shown, hands together, sitting in the flames, to the accompaniment of drums and gongs with a figure in admiring attitude on the right.

In the middle panel, four *apsaras*, celestial maidens with their fly-whisks, escort him up to heaven, but in the top panel, instead of having arrived he is still on his travels, on horseback and carrying a spear. He is followed by an apsara sheltering him under a parasol and led by a guard with a sword and shield. Parasols held above a figure was a device used to indicate royalty or someone of high rank. It is topped with a three-tiered pediment. The whole piece is full of life and movement.

Exhibit 24. This is of particular interest because at the top the hero is shown in heaven represented by a two-storeyed house in some detail. The hero and his wife are inside worshipping a linga, this being an example of a combined hero and sati stone.

Exhibit 22. The oldest hero stone found in Goa. Inscribed on both horizontal spaces between the panels, it is dated 1054, just after Jayakeshi I had transferred the Kadamba capital from Chandrapur to Gopakapattana. It is thought that this honours one of of his generals and shows him in battle at sea. The six heads of the rowers showing just above the ship's hull and their oars form the basis of the composition of the battle scene. This is not so deeply carved as some of the later viragals.

Exhibit 235. A medieval sati stone from Malcornem in Salcete. In the lower panel, the wife namastes before the funeral pyre before joining her husband; in the middle panel they are together ascending to heaven and they are seated together, he holding his wife's hand.

Brahmanical Deities. The first exhibit in this gallery is a dramatic one, the upper part of a figure of Betal, one of the three figures of him in this gallery, together with one of Bhairava. Bhairava is Shiva in one of his most violent forms, a form he adopted when, in an altercation with Brahma, he cut off one of Brahma's heads, leaving him with only four. He is usually shown holding the head in one of his hands, though not here. Bhairava himself has several forms and in Goa is worshipped widely as Ravalnath, but also in his most horrific and terrifying form as Batuka Bhairava or Betal (Vetal) (see p. 18).

Although there is no complete figure of Betal here in the gallery, the one head and torso (Exhibit 237) and headless figure (Exhibit 14) together give a good composite picture and are impressive pieces of sculpture. Both are 12th century and the headless figure comes from Betalbatim, a village deriving its name from the god. The protruding round eyes, serpents writhing in his hair, serpent armlets and ribs showing, are all characteristic, as is the scorpion, which is Betal's vehicle, shown on his belly. The other, headless, Betal is a powerful piece of sculpture. With ribs showing, there is again the necklace of serpents and also a garland of human heads. The girdle with its hanging chains ending in bells is delicately carved. Betal is the only nude god in Goa. The third Betal is less detailed and rather badly worn.

The Bhairava image (Exhibit 18), also 12th century, shows him carrying Shiva's traditional accoutrements, trident, sword, kettle-drum and cup, and he is accompanied by a dog which is also characteristic. However, as already mentioned, there is no sign of Brahma's head. This image is from Cortalim from where the Mangeshi linga was smuggled to Priol and this is perhaps from the original Mangesh Temple there. The Kalbhairava image in the present temple at Priol clearly shows all his typical characteristics including Brahma's head.

There is another very old, 10th-century Uma Maheshwar (Exhibit 1) and two Mahisha Mardini similar in composition to that described in the Key Gallery.

Architectural Pieces. Several fragments that once formed part of the Hindu temples of Old Goa and the surrounding area, including Divar Island, are displayed here.

There is also a smoothly polished Shiva-linga from a temple, about 12th century. On an octagonal base it has Brahmasutra lines, grooving on the shaft, typical of the Kadamba period.

The headless Nandi comes from Loutolim, the original home of the Ravalnath image now installed in the temple at Bandora in Ponda taluka. Sadly, most of the ancient Nandis found are damaged in this way, those from Pilar, Chandrapur and Rachol having suffered the same fate at the hands of the destroyers of their temples.

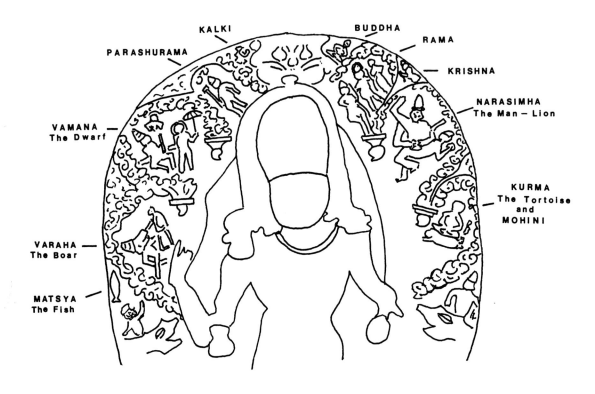

STATUE OF VISHNU.
Indicating the location of the prabhamandala, (the framework)
of the statue, of the illustrations of each of Vishnu's ten avatars,
(incarnations).

APPENDIX II

ST FRANCIS XAVIER – HIS LIFE AND TRAVELS

St Francis Xavier belongs to Goa. He may have been born in Spain, university-educated and, indeed, converted in Paris, spent most of his great evangelical years as a servant of Rome in the far south of India, the East Indies and Japan, with China as his final goal, yet, once having been launched on his life's real work, it was Goa that was the base from which he operated. It was his communication point, and even though he spent so little time here, little more than eighteen months in ten years of journeyings, it was to Goa that he must return, however briefly, to refresh his spirit and re-direct his efforts. In between all his valiant striving to spread Christianity over the Far East he always hastened back to Goa. Five times in ten years he made the journey back, however distant his missions. After his death in China he would return for ever.

In Goa, as well as receiving the complete devotion of Christians, he is held in the highest regard by all communities – Hindus, Muslims and others alike. He is accepted as one of Goa's sons, and his affectionate and gracious Konkani title, 'Goencha Saiba', 'Lord of Goa', sums up Goa's relationship with this Christian saint. He is one of the people of this place.

Francisco Xavier y Jassu was born of a noble family in Navarre, the Basque country of northern Spain on 6 April, 1506. His early years saw much strife and destruction. When he was only six years old, Navarre was caught up in the conflict between Spanish Aragon and France that was to continue, on and off, for the next twelve years. In support of Navarre's independence, first the father and later the two elder sons threw in their lot with the French king. Early defeats led to the destruction of most of Castle Xavier and the confiscation of their estates,

but the brothers fought on, leaving young Francisco at home with their mother.

Among their antagonists, fighting for Aragon, were two whose paths would cross those of the Xavier family again, though not those of the two martial brothers but of the young cleric Francisco. Inigo de Loyola played an outstanding part and fell severely wounded, his leg shattered by a cannon ball, at the battle for Pamplona, and a Portuguese nobleman who took part in the final siege of the fortress of Fuentarabia was one Dom Martim Afonso de Sousa.

At the end of the conflict, Francisco's brothers, treated generously in honourable defeat, returned home, their titles and estates restored. A year later, in 1525, Francisco, whose inclinations were towards an academic life, was sent off to Paris to continue his studies at the university there. Caught up in the whirl of Parisian student life, he soon fell to gambling away much of his allowance and there were many letters home requesting more money. As he was nearing the end of his studies in 1529, an older student obtained admission to the college and by chance was put into the same room as Francisco. It was Inigo de Loyola who, after being wounded at Pamplona, had exchanged the glamour of life on the battlefield and in the courts of Spain for one of religious study and devout spirituality. Older than Francisco by fifteen years, it was his influence that was to change the direction of the younger man's life. Following the example of his mentor he devoted himself to God and, in particular, to the salvation of souls.

In 1534, in a small chapel in Montmartre, together with several other followers of Ignatius Loyola, vows of chastity were taken and the comrades committed themselves to make a pilgrimage to Jerusalem to work for the conversion of the infidels, Jerusalem being in the hands of the Turks at that time. It was another three years before they could

TABLE 1. THE JOURNEYS OF ST FRANCIS

1542	6 May	Arrives in Goa
	September	Leaves for the Fishery Coast
1543	December	Returns to Goa
1544	February	Leaves for Fishery Coast
1545	March	Moves north to Mylapore and leaves for the East Indies
	September	Arrives in Malacca
1546	February	Arrives in Amboina – Visits other islands in the Moluccas
1547	April	Leaves for India
	June	Stop-over at Malacca
1548	January	Arrives in Cochin
	April	Arrives in Goa
	September	Leaves for the Malabar and Fishery Coasts
	November	Arrives back in Goa
1549	April	Leaves for Japan
	May	Stop-over in Malacca
	August	Arrives Kagoshima, Japan
1551	November	Leaves for India
	December	Stop-over in Malacca
1552	February	Arrives back in Goa
	April	Leaves for China
	May	Stop-over in Malacca
	August	Arrives in Sancian Island
	3 December	Dies on Sancian

assemble in Venice to await a ship for the Holy Land and, while waiting, Francis made a visit to Rome where he had audience with the Pope, obtaining his blessing for his ordination which took place on Francis's return to Venice.

The journey to Jerusalem eventually proving impossible, the group moved to Rome and spent the next few years devoting themselves to working for the Church across the length and breadth of Italy. It was during this period that the plan was formulated to create a new order, the Society of Jesus, but this met with strong opposition from the establishment.

By this time, Portugal was well established in the east, but finding sufficient numbers of priests to serve their expanding colonies was proving a problem. The king, Dom Joao III, hearing of the group's activities, asked, through the Pope, for six of them to be sent to the East. In the event only two could be spared, one a young secular priest Paul of Camerino, the other Francis Xavier. So began his real mission in life.

He eventually sailed from Lisbon on 7 April 1541, his 35th birthday, travelling on a ship that was taking out a new Governor General to Goa, none other than Dom Martim Afonso de Sousa who had fought against Xavier's brothers at the siege of Fuentarabia. The voyage took over a year, landing them in Goa in May 1542.

At once Francis plunged into a frenzy of energetic missionary work. A timetable of his activities for the next ten years, bearing in mind the climate and the difficulties and hardships of travel at that time, makes breathtaking reading (Table 1).

Inexplicably, it was only on a visit back to Goa in December 1543 that he learned, through a letter from Ignatius Loyola, that a papal decree of 27 September 1540 had approved the Society of Jesus. This was six months before he had left Lisbon. Ignatius Loyola had been elected General of the order in April 1541 just after Francis had sailed. So Francis took his vows as a Jesuit in Goa.

During the rest of his life, he ranged backwards and forwards across the whole of the Far East, covering the southern coasts of India on both east and west, many of the islands of the East Indies and still further to Japan. As all these expeditions were interspersed with short visits back to Goa, the mileage he travelled was enormous.

His quest was for souls, and the merest suggestion of fertile ground for converts would lead him to set sail in search of them. On his arrival in Goa he described it as 'a city entirely of Christians' but it was here that he established his methods of working, becoming a familiar figure in the streets, ringing his bell to attract a following, singing the lessons to make them as attractive as possible and producing a basic catechism in Konkani. Otherwise he spent much of his time ministering in the hospital and prison. But he was soon on the move.

Before he left on his first visit to the south, starting at Cape Comorin, the southern tip of India, he wrote that he was going to 'a land where all say I shall make many Christians'. Working tirelessly, both on the Malabar Coast and what was then called the Pearl Fishery Coast on the Gulf of Mannar that separates India from Ceylon, he himself baptised thousands of converts, on one occasion 10,000 in a single month.

On one of his visits here he reported, 'I have definite knowledge that in the parts of Malacca the people are much disposed in the service of God and that because of lack of any to work in it, many do not become Christians and there is no increase in our Holy Faith.' So he went to the East Indies. From the Portuguese trading post of Malacca with its great fort, he vigorously pursued his mission in the Malay peninsula and also went still further east into the 'Spice Islands', going as far afield as the tiny islands that form the northern part of the Moluccas. These journeys were particularly difficult and dangerous. One of the events illustrated in a bronze plaque on his tomb in the Bom Jesus Basilica, is where he was forced to plunge into the sea and swim for his life to escape from the savages of the island of Moro. In the face of all these difficulties, he never flagged in his endeavours, spending eighteen months in the 'Spice Islands' before returning to Malacca.

In Malacca he had 'great news of certain very large islands recently discovered in the east called the islands of Japan where there would be better opportunity for the increase of our Holy Faith than anywhere in India because the people have an eager desire for knowledge and instruction.' So, after the almost inevitable return visit to Goa, off he went to Japan, this time braving the perils of the storms and pirates of the already notorious South China Sea for the first time. For Francis, his stay in Japan was frustrating, finding himself faced with devious opposition from vested interests. In spite of the dissatisfaction he felt, by the time he left after two years firm foundations had been laid – to the point where, little more than sixty years after his death, Japanese Christians could successfully petition for part of the Saint's body to be sent there.

On his journey back to India, his ship called in at the island of Sancian off the China coast in December 1551. Learning of China's potential, he determined to tackle it but, typically, still completed his journey back to Goa, another 7000 km. Arriving there in February, he left again in April and, by August, was back on Sancian again and plotting his spiritual conquest of China.

His final throw of the dice, his vision of converting this strange and little-known land, was typical of his refusal to accept that any obstacle was insurmountable. The situation was forbidding, to say the least. China was officially closed to foreigners with trade banned. Sancian, an island outside the mouth of the Yellow River, not far from Macao, was one of the bases for the illegal trading operations that were taking place and this was where the fleets assembled to meet the Chinese traders from Canton. Francis hoped to find someone to take him secretly onto the mainland. He could find no-one prepared to take the risk and, while still negotiating, he was taken ill and soon afterwards, on 3 December 1552, he died.

He died in a wooden hut built for him on the beach by the seamen of the ship on which he had travelled and which still lay at anchor off the island, assembling its cargo. His only companion at the end was a Chinese convert, Anthony, who had been at St Paul's College and who had accompanied Francis from Goa. He it was who organised the simple burial and agreed the suggestion that the coffin should be filled with lime 'to consume the flesh and leave only the bare bones in case anyone in time to come should wish to take them to India'.

The *Santa Cruz*, the ship on which Francis had come to Sancian, remained there until February, when the captain was ready to sail for Malacca. Just before the ship weighed anchor, three months having passed since Francis's burial, Anthony asked that the body should be inspected to see if the flesh had already gone from the bones. A seaman was sent ashore and found the body pure and intact with no signs at all of decay. Cutting a piece of flesh from the leg as proof, he reported back to the ship and it was decided to take the body in its coffin back to Malacca.

The ship arrived there on 22 March 1553 and the coffin was taken to the church of Our Lady of the Mount. The body was buried in a rock-cut grave there but, the grave being too short, the head was bent forward breaking the neck. In addition, when the grave was filled with stony earth, the coffin having been discarded, the nose was crushed and the face bruised.

Five months later a disciple and friend of Francis who was leaving Malacca wanted to see him one last time and, in the dead of night, dug up the body only to find it still untainted. Deciding that such a miraculously preserved body should not be buried again, it was put into a coffin and secreted away. But such a secret could not be kept indefinitely and when the news reached Goa the Viceroy laid claim

TABLE 2.   OFFICIAL EXPOSITIONS

1.	1782	10–12 Feb.	
2.	1859	3 Dec.–8 Jan.	
3.	1878	3 Dec.–6 Jan.	
4.	1890	3 Dec.–1 Jan.	
5.	1900	7–10 Dec.	Eucharistic Congress held in Goa.
6.	1910	26 Nov.–28 Dec.	4th Centenary of Albuquerque's conquest of Goa.
7.	1922	3 Dec.–7 Jan.	3rd centenary of canonisation of St. Francis.
8.	1931	3 Dec.–10 Jan.	
9.	1942	6–17 May	4th century of the arrival of St. Francis in Goa.
10.	1952	3 Dec.–6 Jan.	4th centenary of his death.
11.	1961	14–19 Dec.*	Intercession by the Portuguese ended by liberation.
12.	1964	23 Nov.–13 Jan.*	International Eucharistic Conference held in Bombay.
13.	1974	23 Nov.–13 Jan.*	To celebrate 1975 being declared Holy Year by the Pope.
14.	1984	21 Nov.–13 Jan.*	

* Exposition in the glass casket.

to the body. A ship with the body on board set sail in December, reaching Goa on 16 March 1554, the Friday before Palm Sunday. It was met in state at the quayside by the Viceroy with all the church bells ringing and cannon firing salutes from the forts. It was then taken in triumphal procession to what had been Francis's favourite church, that in the College of St Paul. Here, the open coffin lay for three days while a continuous stream of people filed by to view and touch the body, the first of many public appearances. It also suffered another mutilation – a female fanatic, Dona Isabela de Carom, biting off the little toe of the right foot as a relic. Astonishingly, the foot bled and the lady is reported to have run off screaming but with the toe still in her mouth! Then, in a new coffin, the body was buried in St Paul's.

In 1613, it was moved to the Professed House of the Jesuits next to their new church, where it was kept in an upstairs room above the main entrance.

In March 1622, Francis was canonised, though the news did not reach Goa until May of the following year. Ignatius Loyola was canonised at the same time and, as can be imagined, there were great celebrations and rejoicing. Goa had its own saint.

In 1624, St Francis was moved into the church, the coffin being placed in the chapel in the north transept. A silver casket was ordered and the coffin placed in this in 1637. In 1659, the coffin and casket were transferred to its present home in the chapel of the south transept, where it lay on trestles until the marble mausoleum was erected in 1698.

Apart from these moves, the body's treatment from the time of its first exhumation only underlines the miracle of its continued existence in an incorrupt condition for so long. The coffin was

continually being opened and the body subjected to the touch of devotees and examination by officials and, even worse, to a series of incredible mutilations.

After the battering received in Malacca, there was the loss of a toe, already mentioned. In 1614, even before canonisation, the Pope asked for the right arm to be sent to Rome. It was cut off at the elbow. In 1619, the rest of the right arm was amputated together with the shoulder blade. The upper arm was sent to Japan, the shoulder blade cut into three and sent to Cochin, Malacca and Macao. In 1636 the internal organs were removed and pieces widely distributed as relics. After the body had been ceremonially exposed to public view in 1890, when nearly 100,000 people had kissed the feet of the Saint, another toe dropped off. Two more toes are unaccounted for.

These expositions, when the coffin was opened and the body put on display for the veneration of the public, have proved almost as damaging as the mutilations. At first, these took place every year on the anniversary of his death and there were many private expositions as well. By 1700 the damage inflicted and the deterioration resulting from the combined effects of all these circumstances, caused the authorities to ban any further opening of the coffin. To try and enforce this, the coffin was secured with three locks, the keys of which were distributed: one to the Rector of Rachol, one to the Captain of Bassein and one to the Superior of the Professed House of Bom Jesus. Even then, some exceptions were made.

In 1759, the Jesuits were evicted and control of both the church and the body passed to the Archdiocese of Goa. The policy of keeping the coffin closed continued, but when in 1782 rumours began to circulate that the Jesuits had taken the body with them when they left, it was brought out and shown to the public. In 1859 special permission was obtained for another exposition and again in 1878. From then on they began to be held on special occasions, a reason being found at about ten-yearly intervals (Table 2).

Two expositions are of particular interest. In December 1961, when Goa was under threat from India, Governor General Vassalo e Silva arranged for the coffin to be opened, hoping for a repeat of previous miracles. The exposition ended with the arrival of Indian troops. In 1962, when Chinese troops crossed India's northern border, the Indian Military Governor of Goa ordered a private exposition but this again failed to influence events.

After the expositions of 1952, the authorities again decided, because of further deterioration, that the public should not be allowed to touch the body, and a special glass casket was supplied from Italy into which the body was transferred in 1955. The old wooden coffin is kept in the sacristy at Bom

Jesus. It is in this glass casket that the body has been displayed at the last four expositions and this led to the suggestion that pilgrims visiting the Basilica should be able to see more than just the outside of the silver casket that covers the glass case in which the saint lies. It was decided to remove two panels from the silver casket to reveal the head and shoulders. This proved inadequate and so the other five panels were removed so that the whole length of the body can be seen. It also meant the removal of the silver statue of St Francis that formerly stood in front of the casket. This is now also kept in the sacristy.

The body still survives, though showing the ravages of time and the treatment received over more than four hundred years since his death. It is now accepted that the miracle of the incorrupt body need not be for ever and the remains of St Francis are officially referred to as the Sacred Relics. However, Goencho Saiba still watches over Goa.

APPENDIX III

A SHORT VOCABULARY OF FOOD

It is not possible to ignore the fact that Goan food is quite distinctive. Fish, coconuts and rice form the basic staples of a Goan diet but add to this the long term Portuguese traditions and you have a cuisine that is definitely 'of Goa'.

All forms of meats are eaten, chicken and pork seeming to be the most favoured. Shellfish, in most forms, is rightly prized and sweet and delicious. Goan breads, unlike the rest of India where the norm is to have unleavened breads, have traditionally been leavened and are available in many varieties, the bread stalls in the markets delight the eye and the senses. Pastry shops provide an interesting diversion for the sweet of tooth. Wedding, christening and birthday cakes are an important social and historical tradition, and appear in all their glory.

Below is listed a short vocabulary of the specialities to be found all over Goa:

Ambot-tik – A sour hot curry of fish, shellfish or meat.

Balchao – Of prawn, fish or meat, one of the most delicious of experiences, dark chilli-red in colour, to be eaten with freshly baked rolls or bread.

Bebinca – A delightful confection of layered coconut pancakes baked and turned out to be used as a cake.

Caldeen – A delicately flavoured pale yellow/green fish curry.

Cafreal – Fish or chicken dry-fried after being marinaded for several hours.

Seet Corry—Fish curry rice: a typical Goa fish curry served with coconut-rice, this is the staple food and quite delicious.

Goa sausage – Similar to Portuguese churico, it is red from the chilli content and very spicy.

Kishmur – Crushed dried shrimp to be scattered over the fish curries as a condiment.

Sorpotel – A mixture of pork, liver and black pudding, chopped and cooked with a mixture of spices.

Xacuti – Chicken, beef and pork cooked with pungent spices provide and interesting variation of a textured curry, served with coconut rice.

Add to these the stews, the baked meats, fish grilled or fried, the pastries, savory and sweet, plus a myriad of pickles, and there you have a zestful cuisine of a very lively character.

ACKNOWLEDGEMENTS

With thanks to: John who spurred us on. Dr. P. P. Shirodkar, Dr. B. D. Shastry and others at the Directorate of Archives, Archeology and Museum at Panjim – also for their excellent twice-annual publication *Purabhilek Puratatva*. Staff at the Central Library at the Menezes Braganza Institute who were ever helpful. Father Ivo Souza and Father Ataide at Rachol and Monseignor Carmo da Silva in Panjim all took the trouble to talk to us. Father Teotonio R. de Souza at the Xavier Institute of Historical Research, Porvorim, and Father John Correa-Afonso at the Heras Institute of History and Culture in Bombay. The Asiatic Library in Bombay. The British Library in London and the library of the RIBA.

To Franco, Francis and Peter who over the past few years have cheerfully carried us forth on expeditions and other friends in Goa.

In Bombay and Delhi, thanks to Shernaz and T.N.N. and J.H.M. for all their interest and practical help. J.S. in Cumbria. Last, but definitely not least, to Aries and Maite Dias, translators, lenders and givers of books, mines of information and helpfulness and true true friends.

BIBLIOGRAPHY

Mario Carbal e Sa & Jean-Louis Nou, *Goa*, Lustre Press, New Delhi, 1986.

Mario Carbal e Sa and Lourdes Bravo da Costa, *Great Goans*, Pune, 1958.

Josè Nicholau da Fonsa, *Sketch of the City of Goa*, Thacker & Co., Bombay, 1878.

Golden Goa, Marg Publications, Bombay, 1980.

Rui Gomes Pereira, *Hindu Temples and Deities*, Goa, 1978.

Rui Gomes Pereira, *Gaunkari – The Old Village Associations*, Goa, 1981.

Olivinho J. F. Gomes, *Village Goa*, S. Chand & Co., New Delhi, 1987.

V. T. Gune, *Ancient Shrines of Goa: A pictorial survey*, Goa, 1965.

Ian Hogg, *Fortress: A history of military defence*, Macdonald and Jane's, London, 1975.

Vinayak V. Khedekar, *Goa Cultural Patterns*, edited by Dr. Saryn Doshi, Marg, Bombay, 1981.

Antonio Mascarenhas, *Goa from Prehistoric Times*, Goa, 1987.

Manohar Malgonkar, *Inside Goa*, Directorate of Information and Publicity, Government of Goa, Daman and Dui, Bombay, 1982.

Antonio de Menezes, *Goa – Historical Notes*, vol. I, 1978.

Purabhilek Puratatva, vols. I–VI. (Journal of the Directorate of Archives, Archaeology and Museum), Panaji, Goa, 1984–8.

J. M. Richards, *Goa*, Concept Publishing, New Delhi, 1989.

Professor Lucio Rodrigues (collected) *Of Soil and Soul and Konkani Folk Tales*, Bombay, 1974.

Father Teotonio R. de Souza (ed.), *Essays in Goan History*, Concept Publishing, New Delhi, 1989.

K. M. Sen, *Hinduism*, Penguin, Harmondsworth, 1961.

Percival Spear (ed.), *The Oxford History of India*, Oxford University Press, Oxford, 1964.

NOTES

Introduction

[1] Mormugao taluka was only created in 1917, before then the area being part of Salcete.

Chapter 3

[1] The Brahma Temple at Carambolim, or Carmoli, in Satari Taluka.
[2] The Dattaraya Temple at Sanquelim in Bicholim Taluka.
[3] Goa's 'Village Five' are therefore, Ravalnath, Kalbhairava, Vetal, Lakshminarayana and Shanteri.
[4] *Goa – Cultural Patterns – The Hindu Past*: Marg Publications.

Chapter 6

[1] The latest available official figures for licences issued for stills, show a total of over 6000, roughly equally divided between palm and cashew feni. Salcete leads the way in the production of palm feni; Pernem for cashew feni.

Chapter 9

[1] A recent reprint, in English, of John Hugo Linschoten's *Histoire de la Navigation* gives an absorbing account of the city when he visited it at the height of its prosperity in 1583.
[2] *Golden Goa*, Jose Pereira, Marg Publications.

Chapter 10

[1] For a full account of this operation, see the article by Dr P. P. Shirodkar in *Purabhilekh Puratatva*, vol. v, no. 1, 1987.
[2] In January 1990 this huge portrait fell, breaking into several pieces (it was painted on wood). It is now being restored.

Chapter 11

[1] At that time the whole of the area south of the Zuari River was termed Salcete. Mormugao taluka is a subsequent creation.
[2] Not to be confused with Brahma.
[3] Sadly, hopes have been dashed. An act of vandalism has replaced the superb old tulsi vrindavan with a characterless nonentity. The grandeur of its predecessor is no more, part of the mindless destruction of Goa's heritage that, unhappily, seems to be a growing problem despite the efforts of those determined to preserve such treasures.
[4] The new temple of Gopal Ganapathi at Farmagudi was consecrated only in 1966.
[5] Reached along a turn-off to the right, signposted Opa Water Works, about 5 km from Ponda on the road to Molem.
[6] Along a turn-off to the left on the road to Molem, about 6 km from Ponda and just before the bridge over the river. Less than a kilometre from the main road, a track to the right over open ground leads down towards the river.

Chapter 12

[1] There is an important Salcete village, Cuncolim, which is dealt with in another chapter, 'Fringe Benefits'. It is right on the southern border of the taluka and will be passed through on any visit to the far south, such as an expedition to Cabo de Rama (see p. 188).
[2] For more information on Goa's railway see p. 181.
[3] At times when the church is not open, the priest will usually happily allow the church to be opened for visitors, but it should be noted that church offices themselves only open from 9.00 am to 12.30 pm and 4.00 to 5.00pm. Take into account the fact that siesta is observed in Goa.
[4] The whole of this small area is within a 10 km radius of Margao and is conveniently strung along one of the routes between Margao and the road bridge over the Zuari at Cortalim. Chandor, having its own railway station, can be reached by train. Borim Bridge nearby links the area with Ponda.
[5] To reach the site of Chandrapur from the village square, take the road to Curchorem and Sanvordem that runs down the right-hand side of the church. It is signposted, but this is usually submerged in old posters. Just less than 2 km from the square and just before reaching the bridge over the Kushavati River, there is a fork to the left and a signpost marking the site that can be seen from the road. The site is in the hamlet of Chandra Kott, *kott* meaning 'fort' in Konkani. The other two hamlets making up the village of Chandor are Cavorim (Kovddi) to the south and Guirdolim (Guiddli) to the west.

[6] The other two places are Reis Magos in Bardez and Cansaulim in Mormugao.

[7] Examples are to be seen in the special exhibit at the Museum in Old Goa (see Appendix I).

[8] In fact, the church is most easily reached from the main Panjim-Margao road, taking a turning only about half a kilometre on the Margao side of the junction with the road to the airport.

Chapter 13

[1] Currently open to visitors from 4.00 pm to 5.30 pm, but times require checking.

[2] Moidekkars: 'simple people of innocence and faith that belonged to the ancient world, disarming in their naïveté.' This tale is related in *Of Soil and Soul and Konkani Folk Tales*, collected by Lucio Rodrigues (1974).

[3] There is a modern grotto and an elaborate mortuary chapel.

Chapter 14

[1] *Graffito* – from the verb meaning to scratch – is where a layer of red plaster is applied to a white plastered wall. When the red layer is dry, a further layer of white plaster is laid on top. Before the top layer dries the patterns are scratched on the surface to expose the red layer underneath. There are many examples of graffito art in temples all over Goa.

Chapter 15

[1] Now a Tourist Hostel, the best situated of them all, a visit to the fort provides the opportunity to enjoy the other attractions of this most northern taluka. Bookings can be made at the Tourist Hostels in Panjim at Margao.

[2] From Valpoi, 16 km beyond Sanquelim, the road is signposted Kodal. After approximately 5 km, a turn-off to the left is signposted Bramha-Karmali. The temple is about a further 2 km.

[3] Panjim – Ponda – Tiskar – Darbandora – Sancordem – Temple (62 km). Panjim – Molem (58 km). Molem – Temple (16 km).

[4] **Bondla** – approximately 52 km from Panjim via Ponda and Usgao. The Tourist Department organises one-day visits and a mini-bus makes a return trip Bondla–Ponda every morning and evening. The Sanctuary is open to daily visitors 9-00 am to 5-30 pm except on Thursdays. Accommodation needs to be booked well in advance at Deputy Collector of Forests, Wild Life Division, Junta House, Panjim. All this information should be re-checked with the Goa Tourist Department – things change!

[5] **Molem** – approximately 60 km from Panjim on the main road out of Goa to Belgaum, so can be reached by interstate bus. There is a bus service Molem to Colem. Accommodation should be booked well in advance at the Goan Directorate of Tourism, Pato Bridge, Panjim. Jeeps can be booked only at the Range Forest office. Please re-check all information in advance.

[6] **Cotigao** – approximately 50 km from Margao and 82 km from Panjim.

[7] Tours are organised by the Goa Tourist Development Corporation. Contact their office in Panjim or Margao.

[8] Now in the Archaeological Museum, Panjim.

GLOSSARY

agarshalas	– living quarters, part of a temple complex
amalaka	– flattened globe, grooved to represent a fruit
amrita	– ambrosia or nectar of the gods
antaralya	– vestibule
apsaras	– celestial maidens
balcao	– balustraded verandah
Bhagavad Gita	– great gospel of Hinduism
chaitya	– hall of meditation (Buddhist)
dargah	– tombs and shrine of a Muslim saint
deepastambha/dipmal	– lamp tower
dharalinga	– faceted linga
dharmasalas	– living quarters
dvarapalas	– door-keepers or guardians of the temple sanctuary
garbhagriha	– inner sanctuary of the temple
ghats	– The Western Ghat or Sahyadri Mountains: the mountain range that runs north–south behind the coastal plain. It runs from the north of Bombay to Mangalore
graffito	– scratching: a layer of red plaster is applied to a white plastered wall. When the red layer is dry, a further white layer is laid on top. Before the final layer is dry, patterns are scratched onto the surface to expose the red layer underneath
kott	– fort (Konkani)
kirti mukha	– 'face of glory'
linga	– symbol of supreme reality, the phallic symbol worshipped mainly by Shaivites
Mahabharata	– one of the two epic poems of powerful folk-lore history
mandapa	– pillared hall of the temple
mukhalinga	– linga with a carved face
nacre	– squares of polished oyster shells, previously used in windows instead of glass
nagas	– images of serpent gods
namaste	– form of greeting with hands held together
naubal khana	– room or place for beating drums
Om	– symbol of the supreme Brahman
palki	– palanquin
parivar devatas	– affiliate, or associate, gods
pradakshina	– passageway around the sanctuary
rath	– wooden chariot, vehicle of the gods, used in processions
Ramayana	– the other epic poem of Hindu folk-lore
sabha mandapa	– large pillared, often galleried, assembly hall, often used for music and dance
sati	– ceremony whereby a wife immolates herself on her husband's funeral pyre
satyagriha	– political unarmed demonstration
shikara	– tower surmounting the temple
taluka	– administrative district
tulsi vrindavan	– container of varying size and design established in the garden or courtyard of Brahmin households to hold a tulsi plant
vahanas	– personal vehicle of the gods (Ganesh's vehicle is a rat: Brahma's a swan, etc.)
viharas	– dwelling place for Buddhists
viragal	– 'hero stone'

INDEX